THE ABINGDON PREACHING ANNUAL 2007

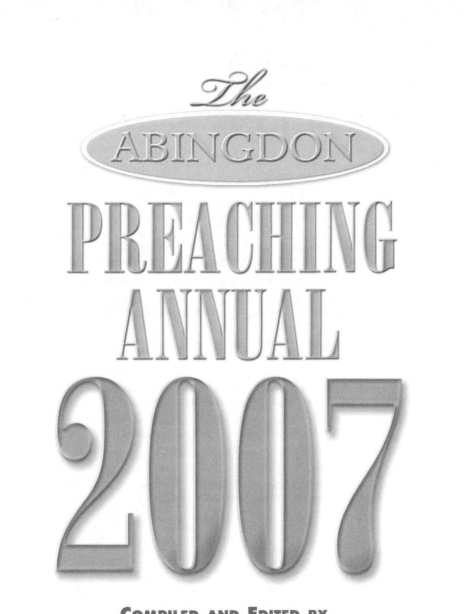

The
ABINGDON
PREACHING
ANNUAL
2007

COMPILED AND EDITED BY
THE REVEREND DAVID NEIL MOSSER

ASSISTANT EDITOR RONDA WELLMAN

Abingdon Press
Nashville

06 07 08 09 10 11 12 13 14 15—10 9 8 7 6 5 4 3 2 1

MANUFACTURED IN THE UNITED STATES OF AMERICA

To Helen, Cassie, and McKenzie
Lovingly dedicated to three vigorous women from
three generations
who try to teach this old throwback what it means to
live in "love and charity"

CONTENTS

꒿꒿ ꒿꒿ ꒿꒿

PREFACE

In one of Christian history's most venerated handbooks on preaching, *On Christian Doctrine*, beloved Saint Augustine wrote: "A man speaks more or less wisely to the extent that he has become more or less proficient in the Holy Scriptures" (*On Christian Doctrine*, book 4, section 7). Following Augustine's lead, I suggest that authentic preaching begins in the Bible and ends in the Bible. Faithful preaching is preaching that deposits the truth of Scripture into the lives of people who compose the church of Jesus Christ.

On Christian Doctrine was Augustine's attempt to teach the church how to read Scripture. Book 4 attempted to teach preachers how to offer biblical truth to their gathered congregations. Sixteen hundred years later, I do not suppose we would be going out on a limb to suggest that we modern preachers try to do the same. The goal of *The Abingdon Preaching Annual 2007 (APA)*, this yearly handbook of sermons and worship aids, is to partner with those who proclaim the gospel week after week in pulpits across America.

Half of the sermons in this collection are lectionary-based, while other sermons are either part of a sermon series or are "stand-alone" sermons fit for a particular day of the Christian year. More than fifteen sermon series have been included this year, on a wide variety of subjects including: the Holy Spirit, Christian faith, exploring rocky relationships, character, forgiveness, relation of church and state, good works, and biblical leadership. Each *APA* sermon is biblically based, either on a lectionary text or on a passage applicable to a particular sermon's intent. The 2007 *APA* collection also reflects the diversity in voice and theological perspective of nearly fifty contributors.

Many preachers find that *The Abingdon Preaching Annual* is a good place to launch their sermon preparation after, of course, a thorough study of the biblical text in its context. That is, after becoming scrupulously acquainted with the biblical passage, the preacher then consults this book. Preachers do this in conjunction with personal knowledge of their congregations. This process begins a sort of conversation between the sermon's author, the congregation, various biblical commentaries, and the preacher's own theological imagination. Out of that fertile mix of minds may emerge a faithful truth useful and unique—it is to be hoped. The sermons offered in *The Abingdon Preaching Annual 2007* are neither canned nor "microwave ready." Rather, they are part of a symposium in the mind of the preacher that takes place weekly in order to proclaim the Word to God's people in season and out of season.

In response to suggestions from our readers, the 2007 *APA* continues to offer the enhancements introduced last year, all designed to aid preachers in worship preparation. Significant changes to the layout and features have also been retained. The General Helps that open the book include: a four-year calendar of significant liturgical events, lectionary listings for the calendar year 2007, and a collection of classical and contemporary affirmations and prayers.

Following the weekly entries of sermons and worship aids is a helpful appendix of additional features: services and sermons for special worship needs that call for a unique word of celebration, comfort, or guidance (funerals, mission commissioning, hanging of the greens, homecoming, and stewardship); classic sermons to inspire and remind us of the richness of our traditions; a listing of our talented and dedicated contributors; and a Scripture index.

We have again included a CD-ROM with the 2007 *APA*. Of course, the full print text is provided. Look for a wealth of added resources and references as well: more pastoral and pre-sermon prayers; stand-alone illustrations for each Sunday; a bibliography of suggested commentaries and other resources to go with each liturgical day; and the text of the lectionary listings, linked to the weekly entries.

The Abingdon Preaching Annual is a resource that preachers have come to use and trust. We hope the features included in the 2007 edition will continue to serve the needs of pastors and preachers.

My prayer is that each reader will discover in *The Abingdon Preaching Annual 2007* a helpful partner in the preaching conversation. To that end we also pray that many congregations may abundantly benefit from the work we all do together "to spread scriptural holiness throughout the land." Amen.

David N. Mosser
June 22, 2005

I. GENERAL HELPS

FOUR-YEAR CHURCH CALENDAR

	2007	2008	2009	2010
Ash Wednesday	February 21	February 6	February 25	February 17
Palm Sunday	April 1	March 16	April 5	March 28
Holy Thursday	April 5	March 20	April 9	April 1
Good Friday	April 6	March 21	April 10	April 2
Easter	April 8	March 23	April 12	April 4
Ascension Day	May 17	May 1	May 21	May 16
Pentecost	May 27	May 11	May 31	May 23
Trinity Sunday	June 3	May 18	June 7	May 30
World Communion	October 7	October 5	October 4	October 3
Thanksgiving	November 22	November 27	November 26	November 25
First Sunday of Advent	December 2	November 30	November 29	November 28

LECTIONARY LISTINGS FOR 2007

Date	First Lesson	Psalm	Second Lesson	Gospel Lesson
1/01/07	Ecclesiastes 3:1-13	Psalm 8	Revelation 21:1-6a	Matthew 25:31-46
1/07/07	Isaiah 43:1-7	Psalm 29	Acts 8:14-17	Luke 3:15-17, 21-22
1/14/07	Isaiah 62:1-5	Psalm 36:5-10	1 Corinthians 12:1-11	John 2:1-11
1/21/07	Nehemiah 8:1-3, 5-6, 8-10	Psalm 19	1 Corinthians 12:12-31a	Luke 4:14-21
1/28/07	Jeremiah 1:4-10	Psalm 71:1-6	1 Corinthians 13:1-13	Luke 4:21-30
2/04/07	Isaiah 6:1-8, (9-13)	Psalm 138	1 Corinthians 15:1-11	Luke 5:1-11
2/11/07	Jeremiah 17:5-10	Psalm 1	1 Corinthians 15:12-20	Luke 6:17-26
2/18/07	Exodus 34:29-35	Psalm 99	2 Corinthians 3:12-4:2	Luke 9:28-36, (37-43a)
2/21/07	Joel 2:1-2, 12-17	Psalm 51:1-17	2 Corinthians 5:20b-6:10	Matthew 6:1-6, 16-21
2/25/07	Deuteronomy 26:1-11	Psalm 91:1-2, 9-16	Romans 10:8b-13	Luke 4:1-13
3/04/07	Genesis 15:1-12, 17-18	Psalm 27	Philippians 3:17-4:1	Luke 9:28-36
3/11/07	Isaiah 55:1-9	Psalm 63:1-8	1 Corinthians 10:1-13	Luke 13:1-9
3/18/07	Joshua 5:9-12	Psalm 32	2 Corinthians 5:16-21	Luke 15:1-3, 11b-32
3/25/07	Isaiah 43:16-21	Psalm 126	Philippians 3:4b-14	John 12:1-8
4/01/07	Luke 19:28-40	Psalm 118:1-2, 19-29	Philippians 2:5-11	Luke 22:14–23:56
4/05/07	Exodus 12:1-4, (5-10), 11-14	Psalm 116:1-2, 12-19	1 Corinthians 11:23-26	John 13:1-17, 31b–35
4/06/07	Isaiah 52:13–53:12	Psalm 22	Hebrews 10:1-25	John 18:1–19:42
4/08/07	Isaiah 65:17-25	Psalm 118:1-2, 14-24	1 Corinthians 15:19-26	John 20:1-18
4/15/07	Acts 5:27-32	Psalm 150	Revelation 1:4-8	John 20:19-31
4/22/07	Acts 9:1-6, (7-20)	Psalm 30	Revelation 5:11-14	John 21:1-19
4/29/07	Acts 9:36-43	Psalm 23	Revelation 7:9-17	John 10:22-30
5/06/07	Acts 11:1-18	Psalm 148	Revelation 21:1-6	John 13:31-35
5/13/07	Acts 16:9-15	Psalm 67	Revelation 21:10, 22–22:5	John 14:23-29

*This list represents one possible selection of lessons and psalms from the lectionary for Year C [January 1–November 25] and Year A [December 2–30]. For a complete listing, see *The Revised Common Lectionary*.

Date	First Lesson	Psalm	Second Lesson	Gospel Lesson
5/20/07	Acts 16:16-34	Psalm 97	Revelation 22:12-14, 16-17, 20-21	John 17:20-26
5/27/07	Acts 2:1-21	Psalm 104:24-34, 35b	Romans 8:14-17	John 14:8-17, (25-27)
6/03/07	Proverbs 8:1-4, 22-31	Psalm 8	Romans 5:1-5	John 16:12-15
6/10/07	1 Kings 17:8-24	Psalm 146	Galatians 1:11-24	Luke 7:11-17
6/17/07	1 Kings 21:1-21a	Psalm 5:1-8	Galatians 2:15-21	Luke 7:36-8:3
6/24/07	1 Kings 19:1-15a	Psalm 42	Galatians 3:23-29	Luke 8:26-39
7/01/07	2 Kings 2:1-2, 6-14	Psalm 77:1-2, 11-20	Galatians 5:1, 13-25	Luke 9:51-62
7/08/07	2 Kings 5:1-14	Psalm 30	Galatians 6:(1-6), 7-16	Luke 10:1-11, 16-20
7/15/07	Amos 7:7-17	Psalm 82	Colossians 1:1-14	Luke 10:25-37
7/22/07	Amos 8:1-12	Psalm 52	Colossians 1:15-28	Luke 10:38-42
7/29/07	Hosea 1:2-10	Psalm 85	Colossians 2:6-15, (16-19)	Luke 11:1-13
8/05/07	Hosea 11:1-11	Psalm 107:1-9, 43	Colossians 3:1-11	Luke 12:13-21
8/12/07	Isaiah 1:1, 10-20	Psalm 50:1-8, 22-23	Hebrews 11:1-3, 8-16	Luke 12:32-40
8/19/07	Isaiah 5:1-7	Psalm 80:1-2, 8-19	Hebrews 11:29-12:2	Luke 12:49-56
8/26/07	Jeremiah 1:4-10	Psalm 71:1-6	Hebrews 12:18-29	Luke 13:10-17
9/02/07	Jeremiah 2:4-13	Psalm 81:1, 10-16	Hebrews 13:1-8, 15-16	Luke 14:1, 7-14
9/09/07	Jeremiah 18:1-11	Psalm 139:1-6, 13-18	Philemon 1-21	Luke 14:25-33
9/16/07	Jeremiah 4:11-12, 22-28	Psalm 14	1 Timothy 1:12-17	Luke 15:1-10
9/23/07	Jeremiah 8:18-9:1	Psalm 79:1-9	1 Timothy 2:1-7	Luke 16:1-13
9/30/07	Jeremiah 32:1-3a, 6-15	Psalm 91:1-6, 14-16	1 Timothy 6:6-19	Luke 16:19-31
10/07/07	Lamentations 1:1-6	Psalm 137	2 Timothy 1:1-14	Luke 17:5-10
10/14/07	Jeremiah 29:1, 4-7	Psalm 66:1-12	2 Timothy 2:8-15	Luke 17:11-19
10/21/07	Jeremiah 31:27-34	Psalm 119:97-104	2 Timothy 3:14-4:5	Luke 18:1-8
10/28/07	Joel 2:23-32	Psalm 65	2 Timothy 4:6-8, 16-18	Luke 18:9-14
11/01/07	Daniel 7:1-3, 15-18	Psalm 149	Ephesians 1:11-23	Luke 6:20-31
11/04/07	Habakkuk 1:1-4; 2:1-4	Psalm 119:137-144	2 Thessalonians 1:1-4, 11-12	Luke 19:1-10

*This list represents one possible selection of lessons and psalms from the lectionary for Year C [January 1–November 25] and Year A [December 2–30]. For a complete listing, see *The Revised Common Lectionary*.

Date	First Lesson	Psalm	Second Lesson	Gospel Lesson
11/11/07	Haggai 1:15*b*–2:9	Psalm 145:1-5, 17-21	2 Thessalonians 2:1-5, 13-17	Luke 20:27-38
11/18/07	Isaiah 65:17-25	Psalm 98	2 Thessalonians 3:6-13	Luke 21:5-19
11/22/07	Deuteronomy 26:1-11	Psalm 100	Philippians 4:4-9	John 6:25-35
11/25/07	Jeremiah 23:1-6	Luke 1:68-79	Colossians 1:11-20	Luke 23:33-43
12/02/07	Isaiah 2:1-5	Psalm 122	Romans 13:11-14	Matthew 24:36-44
12/09/07	Isaiah 11:1-10	Psalm 72:1-7, 18-19	Romans 15:4-13	Matthew 3:1-12
12/16/07	Isaiah 35:1-10	Psalm 146:5-10	James 5:7-10	Matthew 11:2-11
12/23/07	Isaiah 7:10-16	Psalm 80:1-7, 17-19	Romans 1:1-7	Matthew 1:18-25
12/24/07	Isaiah 9:2-7	Psalm 96	Titus 2:11-14	Luke 2:1-20
12/30/07	Isaiah 63:7-9	Psalm 148	Hebrews 2:10-18	Matthew 2:13-23

°This list represents one possible selection of lessons and psalms from the lectionary for Year C [January 1–November 25] and Year A [December 2-30]. For a complete listing, see *The Revised Common Lectionary*.

LITURGICAL COLORS

If the gospel can be proclaimed visually, why should it not be? Color helps form general expectations for any occasion. Traditionally, purples, grays, and blues have been used for seasons of a penitential character such as Advent and Lent, although any dark colors could be used. White has been used for events or seasons with strong christological meaning such as the Baptism of the Lord or the Easter Season. Yellows and golds are also possibilities at such times. Red has been reserved for occasions relating to the Holy Spirit (such as the Day of Pentecost or ordinations) or to commemorations of the martyrs. Green has been used for seasons such as the Season after Epiphany or the Season after Pentecost. The absence of any colored textiles from Maundy Thursday to the Easter Vigil is a striking use of contrast. Colors and textures can be used most effectively in textiles for hangings on pulpits, on lecterns (if any), for the stoles worn by ordained ministers, or for ministerial vestments.*

Advent: Violet (purple) or blue

Christmas: Gold or white for December 24-25. White thereafter, through the Baptism of the Lord. (Or, in the days between January 6 and the Sunday of the Baptism, green may be used.)

Ordinary Time (both after Epiphany-Baptism and after Pentecost): Green

Transfiguration: White

Lent Prior to Holy Week: Violet. Black is sometimes used for Ash Wednesday.

Early Holy Week: On Palm-Passion Sunday, violet (purple) or [blood] red may be specified. For the Monday, Tuesday, and Wednesday of Holy Week, the same options exist, although with variations as to which color to use on each day.

Triduum: For Holy Thursday, violet (purple) or [blood] red may be used during the day and changed to white for the evening Eucharist. Then the church may be stripped.

Good Friday and Holy Saturday: Stripped or black; or [blood] red in some churches on Good Friday.

Great Fifty Days: White or gold. Or gold for Easter Day and perhaps its octave, then white for the remainder of the season until the Vigil of Pentecost.

Day of Pentecost: [Fire] red

Annunciation, Visitation, and Presentation of Jesus: White

Commemoration of Martyrs: [Blood] red

Commemoration of Saints Not Martyred: White

All Saints: White

Christ the King: White**

* James F. White, *Introduction to Christian Worship* (rev. ed.; Nashville: Abingdon Press, 1990), 85-86.

** Laurence Hull Stookey, *Calendar: Christ's Time for the Church* (Nashville: Abingdon Press, 1996), 156-57.

CLASSICAL PRAYERS

Morning Prayer

Almighty and most merciful Father; We have erred, and strayed from thy ways like lost sheep. We have followed too much the devices and desires of our own hearts. We have offended against thy holy laws. We have left undone those things which we ought to have done; And we have done those things which we ought not to have done; And there is no health in us. But thou, O Lord, have mercy upon us, miserable offenders. Spare thou those, O God, who confess their faults. Restore thou those who are penitent; According to thy promises declared unto mankind In Christ Jesus our Lord. And grant, O most merciful Father, for his sake; That we may hereafter live a godly, righteous, and sober life, To the glory of thy holy Name. Amen.

The Book of Common Prayer (New York: Thomas Nelson and Sons, 1928), 6.

Eucharistic

Make this Bread the precious Body of thy Christ, . . . and that which is in this Chalice, the precious Blood of thy Christ . . . transmuting them by thy Holy Spirit . . . so that they may be to those that partake, unto sobriety of soul, unto remission of sins, unto communion of thy Holy Spirit, unto fulfilment of the Kingdom of the heavens, unto boldness toward thee, not unto judgement, nor unto condemnation.

The Divine Liturgies of Our Fathers among the Saints: John Chrysostom and Basil the Great (ed. J. N. W. B. Robertson; London: David Nutt, 1894), 303.

An Orthodox Prayer

I praise Thee, O God of our Fathers, I hymn Thee, I bless Thee, I give thanks unto Thee for Thy great and tender mercy. To Thee I flee, O merciful and mighty God. Shine into my heart with the True Sun of Thy righteousness. Enlighten my mind and keep all my senses, that henceforth I may walk uprightly and keep Thy commandments, and may finally attain unto eternal life, even to Thee, Who art the source of life, and be admitted to the glorious fruition of Thy inaccessible Light. For Thou art my God, and unto Thee, O Father, Son and Holy Spirit, be ascribed glory, now and ever and unto ages of ages. Amen.

http://www.orthodoxphotos.com/readings/prayers/thanksgiving.shtml.

A Covenant Prayer in the Wesleyan Tradition

I am no longer my own, but thine.
Put me to what thou wilt, rank me with whom thou wilt.
Put me to doing, put me to suffering.
Let me be employed by thee or laid aside for thee,
exalted for thee or brought low for thee.
Let me be full, let me be empty.
Let me have all things, let me have nothing.
I freely and heartily yield all things
to thy pleasure and disposal.
And now, O glorious and blessed God,
Father, Son, and Holy Spirit,
thou art mine, and I am thine. So be it.
And the covenant which I have made on earth,
let it be ratified in heaven. Amen.

The United Methodist Hymnal (Nashville: The United Methodist Publishing House, 1989), 607.

A General Thanksgiving

Almighty God, Father of all mercies, we, thine unworthy servants, do give thee most humble and hearty thanks for all thy goodness and loving-kindness to us, and to all men; [*particularly to those who desire now to offer up their praises and thanksgivings for thy late mercies vouchsafed unto them]. We bless thee for our creation, preservation, and all the blessings of this life; but above all, for thine inestimable love in the redemption of the world by our Lord Jesus Christ; for the means of grace, and for the hope of glory. And, we beseech thee, give us that due sense of all thy mercies, that our hearts may be unfeignedly thankful; and that we show forth thy praise, not only with our lips, but in our lives, by giving up ourselves to thy service, and by walking before thee in holiness and righteousness all our days; through Jesus Christ our Lord, to whom, with thee and the Holy Ghost, be all honour and glory, world without end. Amen.

The Book of Common Prayer (New York: Thomas Nelson and Sons, 1928), 33.

Prayer of Saint Francis of Assisi

Lord, make me an instrument of your peace.
Where there is hatred, let me sow love;
Where there is injury, pardon;
Where there is doubt, faith;
Where there is despair, hope;
Where there is darkness, light;
Where there is sadness, joy.
Divine Master,
grant that I may not so much seek
To be consoled as to console;
To be understood as to understand;
To be loved as to love;
For it is in giving that we receive;
It is in pardoning that we are pardoned;
It is in dying that we are born to eternal life.

A Prayer of Saint Chrysostom

Almighty God, who hast given us grace at this time with one accord to make our common supplications unto thee; and dost promise that when two or three are gathered together in thy Name thou wilt grant their requests; Fulfil now, O Lord, the desires and petitions of thy servants, as may be most expedient for them; granting us in this world knowledge of thy truth, and in the world to come life everlasting. Amen.

The Book of Common Prayer (New York: Thomas Nelson and Sons, 1928), 20.

Serenity Prayer

God, grant me the Serenity
To accept the things I cannot change;
Courage to change the things I can;
And Wisdom to know the difference.
                    (Reinhold Niebuhr)

An Orthodox Evening Prayer

O eternal God! Ruler of all creation! Who hast vouchsafed that I should live even down to the present hour, forgive the sins I have committed this day by deed, word, or thought. Cleanse, O Lord, my humble soul of all corporal and spiritual stain. And grant, O Lord, that I may during this night have a peaceful sleep, so that on rising from my humble bed, I should continue to praise Thy holy Name throughout all the days of my life, and that I be victorious over all the physical and spiritual enemies battling against me. Deliver me, O Lord, from all vain thoughts that defile me, and from evil desires. For Thine is the Kingdom, and the Power, and the Glory of the Father, and of the Son, and of the Holy Spirit, now and ever, and unto ages of ages. Amen.

http://ocf.org/OrthodoxPage/prayers/evening.html.

Prayer from Saint Augustine

You are great, O Lord, and greatly to be praised: great is your power and to your wisdom there is no limit. And man, who is a part of your creation, wishes to praise you . . . You arouse him to take joy in praising you, for you have made us for yourself, and our heart is restless until it rests in you . . . Lord, let me seek you by calling upon you, and let me call upon you by believing in you, for you have been preached to us. Lord, my faith calls upon you, that faith which you have given to me, which you have breathed into me by the incarnation of your Son and through the ministry of your preacher.

The Confessions of Saint Augustine (trans. John K. Ryan; New York: Doubleday, 1960), 43.

A Collect for Peace

O God, from whom all holy desires, all good counsels, and all just works do proceed; Give unto thy servants that peace which the world cannot give; that our hearts may be set to obey thy commandments, and also that by thee, we, being defended from the fear of our enemies, may pass our time in rest and quietness; through the merits of Jesus Christ our Saviour. Amen.

The Book of Common Prayer (New York: Thomas Nelson and Sons, 1928), 31.

CLASSICAL AFFIRMATIONS OF FAITH

The Apostles' Creed (ca. 700 C.E.)

I believe in God, the Father Almighty,
   creator of heaven and earth.
I believe in Jesus Christ, his only Son, our Lord,
   who was conceived by the Holy Spirit,
   born of the Virgin Mary,
   suffered under Pontius Pilate,
   was crucified, died, and was buried;
   he descended to the dead. [or "He descended into hell"]
   On the third day he rose again;
   he ascended into heaven,
   is seated at the right hand of the Father,
   and will come again to judge the living and the dead.
I believe in the Holy Spirit,
   the holy catholic church,
   the communion of saints,
   the forgiveness of sins,
   the resurrection of the body
   and the life everlasting. Amen.

The United Methodist Hymnal (Nashville: The United Methodist Publishing House, 1989), 882.

The Nicene Creed (325 C.E.)

We believe in one God,
   the Father, the Almighty,
   maker of heaven and earth,

of all that is, seen and unseen.
We believe in one Lord, Jesus Christ,
    the only Son of God,
    eternally begotten of the Father,
    God from God, Light from Light,
    true God from true God,
    begotten, not made,
    of one Being with the Father;
    through him all things were made.
For us and for our salvation
    he came down from heaven,
    was incarnate of the Holy Spirit and the Virgin Mary
    and became truly human.
    For our sake he was crucified under Pontius Pilate;
    he suffered death and was buried.
    On the third day he rose again
    in accordance with the Scriptures;
    he ascended into heaven
    and is seated at the right hand of the Father.
    He will come again in glory
    to judge the living and the dead,
    and his kingdom will have no end.
We believe in the Holy Spirit, the Lord, the giver of life,
    who proceeds from the Father and the Son,
    who with the Father and the Son
    is worshiped and glorified,
    who has spoken through the prophets.
We believe in one holy catholic and apostolic church.
We acknowledge one baptism
    for the forgiveness of sins.
We look for the resurrection of the dead,
    and the life of the world to come. Amen.

The United Methodist Hymnal (Nashville: The United Methodist Publishing House, 1989), 880.

The Athanasian Creed (ca. 500 c.e.)

Whosoever will be saved, before all things it is necessary that he hold the
    Catholic Faith.

Which Faith except everyone do keep whole and undefiled, without doubt he shall perish everlastingly.

And the Catholic Faith is this: That we worship one God in Trinity, and Trinity in Unity, neither confounding the Persons, nor dividing the Substance.

For there is one Person of the Father, another of the Son, and another of the Holy Ghost.

But the Godhead of the Father, of the Son, and of the Holy Ghost, is all one, the Glory equal, the Majesty co-eternal.

Such as the Father is, such is the Son, and such is the Holy Ghost.

The Father uncreate, the Son uncreate, and the Holy Ghost uncreate.

The Father incomprehensible, the Son incomprehensible, and the Holy Ghost incomprehensible.

The Father eternal, the Son eternal, and the Holy Ghost eternal.

And yet they are not three eternals, but one eternal.

As also there are not three incomprehensibles, nor three uncreated, but one uncreated, and one incomprehensible.

So likewise the Father is Almighty, the Son Almighty, and the Holy Ghost Almighty.

And yet they are not three Almighties, but one Almighty.

So the Father is God, the Son is God, and the Holy Ghost is God.

And yet they are not three Gods, but one God.

So likewise the Father is Lord, the Son Lord, and the Holy Ghost Lord.

And yet not three Lords, but one Lord.

For like as we are compelled by the Christian verity to acknowledge every Person by himself to be both God and Lord,

So are we forbidden by the Catholic Religion, to say, There be three Gods, or three Lords.

The Father is made of none, neither created, nor begotten.

The Son is of the Father alone, not made, nor created, but begotten.

The Holy Ghost is of the Father and of the Son, neither made, nor created, nor begotten, but proceeding.

So there is one Father, not three Fathers; one Son, not three Sons; one Holy Ghost, not three Holy Ghosts.

And in this Trinity none is afore, or after other; none is greater, or less than another;

But the whole three Persons are co-eternal together and co-equal.

So that in all things, as is aforesaid, the Unity in Trinity and the Trinity in Unity is to be worshipped.

He therefore that will be saved must thus think of the Trinity.

Furthermore, it is necessary to everlasting salvation that he also believe rightly the Incarnation of our Lord Jesus Christ.

For the right Faith is, that we believe and confess, that our Lord Jesus Christ, the Son of God, is God and Man;

God, of the Substance of the Father, begotten before the worlds; and Man, of the Substance of his Mother, born in the world;

Perfect God and perfect Man, of a reasonable soul and human flesh subsisting;

Equal to the Father, as touching his Godhead; and inferior to the Father, as touching his Manhood.

Who although he be God and Man, yet he is not two, but one Christ;

One, not by conversion of the Godhead into flesh, but by taking of the Manhood into God;

One altogether; not by confusion of Substance, but by unity of Person.

For as the reasonable soul and flesh is one man, so God and Man is one Christ;

Who suffered for our salvation, descended into hell, rose again the third day from the dead.

He ascended into heaven, he sitteth on the right hand of the Father, God Almighty, from whence he shall come to judge the quick and the dead.

At whose coming all men shall rise again with their bodies and shall give account for their own works.

And they that have done good shall go into life everlasting; and they that have done evil into everlasting fire.

This is the Catholic Faith, which except a man believe faithfully, he cannot be saved.

The Book of Common Prayer (New York: Oxford, 1979), 864-65.

The Creed of Chalcedon (451 c.e.)

Therefore, following the holy fathers, we all with one accord teach men to acknowledge one and the same Son, our Lord Jesus Christ, at once complete in Godhead and complete in manhood, truly God and truly man, consisting also of a reasonable soul and body; of one substance (*homoousios*) with the Father as regards his Godhead, and at the same time of one substance with us as regards his manhood; like us in all respects, apart from sin; as regards his Godhead, begotten of the Father before the ages, but yet as regards his manhood begotten, for us men and for our salvation, of Mary the Virgin, the God-bearer (*Theotokos*); one and the same Christ, Son, Lord, Only-begotten, recognized in two natures, without confusion, without change, without division, without separation; the distinction of natures being in no way annulled by the union, but rather the characteristics of each nature being preserved and coming together to form one person and subsistence, not as parted or separated into two persons, but one and the same Son and Only-begotten God the Word, Lord Jesus Christ; even as the prophets from earliest times spoke of him, and our Lord Jesus Christ himself taught us, and the creed of the Fathers [the Nicene Creed] has handed down to us.

The Book of Common Prayer (New York: Oxford, 1979), 864.

CONTEMPORARY AFFIRMATIONS OF FAITH

A New Creed (United Church of Canada)

We are not alone,
   we live in God's world.

We believe in God:
   who has created and is creating,
   who has come in Jesus,
      the Word made flesh,
      to reconcile and make new,
   who works in us and others by the Spirit.

We trust in God.

We are called to be the Church:
   to celebrate God's presence,
   to live with respect in Creation,
   to love and serve others,
   to seek justice and resist evil,
   to proclaim Jesus, crucified and risen,
      our judge and our hope.

In life, in death, in life beyond death,
   God is with us.
We are not alone.

   Thanks be to God.

"A New Creed" from *Voices United: The Hymn and Worship Book of the United Church of Canada*, The United Church Publishing House, 2003 reprint, p. 918. Reprinted with permission.

The Korean Creed

We believe in the one God, maker and ruler of all things, Father of all men, the source of all goodness and beauty, all truth and love.

We believe in Jesus Christ, God manifest in the flesh, our teacher, example, and Redeemer, the Savior of the world.

We believe in the Holy Spirit, God present with us for guidance, for comfort, and for strength.

We believe in the forgiveness of sins, in the life of love and prayer, and in grace equal to every need.

We believe in the Word of God contained in the Old and New Testaments as the sufficient rule both of faith and of practice.

We believe in the Church as the fellowship for worship and for service of all who are united to the living Lord.

We believe in the kingdom of God as the divine rule in human society, and in the brotherhood of man under the fatherhood of God.

We believe in the final triumph of righteousness, and in the life everlasting. Amen.

"The Korean Creed," *The Book of Worship for Church and Home* (Nashville: The Methodist Publishing House, 1964), 180.

A Modern Affirmation

We believe in God the Father,
    infinite in wisdom, power, and love,
    whose mercy is over all his works,
    and whose will is ever directed to his children's good.
We believe in Jesus Christ,
    Son of God and Son of man,
    the gift of the Father's unfailing grace,
    the ground of our hope,
    and the promise of our deliverance from sin and death.
We believe in the Holy Spirit
    as the divine presence in our lives,
    whereby we are kept in perpetual remembrance
    of the truth of Christ,
    and find strength and help in time of need.
We believe that this faith should manifest itself

in the service of love
as set forth in the example of our blessed Lord,
to the end
that the kingdom of God may come upon the earth. Amen.

"A Modern Affirmation," *The United Methodist Hymnal* (Nashville: The United Methodist Publishing House, 1989), 885.

World Methodist Council Social Affirmation

We believe in God, creator of the world and of all people;
and in Jesus Christ, incarnate among us,
who died and rose again;
and in the Holy Spirit,
present with us to guide, strengthen, and comfort.
We believe;
God, help our unbelief.
We rejoice in every sign of God's kingdom:
in the upholding of human dignity and community;
in every expression of love, justice, and reconciliation;
in each act of self-giving on behalf of others;
in the abundance of God's gifts
entrusted to us that all may have enough;
in all responsible use of the earth's resources.
Glory be to God on high;
and on earth, peace.
We confess our sin, individual and collective,
by silence or action:
through the violation of human dignity
based on race, class, age, sex, nation, or faith;
through the exploitation of people
because of greed and indifference;
through the misuse of power
in personal, communal, national, and international life;
through the search for security
by those military and economic forces
that threaten human existence;
through the abuse of technology
which endangers the earth and all life upon it.

Lord, have mercy;
Christ, have mercy;
Lord, have mercy.
We commit ourselves individually and as a community
   to the way of Christ:
      to take up the cross;
   to seek abundant life for all humanity;
   to struggle for peace with justice and freedom;
   to risk ourselves in faith, hope, and love,
      praying that God's kingdom may come.
Thy kingdom come on earth as it is in heaven. Amen.

Adopted by the World Methodist Council, Nairobi, Kenya, 1986. Used with permission of the World Methodist Council.

II. SERMONS AND WORSHIP AIDS

JANUARY 7, 2007

❧❧❧

Baptism of the Lord/First Sunday after the Epiphany

Readings: Isaiah 43:1-7; Psalm 29 (*UMH* 761); Acts 8:14-17; Luke 3:15-17, 21-22

Baptized to What?
Luke 3:15-17, 21-22

Last summer my wife and I were visiting Santa Fe, New Mexico. We were searching for a piece of art to go in the foyer area of a new addition to our church building. We went from shop to shop, experiencing the local art. We entered one gallery and I was taken aback by a bronze sculpture created by a respected artist named Gib Singleton. Singleton's work appears in the Vatican, the Cowboy Hall of Fame, and he was a favorite artist of Golda Meir, Israel's prime minister. A few years ago he helped restore Michelangelo's *Pietà* when vandals damaged it.

The particular piece that stopped me in my tracks was called *The Dove*. It brings to life that moment when Christ has just been baptized. A dove has descended and landed on the outstretched hand of the Savior. What is so compelling about the way the artist represents that moment in Christ's life? First, Christ's arms are outstretched in a manner that seems to be welcoming all. It is as if Jesus stands ready to embrace anyone who is willing to come to him. Second, Christ's outstretched arms and his body form a perfect cross. The artist's intent is to reveal to us that Christ's baptism commissions him to begin a mission on earth that will culminate in the ultimate saving act performed on the cross. The Christ portrayed by the artist's sculpture is both welcoming to all and ready to die for the sins of all. This welcoming and sacrificial character of Christ is symbolized in the moment of baptism when God's Spirit descends upon him to empower him for all that lies ahead. Christ is baptized to a mission that both welcomes the sinner and redeems the sinner.

Luke tells us that the people were "filled with expectation, and all were questioning in their hearts concerning John, whether he might be the Messiah" (Luke 3:15).

As sometimes happens, the people are close to mistaking the messenger for the message. But John the Baptist clears things up by saying, "I baptize you with water; but one who is more powerful than I is coming; I am not worthy to untie the thong of his sandals" (v. 16).

It is a powerful statement. While John is popular enough to draw a crowd, he is honest enough to admit that he is not the main attraction. While John baptizes with water, the "one who is more powerful" will baptize with something else. John explains that Jesus will baptize with "the Holy Spirit and fire" (v. 16). I'm not sure which is more frightening, being baptized with God's Holy Spirit or with fire. John's point seems to be that Jesus will have an awesome power that will be enacted through baptism. John confirms that Jesus will have the authority to judge souls: "His winnowing fork is in his hand, to clear his threshing floor and to gather the wheat into his granary; but the chaff he will burn with unquenchable fire" (v. 17).

Luke tells us that all of the people were baptized and that Jesus was baptized too. As Jesus is praying, the Holy Spirit descends upon him in the bodily form of a dove. As if that isn't enough, a voice speaks from heaven, saying, "You are my Son, the Beloved; with you I am well pleased" (v. 22). It is a moment of incredible power as the Trinity is joined together in this brief scene.

God's voice affirms three things about Jesus: (1) Christ is God's Son; (2) Christ is loved by God; and (3) God is "well pleased" with Christ.

Perhaps the act of baptism also makes all three affirmations about us: We are God's children; we are loved by God; and God is well pleased with us. I suggest that baptism enables us to follow our part of Christ's mission. We too are called to welcome all and to serve others even unto death in the name of Christ.

John baptizes the sinless Christ into servant and sacrificial ministry. Jesus' baptism represents a moment of empowerment by the Holy Spirit and affirmation by God.

I always get a chill when we begin a funeral service for a sister or a brother in Christ. We lift up the affirmation that this Christian put on Christ in baptism and pray that they may now be clothed with the glory of Christ. Baptism represents the beginning of a journey of sacrificial servanthood that culminates when one enters the very gates of heaven.

Christ lived out his baptism every day as he taught us to feed the hungry, clothe the naked, care for the dying, and share the good news with a broken world. As a people who bear the name of Christian, God calls us to live out our baptisms in the same way, caring for the needy and sharing the good news. We too are baptized to a mission of welcoming and redeeming sinners.

I recently baptized a newborn granddaughter named Allison. The whole process fascinated her four-year-old cousin, Kelsey. She asked her preacher grandpa all kinds of questions about the mechanics of baptism. Another pastor and I were celebrating the baptism. In the middle of the sacrament Kelsey turned to me and said, "More, Papa, more!" Somehow Kelsey understood that this was a moment of great power and affirmation. She wanted to make sure that her cousin Allison got the full dose.

Epiphany celebrates God's unexpected appearances in our lives. Those appearances always remind us of God's equally unexpected forgiveness and love. Baptism celebrates God's love and forgiveness. Jesus commanded his followers to go to all nations, baptizing them in the name of the Father, Son, and Holy Spirit (Matthew 28:19). May we all share some of Kelsey's enthusiasm in fulfilling Christ's command. (Robert Gorrell)

Prayer: An Oprah-Style Sermon

First in a Series of Three on Our Baptismal Vows

Colossians 1:1-14

What is prayer? We will explore this question in an "Oprah-style" sermon. That means it isn't just one-sided—Oprah asks the questions, and her guests or the audience respond.

1. Who taught you to pray?
2. Where is your favorite place to pray?
3. So, what is prayer?

Prayer is all of the answers an audience might give to these questions, plus everything we do to communicate with God. Prayer can be with eyes closed and a bowed head. Prayer can be a big shout of "Thank you, God," when you get the promotion at work, when your spouse comes through surgery, or when your child is born. Prayer can be a walk at dusk spent in awe of the creation. It can be a commute to work with the car radio off— just listening. Prayer is many things.

Because prayer is so many things, I want to share with you what prayers have been helpful in my spiritual life. At different times in my life, different styles of prayer seem to fit. I'm a talker; I don't refresh myself through solitude and being alone. I get charged up and excited spending time in conversation with other people. Consequently, sitting alone and listening for God and to God is not my strong suit. God speaks to me, but not often in the still, small voice that Elijah heard while he sat on that mountaintop and meditated. I hear God in different ways. By observing the world and interacting with other people, I can discern God's will for my life. That discernment is often part of my prayer life, talking with others and asking how they see God at work. One way I pray is to listen to God through other people.

But we all need to change our habits sometimes. My first real job was a miserable experience. My boss was extremely threatening, and I was afraid to go to work. It was such a frightening environment that I was advised to keep a tape recorder on my desk. I would cry every morning in the shower. As I opened the front door of my workplace, I would feel my stomach drop to the floor. I would run up the stairs to my office and hope everything would go all right that day. But as frightening as that job was, I wouldn't take back those six months for anything. Because in the midst of that awful situation, I felt God's protection and presence in a way I never have before or since.

Each day I ran the gauntlet to my office and spent the next hour in prayer. In order to survive, I vowed to give God that first hour in prayer and meditation. Remember, I said I'm not good at listening to God for an entire hour of silence. Since I had trouble focusing in the silence, I found books and written prayers. I tried several different books on meditation until I found the one that fit me. Every morning I used a prayer a friend had given me. And I read a variety of Christian books. Each of these aids on meditation focused me on God. Being so caught up in what was going on in my life and surviving that job, I needed these Christian resources to help center me back on God. That is another type of prayer, using the works of other Christians to help us find our way to God.

When my father died I came to understand another form of prayer that really saved my life. It was a difficult time with many unanswered questions. Through the dreadful time of his funeral, I found the Psalms helpful. In the book of Psalms, you can find every human emotion. There are passages in which we can yell at God through our anger, cry with God in our sorrow, rejoice, and give thanks. Whatever our emotion or state of mind, the Psalms can help us reach out to God. So, at my dad's funeral, I found a breath prayer from the Psalms helpful. A breath prayer is a sentence that you say over and over to yourself, sometimes in bad situations and sometimes in good ones, where you refocus yourself on God. My breath prayer is from Psalm 121: "I lift up my eyes to the hills—from where will my help come? My help comes from the LORD" (v. 1). When I am in difficult situations and anger or fear grips my life, I remember this breath prayer, and I know that God is present in my life and that God is the only help I need.

In your bulletin you will find a space for a breath prayer. Please take a few minutes. What sentence will remind you to refocus on God? *[Give the congregation a few moments to record prayers.]*

Would any of you like to share your breath prayer? Remember, this is an "Oprah-style" sermon. *[Be sure everyone can hear those who choose to share their prayers.]*

When all else fails, and you don't know what to say and have nothing to read, thanksgiving is always a good place to start. Today we are going to give thanks and praise. In the Colossians passage, Paul gives thanks for the little church at Colosse and the people there struggling to grow in their knowledge of God. Paul shows us that giving thanks is another way to pray. In all of our situations, there is always at least one thing for which we can give God praise. When we don't know what to say, or just have not talked to God in a while, giving thanks is a good place to start.

Take another moment to pray by writing down your thanks. This is a time to push everything else aside and focus your life on the blessings that you have received through your Lord.

Okay, "Oprah" is back.

1. What are you thankful for?
2. What is God doing in this world to be thankful for?
3. What is God doing in this church for which you would like to give thanks?

[Listen to and celebrate the congregational sharing.]

Amen. (Jennifer H. Williams)

Worship Aids

Call to Worship

"O LORD, our Sovereign, how majestic is your name in all the earth! You have set your glory above the heavens. Out of the mouths of babes and infants you have founded a bulwark because of your foes, to silence the enemy and the avenger ... O LORD, our Sovereign, how majestic is your name in all the earth!" (Psalm 8:1-2, 9).

Prayer of Confession

Dear God, as we stand on the edge of this new year, we pray to be forgiven for our sins of omission and sins of commission committed in the past year. May insights into our culpability serve to steer us into lives more wisely dedicated to your will and ways in the days ahead. Grant us a sense of being forgiven so that we may live more confidently in an uncertain world. In Jesus' name we pray. Amen.

Benediction

We pray, dear God, that our having gotten together in this place of worship today will amount to something worthwhile in our lives. Now may grace, love, and peace direct your way all week long. Amen. (Thomas Lane Butts)

JANUARY 14, 2007

❧❧❧

Second Sunday after the Epiphany

Readings: Isaiah 62:1-5; Psalm 36:5-10 (*UMH* 771); 1 Corinthians 12:1-11; John 2:1-11

God's Powerful Promise!
Isaiah 62:1-5

During the First Gulf War, a young husband from our small-town church was called up to serve. While he was in Iraq his wife had a very public affair. Upon returning home he heard about the whole thing. He had a great love for his wife and a strong desire to keep his family together for the sake of their two small children. He forgave her.

One night, in a large Bible study group, she broke down and shared the whole story. She concluded by saying, "The question for me is this: How can I live with his forgiveness?"

Israel faced a similar dilemma. In chapter 56 Isaiah points out that Israel's leaders are corrupt. In chapter 57 he condemns Israel's worship. In chapter 58 he calls them to obedience. In chapter 59 Isaiah calls the people of Israel to confession and to prepare for judgment. God's glory is the theme for Isaiah in chapter 60 as the prophet reminds his people of God's power. He tells the people that God will gather all the nations together. In chapter 61 Isaiah shares his prophetic call to preach good news. He even makes reference to the law governing the release of slaves after a period of six years of service. In this way the reader is given a hint of what is to come.

Finally, in chapter 62, Isaiah lifts up this incredible image of love and restoration. God will not rest, Isaiah explains, until Zion and Jerusalem's "vindication shines out like the dawn, and her salvation like a burning torch" (v. 1).

In verse 2 Isaiah explains that the people will receive a new name from the mouth of God. The name, given by the Lord, is a sign of vindication. Israel will become like a crown or diadem, beautiful in the hand of God. Then God's renaming process swings into full force: "You shall no more be termed Forsaken, and your land shall no more be termed Desolate; but you shall be called My Delight Is in Her, and your land Married" (v. 4).

Isaiah tells the people that God will delight in them "as the bridegroom rejoices over the bride, so shall your God rejoice over you." Verse 5 also adds that the builder will marry the bride. The builder is God and the bride is Israel.

It might be helpful to note the corporate nature of both the sin and the redemption pictured by Isaiah. God's people are at fault, but God's love redeems the entire nation. Scripture fully takes into account that while sin often has a corporate origin, it always has a community effect. Because sin affects so many, the need of redemption is even greater. Therefore, the redeeming force must be tremendously powerful.

Last summer we were trying to kill the weeds in our yard. Unfortunately, no matter how we tried, we failed. The home next to us was empty. No one was caring for the yard there, and the weeds had taken over. No matter what we did, the weeds from next door soon found a way to spread into our yard.

In a similar way, Isaiah's Israel is caught up in shared sin. Leaders influence citizens. The demands of the citizens influence leaders. The clergy end up in the middle of everything. When one group gets a little better, another group drags them back down into the pit of sin. Israel needs a complete sin control solution. God's love will provide the answer.

This text from Isaiah offers a powerful symbol of redemption. It will remind some of the image of Christ as the bridegroom found in Revelation. It is also reminiscent of the story of the prophet Hosea and his wayward wife, Gomer, who is also redeemed to demonstrate God's love.

The Gospel reading for this day is John 2:1-11, the story of Jesus at the wedding in Cana. Among other meanings, the story gives us a glimpse at the joy of a wedding. Within that joy the glory of Christ is revealed.

God's glory is revealed in Isaiah's wedding scene as well, not by turning water into wine, but through a similar miraculous process. Jesus takes common water and turns it into precious wine. In like manner, God takes common sinners and turns them into a royal bride. By uniting with God in spiritual marriage, the nation is redeemed and made new again despite its sinful past. In the ancient world, a bride's purity was of ultimate concern. The purity of the bride assured the purity of the marriage. In this scenario, however, Isaiah recognizes that the bride, Israel, is less than pure. The bride is made pure through the act of marriage. The bride is purified not because of any action on the bride's part; the bride is redeemed and made pure due to the gracious and pure love of the bridegroom.

I grew up in a small Midwestern town. A young girl I went to school with had a difficult life. She went out with the wrong kind of boys and at much too early an age. When she was a junior in high school she had a baby out of wedlock. In those days there was a great stigma attached to such an event. The girl's sad life became even more miserable. A boy from a fine local family asked the girl to visit his church youth group. He felt that was what Jesus would want him to do. She went. Eventually they became great friends and were married. Today she is a wonderful wife and mother. Many of the man's friends consider him very lucky to have such a wife.

Love can redeem anyone from any situation. That is God's powerful promise! (Robert Gorrell)

Presence: Why Are You Here?

Second in a Series of Three on Our Baptismal Vows

1 Corinthians 1:18

Why are you here in church this morning? Why are you here? Seriously, ask yourself the question and really ponder it for a moment. Why are you in church this morning?

Your answers may range anywhere from it is just what you do on Sunday morning, or you woke up early and thought you would see what was going on, or because you're supposed to be, or to see what everybody is wearing, or to find out how your friends are doing. These may be some of your initial responses, but we all are here to worship God in community. We come to meet God here in this sanctuary and to learn about our faith and how to serve Jesus Christ. That is our promise at baptism, that we will be present with the people of God.

But what must our coming together and giving ourselves to the church look like to outsiders? Paul says in 1 Corinthians 1:18, "For the message about the cross is foolishness to those who are perishing, but to us who are being saved it is the power of God."

If you put yourself in the place of our neighbor, who is still at home this morning, sleeping in or enjoying a second cup of coffee as she or he leisurely reads the newspaper, this must seem crazy. Paul says it must truly look foolish to the outsider. If you were sitting at home right now, and didn't know about Jesus Christ and the wonders that he can do in your heart and the amazing power Christ has to offer salvation, this church stuff might really look foolish. Why in the world would you get up early on a Sunday morning? Yes, this must really look crazy to our neighbors who sit inside their cozy, warm homes on Sunday mornings.

That, or something like it, is what Paul is saying in this verse. He is pointing out the obvious—the rest of the world thinks we believers are crazy, and that isn't a bad thing. "For the message about the cross is foolishness to those who are perishing, but to us who are being saved it is the power of God." If you don't go to church, if you don't know about the salvation Jesus offers, if you don't know about the family that can be formed between common strangers, then the church is foolishness.

But we know why we are here.

We know that it isn't foolishness or craziness. We are being saved, and it is the power of God. We know that when we sit in the pews, when we talk to one of our sisters or brothers in the faith, when we listen to the beauty of the organ or the choir lifts their voices in song, when we hear the words of Christ proclaimed, we know why we are here. We know that Christ has given us a wonderful and powerful gift and that it isn't foolishness. We are here to be present with one another, our families, and to be in the presence of God. We come to worship God and to be filled with the power of the Holy Spirit.

The message of Jesus must truly seem like foolishness to outsiders. We follow a Savior who died on a tree and rose again after three days.

That's pretty unbelievable, but it is true. We believe that Jesus rose from the dead. We know that a little old rugged cross couldn't hold Christ down, or a tomb with a gravestone; a cave with a big old rock rolled in front could not hold him down. Christ took on all our pain and suffering, became like us, so he could identify with us and we could relate to him. Jesus became human so we just might get a better idea about God's unconditional, absolute, never-ending, never-changing, forever-stable love. In Jesus Christ, God shows us how deeply God cares for us.

We know our future, and that means we know why we are here.

Our faith is not just about remembering some past act. Our faith is about filling us for the present and preparing us for the future, and that is not foolish. As I said, you come here on Sunday mornings; you leave the paper, the television, and the warmth to come to church. You spend your evenings in committee meetings. You miss the evening news, you leave your families who are just finishing dessert, and you come to the church to talk about doing the stuff of ministry for others, planning activities for other people's children, painting the church when your own house still needs another coat of paint. Then, to top it off, you give your money. You sacrifice a trip to the movies, a pizza from the local pizzeria, or another new outfit on sale at the mall, for the church. You give out of your first-fruits, not to get another tax rebate, but because God invites you to do so.

We do all this because we know there is something greater than our lives in the world. We are present with one another in the church to give just a little back, because God has given us so much in Jesus Christ and because God is a constant presence with us.

Why are you here? Why do you give your time, your money? Why come and be present in the church?

"For the message about the cross is foolishness to those who are perishing, but to us who are being saved it is the power of God." We really can't answer any of those questions because, unless you know the power of God and the awesomeness of a faith in Jesus Christ, it just seems like foolishness.

Be filled this hour with the very power of God and then go, and show someone why you are here. Amen. (Jennifer H. Williams)

Worship Aids

Call to Worship

"O LORD, our Sovereign, how majestic is your name in all the earth! . . . When I look at your heavens, the work of your fingers, the moon and the stars that you have established; what are human beings that you are mindful of them, mortals that you care for them? . . . O LORD, our Sovereign, how majestic is your name in all the earth!" (Psalm 8:1, 3-4, 9).

Prayer of Confession

Dear God, Creator and sustainer of all life, as much as lies in our power to do so, we bare our hearts and minds before you. We pray to be forgiven not only of those sins of which we are painfully aware but also of the sin that has become so much a part of daily life and practice that we do not notice it anymore. Restore us by your grace that we may leave this place today feeling like the renewed creatures we are. In the dear name of Jesus we pray. Amen.

Benediction

May the grace, love, peace, and joy offered in this service today fill your hearts and minds with fresh hope and resolve, through Jesus Christ our Lord. Amen. (Thomas Lane Butts)

JANUARY 21, 2007

❧❧❧

Third Sunday after the Epiphany

Readings: Nehemiah 8:1-3, 5-6, 8-10; Psalm 19; 1 Corinthians 12:12-31a; Luke 4:14-21

The Body of Christ
1 Corinthians 12:12-31a

It has always amazed me how many different types of people make up the body of Christ. We gather together each week in our individual congregations to study, to fellowship, and to worship God. In one pew sits a lawyer, while in one pew up sits a farmer. Wealthy businessmen sit with poor widows. Together we are the body of Christ.

Paul calls us out of our everyday routines to serve one another for the greater good. God equips the saints for service and gives us the ability to serve Jesus in ways that glorify Jesus' name.

Many pastors become discouraged when someone leaves their church for another. Perhaps God leads individuals to the places where they can serve the body of Christ to the utmost of their abilities. After many years of poor church attendance, I decided it was time to return to the weekly worship routine. I attended a large church in my city that was known for being an active force within the community. In this large congregation, I found myself lost in the pews. It is difficult to lay blame for this occurrence; it is just something that happened. The people of the church were good people. There were just too many of them, and it was easy for someone to slip through the cracks.

One day as I prepared to go to the large church, a friend called me and invited me to her church. Her church was actually closer than the big church in town, but it was quite small, and there were not a lot of folks my age. I decided to attend church with her. Something from that very first day drew me to the church. The people were gracious, the pastor spoke of God's love for me, and I left that day feeling I had found my place of worship. The church provided many opportunities for me to grow in my walk of faith and develop God's call in my life to become a pastor. One of the greatest gifts I received from the pastor at the church was this: we need to worship and attend church where we feel closest to God. I have tried to remember that to avoid disappointment when someone leaves the congregation. God places people where they can truly serve the body of Christ to their fullest.

Anyone who has had a broken appendage knows exactly what Paul writes about in his letter to the church at Corinth. As a teenager, I broke my right thumb. As a right-handed person, I struggled through several long months of doing almost everything with my left hand. God creates each of us with an incredible machine called the body. The parts work together to do some of the simplest and some of the most incredible things imaginable. To a child, holding a fork or a spoon seems quite impossible, but as they grow and practice, this becomes routine and the difficulty is quickly forgotten. As individuals in the body of Christ, it seems difficult, at first, to trust Jesus in all we do, but with practice and spiritual discipline it may even become commonplace. A church runs best when everyone serves God using the spiritual gifts they have been given, gifts that align with our deepest joys and passions. In general, people seem to be happier when they are doing something they enjoy. It is ironic that we understand this to be true when seeking employment, but struggle with it when volunteering for or answering the call to ministry within the congregation.

It is important for Christians to remember that one church is no greater a part of the body of Christ than another. God equips each congregation to serve their community in various and unique ways. The large church I spoke of earlier has become quite adept at serving the poor in the city that surrounds it, while the smaller church does a wonderful job nurturing new Christians and helping individuals distinguish God's call in their lives. Both are important members of the body of Christ, but each serves God in different ways.

The Corinthians seemed to be worried about who possessed the best gift or gifts for ministry. They were concerned about religious power and prestige. Churches today should see this as a valuable lesson as to what is really important in their missions and visions for the future. Paul writes, "But strive for the greater gifts. And I will show you a still more excellent way" (1 Corinthians 12:31), and then begins his discourse on love. The term "unity in diversity" has always been a favorite of mine. Whether an organization is a church or a secular business, the more diverse and different the individuals who make up the larger body, the stronger it will be. A dissenting voice requires the body as a whole to consider every aspect of a decision. For God can be heard in the still, small voice just as easily as in the loudest thunderclap or crescendo. (John Mathis)

Gifts and Service: Use What You Got!

Third in a Series of Three on Our Baptismal Vows

Luke 16:1-8

The Broadway musical *The Life* follows a group of prostitutes and their pimps in the late 1970s on New York's Forty-second Street. The play begins with JoJo, the local con artist, singing about using what you have "to get whatcha want, / before whatcha got is gone" (Ira Gasman, "Use What You Got," *The Life*, Sony Music Entertainment, 1997).

The parable of the shrewd steward reminds me of this song. But how can a parable of Jesus be compared to a song about using people? The steward seems like the character JoJo, using everyone and everything to get his own way. This steward doesn't sound like a character that should be in the New Testament, let alone be an example of Jesus. Are we supposed to follow a person who squanders and cheats to get ahead?

There is no initial redemption for the steward; verse 1 shows how the steward has been squandering his master's property. In ancient culture being a steward was a coveted job because it elevated a person's social standing and importance in the community. While the steward was trusted by his master and given the power to look after his goods and property, the passage says, "Charges were brought to [the master] that this man was squandering his property" (Luke 16:1). These were awful charges, and commentators suggest that not only was he squandering the master's property, but the steward was also slandering his name in the process. So far, the steward is like JoJo.

The steward, now caught red-handed, must examine his options after leaving his current position. Not only is he facing a job loss; his entire life will change when the master releases him. Imagine how desperate he feels, about to lose everything. At the point of desperation, the steward asks himself, "What will I do, now that my master is taking the position away from me?" (v. 3). Then, as any logical person would, he begins to examine his prospects for the future. He sits down and weighs his options. The steward says, "I am not strong enough to dig, and I am ashamed to beg" (v. 3). You can almost hear the honesty when he admits to himself that he does not like his options: manual labor or begging.

At this juncture of the story, I imagine Jesus saying that this man will turn from his wicked ways and believe in God. Here he is, desperate, without job or status, facing the prospects of begging or hard labor. I know Jesus will say that the steward will mend his ways just like the prodigal son. The steward will realize that he has done wrong, beg for forgiveness, and apologize for squandering the master's property.

But this is where Jesus gets us. As in many of Jesus' parables, the expected doesn't happen. Instead of turning toward God and admitting his wrongs, the steward decides upon a plan to save his reputation. He decides to lower the debts owed to his master in the hope of making friends when he is out of work. He acts like JoJo again and uses what he's got to get what he wants before he ain't got no more. He is running out of time; the master will soon return to remove the steward from his post. He must act quickly and get what he wants before the master catches up with him.

So here we have the main character of a Jesus parable squandering his master's money and using his power to get an advantage in the future. We expect the steward to face serious consequences, but Jesus gets us again. The steward isn't run out of town on a rail or tarred and feathered or thrown in prison. Instead, the Scripture says the master "commended" the manager for being dishonest and acting shrewdly (v. 8). What is happening when Jesus has a guy getting commended for being a cheat?

Jesus ends the parable this way: "For the children of this age are more shrewd in dealing with their own generation than are the children of light" (v. 8).

I don't believe Jesus is instructing us to go out and cheat our masters or squander money that is not ours. Rather, Jesus is saying something very powerful. Jesus is telling us to use what we got, to get what we want, before we ain't got no more. Unlike JoJo and the steward, however, we as Christians are called to something more than our own selfish desires. We are called to use the gifts God has given us to get what we want. What we want is to serve Jesus and live life every day, not in a self-consumed manner as the steward does, but to live a life rich toward God. Jesus wants us to use what we got, all of our gifts, in service to him.

We *can* learn from the steward. We can examine our lives and use what we've got to get what we want. God has given each of us gifts and calls us to use them. Through our membership in Christ's church, we have pledged to use all we have in service to him.

The possibilities are endless. We must use what we've got to get what we want. But we must remember that what we want is not for ourselves; it is not so that we can keep our jobs or buy new fancy clothes or remain members of the country club. What we want is to use our gifts to serve Jesus Christ.

Remember, "you gotta use what you got" to serve Jesus Christ. Amen. (Jennifer H. Williams)

Worship Aids

Call to Worship

"O LORD, our Sovereign, how majestic is your name in all the earth! ... I will give thanks to the LORD with my whole heart; I will tell of your wonderful deeds. I will be glad and exult in you; I will sing praise to your name, O Most High" (Psalms 8:1; 9:1-2).

Prayer of Confession

We confess, O Lord, that our hearts ache over the sin that we must confess again and again because we have not disciplined our lives in such a way as to turn away from what we know to be wrong. Forgive our willfulness, our carelessness, and our slowness to learn and obey. Touch us again with the grace of forgiveness. In the name of Jesus, amen.

Benediction

We have heard the music, the Scripture, the sermon, and the prayer; now may all that has been given us in this time of worship serve to strengthen us and make us whole. Go in peace. Amen. (Thomas Lane Butts)

JANUARY 28, 2007

≈≈≈

Fourth Sunday after the Epiphany

Readings: Jeremiah 1:4-10; Psalm 71:1-6; 1 Corinthians 13:1-13; Luke 4:21-30

True Love
1 Corinthians 13:1-13

If someone were to ask me, "What is the greatest theological truth?" I would have to say simply, "Jesus loves you." Paul takes time out in his letter to the church at Corinth to explain just what is really important to them as a body of believers. It is not who has the most spiritual gifts, who drives the nicest car to church, or who owns the most oxen or sheep. It is love. God is love. As followers of Christ, we are called to love one another regardless of the circumstances. Sometimes this is difficult and may seem completely impossible. Paul tries his best to describe love so that we may find it easier to love our neighbors as we love God. How can one truly describe something that must be experienced firsthand? Paul attempts to describe the indescribable. His description challenges us to seek God's guidance to teach us how to love—love that is patient, love that does not insist on its own way. God blesses us when God allows us to see perfect love.

Occasionally, we are allowed to see individuals give selflessly of themselves to serve the greater good of God's kingdom. Each year our church youth go on a mission trip within our state. They serve a few hours a day repairing homes for the less fortunate, working in soup kitchens, or spending time with the elderly in nursing homes. When they return each day, you can see the joy and love of Christ in their faces. They feel blessed by those they have served and feel that they have made a difference in someone's life.

Paul begins his discourse by explaining that all the spiritual gifts in the world mean nothing if those receiving them do not love one another. It is important to notice when Paul writes, "If I have all faith . . . but do not have love, I am nothing" (1 Corinthians 13:2). A great faith in Jesus Christ is pointless if the individual does not fully love. Every church seems to have someone who has the greatest faith in the world but does not seem to like too many people, let alone love them. The church in Corinth must have been filled with many individuals like that, people who were difficult to work with or wanted to do everything themselves. No individual can do God's work alone, without a community of support. Fellowship is a vital part of the body of Christ, whether in a small church or an ecumenical gathering. Love bonds believers together to do the work of Jesus Christ in the world.

There is no greater feeling in the world than to be loved. Children experience love from their parents and learn as they grow up what it means to nurture and love another. When God blesses a man and a woman to find each other and fall "in love," no expression can truly describe the joy they have found. Perhaps that is why this passage from Paul's letter is read so often at weddings. It is an attempt to put into words what a couple is experiencing in their relationship. True love is sometimes difficult to find in our world. Divorce rates are high, and the number of singles in our country is on the rise. This passage illustrates to us the power of love to transform and rejuvenate relationships, especially our relationship with Jesus Christ.

Finally, Paul's letter is an attempt to explain eternal truth in an incomplete existence. "Love never ends" (v. 8). It looks as if Paul is telling us that we cannot fully experience all the aspects of life in our earthly lives. We experience a portion of God's love through other people we encounter along the way. We take a part of that love and share it with others. Paul tells us "we see in a mirror, dimly" (v. 12). I did not fully understand this until several years ago when the small town in which I live found itself in the path of Hurricane Isabel. We lost electrical power for more than a week. Flashlights and candles became my only sources of light at night. If you have ever tried to look into a mirror using indirect light from a flashlight, you have an idea of what Paul is writing. You can make out your reflection, but it is not possible to see the entire picture clearly. Our vision is blurred by the darkness that surrounds us. Sometimes the darkness of sin that surrounds us blurs our relationship with Christ. We need the light of Christ to guide us to lead lives of holiness. Living in the light of Christ reveals to others the power of transformation. God transforms us into new beings capable of sharing Christ's love with the world. (John Mathis)

It's About Trust

First in a Series of Three on the Christian Faith

1 Corinthians 8:1-13; Mark 1:21-28

What is Christian faith? Is it believing certain creeds, having a moving experience of God's mercy in Christ, asking Jesus into your heart, doing deeds of mercy and justice, being a member of a church, reading the Bible, being a good citizen, being baptized, worshiping regularly in your church, praying?

These things are desirable and a part of Christian experience and practice, but none of them alone makes one a Christian.

Today we begin a three-part series on the Christian faith. What are the distinguishing marks of a Christian? Today we examine the question, "What does it mean to have faith?"

Classically, Christians have said, "We are saved by grace, effective by faith." God's grace is at the heart of our experiences of life and the hope we have in Christ. This grace is incorporated into our lives through faith. But just what does it mean to say we have faith? Perhaps it is best to start with the things faith is not.

Faith is not intellectual agreement with certain beliefs. Christian faith is not a statement about the nature of God or the work of Christ. Simply agreeing with certain statements about God or Christ does not make one a Christian.

Faith is also not a blind hope that God will make our lives easy or that God will fix the ills we face. Faith does not protect us from illness, accident, betrayal, stress, or death. The Christian faith is not a belief that God will banish trouble from our lives.

If faith is neither acceptance of a set of beliefs or doctrines nor protection from trouble, then just what is faith? Faith is trust. When the New Testament speaks of faith, we would understand the message better if the word *trust* were substituted. Christian faith is a life of trust in God in all times, places, and circumstances.

Today's Gospel lesson points toward this trust. It is Jesus' first healing recorded by Mark and points to Jesus' healing ministry, which was based on trust. After a healing, Jesus often said to the person healed, "Your faith has made you whole." Those who were healed trusted Jesus before he did anything for them. Trust preceded healing. The sequence was not that Jesus healed and then they had faith. No, they had faith in the absence of healing.

Faith is trust in God even in the absence of healing. Christians say confidently, "God can be trusted." We trust not only when life is kind to us, but we trust also in hardship. We say, "We trust not only when we are in the sunshine of God's love, but also when we are in the darkness of despair."

The Christ story marches to a cross and the very worst life can give. We trust that in the Resurrection, God has the last word. God's last word may be late, but it is a word of love and grace. We trust God even when on the cross.

This trust takes many forms.

First, Christian faith trusts God for today. The Lord's Prayer seeks nothing for tomorrow, but only for those things we need today. In the Sermon on the Mount, Jesus asks, "Can any of you by worrying add a single hour to your span of life?" (Matthew 6:27). Christian faith is marked by a quiet confidence that God's grace will be sufficient for today. It is a trust that embraces today's joys and troubles, and worries not about tomorrow.

Further, Christian faith trusts that God's "nature and name is love." There is plenty of evidence to the contrary. A strong case can be made that only the strong survive, that might makes right, and that the world is ultimately a dangerous fearsome place. Christians are aware of this, but trust that God's "nature and name is love."

Finally, Christian faith trusts God not only for this life but also for the life to come. True Christian faith is neither focused on heaven nor a strategy to escape hell. It simply trusts that God's love is not bounded by our deaths. Christians can die at peace not because of a belief in heaven but because of an utter trust in God.

Leonard Sweet tells the following story in the February 2, 1992, edition of *Homiletics*.

> On March 1, 1990, Jean and Ken Chaney, while attempting to negotiate a little-used road in [the Sierra National Forest], skidded off into a huge snowbank. With a blizzard swirling around them, [they] decided to sit tight. As they waited for help to arrive, the couple began to keep a diary of their actions. [They wrote], "We began to realize that we were on a road that isn't maintained during the winter.... We have no idea what lies ahead.... We are completely and utterly in God's hand!!

What better place to be!!" They endured those days by singing hymns together, quoting all the Bible verses they could recall, and praying. Still no one came. On March 18 Jean Chaney made the following entry in their diary: "Dad went to the Lord at 7:30 this evening.... It was so peaceful I didn't even know he left. The last thing I heard him say was 'Thank the Lord. I think I'll be with him soon.... I can't see. Bye. I love you.'"

This utter trust is the meaning of Christian faith. Faith does not depend on a happy ending. It does not require rescue from all ills. It trusts that nothing in life or death can "separate us from the love of God in Christ Jesus our Lord" (Romans 8:38-39). Amen. (Carl L. Schenck)

Worship Aids

Call to Worship

"O LORD, our Sovereign, how majestic is your name in all the earth! ... The LORD sits enthroned forever, he has established his throne for judgment. He judges the world with righteousness; he judges the people with equity" (Psalm 8:1; 9:7-8).

Prayer of Confession

We confess, dear God, the distance we feel from you. In our minds we know all we have been taught about how you are with us always, but on some days you seem far away. Forgive our love of things, our fear of adversity, our trials, and our paltry devotional lives that have distanced us from you. Give us a mind to know of your presence even when we do not feel your presence. In the name of Jesus, amen.

Benediction

When we encounter adversity and temptation this week, may we remember that we belong to the community of Christ in our fellowship with the people with whom we have worshiped today. In the remembered name of Jesus, amen. (Thomas Lane Butts)

FEBRUARY 4, 2007

❦❦❦

Fifth Sunday after the Epiphany

Readings: Isaiah 6:1-8, (9-13); Psalm 138 (*UMH* 853); 1 Corinthians 15:1-11; Luke 5:1-11

The Greatest Book, the Greatest Call
Isaiah 6:1-13

Psalms may win the title of "Most Popular Old Testament Book," and the first five books (the Pentateuch) are the most important to Judaism. But for Christians, Isaiah may be the greatest book of the old covenant. Jesus often quoted Isaiah, including an extended quote Jesus used as a prelude to his own ministry (see Luke 4:17-19). Isaiah is filled with messianic prophecies, which the Gospel writers tell us were fulfilled in Jesus. We find many familiar passages and pithy quotes in the book of Isaiah. And the book is beautifully written, a masterpiece of prose and poetry, so it is hardly a surprise that many of our hymns use Isaiah as their text, including one of the most popular contemporary hymns, "Here I Am, Lord" by Dan Schutte, who cites Isaiah 6:8 as his inspiration.

The name Isaiah in Hebrew is Yesh'yahu, which means "the salvation of Jehovah." He was the son of Amoz, who was apparently a common man, not a peasant but certainly not royalty. Nevertheless, young Isaiah became part of the royal court in Jerusalem, as a religious adviser and prophet to Uzziah, king of Judah. Gaining such an honored position and moving into the royal palace would seem like a high enough achievement for a young man of common blood, and Isaiah was surely tempted to rest on his laurels. But a prestigious job does not exempt us from an even higher vocation; in the literal sense of the word, Isaiah was called by God.

Interestingly, the call was not explicitly direct or personal. Isaiah was not called by name, but in his vision, merely overheard a general call from God: "Whom shall I send? And who will go for us?" And Isaiah responded, "Here am I; send me!" (Isaiah 6:8). Can we be so bold? Why do we wait for some direct, specific instruction from God or a "burning bush" experience before we take up the call to be ministers and missionaries for God? The call of God is indeed general. It is a call laid upon all believers. The greatest call of God is not the famous "call to preach," but rather the call to whatever you personally hear and, most important, answer! Yes, the vision came to Isaiah; perhaps Isaiah was singled out because of his royal office, but the totality of Scripture supports the idea that God's call extends to everyone, not just to a chosen few. The whole purpose of Jesus' calling the Twelve was so that they could, in turn, go into the whole world and call others. Isaiah was bold to answer the call from the One seated high on the majestic throne of heaven. We are summoned to a similar boldness in claiming our place of ministry in the kingdom.

After his powerful vision, Isaiah went on to exercise an even greater boldness in a lifetime of ministry. With uncompromising firmness, he brazenly criticized whichever king happened to be on the throne. Isaiah's challenge to his listeners was usually focused through two simple themes: turn to the Holy One of Israel and worship God only; and care for the poor and the oppressed. These themes were central to Christ's message as well. The message is one we are called to receive and, in turn, share with others.

Another theme recurrent in Isaiah's writing is that there was still hope for Israel (and likewise, for us). But our hope depends on how we answer God. Isaiah told the king and the nation that if they turned back to God, began to live rightly, and treated the poor with justice, the consequence would be a land of peace and joy and prosperity. This promise of the potential for a golden age, or paradise, is often connected with the messianic promise, which emerges later in the book of Isaiah. It was not a message of "pie in the sky." Isaiah was concerned with the here and now. He called his people to reform their social behavior, not just their individual piety. In other words, developing a just society that treats the poor fairly and the infirm with compassion is as important as personal holiness. That is a call that seems equally relevant in our time, as we face the greatest gap between the rich and the poor in history.

God's call upon Christians today begs for boldness like that of Isaiah. Do not wait for a FedEx from God. Stand up where you are, wave your hands in the air, and cry out, "Here am I. Send me!" (Lance Moore)

Drawn to Jesus

Second in a Series of Three on the Christian Faith

Isaiah 40:21-31; Mark 1:29-39

Last week we began a three-part sermon series on the Christian faith. You may remember we concluded that Christian faith was utter trust in God regardless of the circumstances. This trust is the foundation of the Christian life of faith, but it is not the whole structure. Without the foundation, everything crumbles. Without the rest of the structure, it remains incomplete. So today we will build an additional part of the structure of faith as we consider the devotional life.

Christians are drawn to Jesus Christ. Christ reveals to us the nature of the God we trust in faith. Without an acquaintance with Jesus, we do not know, understand, or fully experience God. Christian faith seeks Christ. It is drawn to Jesus. It responds to a tug on the heart and mind that connects us to Christ. The budding Christian faith is drawn to Jesus just as the people of Capernaum were in today's Gospel lesson. They found Jesus and his power irresistible. So will we if we just get acquainted with him. Yet, tragically, many who call themselves Christians are largely unfamiliar with Jesus. They give him lip service, but do not know him. They have not responded to the lure of the Christ.

To respond to the lure of Christ is to immerse oneself in the Gospels. It is amazing how many people say they know Jesus, but don't have a rudimentary grasp of the life and teaching of Jesus. Their biblical knowledge seems to skip from Christmas to Easter without touching down anywhere in between. Their knowledge of Jesus is largely made up of a few stray sayings or stories and a phrase or two from a familiar hymn, mixed with their own subjective wishes and impressions of what Jesus ought to be like. This ignorance leaves these uninformed believers with a Jesus who never confronts their cherished ideas and who never challenges their comfortable beliefs.

The only real antidote for this imaginary Jesus is a healthy shot of the real thing. Perhaps the only place to get that shot of the real Jesus is in the presentation of him in the Bible. There simply is no substitute for regular exploration of the life of Jesus as presented in the four Gospels. Even listening to preaching will not teach us about Jesus as well as a few minutes each day spent sitting with Jesus as we read about him in the Bible! We have all kinds of excuses. We are busy. Sometimes the Bible is difficult to understand. We have heard them all. But the reality is that there are many accessible translations of the Scriptures that are very readable. And let's face it, we find time for the things we believe are important. Get to know Jesus directly through the eyes of the Gospel writers. This reading is as close to Jesus as we can get.

But reading about Jesus isn't enough. The practice of the Christian faith also includes prayer. As with Bible reading, we can sometimes find prayer difficult, but daily time with God in Christ is essential. I like to think about prayer not as a way to get something, but as a way to be in relationship. Too often our prayers become wish lists of all the things, all the changes, and all the blessings for which we long. Unfortunately, if that is the only way we pray, God is reduced to some kind of celestial Santa responding to our prompting.

Healthy prayer, rooted in Christian faith, is more like a relationship. It is our private interaction with God. Prayer is the time when we share with God the hopes and hurts of our hearts and when we experience God's intimate presence in our lives. Relationships require time and they require honesty. We could not sustain a healthy marriage or friendship without time and honesty. So it is in our relationship with God. Our time in prayer should be long enough to sustain a relationship and honest enough to prompt intimacy. This means that we share with God not only our hopes and concerns but also our fears and failures. We let God know of those ways in which we may feel God has let us down. We celebrate the gifts of life and creation. In these and other ways, prayer becomes a relationship with God that nothing in this life can take away from us. That relationship protects and strengthens the trust that is the foundation of faith.

Finally, the Christian faith cultivates community. Association with others who share the faith helps us hold steady to our faith. The communal aspect of the Christian faith has many forms. Worship is central. When we sing the songs, pray the prayers, hear the Scriptures read and proclaimed, and give of our resources in community, our faith is restored and strengthened.

In addition to worship, Christian community forms in classes, choirs, fellowship meals, shared sacraments, and shared work. Every time we interact with another person who lives the faith, we are formed in ours. There is no solitary Christianity. Jesus himself began his ministry by calling others to join him. His ministry attracted a few intimate disciples, hundreds of followers, and even more interested listeners. The Jesus story is the story of community. Our faith goes nowhere and does little unless it is combined with the faith of others.

Bible, prayer, and community are vital components of the Christian faith. They spring from our trust in God, and they develop that trust into a deeper and more profound experience. The three elements are indispensable components of Christian faith.

But faith is not only about us and about building up our trust in God. It also has an essential external dimension that connects us, not only with Christ and one another but also to the world. Next week we will turn to the Christian faith at work. (Carl L. Schenck)

Worship Aids

Invocation

Dear God, we have come here today to find some refuge from the busyness of the world and the pressure of unresolved problems in our lives. May we hear your voice in the Scripture, the sermon, the music, and the prayers; and feel your presence as we brush elbows with strangers and friends. Amen.

Prayer of Confession

Hear us as we confess our sin. We confess how, from time to time, we have forgotten who we are. Sometimes, in our arrogance, we think more highly of ourselves than we ought to think; and sometimes we think so little of ourselves that we disgrace the Creator in whose image we are made. Grant us godly balance so that we may see ourselves as we really are. In Jesus' name, amen.

Pastoral Prayer

Almighty God, our heavenly Father, whose mighty acts in the small circle of human life continue to amaze us as much as your mighty acts in the boundless universe; we come before your throne of grace today with a deep sense of gratitude.

We are thankful, not only for what we know you have done in our lives but also for your care for (and watchfulness over) those aspects of human life and physical existence that move beyond our consciousness and our understanding. You have given orderliness to the vast universe and sensible cycles and intricate orderliness to our individual lives. And while we cannot see what you have done, and what you are doing from the beginning to the end, we trust your wisdom in all that we cannot see or do not understand.

We confess to the sin of disobedience, in which we have acted in a manner we clearly know to be wrong, or when we have entertained thoughts and attitudes we clearly know to be in conflict with your eternal purpose.

We give thanks for workers of the world whose labors keep the fabric of society together. Keep us mindful of our places as contributing members of society in the community of which we are part. Save us from the sin of shirking our responsibilities.

We pray for all those human conditions that have reduced people to misery and defeat.

Hold us as we reach out to touch people whose suffering is more than we can bear alone. Stretch our vision of what we can accomplish as a congregation in our resolve to be a servant people. In Jesus' name, amen. (Thomas Lane Butts)

FEBRUARY 11, 2007

❧❧❧❧

Sixth Sunday after the Epiphany

Readings: Jeremiah 17:5-10; Psalm 1 (UMH 738); 1 Corinthians 15:12-20; Luke 6:17-26

Like Trees
Jeremiah 17:5-10; Psalm 1

Jeremiah and the psalmist agree: anyone who trusts and obeys God is like a tree "planted by streams of water" (Psalm 1:3), ever green, ever growing, ever fruitful. Jeremiah adds a curious attribute for a tree to model: "not anxious" (Jeremiah 17:8). I have to admit; I've never seen an anxious or nervous tree. Even dead trees have a certain calm about them, with a sculptural beauty that remains long after the last leaf falls. The poem most memorized by high school English students is "Trees," written by that oddly named man, Joyce Kilmer. "I think that I shall never see a poem lovely as a tree." So we all agree that trees are mighty metaphors of tranquillity and beauty. Imagine how much more beautiful a tree appeared to desert-dwellers such as Jeremiah and the other Hebrew writers. A tree provided a wonderful respite from the heat of the desert sun. Usually, the tree marked a spot of vegetation or even an oasis. Thus, a tree in the desert could be a true lifesaver as well as a place for relaxation and replenishment.

As Christians, we can find ourselves lost in the wilderness or weary in the desert. Life has a way of weathering us, sucking from us creative juices, leaving us thirsty and aimless, like nomads lost in the wasteland of worry and work. Scripture calls us again and again to pause and plant ourselves by living water, to drink deeply of God's replenishing spirit.

I was one of thousands of residents in Alabama and Florida whose homes were hit hard by Hurricane Ivan. Most of the damage involved trees, uprooted by the category 4 storm winds, then falling on homes, barns, and businesses. The timber industry was devastated by the loss of literally millions of pines and hardwoods. The landscape has been dramatically changed for the worse. We grieve the loss of our trees. After the storm, I noticed the large pecan tree that fell in my yard managed to stay alive for at least a week after it had been uprooted. The tree trunk itself held enough residual water and nutrients to keep the leaves green for many days.

We are like that. Torn away from our spiritual roots, disconnected from God, we do not immediately shrivel up and die. Some communities manage to live a hundred years without any meaningful faith connection. God created us and imbued us with life, and this life has a certain "residual" vitality. But sooner or later, a life cut off from God's spirit dries up. We shall all, eventually, die a physical death, and many of us are already dying spiritually. But Jeremiah reminds us, "Blessed are those who trust in the LORD... They shall be like a tree planted by water, sending out its roots by the stream. It shall not fear when heat comes, and its leaves shall stay green; in the year of drought it is not anxious, and it does not cease to bear fruit" (vv. 7-8).

Jeremiah continues with this imagery in verse 13, where he calls God a "fountain of living water." Jesus would later use the same expression in order to convince the woman at the well that true satisfaction can be found only in the "living water" of God. She came to the well obsessively because she was thirsty—not for water, but for inner satisfaction. She had gone from one lover to another, trying to find fulfillment in obsessive, grasping behavior.

Such is the human condition. We live in a society that has not learned the lessons of Jeremiah and Jesus. We continue to seek satiation in material trinkets and fleeting pleasures. Our culture is commonly thrilled, but rarely fulfilled. We bounce from one craving to another hunger to yet another longing and even to addiction, never finding gratification.

"Returning to our roots" has a double meaning in this context. We need to return to the roots of our faith, to the ancient words of Scripture that remind us again and again to trust in God, to stay "rooted" in the Divine. The words of the psalmist, the prophet, and the Christ have never been more relevant. Strength for living does not come from trusting in our flesh. It comes directly from the spiritual power of God, from that eternal spring welling up into eternity. If we are to find contentment and refreshment, we must slow down and plant ourselves by the streams of living water—like trees. (Lance Moore)

Faith without Works

Third in a Series of Three on the Christian Faith

2 Kings 5:1-14; Mark 1:40-45

Over the past two weeks we have looked at aspects of our Christian faith, and today we bring this review to a close. We began by saying that Christian faith is absolute trust in the goodness and care of God regardless of the circumstances. This is in sharp contrast to a distortion of the Christian faith that suggests those who have strong faith will always find themselves in the best of circumstances.

Last week we took this trust theme a step further to explore how our trust in God can grow through the devotional life. Christian faith is a relationship, a connection with God through Jesus Christ. This connection relies on God and grows in this reliance through relationship, especially a relationship reflected in prayer.

If these two building blocks of Christian faith were the whole story, faith would be all about us. It would consist of our trust in and relationship with Christ. But such a "faith" would ultimately fail because it is centered on self. Our trust in Christ causes us to follow him on the paths he walks. If we believe Christ is trustworthy, then we have no hesitation to walk in his ways. We seek to be where Christ is. We align our lives with the projects of God in the world.

Christian faith trusts God so completely that it seeks to identify the places where God is most significantly at work and to join in that work. We do not join in God's labors in order to appease or impress God. No, we join in God's work because we trust God so completely that the only place we want to be, the only place we feel safe and at peace, is in partnering in God's efforts. The deep mystery and miracle of this faith are that we may find ourselves in quite unpopular or uncomfortable places as we seek to find peace and association with God in Christ.

Where do we find God at work in our day? Our best indicator of God activities is to look at the activities of Jesus. Today's Gospel lesson gets us off to a good start with the story of the healing of the leper. What is going on in this story?

First of all, Jesus involved himself in the life of someone on the margin. In Jesus' day, so-called lepers were considered both religiously unclean and dangerous to be around. These people were thought to be sinners who were being punished by God for their transgressions. Most people thought these "sinners" got what they deserved. They were suffering because they were bad people, and good people kept their distance from bad folks.

Jesus would have nothing to do with this kind of thinking. Rather than shunning the man, Jesus reached out and responded to his hurt with healing. Without blame and without hesitation, Jesus got involved with this person who was considered a hazard to the moral and physical health of others.

If Christian faith calls us to trust God so much that we can follow Jesus, then we will be following Jesus into the lives of persons others find unfit, dangerous, or sinful. Who might that be in your life? It is extremely hard for some of us to go to a hospital or a nursing home. Others of us believe the poor are at fault for their poverty, and we are reluctant to become involved in their lives and problems. Still others are reluctant to have an AA group meet in their church or to be in ministry to persons with AIDS. Yet, in Jesus we see One who did not shy away from the people others saw as unworthy outcasts. God was in Christ, and if we are to be working in partnership with God, then we must find ourselves involved in the lives of persons at the margins.

A second dimension of Jesus' response to the suffering man was to change his situation. Jesus' response was not limited to sympathy or superficial warmth. Jesus changed the man's life for the better.

If we are looking for God's work in our world, we do well to look for any place where people are being helped to have new and better lives. Some of those ways may be safe and conventional. Sponsoring a youth group, working with a Scouting program, and building houses with Habitat for Humanity are ways people's lives are made better. These are comfortable places where God is at work. In them it is easy to be partners with Christ.

Harder are the places that are less conventional and less accepted, but where people's hardships are being lifted. Prison ministries are uncomfortable places where lives are made better. The same is true of ministries that seek to improve the lot of farmworkers, single parents, pregnant teenage women, or drug users. Working for and with these people in our time would be very much like the work Jesus did when he healed the leper.

If we trust God, we will go where God is—even if that place seems unconventional or dangerous. We began this series with the affirmation of faith that God can be trusted. We believe God was in Christ. As counterintuitive as it may seem, our comfort may be found in uncomfortable places. God is in those places, so we can trust there is no better place to be.

In New Testament times there were those who believed that believing was enough. They thought Christian faith was a cozy way of life. The writer of the letter of James challenged this thinking with the bold declaration, "Faith without works is dead" (see James 2:17). So it is today.

The Christian faith begins with unconditional trust. It leads to a growing connection with God through Christ. It produces people ready to make a difference for others. (Carl L. Schenck)

Worship Aids

Invocation

Dear God, we pray that we may see in this service today those virtues in and for which we may experience blessedness. Open our hearts and minds to the divine realities that we are not likely to see in the secular world. In the dear name of Jesus, amen.

Prayer of Confession

We confess, O God, how prone we are to turn away from those people and circumstances in which you would reveal yourself to us. Forgive us, for being afraid of the poor and oppressed through whom you are always revealing yourself. Grant us the courage of vulnerability and save us from the sin of always looking out for number one. Amen.

Pastoral Prayer

Dear and loving God, in whom we find the perfect arrangement of Father and Mother for our spiritual understanding of reality, we come in prayer and with thanksgiving for all the benefits we have received from your bounty. For whatever circumstances we now experience, we are grateful to be alive. Our gratitude does not denigrate the hope we have for what you have in store for us beyond this life, yet it comes of hearts happy to have a bit more time to do what we believe you sent us into this world to do.

Teach us to number our days, to be aware of the frailty and brevity of our lives, so that we may apply our hearts with wisdom to the tasks before us. You have made us stewards of a certain amount of this world's wealth; teach us how to use it wisely. Save us from being greedy about material things. Teach us in what ways we should value what we own in this mate-rial world, so that we will not be careless and flippant about the value of wealth. But we also pray that what we own will not own us. Show us again and again that our ownership is not permanent. Help us to pause and to see how things inexorably pass into the hands of others. May all our giving to the church and all other causes be consistent with your design for life, reflecting a basic respect for where it all came from and what it is all about. And, for thy sake and for our sake and for the sake of the sanctity of life, don't let us become fools about something we have but cannot keep. In the name of Jesus, amen. (Thomas Lane Butts)

FEBRUARY 18, 2007

❧❧❧❧

Seventh Sunday after the Epiphany/Transfiguration Sunday

Readings: Exodus 34:29-35; Psalm 99; 2 Corinthians 3:12–4:2; Luke 9:28-36 (37-43*a*)

Whoever Goes Up, Must Come Down
Luke 9:28-43*a*

Several years ago, Dallas Cowboy personalities Deion Sanders and Jerry Jones made a pizza commercial. In the commercial Jerry asked Deion: "Deion, is it fifteen million or is it twenty million?" Deion replied, "Both!" Should Christians be devoted to God or devoted to people? The answer is both.

Jesus has predicted his suffering, death, and resurrection to his disciples. Jesus has called on them to "take up their cross" (Luke 9:23), warned that those who hear the gospel but fail to trust in it will be condemned, and has promised that some present will see the realm of God. Now Jesus and three special disciples ascend "the mountain."

We have heard this transfiguration story, as related by Matthew, Mark, and Luke, each year on "Transfiguration Sunday." Even if we have never been to the mountaintop ourselves, we still like to hear about others having the experience.

What happens after the mountaintop experience? We all know that if you go up to the mountain, you must come down. What happens to Peter, James, and John when they come down? [*Read Luke 9:37-43a.*]

From a mountaintop moment, disciples go back to the drudgery of the human world of pain, disease, and death. No wonder Peter said it was good that they were on the mountain and should build three dwelling places. When we are in a place of joy, rarely do we want to return to the ordinary world. Yet, Jesus, as the prophets before him, always forces disciples to look at their world—where the rain of God's grace falls on the just and the unjust (see Matthew 5:45). A prophet is a person "who afflicts

36

the comfortable and comforts the afflicted" and Jesus' lesson concerns prophetic discipleship.

The story of the healing of an epileptic child offers at least three lessons on discipleship. First, disciples alternate their lives in Christ between the mountain of joy and their Christ-needy world. Given people's nature, however, we tend to overindulge one side of the human-divine equation. Two candles always adorn the church's altar. These candles represent Jesus' incarnation. One candle symbolizes Jesus' divinity, and the other candle signifies Jesus' humanity. Consequently, we understand Jesus' essential nature as fully human and fully divine. Jesus represents the fusion of God with humankind.

In the earlier part of the twentieth century, American Christianity wrestled with two primary heresies, heresies as old as the Jesus movement. One side of the dispute included people who retreated from the world's problems. These persons focused on their own spiritual needs while ignoring the world's troubles. People often used the transfiguration story of the disciples with Moses, Elijah, and Jesus to support a theology of retreat. Conversely, others observed "the Social Gospel." Although deeply dedicated Christians, their focus was to put the world's affairs in order. Sometimes they neglected their own spiritual lives. Through the story of the Transfiguration and the healing of the boy with a demon, Luke helps believers understand the vitality of both the personal and the communal characters of discipleship. Could this be why Luke links these two very different stories together?

A second lesson of discipleship teaches us that Jesus' power over evil is what enables disciples to do what needs to be done if we are to share the realm of God with the people of God. A balance between heaven and earth, or the divine and the human, keeps our lives between the poles of joy and service. If we look too much toward heaven, we miss our calling. If we worry too much about how to live out the nuts and bolts of Christian service, we may forget God's power that sustains every benevolent effort.

I heard an amusing story about former heavyweight boxer James (Quick) Tillis. He was a cowboy from Oklahoma who also boxed in Chicago in the 1980s. He remarked about his first day in Chicago arriving from Tulsa. "I got off the bus with two cardboard suitcases under my arms in downtown Chicago and stopped in front of the Sears Tower. I put my suitcases down, and I looked up at the Tower and I said to myself, 'I'm going to conquer Chicago.' When I looked down, the suitcases were gone."

The point is simple. We cannot do God's work if we are preoccupied with looking only to our needs. Likewise, if we do not often look up for God's guidance, then we do not have the strength that God gives to spread healing grace.

Luke's third lesson on discipleship reminds us that the greatest stumbling block for disciples is the tediousness of our hard and often disappointing work. Boredom is a most seductive enemy of the Christian life because many of the most important things we do are routine. We do the same kinds of activities over and over. Bible study is unlike any other kind of studying that we do. It is too deep and too important to ever be mastered. I have never heard anyone say that she or he knows Scripture well enough. We must return to it again and again. The same is true of prayer. Prayer is a relationship with God that can never be complete. It is always growing and evolving. None of us are ever finished praying.

We all know what it is like to give our best effort and hear someone say in appreciation, "Thank you for that wonderful Sunday school lesson. I look forward to next week. I'm sure your next lesson will be just as good." These compliments have the potential to destroy. Every time we do something well, a similar opportunity rolls around again. We live the Christian life in a habitual, but important, manner again and again. It is easy to simply give up and put our discipleship on "cruise control."

Whether one is a Sunday school teacher, a Stephen minister, a teacher or student of Disciple Bible Study, a VBS worker, or whatever—whenever we finish one task, there is another waiting for us. The Christian life can make one both a bored and a boring person, if one is not captured by its beauty and grace. We need the fire of the Spirit to continue to bring energy and creativity to those repetitive but important tasks that Christ has called us to do.

Jesus seems to tell us that looking up is vital to our relationship with God, but that by our looking down, we can do God's will. (David N. Mosser)

Love or Romance
1 Corinthians 13:4-7

If you are looking for a bargain, go into the stores right now and buy your Valentine cards, candy, centerpieces, and lawn flags for next year!

Secular holidays seem to be growing in their popularity and merchandising. Yet Valentine's Day, for the Christian, should be like Easter, a daily celebration.

Valentine's Day is a day for romance. Many couples' wedding anniversary is February 14. The roses, the candy, the outward signs of affection, but which comes first—romance or love? Can you have one without the other?

This may surprise some people, but if I had the choice to officiate at a funeral or a marriage, I would choose the funeral. A funeral marks the end of an individual's life, but a marriage is a beginning. With the divorce rate in the United States at 50 percent, I feel greater challenge and responsibility in joining two people in holy matrimony than in comforting a grieving family. I ask the couple, "What do you expect from love? What do you expect from marriage?" The difference between romance and love is played out in the day-to-day life of the relationship.

Hollywood would like us to believe in the fairy-tale ending following the perfect wedding. In my experience, many couples spend more time on details regarding the wedding than anticipating obstacles surrounding money, family, and division of housework.

Over the past few years, I have done an informal survey of couples married for more than fifteen years. I ask, "What is the one thing that has contributed to the success of your marriage?" The most frequent answer is, "Willingness to compromise."

Jesus said this in another way: "Love is never selfish; it never demands its own way."

Compromise, in recent years, has gained a negative connotation. It seems to mean "weakness," as in giving up or giving in to a stronger force. What compromise really means, whether in business or in marriage, is doing what is best for the union, for harmony; and yes, that might mean giving in to promote the greater good. Harmony is jeopardized when keeping score becomes as or more important than the compromise.

Motivation is an issue we cannot ignore. In a working marriage, when one compromises, both sides will even out. Don't think just because you gave in and cleaned the toilet that you are relieved of any responsibility to go to the next dinner at your in-laws! As in war, you can win the battle but lose the marriage.

Women and men need different things and express things in different ways. One common mistake is assuming that what makes us happy or encourages us is what will make our spouses happy. When I am a little discouraged, I like to go shopping. Let me assure you, when my husband is a little discouraged, the very last thing he wants to do is go shopping. Okay, shopping is never the first thing he ever really wants to do, except for, maybe, a power saw. When I am discouraged, a little pat on the shoulder or a hug works very nicely to show support. My spouse wants to go into his cave, the garage, and work things out by himself. He needs some time and space to work out a plan, determine some strategy. Going out to the garage to give him a pat or a hug is accepted, but is the pat and hug for him or for me?

In some Native American weddings, the man vows, "I give you my life and my honor." The woman answers, "I accept your life and your honor, and shall treat it as my own." This value of honoring each other is of utmost importance; it is integrity in its highest form. Television sitcoms depicting marriage discount the marriage vows and the honor of both parties. Lying and ridiculing one's partner is a joke, complete with laugh track. Our youth are learning this as the norm for marriages. I watch as young couples put each other down in front of others, and sometimes even get laughs and encouragement from their peers. But what happens when the couple is alone, the sitcom retorts are thrown back and forth, and no one is laughing? In fact, the opposite is happening, and tears and hurt feelings will be followed by hours of silence or anger.

The word *love* is very confusing. It is a noun, a verb, a feeling, an emotion, and an act. In most instances, *love* is a verb. I love you. Love is working to help your partner become the person God wants him or her to be. Love is not always romantic. Ask the wife who must care for her husband following chemo treatments, or the husband who visits his wife in the Alzheimer's ward faithfully for years.

Can you have romance without love? Yes, this is the love that depends on the warm, fuzzy feelings, but no matter how much you love your partner on your wedding day, those feelings don't last, and someone has to clean the toilet. Divorce lawyers profit from those people who want infinite warm, fuzzy feelings.

Can you have love without romance? I don't believe so. The love one feels is expressed outwardly in some way; it just may not be the way the other person needs, recognizes, or appreciates. Many divorced workaholics will tell you that they worked hard so their families could have everything they needed or wanted, materially. Yet an afternoon in the park or attendance at a soccer game would have said a lot more in the long run.

Love and romance—if you find you are lacking in one of these areas, fix it. Talk to each other and be willing to listen to what the other needs. Never assume you know what your partner needs; we are human beings, growing and changing, so what worked ten years ago probably won't work now.

The roses will wilt, the chocolate will be eaten, but with work, communication, and no scorekeeping, the marriage will last. I invite you, if you are married, to choose to be examples for those who are just beginning. Let your love be like Easter, a daily celebration, and acknowledgment, of God's blessings. (Raquel Mull)

Worship Aids

Invocation

Dear God, we each come to this occasion of worship with our private set of needs. May the prayers and music, Scripture and sermon have something for each of us. In the name of Jesus, amen.

Prayer of Confession

Dear God, our hearts yearn for your forgiveness. Our sin weighs heavily on us. We come before you depending on your mercy and grace. We are not leaning on any virtue of our own that we suppose would make us worthy. Hear our confession and grant us your absolution. In the name of Jesus, amen.

Pastoral Prayer

Dear God, Father and Mother of us all, we come before you today not only as a congregation but also as individuals. There are people and circumstances that keep playing across the backdrop of our minds as we worship. You know so much more about them than we could ever know. We recall some of them in your presence because, if we do not speak of them, we may forget. We pray for the sick and disabled among us. We pray for the troubled and disquieted spirits of those we know and love, in whose lives some important aspect is not manageable, and who are anxious, sad, depressed, discouraged, or worried in ways you never intended. We pray for the poor, the oppressed, the dispossessed, and for those whose lives are wounded or distorted by their own ignorance or the malice of others. Help us all, O Lord, when life gets off course or comes unhinged.

Bless us as we try to be "church" in the way you intended church to be. Forgive us when we "play" church and substitute our little games for the real thing. Forgive us our sins, those that are real and those that are imagined. Help us not to invent sins and feign weaknesses. Teach us to be content to shoulder and confess what is real, knowing that it will be about all we need to handle, and all you expect us to handle. We pray in the name of Jesus. Amen. (Thomas Lane Butts)

FEBRUARY 21, 2007

❧❧❧

Ash Wednesday

Readings: Joel 2:1-2, 12-17; Psalm 51:1-17; 2 Corinthians 5:20b–6:10; Matthew 6:1-6, 16-21

Lent Is a Gift for You
Matthew 6:1-6, 16-21

The gospel text for Ash Wednesday mentions many of the primary spiritual disciplines of a Christian's life: almsgiving, prayer, fasting, and stewardship.

Almsgiving is the practice of sharing of one's financial resources for charitable causes. Prayer is the spiritual discipline of focusing our minds and our spirits on God to both speak to and listen for God's Spirit. Prayer is an opportunity for confession, petition, thanksgiving, and intercession. Fasting—an often-overlooked spiritual discipline—is a means of physical self-denial in order to physiologically and spiritually focus on God. Far from dieting, fasting is a practice that allows us to rely more on the Spirit than on our bodies for nourishment and strength. It is another means of removing our needs from the center of our lives in order to focus on the One who is the center of life.

Lent is a gift, a season of the Christian year whose name comes from the Latin for "lengthening of days." Lent is for preparation, a journey of preparing our souls to encounter the amazing mystery of Christ's life, death, and resurrection. Easter can never mean quite as much without the journey through Lent.

Ash Wednesday marks the start of our preparation period. The journey begins with contrition, owning up to our sin and brokenness, and evaluating the state of our relationship with God. Ash Wednesday, by its very name, reminds us of our mortality. We are created from dust, and to dust we shall return. Even our acts of praise, the palm branches of the Palm

Sunday celebration, are but ashes in comparison to the majesty of God and the sacrifice of the Christ.

What stands in our way of a closer walk with the Holy One? Our attitudes toward spiritual disciplines can be especially dangerous when they become a means of self-aggrandizement and arrogance. Such is the warning of Jesus' teaching in Matthew 6.

God always desires to be close; have we moved away from God? A woman wrote to the financial secretary of a church in an affluent community. She said she was unable to afford the cost of membership in such a church and wondered if this staff person had any suggestions. The financial secretary passed the note along to the pastor, who replied: "The price of belonging to Christ's church was paid long ago. Anything we do today is but an opportunity to walk more closely with God. Come home; God is waiting. There is no admission fee, only the need for an open heart."

Lent is a gift. Lent compels us to return to Christian disciplines and to make time for genuine spiritual care for ourselves. Spiritual disciplines are a tool, a gift of God to center us and to remind us that we are spiritual people on a physical journey. Spiritual disciplines are a means of grace. They are a method and practice of focusing on God's Spirit rather than on ourselves.

We can use spiritual disciplines as a means of grace or a method of grandstanding. My father often said, "The real art of conversation is not only to say the right thing at the right time but also to leave unsaid the wrong thing at the tempting moment." The true art of Christian discipleship is to be disciples who are servants of God and leaders for Christ, not selfish lovers enthralled with ourselves. (Gary G. Kindley)

Too Painful to Forget
1 Corinthians 15:1-2, (3-58)

"Ashes to ashes, dust to dust." These are the words of committal heard at the cemetery. But we go to such great lengths to disguise death. How many times at the funeral home have you heard someone say, "She looks so good" or "He looks so natural"? And, we mean it! The person in the casket hardly looks dead at all. The embalmer's art, soft, pastel lights overhead to cast the perfect glow, an upholstered casket that looks, well, comfortable. My grandmother wore her glasses in her casket. Was she suddenly going to wake up and need them? And a necklace—the same necklace she had worn at her ninetieth birthday party several months before she died. I don't think St. Peter is going to say, "That necklace goes perfectly with the dress you are wearing."

When we come to the cemetery, the gravesite is draped with a green, grass-like cloth. It goes over the sides and down into the grave. It doesn't look like a hole in the ground at all, and the mound of earth that will cover the grave is nowhere to be seen.

Finally, after the committal, the family is gently ushered away. Seldom does anyone stay long enough to see the casket lowered into the ground. And if you go back to the cemetery later in the day, the ground is covered with flowers. You couldn't find the spot where you stood and wept if you had to. We remove ourselves as far as possible from physical death. It's understandable, because death is painful, and who wants to hurt? We don't come easily to the end of relationships with those we have loved.

On this Ash Wednesday we begin a journey that will take us to the cross, where Jesus died a torturous, brutal death. It is sad and scary to stand at the foot of the cross and watch Jesus die. For the next six weeks, you won't be hearing any hallelujas in the church, no triumphal music, no song choruses of victory in Jesus. Instead, the tone of worship will be somber, even mournful. During these next few weeks we will be asked to take a serious look at who we are and how we have become less than the people God created us to be. That is the purpose of Lent: self-examination.

When Jesus died on the cross that Friday afternoon, those who loved him didn't have much to say. Those who had come to mock and ridicule had plenty to say. But those who really cared were silent, probably numb with shock and sorrow. When you lose a loved one, there are no words adequate to express your grief. Watching Jesus die must have been a horrible experience for those present. The sound of hammers and nails tearing through flesh and bone was horrendous. There was no comfortable disguise of death that day. When they took his body down from the cross, there was no easy way to remove the nails from his hands and feet. There was no embalming makeup or flattering lights, just a tortured, dead body for everyone to see.

Sometimes I think we in the church have romanticized Jesus' death. We "spiritualize" the story, make jewelry out of the instrument of his death, and hardly notice the body at all. It reminds me of going to the rodeo in Houston a number of years ago. One of my friends remarked that it wasn't a real rodeo, although there was bull riding, calf roping, and bronco riding. He said it wasn't like a real rodeo because we were so far away you couldn't smell it. No one wants to stand near a cross and see a man die. It is too awful, too wrenching, so we distance ourselves. Life is difficult enough without being reminded of the pain of death.

The truth is, living and dying can be painful. We don't want to hear that or be reminded of it. Life is difficult enough without coming to church and being reminded of it. The twists and turns, the unexpected, unanticipated tragedies, great and small, are difficult to negotiate. Some people, in fact, find it impossible. When life deals them a blow, they retreat, hoping to avoid more pain or not be hurt again. Day by day their existence becomes more restricted.

I've often wondered why we repeat some stories in the church over and over again. We know this story of Jesus' death. We know he is going to Jerusalem and no good end will come of it. We already know about the betrayal and arrest, the beating and mockery. We already know about the cross, the nails, and the tomb. But repetition is essential lest we forget the essential elements that are too painful to remember.

We also know about the Resurrection, and we need reminding of that as well. Life doesn't quit. We will continually be challenged, disappointed, and hurt over and over again. There is no end to it. That is why we need to be reminded of the Resurrection, as many times as it takes. We will all die, either by degrees or suddenly, and draw our last breath. We know it's coming. Along the way we will visit our own Garden of Gethsemane, walk our own *Via Dolorosa*, and face the tomb. But all these experiences become bearable when we know that Jesus has been there before us. We handle life's hardships much better when we are reminded that life with Jesus doesn't end on Friday at the cross. Sunday is coming and with it, victory over death. Today we begin that journey. Remember where it ends and your way will be graced with hope. (Robert D. Penton)

Worship Aids

Call to Worship

> Leader: We begin a journey this evening.
>
> **People: A journey that begins in the twilight and that con-
> cludes at a dawn that is yet to come.**
>
> Leader: We journey to the dawn of Easter morning.

People:	**Along the way, we pause under dark and rumbling skies of Good Friday.**
Leader:	Let us confess our need for God.
People:	**Let us confess our sin and claim God's promise. Amen!**

Invocation for Ash Wednesday

Holy God, we gather this evening to face the reality of our mortality. We stand in need of your grace and we kneel before your majesty. Merciful One, help us to understand that our sin is not a sign we are worthless, but a reminder that we, the created, need the Creator to reclaim our sacred calling. Let us worship God and celebrate the sacred journey we share together. Amen.

Benediction

Go into the night as a people of the dawn. Be light where there is dark-ness. Share the hope of God's immeasurable love. Amen. (Gary G. Kindley)

FEBRUARY 25, 2007

❧❧❧

First Sunday in Lent

Readings: Deuteronomy 26:1-11; Psalm 91:1-2, 9-16 (*UMH* 810); Romans 10:8*b*-13; Luke 4:1-13

I Promise I Will Find You!
Psalm 91:1-2, 9-16; Luke 4:1-13

Hear these biblical words that strengthen my weak heart and calm my frantic thoughts: "God is my refuge and fortress. God is my strength. God is my very present help in time of trouble."

Throughout the pages of the Bible, those affirmations of God's protective love for people are found in varied places. In the Holy Scripture there is always confidence in God's protective presence. The prophet Isaiah voices the truth, saying, "I have taken you by the hand and kept you" (42:6). The psalmist affirms, "The LORD is my Shepherd, I shall not want" (Psalm 23:1). And Jesus says: "I am the good shepherd; I know my own" (see John 10:11). "I will not leave you desolate; I will come to you" (John 14:18 RSV).

These words from the Bible reassure. Yet, as we live our lives, there are the daily reminders of the fragile nature of human life, which awaken uneasy feelings. As you consider the hurricanes and tornadoes and tsunamis that rip through our communities and claim the lives of human beings by the thousands, sometimes it is easy to wonder if perhaps God has not lost God's grip.

Where is God's protective spirit, watching over the least and the last of society? The world's poor didn't ask to be born with so little, and they didn't choose to live in vulnerable places, but there they are. Why did God not take hold of the hands of the people of Southeast Asia and lead them to higher ground when the deadly tsunami struck in the aftermath of the Christmas celebration of 2004? One of the many stories that came from the people of Indonesia is the brutal memory of a mother who was

48

holding the hand of her six-year-old when the waters separated them forever. Where was God when the force of the water separated mother and child?

Some have suggested that God sends destruction as a judgment against sin, and that's the reason for disasters that claim so many lives. Don't you believe it!

It is certainly true that "what goes around comes around." It is true that if you violate the moral principles of the universe or the commandments of God, then you will be judged harshly and will pay a price. If you violate the spirit of Jesus, which is the way God has clearly taught that God wants us to live, there will be a price to pay. If you sin, you will reap the whirlwind!

But really, when the innocent suffer and earth's fragile structure is shattered, does God inflict this kind of senseless death? Not on your life. As Rabbi Harold Kushner, struggling with this troubling issue, affirmed, "Bad things happen to good people."

The truth is, there are earthly powers beyond our control: global weather changes produce whirlwinds of tornado and hurricane force, the shift of the plates of the planet beneath the waters that cover the earth stir those waters and flood the islands. Many things just happen: accidents, disease, malformations of nature and human life. We are born and we die, sometimes at untimely moments.

Although we must recognize and acknowledge this vulnerable nature of the human condition, still we hear affirmation of the faith from the giants of Scripture: "God is our refuge and fortress. He is our strength. He is our very present help in time of trouble" (see Psalm 46:1). When William Sloan Coffin dealt with the unexpected death of his son, he wrote that God gives us "minimum protection, maximum support."

When Jesus faced the temptations in the very beginning of his ministry, there was an inner confidence that enabled him to reject the offers of easy answers: sensationalism, miraculous and military powers as means of communicating the message of God's protective love. Jesus' confidence was in God alone, not in the things of God. God came to earth in Jesus embodying God's searching, shepherding, and protective love. Remember the story of the one sheep that was lost for which the good shepherd would search until it was found. So, also, will God find us.

There is a wonderful children's book, written by Heather Patricia Ward, that captures the love of a parent for a child, but points in the direction of God's eternal love for all children. I believe that it affirms the biblical truth of God's never-failing love for God's people. The book was dedicated to the "Foundation for Missing Children." The title is, *I Promise I'll Find You* (Ontario: Firefly Books, 1994). Read some of the words. The imagery is vivid—a mother or father rows a rowboat, rides a horse, drives a race car, or shoots through space in a rocket ship until the child is found, brought back home, and enveloped in love and safety. And the parent says, "I'll find you!"

For those today who feel lost, confused, or abandoned, hear these words: "I Promise I'll Find You." "God is our Refuge and Fortress." (Henry Roberts)

Do You Believe That I Am Able to Do This?

First in a Series of Five: Questions Jesus Asked

Matthew 9:18-31

I imagine it took about twenty minutes after the bumper was invented for someone to apply a bumper sticker that said, "Jesus Is the Answer." My usual and immediate response is, "Yes, but what was the question?" There are questions for which the answer is "Jesus." What is my greatest source of encouragement? Who is the hope of my salvation? Who is the Son of God? Still, some clarification seems needed.

It might be better to say that Jesus is the "Answer Person." Indeed, the Gospels are crowded with stories of people coming to Jesus seeking answers to their questions. "How can I enter the kingdom of heaven?" "My daughter is ill. Will you come?" "Will you heal me?" Sometimes his answers were like riddles. Often though, Jesus' answers far exceeded the questioners' expectations.

Is Jesus the Answer? Yes. Is Jesus the "Answer Person"? Sure; but Jesus is also the "Question Person." Jesus asked questions of his own, and sometimes when he answered others' questions, he did so with a question. In Matthew alone, Jesus asked more than forty different questions. Some are basic, almost rhetorical. "Haven't you read the Scriptures?" "Don't you understand?"

Some of Jesus' questions are more specific, heart-stopping kinds of questions. "What is your name?" It sounds innocent enough, but I remember how I felt in second grade when I was hauled into the principal's office and she asked, "What is your name?" Or, "Who do you say I am?" Suddenly, with this question, we can no longer point to others or cite the experts. There comes a time when we have to speak for ourselves.

It seems right to consider questions Jesus asked as we move through Lent. Jesus' questions often cause us to consider how it is with us, how our faith is coming, or how our relationships with Jesus fare. If Lent is a time for somber introspection, Jesus' questions force us to take a spiritual inventory.

"Do you believe that I am able to do this?" Jesus asked two blind men wanting him to restore their sight. This is in a portion of Matthew in which several people approached Jesus asking for miracles (Consider the events in Matthew 9:18-31).

There are three stories of faith here. The first is a story of faith as a last resort. A synagogue leader would have avoided any association with Jesus and would surely have first tried every possible cure for his daughter's illness. Nothing worked. Finally, grasping at straws, he came to Jesus. How Jesus must have longed for people with enough faith to come to him first!

Second is a story of a woman with severe bleeding who seemed to treat faith like a good-luck charm. *If I can just touch his robe!* she thought. She wore her faith the way people might wear a good-luck charm on a chain around their necks. Jesus allowed that her faith had made her well, but surely Jesus longed for people who would come to him face-to-face rather than sneak up behind him.

A third incident illustrates faith based on bad theology. Two blind men called out, "Have mercy on us, Son of David!" While Jesus is a son of David, Jesus is so much more. Besides, there were lots of sons of David; so many, in fact, that there had been no room for the holy couple at the inn in Bethlehem, David's town.

The blind men came seeking mercy, hoping Jesus would restore their sight. Jesus asked, "Do you believe that I am able to do this?" Two things must be said about this question.

First, Jesus did not ask the question until he had taken them into the house where they were alone with him. It is good that Christians gather to sing God's praises, pray, recite the creeds, hear the Word of God proclaimed; but there comes a time when each of us must go into the house with Jesus and face him alone. We must stand before Jesus on the strength (or weakness) of our own faith. When we stand before Jesus and he asks, "Do you believe that I am able to do this?" it will not do to answer, "My mother thinks so," or "My Sunday school teacher says so." We will have to answer for ourselves.

Second, it makes a difference how we answer this question. Did the blind men believe Jesus could heal them? Faith is always the deciding factor. No doctor can heal a person who does not believe he can be well. No counselor can heal a person who does not believe she can be well. Jesus could do nothing with these men unless they believed he could make them see. Just because you believe does not mean everything will always go your way, but without faith, nothing will happen.

When Jesus gave them sight, he told them not to tell anyone. They immediately went out and told everyone! We've seen faith that was weak or ill-informed, and now we see blatant disobedience. Still, the miracles stood.

This means we don't have to wait until we are perfect to approach Jesus. We don't have to wait until we are giants in the faith. We can come to Jesus as we are, without understanding perfectly, without a complete grasp of theology, and even from our positions of disobedience and sinfulness. It doesn't matter how we come to Jesus. What matters is that we come.

What is it you need Jesus to do for you? Jesus said to the blind men, "According to your faith let it be done to you" (Matthew 9:29). Whatever it is you want Jesus to do for you, do you believe that he is able to do it? Either way you answer, you are correct. (Douglas Mullins)

Worship Aids

Invocation

We come before you, O God, seeking strength and courage for our lives, and the life of this fellowship. We pray for such spiritual reinforcement as would guide us safely through the times of temptation in life. Grant us such powers of discernment that we may not yield to temptations that look good but will erode our souls. Amen.

Prayer of Confession

We confess, O God, that we are attracted to false gods and easy answers in life. We are vulnerable to temptations that could damage us in ways that are not obvious. Forgive us that we are drawn like moths to the flame. Restore us and fill us with godly resolve. In Jesus' name, amen.

Pastoral Prayer

Gentle Jesus and loving Lord God, here we are again today, hoping that the sanctity of this place will reinforce the sincerity of our petitions.

Here we are again today, sitting in the same place, asking the same questions, even confessing the same sins. Unworthy though we may be in our own sight, and perhaps in the sight of others, we remember that you regard us as persons of worth no matter how much garbage we have dragged our lives through to get here. So, here we are, Lord—again.

We know that in this brief time we cannot find answers to all the questions our minds can frame, or heal all the hurts our hearts have sustained, or untie all the knots in our lives; but we pray that you will help us get started.

We confess, O God, how difficult it is to be honest with you and ourselves, much less with all these other people. We confess how often we try to look better than we really are. It seems to be a part of our dark sides to pose, and fake, and give false impressions. And we do not do it entirely in the interest of peacekeeping and diplomacy. Forgive us that so much of our insincerity has to do with pretense, face-saving, and masking the true feelings we are afraid to express and face. We confess that we have not come to terms with the dark dimensions of our natures or the sins of self that are so destructive to others and ourselves. Uncertain of ourselves, our worth, and our God-given dignity, we are afraid of honest anger and constructive criticism that seek to right wrongs. As we give voice to our personal and community confessions, hear our deep desire to control our anxious feelings rather than let them control us. Enter into the ambivalence that tears us apart and damages so many important relationships. Help us to such honesty in attitude and selfhood that we will be able to reconnect all the fragmented parts of life. In Jesus' name, amen. (Thomas Lane Butts)

MARCH 4, 2007

❧❧❧

Second Sunday in Lent

Readings: Genesis 15:1-12, 17-18; Psalm 27 (*UMH* 758); Philippians 3:17–4:1; Luke 9:28-36

Jesus—Listen to Him
Luke 9:28-36

The story in Luke 9:28-36 tells of a turning point in Jesus' life and in the lives of the disciples who experienced this unusual occurrence. The story is told in the manner of an Old Testament theophany. Unusual things happen; there is a new revelation, or epiphany—a new understanding. As in the story of Moses on the mountain receiving the Ten Commandments, there is a cloud and an encounter with the divine. There is a voice from above and a transfiguration. Like Moses, who glows after the mountaintop encounter, so Jesus, Elijah, and Moses are portrayed as appearing together in a strange light. Immediately following this event, Jesus sets his course toward Jerusalem, just as Moses moved from the mountain to lead the Israelites to the Promised Land.

The Transfiguration was certainly one of the major events in Jesus' life, along with his birth, baptism, death, and resurrection. Interestingly, as a voice from above is heard at his baptism: "This is my beloved Son, in whom I am well pleased" (Matthew 17:5 KJV), so also, in this event, a voice is heard: "This is my Son, . . . listen to him!" (Luke 9:35).

The disciples realize for the first time that Jesus is the culmination of the great prophets, represented by Elijah and the great lawgiver, Moses. In approximately 1200 B.C.E., Moses led the Israelites to freedom and gave them God's law, which would define them forever as God's moral people, unique and special. Elijah was an Israelite prophet in the ninth century B.C.E. The former slaves of Egypt were trying to establish their identity now that they were living in the "promised land." Through a dramatic confrontation between Elijah, the prophet of God, and the prophets of Baal, an agricultural deity, Elijah reminded the Israelites that they were to have no other "gods" but God alone.

On the mountaintop, Jesus engages in deep conversation with these historical giants and a voice declares, "This is my Son. Listen to Jesus." It is a clear message to us today: "Listen to Jesus! You listen to everything else, but you must listen to him who is the author of life at its best."

The average American home has the television turned on more than seven hours per day. Each individual watches approximately four and one-half hours of TV each day. When young people graduate from high school, they have spent more hours watching television than they have spent in school and church combined. It is estimated that when they finish high school, young people will have watched five hundred thousand commercials. I support the families in our church who turn off their televisions on three out of five school nights. With schoolwork, the computer, and home chores, we must start being selective.

Let us listen to Jesus. Let us listen to the One who is the Son of God as he seeks to speak to us through the noise and clutter of today. Let us listen to Jesus, first of all, because he gives to us our clearest understanding of God. In Jesus, we see as much of the Creator of the universe as we can ever hope or need to see. Anything you think about God that is not found in Jesus should probably be suspect.

Because of Jesus' teachings, we have come to understand God in three ways. We call this "the Trinity." There are, in God, these three dimensions: Creation, Redemption, and Holy Presence. God is a creating Father, a redeeming Son, and an ever-present Spirit—Father, Son, and Holy Spirit. We do not worship three separate entities; we worship one true God, who has made the divine known in creation, redemption, and ongoing involvement with creation.

As one of our church families sits down for dinner in the evening, the father asks, "Where have you seen God today?" Each person shares where he or she experienced God in life that day. Sometimes the responses of the children are quite interesting, but nonetheless the exercise is wonderful.

Keep your thoughts on God's involvement in your life and you will experience a peace that surpasses all human understanding. A word of caution here: take care that you do not blame on God every cancerous disease, germ, or careless mistake.

A young friend began to cultivate seeing God in everything, and when he left his class notebook at home, he said, "Well, God didn't want me to take my notebook to class today." Not having his notebook with his homework in it meant that he received a zero on his work for that day. Don't blame God for your carelessness.

An older friend often arrived to work late, had a bad attitude with fellow workers, and, another serious mistake, a bad attitude toward her employer. When the business changed some priorities and downsized, she lost her job. Trying to maintain a perspective of God's involvement in her life, she said: "Well, God wanted me to lose that job." Don't be tempted to shift responsibility from yourself. God equips you to use your gifts every day for God's purposes, and God will see you through difficult times, but God is not the author of every tragedy that strikes our lives. Take responsibility for your own carelessness; don't blame it on God. God is the Creator, the Redeemer, and the ever-present Spirit. Listen to Jesus and watch for him.

Listen to Jesus when he talks about the importance of prayer and acts of kindness. In Jesus we sense a rhythm of being and doing, silence and speaking, prayer and action. We are probably better at doing than we are at praying, better at action than we are at silence. Yet Jesus made a place for both in his life, and if we listen to him, we will make a place for both in our busy lives.

Lent has now begun, and it can be a unique opportunity for us to intentionally spend time in prayer, worship, and silence. Increasingly, I find it more difficult to discover God in noise and restlessness than in quietness and reflection. I have come to believe that God is a friend of silence. In nature, the trees, flowers, and grass all grow in silence. Springtime comes quietly in silence. In silence, the stars, the moon, and the sun move along their established tracks in the darkness of the universe. Perhaps Mother Teresa was correct when she wrote: "The more we receive in silent prayer, the more we can give in our active life."

John Wesley had much to say about the nature of that active life. Steven Manskar has written a fresh rendering of Wesley's "A Plain Account of Christian Perfection" (Steven W. Manskar, Diana L. Hynson, Marjorie Hewitt Suchocki, *A Perfect Love: Understanding John Wesley's "A Plain Account of Christian Perfection"* [Nashville: Discipleship Resources, 2004]). He provides a nice updating of the original work in more modern language and vocabulary while maintaining Wesley's emphasis on perfection. Listen to the words of John Wesley (updated by Manskar): "We willingly allow and constantly declare that there is no perfection in this life that suggests either an exemption from doing good or attending all the ordinances of God."

Lent is a time for us to seriously consider our going on to perfection, moving toward a complete and total commitment to love God with every part of our being, and to love our neighbors. It is a time for listening as we selectively shut out some of the noise of our busy world. Choose carefully the voices to which you listen.

Just as the voice long ago said, "Listen to my Son," so God says to his disciples today, "Listen to Jesus, and you will learn of God and you will learn of the very careful balance in doing and believing." (Henry Roberts)

What Is Your Name?

Second in a Series of Five: Questions Jesus Asked

Mark 5:1-9

This Lenten season we are taking stock of our faith and spiritual health by considering some of the questions Jesus asked. Today we hear Jesus ask the demon-possessed man in the Gerasenes, "What is your name?" which may or may not be a simple question.

Before we consider the question, consider how Jesus dealt with people. The man among the tombs had been treated poorly by the townspeople. They tried to contain him with fetters and chains; he simply broke the chains and ran loose among the tombs in the place to which he had been banished. They used force; force rarely works, and never works for long periods of time. Jesus' model for dealing with the man rejects the use of force in favor of calm and courageous persistence and kindness. World history is full of attempts to deal with people in forceful ways. How different the world might be if gentler, kinder ways had been tried! Jesus' way has many applications, not only in world politics but also in the office, classroom, and home.

Jesus asked the wild man, "What is your name?" It is a question that ought to make any one of us quake in our boots. This isn't about polite introductions at some reception. This is different. When in second grade, I once crossed the street in front of the school without the assistance of a crossing guard. I was hauled into the principal's office, and I can still remember how I felt when she said, "What is your name?" Jesus asks the same question of each of us, and if there is any guilt in us, this question will make us squirm.

Names are incredibly important. They are more than mere labels. If they were only labels, numbers would do. We could number people sequentially;

Social Security numbers would suffice. But each of us is more than a number. In some cultures a name is thought to embody the very personality of the person. In cultures like the one described by Alex Haley in *Roots*, the parent whispers a child's name into the infant's ear so the child is the first one to hear its name. Some cultures won't name a child after any living relative, while others take great pride in doing exactly that.

One of the most important things a parent ever does is name a child. A child's name may exert great influence on his or her life. I think of the number of United Methodist pastors I've known who had the name Wesley. I recall a pastor with the last name of Bible. I also remember a pastor named Paul, on the staff of a St. Paul's Church. He took great pleasure in answering the phone, "St. Paul's Church. Paul speaking." Johnny Cash told us of a boy who would have to be tough in order to survive, so his father named him Sue.

We may or may not like our names, and few of us appreciate our middle names, but all names are good—at least until someone spoils one. David, Moses, Mark, Matthew, and James are good names, but not Herod or Judas. Sarah, Rachel, Hannah, Ruth, and Mary are good names, but not Jezebel. Perhaps you know a perfectly good name that you would never give your child because of a bad experience with someone with that name. Names are important, and Jesus wanted to know the name of the man among the tombs.

"Legion," he answered, referring to the Roman legion, the basic fighting unit of six thousand men. The man was saying that he felt so fragmented it was as if six thousand forces were competing within him for control, each wanting to pull him in a different direction. Even in his conversation, if you will take notice of the text, he flip-flopped between the singular and the plural as he referred to himself.

I imagine there are days when each of us feels like that. Sometimes we are pulled in so many different directions we don't know which way to turn. How are we to manage all the conflicting forces in our lives? One thing Jesus can do for a person is to unify the conflicting spirits within. Jesus can give us the one, central focus that overshadows all else and gives meaning and order and purpose to our lives.

In the end, we shall be given a new name. "Let anyone who has an ear listen to what the Spirit is saying to the churches. To everyone who conquers I will give . . . a white stone, and on the white stone is written a new name that no one knows except the one who receives it" (Revelation 2:17). The symbolism of the book of Revelation is anything but simple.

Still, the white stone seems to suggest purity. When we enter that new kingdom, we do so clean, forgiven by the grace of God. And on the stone we are given is written a new name. It represents a fresh start. The uniqueness of our new names teaches us that even as Christians we are not all cast in the same mold. We are individuals, each a person of worth, each with his or her own name given by God. Even so, through our baptism we realize that we all have the name "Christian" in common.

Jesus, providing a model of calmness and gentleness while approaching troubled people, asks, "What is your name?" We answer, "Legion," for we are often a confused and disturbed people with conflicting motives. Then Jesus calls us to order and gives us direction, purpose, and peace.

Again Jesus asks, "What is your name?" And now we can answer, "Christian."

If there is yet a later question, it might be Jesus asking, "Christian, are you living up to your new name?" (Douglas Mullins)

Worship Aids

Call to Worship (Psalm 27:1-3)

Leader: The LORD is my light and my salvation;

People: Whom shall I fear?

Leader: The LORD is the stronghold of my life;

People: Of whom shall I be afraid?

Leader: When evildoers assail me to devour my flesh—

People: My adversaries and foes—they shall stumble and fall.

Leader: Though an army encamp against me,

People: My heart shall not fear;

Leader: Though war rise up against me,

People: Yet I will be confident.

Prayer of Confession

Forgiving God, we confess how we have rebelled against you. We have allowed doubts and fears to hold us back from the freedom to which you have called us in Christ Jesus our Lord. We have been quick to blame others for our weakness and slow to accept responsibility for ourselves. Forgive us, and grant us your peace, through Jesus Christ our Lord. Amen.

Pastoral Prayer

Almighty God, Father of our Lord Jesus Christ, we come before you today, in the shadow of the cross, to offer the prayers of this congregation. We thank you for the hope we have that is born of our faith in Jesus. How grateful we are for the sacrifice Jesus made for us, and for the example for living we see in his life. Grant us the strength and courage to follow him closely. We confess how we have failed you by our commitment to lesser values and selfish goals. Open our eyes to what is of lasting value in this world and the next.

We pray not only for ourselves, but for others—many others, known and unknown, named and unnamed—from whose lives health or happiness has fled, leaving hollow remnants of the persons they once were. Make us more eager to help others than to criticize or give them bits of our wisdom that we think they need. Help us to learn by heart what Jesus knew so well: that the hungry, the hurt, the sick, and the oppressed do not care about how much we know until they know about how much we care.

Touch our lives with grace through the worship we experience here today. In the good name of Jesus, amen. (Thomas Lane Butts)

MARCH 11, 2007

⊱⊰⊱⊰⊱⊰

Third Sunday in Lent

Readings: Isaiah 55:1-9; Psalm 63:1-8 (*UMH* 788); 1 Corinthians 10:1-13; Luke 13:1-9

You Want Answers? He's Got Questions
Luke 13:1-9

Obadiah wrote, "You should not have gloated over your brother on the day of his misfortune; you should not have rejoiced over the people of Judah on the day of their ruin" (v. 12). The prophet laments the tendency his people have to find some sense of satisfaction in the troubles of others. We do not like to admit, in polite company, that we have such feelings, but we do. Why else buy *National Enquirer* or watch *American Idol*?

Sometimes, truth be told, what we feel in view of another's calamity is nothing short of fascination—celebrity trials, wars—it's like watching a train wreck, and who can resist? Sometimes, what we feel and think is more sinister, a satisfaction both malignant and cruel: "It couldn't happen to a nicer guy!" Other times, however, what we feel is far more complex, and rejoicing only a part of it.

There is a German word, *Schadenfreude*, which describes a more or less universal human trait: the sometimes sad and always anxious relief, which, for example, certain soldiers feel during battle when the infantryman next to them is wounded or killed while they are spared. Two are in the field; one catches a bullet but the other does not. There is sadness, but there is relief, too—not rejoicing, exactly, but something else. It is hard for a survivor not to read some "pattern" or purpose into such a stark episode. It is hard, in fact, not to posit divine intent or involvement in the moment: "I must have been spared for a reason." And perhaps that is the case.

A tornado comes, and one house is utterly destroyed while next door there is not even a scrap of paper in the yard. The folks whose house still stands are sorry as they can be about their neighbors, and they will help all they can, but at the same time there is a sense of great relief that *they* got hit and *we* didn't. We should not feel this way, but we often do. We sigh. But maybe we were spared for a reason, we say to only ourselves at first, or maybe they were likewise being punished.

Such thoughts are not without precedent. After all, even the psalmists affirm divine protection for the righteous.

A thousand may fall at your side, ten thousand at your right hand, but it will not come near you. You will only look with your eyes and see the punishment of the wicked. The Lord is our refuge and our fortress, sings the psalmist, who delivers us from the snare of the fowler and whose faithfulness is a shield (see Psalm 91:1-8).

Still, we must be careful lest warm thanks and praise become cold judgment and self-righteousness. Some of the most condescending words ever spoken are "There but for the grace of God go I." It may sound like piety to undiscerning ears, but it is much more self-serving than grace-filled.

"Who sinned, this man or his parents, that he was born blind?" the disciples asked Jesus (John 9:2). What a safe, sterile question for the sighted to ask, although as the story reveals, there is more than one kind of blindness. It is not the Pharisee who prays, "Lord, I thank you that I am not like *this* man," a prayer that, according to Jesus—although it is as ancient as the text and as current as ethnic and national bigotry—justifies no one. When we say, "There, but for the grace of God, go I," we may not be nearly so graced as we think.

In our lesson for the morning, we have an example of ancient Near Eastern *Schadenfreude*: people come to Jesus to tell him about two tragedies that have occurred and perhaps, ostensibly, in hopes of an explanation. They say Pilate has murdered some Galileans, right there "in church," while they were in the very act of worship! Maybe they were just seeking plausible answers, as we did when we asked the "Why?" questions after September 11 and the tsunamis of 2005. But Jesus, perhaps sensing a kind of relieved smugness in them, serves up questions instead: "Do you think these suffered in this way because they were worse sinners than others?" (see Luke 13:2). Jesus asks, in effect, "Do you imagine yourselves as better than they because you did not suffer in this way?"

"No, I tell you; but unless you repent, you will likewise perish" (see v. 3). Jesus will not allow them to content themselves in such a way. He will not permit his questioners to objectify the suffering of others in any way as to make it self-serving.

Jesus strikes again, while the iron is hot, and reaches quickly for another example to drive home the point. In Jerusalem, he reminds them, the Siloam tower fell and killed eighteen people. "Do you think they were worse sinners than any other person in the city?" (see v. 4).

The obvious answer is no. Towers sometimes fall; the Pilates of the world sometimes kill people cruelly and irrationally. That does not mean, however, that there is a reason to bless ourselves by cursing others in such a tragedy, or to satisfy ourselves as to the reasons for our own security or righteousness over against other of God's children. Towers sometimes fall, and the Pilates of the world are sometimes incredibly sadistic. There is no security in this world, and so we too must repent; we may perish in the same way as the others.

In theological language, Jesus is upending the old Deuteronomic theology that equates blessing with righteousness, suffering with wickedness. But it is not that simple, he says. We should not rejoice or stare at our neighbor's calamity. We must not content ourselves or denigrate others in view of their suffering, or imagine it justice that some suffer and others are spared. No, things happen in this world. There are towers that fall and murderers who kill, and we best not rejoice, only repent. We too must repent. (Thomas R. Steagald)

Why Do You Worry?

Third in a Series of Five: Questions Jesus Asked

Matthew 6:24-34

"And can any of you by worrying add a single hour to your span of life?" Jesus asked. Matthew 6:27 is translated in a variety of ways. The KJV says, "Which of you by taking thought can add one cubit unto his stature?" For those who have forgotten how to measure Noah's ark, a cubit is about eighteen inches. What adult would really want to be eighteen inches taller?—a few maybe, but not most. The RSV reads, "And which of you by being anxious can add one cubit to his span of life?" This is clearly a case of mixed metaphors.

This is a rhetorical question. We cannot add a single hour to our lives. We know that, but we worry anyway. Worse yet, the stress of our worrying may actually shorten our lives. Jesus asked, "Why do you worry?"

It should be noticed that this question surfaced in the Sermon on the Mount. Matthew told the story by collecting all of Jesus' sayings and arranging them in great discourses as if spoken to various audiences. In this case—the first of these discourses—we have a collection of Jesus' sayings to his disciples. Therefore, Jesus' admonishment of his listeners to not be anxious or worried is a teaching for those who believe in and follow Jesus. The person on the street may have good reason to worry, but the disciples of the Christ do not. This is a teaching for the person who takes his or her Christianity seriously. Fully 10 percent of the Sermon on the Mount is an explanation of why we should not worry. This is an important teaching!

Also, Jesus seems to be doing more than offering kindly advice here. This isn't just a suggestion that one not worry. Jesus isn't saying, "Gee, I wish you wouldn't worry so much." He seems to be creating a new commandment: "Thou shall not worry."

Throughout the Gospels you will find Jesus, and even the angels, saying, "Do not worry; do not be anxious; do not be afraid." It was the admonition of the angels to Mary, Joseph, and the shepherds. It was what Jesus said to the disciples when he walked on the water and approached their storm-tossed boat. This is such a serious teaching, occurring throughout the Bible, that one almost cannot believe how many times we are told not to worry, be anxious, or afraid. If you take this directive in all its permutations, you will be amazed to discover that it turns up in the Scriptures 365 times. That's right! One "Do not worry" for each day of the year.

Jesus tells us why we should not worry, why we have no reason to worry. In the first place, Jesus argues that worry is not necessary. It is needless, it is useless, it is a waste of time, and it may actually be injurious. Worry doesn't change the past. The past is past. Our own folk sayings attest to that. "Don't cry over spilled milk." That doesn't help. The milk is running over the table, dripping through the crack in the middle of the table, and is already on the floor. Worry won't get it back in the pitcher.

Worry about the future won't change the future either. We worry about something that may happen. It either happens or it doesn't. If we worry about a thing and it happens anyway, our worry was a waste of time. If we worry about a thing and it doesn't happen, our worry was a waste of time. Not only that, it has been argued by all but the most die-hard pessimists that the future rarely turns out as bad as our worries anyway.

Worry may actually harm us. Worry may cause ulcers and headaches; it elevates blood pressure and contributes to heart disease. Worry is not necessary. Why do you worry?

Jesus also argues that worry ignores the evidence. It ignores the lessons of nature. Birds are fed and the flowers are beautifully clothed. Worry ignores history. The Bible is a repetitive reciting of God delivering God's people, rescuing God's people, saving God's people. Worry ignores the lessons of our own lives. We have lived through the impossible and unbearable before. We have experienced great darkness and seen the dawn. We have passed the breaking point and did not break. Why do you worry?

Jesus offers two teachings on how to overcome worry. One is to "strive first for the kingdom of God" (Matthew 6:33). Focus your life on God and God's kingdom. All of our cares—money, food, clothing, retirement plans—are legitimate concerns, but should not be first. God's kingdom is to be first and foremost in our thinking. Put God first, and all else falls into place.

Jesus, teaching us not to worry, also said, "Do not worry about tomorrow" (v. 34). Handle today's task today. Those who have overcome addictions or dread diseases know that health and wholeness return one day at a time. Live your life one day at a time, and worry will not have a foothold.

Finally, take your worry and lay it at the throne of God. It's like in the old gospel hymn "What a Friend We Have in Jesus": Do you have any care, is there trial or tribulation, do you have any worry? "Take it to the Lord in prayer" ("What a Friend We Have in Jesus," *The United Methodist Hymnal* [Nashville: The United Methodist Publishing House, 1989], 526).

There are surely greater sins than worry, but few are more destructive or disabling. Jesus asked, "And can any of you by worrying add a single hour to your span of life?" Jesus asked, "Why do you worry?" He went on to say, "Do not worry." It is a commandment. It is also the way to inner peace. (Douglas Mullins)

Worship Aids

Call to Worship (Psalm 63:1-4)

Leader: O God, you are my God, I seek you, my soul thirsts for you;

People: My flesh faints for you, as in a dry and weary land where there is no water.

Leader: So I have looked upon you in the sanctuary, beholding your power and glory.

People: Because your steadfast love is better than life, my lips will praise you.

Leader: So I will bless you as long as I live;

All: **I will lift up my hands and call on your name.**

Prayer of Confession

O God, we confess that we have surrounded ourselves with crosses without realizing the meaning of the Cross. We have turned the symbol of the cross into a trinket that is lovely to behold, but we tend to forget its origin and meaning. Forgive us for taking something so serious and treating it so casually. May the way of the cross become our pilgrimage, so much as in us lies. In Jesus' name, amen.

Pastoral Prayer

Almighty God, our heavenly Father, whose way is mercy and whose name is love; we come today in grateful praise for the blessings that have fallen upon our lives from your hand. You have blessed us a thousand times when we didn't deserve it, and sometimes when we didn't notice it. Keep us ever-mindful of the source of all the good things that have come to us.

We lift the needs of your people today in prayer. We pray not only for those of us here in this sanctuary. We pray for all who are apart from us, wherever they are. We pray for those who are estranged, lost, and missing from the fellowship. We pray for those who have once found meaning in worship, but who now wander restlessly in the contemplation of eternal things. We pray for those who have never known what it means to believe that God cares, and who have never experienced a relationship that made them feel anyone cares. May the loving intent of this church reach the hearts and lives of the lonely, the lost, and the estranged.

We pray for the sick and the hurt today, whoever they are and wherever they may be. We pray for those who suffer daily undiluted physical, spiritual, or emotional pain. Save us from insensitivity to the tangible and intangible hurts of those people who walk past us each day.

Forgive our sins—even the sin that clings so close we hardly know it is there. Take away our guilt, and lead us in lives of daily commitment to the highest and the best we can know. This we pray in the strong name of the Master, Jesus Christ, our Lord. Amen. (Thomas Lane Butts)

MARCH 18, 2007

❧❧❧

Fourth Sunday in Lent

Readings: Joshua 5:9-12; Psalm 32 (*UMH* 766); 2 Corinthians 5:16-21; Luke 15:1-3, 11*b*-32

Ministries and Messages
2 Corinthians 5:16-21

"Christ our Lord invites to his table all who love him, who earnestly repent of their sin, and who seek to live in peace with one another." Every time I hear that invitation to Holy Communion I shudder a bit, for there are many Sunday-go-to-meetin' Christians who seek no such thing, and my own father one of them, God rest his soul.

Dad went around the world a couple of times, but he never took the longest and most important trip any of us need to take; the fifteen-inch journey from head to heart. That is to say, although he was a preacher of the gospel for many years, he never quite got this verse worked out in any way that was the least bit obvious to the rest of us: "We no longer regard anyone from a human point of view."

In some ways, of course, I understand. He was born in the Deep South and formed in the days of Jim Crow and stark segregation. He could never see past that particular picture of divided humanity.

He fought in World War II, and spent his tour directing artillery fire against the Nazis and Fascists. He never got used to the alliances that emerged soon after the war. My father hated the Communists too, even more than he had hated Germans, Italians, and Japanese.

He raised children through the sixties, when most every value he had lived by, gone to war for, and very nearly died on account of was questioned, denied, usurped, or burned. And although my sister and I were pretty well-behaved, I can still remember him sitting in his chair, railing at the TV, yelling at the news, shaking his head with disgust.

Until the end of his life he regarded many things not only from a human point of view but also from a very particular human's point of view. My father never got outside himself or his experience to see things from a different perspective—the perspective of Paul, say, or the perspective of grace. Oh, he knew these words of Scripture. He had them memorized, and other good words too, such as Galatians 3:28. And in fact he preached a lot on grace, but it never made him particularly gracious.

When my father preached from Paul, very often the limit of his interest seemed similar to Luther's: how can sinful persons stand righteous before a holy God? How can we hope for God to love us? How can we get to heaven? Never, so far as I know, did he ask the parallel question, "How can I or we become more loving?" His reading of the text dealt with fear of God's judgment, not love of God's children.

Paul answers the question of salvation, of course—even in our text for the day—but he does not stop or get stuck there. Instead, he moves on to the need and call for community-building.

Paul affirms that we who are Christians are "in Christ." This is the amazing gift of an amazing grace, a grace that creates a new creation. All the old things have passed away, Paul says, and among them enmity, prejudice, and hatred. We have been reconciled, brought near to God through Christ. That reconciliation to God draws us nearer, in turn, to our brothers and sisters. God loves us with heart, strength, and Son, so we can love our neighbors as God does.

That is what the "ministry of reconciliation" is, then: the bridging of old gaps, the healing of old wounds, the forgiving of old enemies, and the forming of new friends. It is not only hospitality and welcome; it is more like the practice of loving one another as Jesus has loved us. Seeing one another as God sees us, loving one another as Jesus loved, we find a unity that is both profound and profoundly countercultural. We no longer see one another according to human values, but learn to look through the lens of the precious price paid by Christ.

On the cross all the dividing walls of hostility have been broken down—between us and God, and between us and one another. We are now one people, a new creation.

Reconciled to God, we become reconcilers among God's people, and it seems Paul is referring to members of the church. But this "in-house" ministry of reconciliation becomes a message to those outside; indeed, the message of reconciliation. In sum, what we practice on each other we proclaim to everyone else, and as we learn how to love and forgive, how to confess and pardon, how to live in mutual service and fellowship, we take that message of life together into the world: "Christ for the World We Sing" (*The United Methodist Hymnal* [Nashville: The United Methodist Publishing House, 1989], 568).

Until the day when Christ is all in all, we do this ministry and we proclaim this message, Christ making his appeal through us, his ambassadors.

The man of the house stopped by to tell me his family was going to join another church. They had visited us a few times, and really liked some things about us, he said, but we fought too much and not about the important things. I don't mind a good argument, he said, but you folk sometimes just fuss.

I was reminded of that time in Mark 9, right after the Transfiguration, when a man had seen so much of the disciples' incompetence that he questioned the person and work of Jesus. I wonder how often our ministry of reconciliation, or the lack thereof, renders our message moot.

If we can't learn to be reconciled to one another, how can we preach reconciliation in the world? If we continue to see each other and talk to each other, or not talk to each other on account of our human points of view, then we will never be the kind of ambassadors for Christ who will evoke God's new creation. (Thomas R. Steagald)

What Is It You Want Me to Do for You?

Fourth in a Series of Five: Questions Jesus Asked

Mark 10:35-45

This Lent, our thoughts are turned inward by the questions Jesus asked. Jesus asked, and asks yet again, "What is it you want me to do for you?" (Mark 10:36). The question was asked of disciple brothers James and John, sons of Zebedee. Seeing Jesus alone and out of earshot of the others, they came to him and said, "We want you to do for us whatever we ask of you" (v. 35). Incredible, isn't it, that they would say such a thing to Jesus or to anyone else? It's the stuff of fairy tales and genies and magic lamps. Incredible too is Jesus' response to their presumptuous request: "What is it you want me to do for you?"

James and John approached Jesus in a way that might make us envious. They simply walked up to Jesus, stood there face-to-face with their Lord, and spoke their minds. While we may have a personal relationship with our Lord, we must approach him through prayer. I don't know about you, but to me it never quite feels face-to-face. I'm okay with that, but James and John really were blessed in that regard.

Sadly, they went seeking special favors. They wanted special places in the kingdom, one on each side of Jesus. Their request was honest and sincere, but it was wrong! It wasn't just that their request was self-serving, or that it ignored the feelings and rights of all the others. What was wrong with their request was that they were asking Jesus to fit into their plans. Prayer and supplication are always suspect when one says, "Do what I want!"

It is all right to be honest with Jesus. In fact, we must. Never hesitate to tell Jesus what is on your mind. Jesus did exactly that when he approached his Father in prayer just a few nights later in the Garden of Gethsemane. "Remove this cup from me" (Mark 14:36), said Jesus. No one wants to go to the cross, and it is perfectly all right to express our fears, our hopes, and our personal desires. But the rest of Jesus' prayer was, "Yet, not what I want, but what you want." Jesus was practicing what he had taught the others about prayer in the Sermon on the Mount. "Pray then in this way" (Matthew 6:9), said Jesus, and it was there he taught them to pray, "Thy will be done" (v. 10 KJV). We may speak our minds to God, but in the end, we must temper our requests by asking what Jesus wants and what our God wills.

I appreciate Mark's honesty in telling this story about James and John although it puts them in a bad light. It opens the door to ill thoughts about these two major disciples. It's all right to bad-mouth Judas, or to poke fun at Thomas's doubting, but here are two leading disciples. John, in the Fourth Gospel, never mentions this incident. Luke, who gives a thorough account, never mentions it. While Matthew alludes to it, he whitewashes it, having their mother make the request. Mark puts it right out there. Mark insists that Jesus could change the world with the likes of these two self-centered, arrogant disciples. This is good news, for it allows that Jesus can change the world with the likes of you and me.

James and John said, "We want you to do for us whatever we ask of you." Jesus asked them, "What is it you want me to do for you?" It is the most wonderful invitation, isn't it? Of course, when Jesus heard what they wanted, he asked them if they could pay the price, and then went on to talk about what true greatness might mean.

In Jesus' question there is good news and bad news. The good news is that Jesus' invitation to tell him what we want him to do for us is an honest invitation. It's what he meant when he said, "Knock, and the door will be opened for you" or "Ask, and it will be given you" (Matthew 7:7). I believe Jesus would really like to do for us whatever we ask.

The bad news is reflected in a couplet by poet Ralph Waldo Emerson:

"What will you have? quoth God; pay for it and take it" (Ralph Waldo Emerson, *Essays and English Traits*, vol. 5 [New York: P. F. Collier & Son, 1909–1914], 51).

Whatever we want we can probably have, but the bad news is that we have to pay the price for it. We can have happiness if we are willing to escape the prison of self and have a childlike trust in Jesus. We can have peace if we make an absolute commitment to justice for all. We may see the kingdom come if we put away greed, pride, prejudice, and self-centeredness, and realize that we have been among the obstacles to its coming. Some wanted discipleship, but it cost them their fishing boats and tax-collecting booths. Some wanted forgiveness, but it cost them repentance and a serious and certain effort at changing the way they lived and thought and spoke. Some wanted new life, but it meant dying to their old lives. Jesus asks, "What is it you want me to do for you?" He also asks, "Are Ye Able?" (*The United Methodist Hymnal* [Nashville: The United Methodist Publishing House, 1989], 530).

Finally, Jesus taught James and John what greatness might really mean. It wasn't about preferred seating; it was about humility. It wasn't about being served; it was about serving.

Jesus asks, "What is it you want me to do for you?" Before you answer, test your desires against the will of God. Then go ahead and tell God what you want, but only if you are willing to forget about yourself, give yourself to a higher cause, put God at the center of your life, and be the servant of all.

A life lived like that will make a difference in the world. (Douglas Mullins)

Worship Aids

Call to Worship (Psalm 32:1-2, 6-7)

Leader: Happy are those whose transgression is forgiven, whose sin is covered.

People: **Happy are those to whom the LORD imputes no iniquity, and in whose spirit there is no deceit.**

Leader:	Therefore let all who are faithful offer prayer to you;
People:	**At a time of distress, the rush of mighty waters shall not reach them.**
Leader:	You are a hiding place for me; you preserve me from trouble;
All:	**You surround me with glad cries of deliverance.**

Prayer of Confession

We confess, O God, that our lives have been filled with poor beginnings and bad endings. We have intended to do and be better than we are. We have wished for good outcomes, but we have not followed the disciplines that would make them so. Forgive our negligence of those ways we know from the life and teachings of Jesus Christ our Lord, in whose name we pray. Amen.

Pastoral Prayer

Dear God, we come here today to praise you and ask you to help us, at least for the time it takes us to pray, to set our minds on your blessings and give up feeling sorry for ourselves. You have blessed us with the gift of life—surrounded us with friends, trusted us with responsibility, provided for our needs, set your love over us.

In the quiet of this moment, Lord, we pause to remember those whose sacrifices have secured the goods that we enjoy—parents, teachers, soldiers, inventors, scholars, pioneers, and prophets. But mostly we remember Jesus Christ—his selfless life, his voluntary death, his victorious resurrection, his continuing power to save.

We pray this morning for those who live with a sense of running out of what they need:

- Those who are running out of time with their dreams still unfulfilled
- Those who are running out of patience, wondering how long they can endure
- Those who are running out of health, who feel their powers waning
- Those who are running out of money, fighting rising costs on a fixed income

- Those who are running out of excuses, nearing the time when they must assume blame for their failures
- Those who are running out of love, finding it easier to accuse and criticize and hate

Lord, you alone can keep us from fading. Fill us again, we ask, for we want to endure to the end. Lead us in paths of love and service. In the name of Jesus we pray. Amen. (Thomas Lane Butts)

MARCH 25, 2007

❧❧❧

Fifth Sunday in Lent

Readings: Isaiah 43:16-21; Psalm 126 (*UMH* 847); Philippians 3:4*b*-14; John 12:1-8

An Assassin, a Devotee, and an Enigma
John 12:1-8

There are two major figures in this story besides Jesus—Judas and Mary. They present interesting contrasts.

Jesus chose Judas as a disciple. The group trusted him to handle their finances. Judas fully participated in the disciples' ministry, yet he will always be remembered as a traitor. If Jesus' death was an assassination, Judas was the assassin. How did it happen that one of Jesus' own disciples betrayed him?

Somehow he had lost faith. It is evident in this passage that Judas does not approve of Mary's act of devotion. John's evaluation of Judas's motives may or may not be true, but what is evident is that Judas is distancing himself from Jesus.

One of the surprising parts of this story is the setting. Lazarus has been raised from the dead and is seated at the table with Judas. Other Jews are placing their faith in Jesus because of this miracle. Yet even the raising of Lazarus has not changed Judas's mind. This should not be surprising, since Jesus had observed about skeptics, "If they do not listen to Moses and the prophets, neither will they be convinced even if someone rises from the dead" (Luke 16:31).

Judas wasn't moved by the hospitality of his host, the devotion of Martha, or the gift of Mary. He wasn't influenced by the changed lives of his fellow disciples. Judas wasn't convicted by his own sin. Not even Jesus' love and acceptance could win him over. Only days later, Jesus would wash his feet and serve Judas at the Last Supper.

Why did Judas do it? That is the question every reader wants to ask. There are several answers that offer possibilities: he was trying to force Jesus' hand, or he misunderstood the kind of Messiah Jesus wanted to be. What we know for certain is that God did not cause him to betray Jesus. Judas chose to follow Jesus, and Judas chose to betray him. Perhaps there is no simple answer to the betrayal question. My own best explanation is that Judas was a man who never quite allowed himself to be conquered by Jesus.

Now contrast Judas with the other major figure in this story—Mary. She chose Jesus. We might guess at the reasons. He was a charismatic leader. He was a man among men, yet he was comfortable around women. Jesus was a religious man—a rabbi whose spirituality was unself-conscious. He cared about people, especially hurting people. Jesus was open to all and a friend to many. He had been a friend to Mary and her siblings, Martha and Lazarus. And when Lazarus died, Jesus had come (late, admittedly) to save the day by calling Lazarus from the tomb. It could have been any one of these things or something we don't even know about, but Mary was a devoted follower of Jesus.

Just as Judas's motivations seem to have been self-serving, hers seem to have been unselfish. She loved Jesus and wanted to show her devotion, not by anointing his head, but by anointing his feet. The wiping of his feet with her hair is the very picture of humility. And yet she is questioned, even criticized, for this act of devotion. Jesus' prediction has been fulfilled. Her devotion is celebrated and, conversely, Judas's treachery is despised. I am reminded of a response I once heard from a woman whose gift was deemed to be "too much." She said to the recipient, "Love is not afraid to give too much."

Perhaps it was John who understood Mary best. He's the one who wrote, "We love because he first loved us" (1 John 4:19).

For the modern reader of this story, John has told it in such a way that it is almost too easy to categorize everyone in black or white. Judas is the despicable traitor, and Mary is the devoted disciple. The problem in this depiction is that in most modern disciples there is a good mixture of dark and light, evil and good, Judas and Mary. I'm not convinced that the same mixture wasn't present in Judas and Mary. Judas did, after all, return the blood money and hang himself. There is a clear sense of remorse in his words "I have sinned by betraying innocent blood" (Matthew 27:4). Mary's motivations for washing Jesus' feet may have been mixed, as are ours when we do some act of devotion. She did, after all, show her devotion in the most public of places.

To compound our ambivalence, there are the words of Jesus. They seem both morbid and callous. Jesus seems to talk easily about his own death in a way that we find odd and disturbing. Did he know that he was going to die in a few days? Was he determined to force the hand of the religious leaders in Jerusalem? Did he feel that his fate was somehow sealed? We can't know of course, but death is certainly at the front of Jesus' own consciousness.

And what are we to make of his comments about the poor? These are not words we expect to see carved on the front of a Christian rescue mission. Was Jesus speaking in realistic rather than idealistic terms? Does he not care about those consigned to poverty? Jesus' whole mission and ministry serve as counterweights to those questions. Jesus was responding to Judas's pious question, "Why was this perfume not sold for three hundred denarii and the money given to the poor?" (John 12:5). Ever the teacher, Jesus is calling for clarity in the thinking of his disciples. Now is not the time to focus on the poor; they have been doing that for three years. Now is the time to focus on what Jesus must do in Jerusalem. (Philip D. Wise)

Does It Come from Heaven, or Is It of Human Origin?

Fifth in a Series of Five: Questions Jesus Asked

Matthew 21:23-27

Because fully one-fourth of Matthew tells what happened after Palm Sunday, I want to leapfrog to the following day. After the triumphal entry into Jerusalem, Jesus cleansed the Temple, then left town. Jesus was back on Monday, and when he entered the Temple, the chief priests and elders challenged by what authority he did these things. "Who gave you this authority?" they asked (Matthew 21:23). Jesus responded, "I will also ask you one question; if you tell me the answer, then I will also tell you by what authority I do these things. Did the baptism of John come from heaven, or was it of human origin?" (vv. 24-25).

On the surface, it is a simple enough question. However, for the temple officials, it was a catch-22. If they answered that the baptism of John was from heaven, Jesus would ask why they did not accept John's teaching. If they answered that John's baptism was of human origin, many of the people in the Temple would have been up in arms because they believed John's teaching. The temple officials did not want an uprising on their hands, so they begged the question, saying, "We do not know" (v. 27).

Jesus asked, "Does it come from heaven, or is it of human origin?" First, let's acknowledge that this question addresses every facet of our lives. Second, we should consider the temple officials' answer.

Apply the question "Does it come from heaven, or is it of human origin?" to all aspects of our faith and life. We are each nurtured in the faith by the many people of faith who have surrounded us through the years: Sunday school teachers, preachers, good Christian folks, parents, and other relatives. Still, these witnesses have only passed on what they first received from God. One of the rituals for baptism asks the parents, "Will you keep this child under the ministry and guidance of the church until he or she is led by God into a life of faith whose harvest is everlasting peace and joy?" Our faith comes from God. It is from heaven.

Does Jesus come from heaven, or is he of human origin? This is where people of faith are separated from those who may believe Jesus' teachings are worthy, but are unwilling to go further. Jesus is a good teacher, but he is much more. He came not only to teach but also to restore the creature's relationship with God. Jesus is from heaven.

What about the church? If the church is the creature's creation, it is nothing more than a club—a self-serving fellowship of like-minded thinkers. Yet one ritual for the confirmation and reception of members reads, "The church is of God." That is what makes the church more than a "feel-good" place. Only if the church is building up the faith, serving those in need, making disciples of all, is it from God. Only if it is from heaven is it the church.

Every facet of our faith is judged and every facet of our life is to be tested by Jesus' question: "Is it from heaven, or is it of human origin?" Do we understand that our very lives come from God? Do we understand that everything we have is a gift from God? When the offering plate is passed, are we more concerned with what we think we can spare or with how best to use our God-given resources to fulfill God's will?

Jesus inquires about every ounce of our being, "Is it from heaven, or is it of human origin?" We must answer with integrity.

The people to whom Jesus first addressed this question were chief priests, Pharisees, and members of the Sanhedrin. Their duty was to settle religious matters. Specifically, they were to distinguish between true prophets and false. When they realized that they dared not answer Jesus' question, they said, "We do not know," shirking their responsibility.

There are times when "We don't know" is the acceptable and preferred answer. When we really don't know, it is best to say so rather than make up answers that only confuse the issue more. The problem with the temple officials was that they did know the answer, or at least thought they did, but were too cowardly to speak their minds. They did the safe and expedient thing.

Evidently most of the people in that Palm Sunday crowd did the same. The crowd was rowdy, and it was easy to join in with their "Hosanna!" Yet, by Friday, many of these same people were in a different crowd where it seemed safer to shout, "Crucify him!"

Simon Peter chose the expedient route when questioned around the campfire the night Jesus was arrested.

"You also were with Jesus the Galilean."

"I do not know what you are talking about."

"This man was with Jesus of Nazareth."

"I do not know the man."

"Certainly you are also one of them."

With curse words, Peter said again, "I do not know the man!" (See Matthew 26:69-74.)

Peter took the expedient and safe way and denied even knowing Jesus rather than proclaim his faith and take the consequences.

It is often a question of expediency versus principle. Choose expediency, and you will be driven to say, "I don't know." We say it when we know the truth but are afraid to speak it for fear that the truth will not serve our purposes. Too often we ask, "What is it safe to say?" rather than "What is it right to say?"

Jesus asks, "Is it from heaven, or is it of human origin?" Let that question guide our taking account of every facet of our lives and faith. It all comes from God; it is all from heaven. Stand up, say so, be counted as one of God's people, and change the world in the name of God. (Douglas Mullins)

Worship Aids

Call to Worship (Psalm 126:1-3, 5-6)

> Leader: When the LORD restored the fortunes of Zion, we were like those who dream.

People:	**Then our mouth was filled with laughter, and our tongue with shouts of joy;**
Leader:	Then it was said among the nations, "The LORD has done great things for them."
People:	**The LORD has done great things for us, and we rejoiced.**
Leader:	May those who sow in tears reap with shouts of joy.
All:	**Those who go out weeping, bearing the seed for sowing, shall come home with shouts of joy, carrying their sheaves.**

Prayer of Confession

God of grace, we confess to being a part of a sinful society that worships so many of the things you have called false gods, and has neglected the things that feed the soul. Help us learn how to set ourselves apart and pledge our loyalty to the highest that we know. We confess to sins of the self, sins that are ours only, sins nurtured by neglect of the soul. Forgive us and restore us for Jesus' sake. Amen.

Pastoral Prayer

Almighty God, Father and Mother of us all, we seek your favor and guidance as we try to strengthen our spiritual lives. We know that we were made in your image, but some days we feel that we need to be remade. Somewhere along the way we have lost or obscured some essential elements of divinity, and we sorely miss what we have lost. You made us in love, but we let bitterness take root in us and we let hate grow. You made us to be merciful and kind, but we have permitted jealousy to ruin that spirit. You made us to be people of reason, but we tend to be ruled by our passions. You made us to be just and loving toward others, but we devise ways to get even with and ahead of our brothers and sisters. Remake us, O Lord, in your image. In the name of Jesus, amen. (Thomas Lane Butts)

APRIL 1, 2007

✦✦✦✦

The Liturgy of the Palms

Readings: Luke 19:28-40; Psalm 118:1-2, 19-29 (UMH 839)

The Liturgy of the Passion

Readings: Isaiah 50:4-9*a*; Psalm 31:9-16; Philippians 2:5-11; Luke 22:14–23:56

Can Faith Guarantee Success?
Psalm 118:1-2, 19-29

Have you ever wanted something so badly that you offered God a deal? I've talked with many people who have. Middle-aged folks, who have never married but desperately wanted to, have confided that they made a deal with God, that if God would provide someone who would fall in love with them, they would do such-and-such. I know businesswomen who have made deals with God over a new job or a big sale. I've known spouses who have made deals with God if God will just keep their sin secret. I've known men who have made deals with God in relation to financial security. I've counseled patients who have already made a deal with God about surviving surgery. I've even made a few deals of my own concerning my children's health or spiritual well-being.

Naturally, the results from these deals have been very mixed. Some felt that they made a good deal. They have given God the credit and fulfilled their vows. Others did not get what they bargained for and blamed God for their misery. Some felt that their results were mixed. When they got what they bargained for—or a portion of it—they gave God the credit. When they did not get what they asked for, they blamed themselves and concluded they would have been successful, "If I had only . . ."

I've heard and read theological critiques of each of these results. Some argue that thankfulness in light of blessings should be expected. The real theological question is: does God love only those who get what they bargain for? To the disappointed, the more spartan theologians ask, "Is God supposed to make our lives easy?" And to those who credit God for good things that come their way and blame themselves for the bad things that happen, theologians often observe that these folks are simply superstitious.

On this issue, everyone qualifies as a theologian. Some say that God determines everything. There are no accidents. Others conclude that God gave us minds so that we would make our own decisions, and we must live with the consequences. Some believe that God doesn't intervene in history. Others believe God gives us what we want if we pray. Some believe God has a detailed plan for every life. Interestingly, these beliefs are not novel. In fact, each one of them may be found in one or more of the psalms.

Psalm 118 addresses the whole question in a beautiful way that throws light on the events of Palm Sunday. On that day, it seemed Jesus' success was guaranteed—that God had uniquely blessed Jesus to be the promised Messiah. Jesus rides into Jerusalem in triumph. The psalmist would have understood Jesus' supporters' welcoming greetings. He wants God's blessing too. In that way he is no different from Cain or Moses, Saul or David. The psalmist is like the disciples who long to be the greatest in the kingdom of heaven.

In order to be successful, the psalmist asks for God's help. Assuming that one's goal, motivation, and plan are worthy, there's nothing wrong with asking for such help. Jesus repeatedly asked God to help him—most notably in Gethsemane. The psalmist asks on the basis of God's prior help. But the situation has changed. He feels chastised by God. Others have written him off. Why has God kept him alive? It is because he wants him in the camp of righteousness again. Perhaps he had come to believe that God would always bless him no matter what he did.

But the psalmist knows what God expects. He must return to the camp of the righteous. The Lord has provided a gate to the camp, but the psalmist (like all the righteous) must enter through it. Only then will God act.

So what should we conclude from this psalm? When we do our parts, God will respond. It isn't a trade, but God will not help us until our goals and motives are right, and then only if we ask. It's interesting how often those who have a good goal and proper motivation don't ask for God's help. The psalmist has the right idea. We should begin by rejoicing in what God has already given us, including life itself. We should have confidence that God will prevail. We should continue to trust that if we are on God's side, we will prevail as well.

Does God guarantee success? Yes, but on God's scale of success, not ours. This means that we may lose the game, our job, or someone we love, but we cannot lose God's love. Peter had it right: "The goal of your faith is the salvation of your soul" (see 1 Peter 1:9). (Philip D. Wise)

Telling the Story without Expectation

First in a Series of Three

Mark 14:12-16, 22-24

It was a good meal. Passover always was. It was a time of rituals, food, and fellowship. Of course, there was probably some talk among the disciples about the strange way in which they found the location for their celebration and the means by which they made the preparations. They had followed Jesus' instructions, despite the oddity of those instructions. They were probably delighted that the preparations for this meal were lighter than usual—they had found a room, with Jesus' help, of course, that was furnished and ready for the Passover meal.

The preparations were made. The meal had been served. Everyone around the table was getting along. It was a typical Passover meal. The evening was progressing nicely. You can almost hear the disciples breathe a sigh of relief and pride in honor of their accomplishments for the evening.

The disciples thought they knew what to expect. They thought they knew everything that was happening. They thought they knew Jesus. Having heard the story before, we are not surprised at what comes next. We know Jesus is not an individual of routine. We know to expect the unexpected.

But imagine how the disciples felt. They came to the meal expecting to be physically fed, to participate in fellowship and friendship, and to spend time with Jesus. In the unexpected events that interrupted the Passover meal, Jesus offers them more than the food filling their bellies and the wine quenching their thirst. Jesus offers them a covenant sealed with his own blood and body. Jesus offers them a holy gift that would change the face of the world forever.

Holy Week is about expecting the unexpected. In Holy Week we tell the story of ultimate highs and depth-defying lows. We tell the story of life conquering death, and salvation dominating sin. We tell this story because it is part of our story, as we have become journeyers with Jesus. We participate in the telling and retelling of our story as often as we partake in Communion.

We have come to expect the elements to be set before us on specific Sundays of each month. We anticipate hearing the story and resonating in the familiar words from our passage for today. We know what is coming. The bread is broken, blessed, and offered. The cup is poured, blessed, and offered. There are blessings and affirmations. We know what happens around this table, as we are lovingly invited to come to it over and over again.

But let us not forget that the first time this meal was offered, the disciples had no idea what it meant or what would come to pass to enlighten this holy ritual. They may have even seen Jesus' words and actions as interruptions of the ritualistic Passover meal. They did not know what we know. They did not know that Jesus was offering them the only meal they would ever need, one that fills the hunger of eternity and quenches the thirst for everlasting life.

We see this meal in light of Christ's death and resurrection because we know the events that follow. We know what happens when Jesus and the disciples leave the Passover meal. We recognize that Holy Week culminates in Christ's victory over sin and death. The disciples would not grasp the intensity of their surroundings for days, if not months or even years. At this point we typically vilify the disciples, pitying them for their lack of foresight and their inability to recognize the gravity of their interactions with Jesus.

Perhaps our knowing the rest of the story is not always to our benefit, at least in terms of being able to appreciate the newness of each journey to the Lord's Table. Is it possible that in our telling and retelling of Christ's story, we have become so familiar with what we know comes next that we miss something? The disciples experienced what we know as "the Lord's Supper" as an intimate moment with their friend and leader. Their eyes were focused on Jesus. Something new and unexpected was happening, and they did not want to miss any of it. How often, I wonder, are we that focused when we approach the Lord's Table? How fresh are our eyes? How new is this experience? Maybe the disciples really did get it that night with Jesus. Perhaps we should approach Communion as they did, as an interruption of our routines, as Christ announcing an unexpected message of grace, thanksgiving, and commitment to us when we expect it the least.

In this Holy Week, expect the unexpected. Expect the crucifixion of a King. Expect the masses to turn against that which is blameless and perfect. Expect life after death. But do not forget to expect something unexpected. Open your eyes to interruptions in routines, welcome those who want to make commitments with you, and approach the Table with the reverence of the first time. Jesus Christ is not bound to routines. Expect the unexpected, and prepare the way of the Lord. Amen. (Victoria Atkinson White)

Worship Aids

Call to Worship (Psalm 118:1-4)

Leader: O give thanks to the LORD, for he is good;

People: His steadfast love endures forever!

Leader: Let Israel say,

People: "His steadfast love endures forever."

Leader: Let the house of Aaron say,

People: "His steadfast love endures forever."

Leader: Let those who fear the LORD say,

People: "His steadfast love endures forever."

Prayer of Confession

We confess, O God, how we love the celebration and personal anonymity of the crowd. We love the smell of victory in the air. Forgive us when we turn and run because the parade did not lead where we thought it might. Forgive us when we leave our principles on the parade ground and follow the crowd instead of following Jesus. Forgive us and restore us in the name of Jesus. Amen.

Pastoral Prayer

O God, we know that you have watched the passage of thousands of Palm Sunday parades, knowing how short they would be. Forgive us for cheering so loudly when we thought Jesus was going to win one for our side; and running so quickly when things did not turn out as we thought they would.

Deliver us from the worship of false values and selfish goals so that we will not waste our lives on things and thoughts and hopes and dreams with no eternal significance. Save us from selling the highest and best we know for a few pieces of silver or a cheap victory over a perceived enemy or an advantage in some ultimately meaningless competition. Strengthen us for the betrayals and disappointments we will face when we refuse to give in to the temptations that come to all who follow Jesus.

We pray for health for those are ill in whatever way illness may come in life. We pray for wholeness for all who feel fragmented and broken. We pray healing for all who have been hurt in any of the ways that hurt may happen. Guide us in ministries of healing and help not only for others but also for ourselves. Help us to seek out atmospheres of love and teach us how to create what we cannot find. In the name of Jesus, amen. (Thomas Lane Butts)

APRIL 5, 2007

❧❧❧❧❧❧

Holy Thursday

Readings: Exodus 12:1-4, (5-10), 11-14; Psalm 116:1-4, 12-19; 1 Corinthians 11:23-26; John 13:1-17, 31*b*-35

The Ritual of Remembrance for a People on the Run
Exodus 12:1-4, (5-10), 11-14

In our church we celebrate weekly what we euphemistically call the "Ritual of Friendship." Perhaps we are a little formal, because other churches call this ritual of welcome the "Greeting Time." The intent, of course, is to welcome those who are guests among us. It is an important moment in worship where people in our congregation offer signs of hospitality to those who are new among us, or at least those who are visiting our congregation. It may be that we go a little overboard in using the term "ritual" for this time in our worship, but in fact we want to inculcate this idea of congregational hospitality. So we formalize this practice of hospitality by the use of the word *ritual*. Ritual is normally simply thought of as a custom or a tradition that a group or individual regularly practices.

But ritual is much more than simply a custom or a tradition. It also has a deep and what we might call a teaching purpose. Ritual helps us pass along those meanings of our common life together that are bigger than the words we use to explain them. This is why ritual is so important in life. Ritual communicates many things we hold dear, although few of us could articulate why these things are so important.

Ritual is practiced in many places and in many ways. By way of example, many families have traditional rituals. Some families have a special series of observances that they use for the holiday of Thanksgiving. In my family we always alternated going to Grandma's house (it, for some reason, was never Grandpa's house). As it worked out, we went to my father's parents' house in even-numbered years, while in odd-numbered years we traveled to my mother's parents' house. When we arrived we hugged and kissed, visited for a while, waited for a grand turkey dinner to be prepared, my father then took a nap, and so on. It was a ritual in the sense that each year—every year—the practice remained identical. Our ritual never changed, and it reminded us of what Thanksgiving consisted of for people in our family. Christmas had its unique ritual, as did Easter. Many of the holidays we celebrated consisted of the same kinds of routine integral to the particular festival day we remembered.

In 2004 I was part of the ritual of a new baseball season's beginning. The Texas Rangers baseball club invited our church staff to lead the opening-week banquet. Our choir director sang the national anthem, and I offered an opening prayer. The players were introduced, and generally we followed the identical format that has been in place for more than twenty years. Ritual helps us understand things in ways that often defy mere words.

Our Scripture lesson for Holy (Maundy) Thursday night relates to us a ritual that preceded the events it describes. *[Read: Exodus 12:1-14.]*

What we notice from the text is the absolutely controlled fashion by which the Lord coaches Moses and Aaron concerning the preparation and eating of what eventually becomes known as the Passover or Seder meal. Yahweh tells them that this "shall be the first month of the year for you" (v. 2). Yahweh tells them that they are to "take a lamb for each family, a lamb for each household" (v. 3), and if the household is too small then people may share. In fact, the lamb is not just any old lamb, but rather "without blemish, a year-old male; [and] you may take it from the sheep or from the goats" (v. 5). One thing that cannot escape notice is that these directives are quite explicit. Yahweh does not leave much "wiggle room" in the guidelines for this particular meal.

Likewise, Yahweh charges Moses and Aaron as to exactly how long this feast is to last, when the people shall slaughter the lamb, and offers details concerning where to sprinkle the blood on their doorposts and lintels. Beyond these explicit commands, Yahweh also commands that the people roast the lamb in a certain manner and dictates with what other foods they are to eat the lamb. The people, God tells Moses and Aaron, shall dispose of the remainder of the meal in a certain restricted way. Indeed, they are to eat the meal with "your loins girded, your sandals on your feet, and your staff in your hand; and you shall eat it hurriedly" (v. 11). "Why?" is a question we might ask at this point of the instructions. The answer is simple: "It is the Passover of the Lord."

This Passover meal is a ritual for the people for whom it was intended. It teaches through the very nature of the exacting way the people are to prepare the meal and how they are to eat it. It reminds them of the entire exodus from Egypt story, a story that defines and teaches its people. As Exodus concludes this story, it reminds all who hear it or read it that "this day shall be a day of remembrance for you. You shall celebrate it as a festival to the LORD; throughout your generations you shall observe it as a perpetual ordinance" (v. 14). It is a salvation story reenacted through a ritual.

When the Hebrews of old saw the preparation of the Passover meal, they remembered their story. They remembered that once they were slaves in Egypt, but now God has come and freed them. When we Christians celebrate the ritual of Holy Communion, we too remember our story and who we are. Ritual gives us a sense of identity as the people of God. Ritual helps set the context of our lives. When we celebrate the ritual meal of the Eucharist on this Holy Thursday, it also tells the story of Jesus and it tells our story as believers too. When we see the bread broken and the wine offered, we find ourselves in the midst of the greatest of all stories. Sometimes words are unnecessary. This night is one of those nights.

Jesus reminds us of what happens to people who grasp their relationship with God—liberation and freedom. May we all eat with Jesus and experience the freedom God offers us in Christ. Amen. (David N. Mosser)

When the Cock Crows
Luke 22:31-38, 54-62

Events in and around the life of Jesus move with increasing rapidity, from the triumphal entry on Palm Sunday to the tragic end on Good Friday. The days of Holy Week are so much of one fabric that it becomes more and more difficult to separate one day from the next or to isolate one event from those that precede and follow it. By the time we reach Maundy Thursday evening, there are multiple mini-dramas being played out in and around the main drama.

There are so many things that need to be brought into manageable units, and there is so little time left. It seems unbelievable, given the situation at hand, that the disciples arrive for the Passover meal on the tail end of a dispute among themselves about "which one of them was to be regarded as the greatest" (Luke 22:24). A reprimand and a lecture from

Jesus are not adequate. It takes a foot washing before they see themselves. The Romans and the Jews have an "APB" out on Jesus. One of the Twelve, Judas Iscariot, had made arrangements to betray Jesus. With a decision that must have broken his already troubled heart, Jesus sends Judas out into the night to do the dark deed for which his name is destined to live in infamy. Satan is tugging on the coattail of Simon Peter, the disciple to whom Jesus has given the "keys of the kingdom" (Matthew 16:19). In the midst of all that is swirling around the table that night, Jesus takes time to warn Peter, empathetically but directly, about what lies ahead.

Let us turn our attention to this minidrama, which is about to be played out in the life of Simon Peter. It is an unhappy example of what can, and often does, happen to followers of Jesus in any age. In this we are not to see Simon Peter as a model, but a mirror in which we may get a glimpse of that dark side of the self we so much dread to see. We do not like to believe that our actions can so quickly be driven by circumstances rather than the courageous ethics we glibly espouse. This is what happened, and it must be true, because all four Gospels give an almost identical account of it.

Jesus warns Peter that Satan is "sifting" him. The warning and prediction are more specific in Matthew and Mark than in Luke (see Matthew 26:31-35 and Mark 14:27-31). Jesus says that they will all fall away from him, but that after he is raised he will meet them in Galilee. Ignoring the profound statement of resurrection, Peter picks up on Jesus' prediction of their collective cowardice. He says that even if everyone else deserts Jesus, he will not. Luke has Peter say: "Lord, I am ready to go with you to prison and to death!" (22:33).

In the emotion of the moment, Peter was too sure of himself. He forgot his own weakness. He could not envision how he might respond when the circumstances became such that his life really was in danger. I am not sure Peter really understood what was about to happen to Jesus. It is easy to be brave before the battle. But Peter's heart was in the right place. Jesus could see what Peter could not see in himself and in the circumstances of the next twenty-four hours. Jesus said bluntly to Peter: "I tell you, Peter, the cock will not crow this day, until you have denied three times that you know me" (v. 34).

When Judas did his dark deed and Jesus was taken into custody, true to his predictions, they all headed for tall timber, all except Peter. He was obviously frightened, but to his everlasting credit, he did not run. In the course of the evening, Peter was recognized as one of Jesus' disciples on three separate occasions, and Peter denied that he knew him each time. While he was still speaking the third denial, the cock crowed. And it so happened at that time Jesus was being taken from one place to another, and "the Lord turned and looked at Peter. Then Peter remembered the word of the Lord, how he had said to him, 'Before the cock crows today, you will deny me three times.' And he went out and wept bitterly" (Luke 22:61-62).

Is there anyone, other than Peter himself, who could have known the details of this failure? It must have been Peter who told it to the others! God bless him! He did the deed. He wept and he confessed. Are there any among us who have not experienced the embarrassment and the pain of having promised in good faith to do something and then suffered a failure of nerve? We have all heard the cock crow at some time in our lives. We cannot know its effect on Peter unless we have had a similar experience.

Neither Holy Scripture nor secular history gives us an account of the last chapter of the life of Peter. There are many legends. This is one of them.

When Peter was old he was preaching to the Christian community in Rome with such power that he converted the concubines of Albimus, a friend of the emperor. This so angered the emperor that a door-to-door search was made for Peter. The leaders of the embattled church persuaded Peter to flee Rome. He departed at night with a companion to guide him. Just outside Rome, Peter saw a vision of Jesus walking toward Rome. Peter cried out: "Domine, quo vadis?" (Lord, where are you going?) Jesus answered: "To Rome to be crucified again." "Again?" asked Peter. "Yes," said Jesus, "again." Then it dawned on Peter what Jesus was saying. It was as if, from the distant past, he heard the cock crow again; he turned around and walked back into Rome. He had once denied Jesus three times, and he was not going to do it again. Peter was taken by the Romans and crucified upside down, at his request, because he did not feel worthy to be crucified in the same manner as Jesus was crucified.

Strange the things we forget, but stranger still how the cock crows to remind us who and whose we are. Listen! Listen! Listen! (Thomas Lane Butts)

Worship Aids

Call to Worship (Psalm 116:1-4)

Leader:	I love the LORD, because he has heard my voice and my supplications.	

People:	Because he inclined his ear to me, therefore I will call on him as long as I live.
Leader:	The snares of death encompassed me; the pangs of Sheol laid hold on me; I suffered distress and anguish.
People:	Then I called on the name of the LORD: "O LORD, I pray, save my life!"

Prayer of Confession

Gracious God, we come this night as a people who desire to be healthy, wealthy, and wise. Yet part of wisdom is to recognize that each of us has a "shadow side" to our personalities. Our shadow side surfaces when life's events swirl around us and frighten us. Or, perhaps, this part of us comes into view because we crave the control that we can never ultimately possess. In our anxiety to control our life and our circumstance, we make mistakes, overstep our boundaries, and fail to trust you, O Lord. Your promise is that you will always abide with us and provide for us. Forgive us our lack of trust and once again believe deeply in your eternal promises offered in Jesus Christ. Help us revisit your covenantal promises as revealed in Scripture. Where we are weak, please let us rely on your strength. Where we are foolish, we beseech you to inspire us to lean upon your divine wisdom. Most of all, O God, allow us to offer our humble contrition for our failure of faith. Make us once again your people who rest in your unfailing grace in Jesus, our Lord and Savior. Amen.

Offertory Prayer

As we bring our firstfruits and offerings to your throne of grace, O God of the Ages, accept them as a sign of our part of the human-divine covenant that you have cut with those who call on your holy name. Please bless not only we who give these gifts but also those who receive this small portion of our great bounty. We pray this in the name of the one who offered his life for us that we may live in abundance. Amen. (David N. Mosser)

APRIL 6, 2007

❧❧❧

Good Friday

Readings: Isaiah 52:13–53:12; Psalm 22; Hebrews 10:1-25; John 18:1–19:42

The Day of Preparation
John 19:31-42

Today and, in many cases, tonight, churches around the world celebrate—or at least remember, Good Friday. Good Friday is perhaps the most misnamed day of the liturgical year, or even any day of the calendar year—at least from our typically commonsense point of view. After all, what could be "good" about the death of a righteous and sinless man? Yet, this story of the death of Jesus has shaped many millions of lives over the Christian centuries. To this story we turn tonight. *[Read John 19:31-42.]*

Before we attend to the text, it is important to remember what has preceded our lesson for the evening. Jesus has just uttered his last word from the cross. He has confessed that "it is finished" (John 19:30). For us to understand Jesus' phrase "It is finished," we must first recognize John's insight into Jesus' crucifixion.

In John's story of the Crucifixion, Jesus is executed at the same moment that the lambs are sacrificed in the Temple. This timing is one day different from the Synoptic Gospels' telling of the story of Jesus. This is because, for John, Jesus does not represent or symbolize the Passover lamb—Jesus *is* the Passover Lamb. Just as Passover represents for Jews liberation from the bondage and oppression of Egypt, so too does Jesus provide liberation for all human creatures from the shackles of sin and death.

What clue does our lesson from John offer that would lead us to this conclusion? The clue resides in the allusion to hyssop—a small, flimsy plant. For those "botany-types" who would recognize such an oddity, they might arch their brows when we read in the text: "They put a sponge full of the wine on a branch of hyssop and held it to his mouth" (John 19:29).

This hyssop plant would be a strange choice to lift a more or less heavy sponge full of wine to a height of seven, eight, or more feet from the ground. The hyssop plant is much too flimsy to do the job. However, John is not so much interested in botanical practicalities as he is interested in theology. This is why John mentions the hyssop plant.

Way back in the book of Exodus, we read the Lord's direction for Passover to Moses and Aaron in the land of Egypt: "Take a bunch of hyssop, dip it in the blood that is in the basin, and touch the lintel and the two doorposts with the blood in the basin" (Exodus 12:1, 22*a*). Later that night, as the angel of death makes the sweep over the land of Egypt, God protects the Hebrews from the avenging angel by sparing their firstborn. Thus, hyssop plays a role both in liberation of the children of Israel and now here in the deliverance of human beings from sin and death.

No matter what John tries to convey theologically with his biblical allusions, we still have a problem. This problem is that when Jesus says, "It is finished," most practical-minded folks like us to think this means "He is finished." That is, Jesus is finished. These words do not inspire the confidence of faith most of us need. Rather, they remind us of a thousand different ways to say things, such as "He is history," or "He is done for." In sports, young people often speak of a victory over an opponent with words like "We smoked them," "We burned them," or "He is finished." Thus, to our ears, or at least the ears of the modern people who live around us, when Jesus says, "It is finished," we hear, rather, "I am finished." The remainder of our text for Good Friday certainly confirms such a negative conclusion to the fate of Jesus. We will have to wait until Easter morning to see how the story turns out.

On the Day of Preparation, because of certain Jewish ritual taboos, arrangements were made to remove the bodies from the crosses so that they would not remain there during the Sabbath. In a touching tie to the Passover provisions in Exodus 12:46, John writes regarding the Passover Lamb, "None of his bones shall be broken" (19:36).

Later in the day, a secret disciple of Jesus, Joseph of Arimathea, got permission from Pilate to take Jesus' body. Joseph and Nicodemus helped prepare Jesus' body for burial and did so "according to the burial custom of the Jews" (19:40). These two faithful Jews, and we might even say cloistered disciples of Jesus, laid him in the tomb that would be so vital to the announcement of the good news—"He is risen!" But, of course, that all comes later.

The phrase "Day of Preparation" is a pertinent one for Christians, just as it was for the Jewish nation of the first century. For Jews, it may have meant either the day before the Sabbath or the day before Passover. Either way, it was a day in which the people prepared for a significant event in their religious lives. Can we understand Good Friday and Holy Saturday as days of Christian preparation? As we all know, many Christians, especially in our modern world, want to skip pain and embrace pleasure. We see this mind-set, for example, at Christmas when many congregations prefer to skip any Advent hymns in a minor key (read here: "In the Bleak Midwinter") and go straight for the more joyous hymns of Christmas. Yet before we can embrace the good news of Jesus Christ, perhaps it would spiritually enrich us to reflect on the world's bad news, which Jesus came to redeem. In our days of preparation we might embrace Jesus' travail in order to appreciate his sacrifice. For Easter to be an occasion of joy, we must entertain the pain of Jesus' death. (David N. Mosser)

The Triumph over Tragedy
Matthew 27:45-50

We come now to that unspeakably terrible last day in the earthly life of Jesus. He was young when he died, even by the standards of longevity of his time. He started so late in his ministry.

He had only three years to do the most important thing in the world for all time. There are many sad things about how and why it all happened the way it did! The sense of tragedy is in almost everybody and everything. Even dumb nature rebels.

The earth trembled. Rocks split. Tombs broke open. The sacred veil of the Temple split open from top to bottom. Darkness fell over the whole land. The battle-hardened execution team, including their leader, became afraid and said: "Truly this was the Son of God" (Matthew 27:54 KJV). A thief on the cross beside Jesus asked to be remembered by Jesus in his coming kingdom. His enemies taunted him and said that if he were who he said he was, he should save himself. His friends and family wept. The whole atmosphere of that day was one of unrelieved tragedy.

Yet there was something happening on that rough hilltop that was beyond the knowing of everyone present except Jesus and his heavenly Father, whose spirit hovered over the place like a heavy fog. This is the focal point of the Atonement in time and history. It is God acting on behalf of all humankind for all time. This is the raw material from which the great atonement theological formulations are later made. It is too soon for the Gospel writers to find adequate words and phrases to communicate the meaning of this divine transaction. It is a holy mystery, yet none present could doubt that it held meaning beyond their present knowing.

The crucifixion and death of Jesus caused many questions, then and now. When you immerse yourself in this holy mystery, however, meaning is so palpable that it seems sacrilegious to raise questions and discuss exegetical and language problems. You get the feeling that you do not need to mess with the mystery. As one observer said, it would seem like "geologizing on holy ground."

This is not just talking about what is going to happen. This is not the "Mass" acted out in symbolism and institutionalized in the sacrament of the Last Supper. This is *the* Mass! This is the real thing! Its meaning is a holy mystery beyond description.

The Gospels were not written to boost the power of the Atonement by the psychological effect on the reader. The Good Friday narrative is not "juiced up" in order to get the attention of the reader or to get it on some best-seller list. The Gospel writers simply tell the story. They neither pose imponderables nor presume to resolve inherent mysteries.

Unlike some Hollywood versions of the passion of the Christ, the Gospel writers avoid the gory details of the flogging, the Via Dolorosa, and the Crucifixion. This is not to withhold or obscure important features in giving a factual account of what happened. They understand that the efficacy of the suffering and death of Jesus for humankind does not turn on the intensity of the psychological effect it has on subsequent readers.

Those of us who handle "holy things" every day and whose conversation is sprinkled with "God language," and whose sermons, prayers, and lessons presume to describe and interpret those inexplicable mysteries that mean everything, else they mean nothing, must be very cautious about reducing the mystery of the Passion and the Atonement to simplistic sentences and "bumper-sticker" interpretations. To trivialize by oversimplifications and strip the mighty acts of God in Christ of mystery is to miss the meaning.

Those who loved Jesus hung on to every word he spoke from the cross. Some things he said were so graphically etched into the minds of the Gospel writers that they remembered his exact words in the language in which he spoke. Near the very end he cried out: "Eli, Eli, lema sabachthani?" (My God, my God, why hast thou forsaken me?) (Mark 15:34b KJV; Matthew 27:46). Those haunting words were too heavy to translate. All the Gospel writers say that Jesus gave a great shout and died. John tells us what he shouted: "It is finished" (19:30).

Dr. William Barclay brings a thrilling insight to that last great shout. In English, "It is finished" is three words, but in Greek it is one word—*tetelestai*—as it would also be in Aramaic. In classic Greek, *tetelestai* is the victor's shout (William Barclay, *Matthew*, vol. 2, Daily Study Bible Series [Louisville: Westminster John Knox, 2003], 408). It is the triumphant shout of one who has survived the struggle and the pain and now stands in the winner's circle. What a great difference this makes at the end of this tragic day. Jesus does not go down in defeat. His life has not been taken from him. He has willingly and purposefully laid down his life. *Tetelestai!*

This understanding is not an attempt to put a nice facade on what has been a terrible day. *Tetelestai* is a fitting precursor to the next surprising mystery on which we all bet our lives—the Resurrection.

The story does not end with a tragic death on the cross on Friday. Get ready! Sunday is coming. *Tetelestai!* (Thomas Lane Butts)

Worship Aids

Invocation

Almighty God, as we meet this day called "Good Friday," help us feel our way into the story of Jesus' suffering and passion. Help us recognize Jesus' sacrifice upon the cross and help us live more faithfully in the cross's shadow. As we look upon the distress and misery of our brothers and sisters, make us mindful of the great gift of sacrifice that Jesus performed on our behalf. Make us people who are willing to pour ourselves out for others in the spirit by which Jesus poured out himself for us. In this time of worship, O God, help us connect ourselves to the saints of the church, those sisters and brothers who lived full and faithful lives. We pray this in the name of Jesus, who gave us all so that we could have all in his holy name. Amen.

Pastoral Prayer

In the darkness of the day and in the darkness of our sanctuary, O God of Mercy and Charity, help us quiet the inner cauldron of emotions we feel when we ponder Jesus' cross. Help us receive the gift of your unspeak-able grace as we distinguish the unconditional love from the many other kinds of provisional loves we embrace. It is, of course, this unconditional love that Jesus not only offers us but also demonstrates for us plainly on this Good Friday. As we ponder the stations of the cross, put us in the place of the disciples who all fled panic and grief. When Jesus speaks of betrayal, we, like the disciples, ask, "Is it I, Lord?" Help us this day, O God, to own up to our failure of nerve and accept our part in the passion story. Help us learn from the mistakes and experiences of those who have gone before us. Help us remember and appropriate the words of the Psalmist who prayed to you: "Create in me a clean heart, O God, and put a new and right spirit within me" (Psalm 51:10). Grant us peace at this time when there seems to be so little peace. In Christ's name we pray. Amen.

Benediction

Take the yoke of the cross and turn it from a symbol of shame into a symbol of light. Jesus is the light of the world and asks us to be the lesser lights of the world. As your people, O God, make us to be a city built on a hill that cannot be concealed. Go now in power, mercy, and the strength of God, our creator, redeemer, and sustainer. Amen. (David N. Mosser)

APRIL 8, 2007

❧❧❧

Easter Sunday

Readings: Isaiah 65:17-25; Psalm 118:1-2, 14-24; 1 Corinthians 15:19-26; John 20:1-18

Fight or Flight?
Isaiah 65:17-25

Supposedly, the "fight vs. flight" instinct is one of the most basic wirings in our brains, helping us decide how to act in the face of danger in order to optimize our chances for survival. I seriously doubt that any consideration was given to this "fight vs. flight" instinct by the organizers of the lectionary, but I propose that today's texts invite just such a discussion, if not on a biological level, certainly on a theological one. On this Easter Sunday, humanity faces a crisis. Should we take flight out of the realities of daily living, or should we stay in the grittiness of the world and fight it out? Let go and let God, or do unto others as God has done unto us? How do we survive as the people of God?

Let's start, as I did, with an alternate text for this Easter Sunday, namely Isaiah 65:17-25. (I couldn't resist the challenge of writing an Easter sermon from the Old Testament!) Here is an apocalyptic vision of creation reordered by God. It is a flight into the not-yet, with a promise of what will be. The author speaks of a new heaven, a new earth, even a new Jerusalem. People live to be a hundred years old and are called youth. Surely this is an idealistic daydream of what Isaiah wishes God would do for God's people. If this is the text the lectionary offers as a response to Easter, then our quest for survival lies in our dreams of God's re-creation.

An alternative reading for today is Acts 10:34-43. Peter, having fought with God concerning the Gentiles, embraces God's calling and preaches Jesus' gospel to Cornelius and his friends. Far from a daydream, this experience is reality for Peter. Peter is called to be present in concrete terms to these Gentiles. Peter stands up to this reality, he grapples with it, he

98

offers up his best fight for the sake of God's work in Cornelius. From this point of view, the lectionary's response to Easter is to call us into the reality of day-to-day ministry. God's people survive because they act.

Taking a closer look at Isaiah, however, we can note that as part of this apocalyptic vision the people of God are not removed to some "higher" realm, but remain as part of the re-created order. Such is the power of this text—God's people are empowered to act. An infant and an old person live out a lifetime. This one builds; that one plants. This one labors; that one bears. God does not take away people's activity in this world, but rather enables them to live life more fully. Sound familiar? Likewise, the story of Peter and Cornelius has its own dreams, those through which God directs Peter to visit Cornelius.

In both Isaiah and Acts, God and people work together to bring about the vision, the dream, if you will, God has for the world. The resurrection of Jesus Christ did not suddenly create a reordered world. God still needed Peter to go to Cornelius. The reordered world envisioned in Isaiah does not speak of people simply existing in the presence of God. The verbs in the vision attest to their continued action. Just as the people in Isaiah are empowered to act, so the individuals living in the wake of Jesus' earthly life are also expected to act. In fact, God's salvation for the world depends upon their actions. Easter resurrection happened to one individual, Jesus Christ, through the sole power of God our Creator. Humanity's response to the Easter resurrection spreads salvation to all of creation, just as Peter's response to God spread the good news to the Gentile Cornelius.

With our lectionary organizers, who included both texts of dreams and of reality, I suggest our own responses to Easter should weave both real-life action and anticipation of future redemption together. The reality of Easter resurrection gives us the assurance that God has first loved us. Isaiah, too, speaks words of assurance, describing God as answering before we even call. Through the resurrection of Jesus, the stories of early Christians like Peter, and the visions of a world re-created by God, we gain courage to engage in action. Such courage stems from the knowledge that we do not control this world, but we are vital to the process through which it is redeemed. And in the visions of God's ultimate salvation, we glean hope that the world can be, in fact will be, a better place.

Assurance, courage, and hope—all gifts of God—enable us to not merely accept but to embrace our responsibility of being God's people in the world. God's kingdom is advanced one person, one soul, at a time when resurrection happens in a heart today. Jesus said he gives power to his disciples, power even to raise people from the dead. I suggest that resurrection is the sole gift of God, but that resurrection, as is witnessed in lives transformed and renewed, is the gift of humanity to one another.

It takes both imagination and reality to live as the people of God. Imagination empowers us to act. Events, both past and present, call us to act. Together they provide courage, hope, and assurance to each of us so that we can embrace our call to be the people of God in this world. It is a calling born, not out of guilt, but out of power. Stay in the world and fight for your neighbor, being always renewed by the flights of your spirit into the vision of a world fully redeemed by God. Strengthened by courage, hope, and assurance, we can believe in God's ability to act with humanity. In so doing, the people of God are sustained. (Karen Hudson)

Tell the Story

Second in a Series of Three

1 Corinthians 15:1-11

Today is the day we tell the story. It is the story of all stories. It is the story that changed the face of the earth so many years ago, and the story that continues to change our lives every day as we relive and retell the Easter story. It is the story of Jesus Christ and his victory over death. Let us not make light of the story—did you hear it?—victory over death! This is no small feat.

Psychologists, psychiatrists, ministers, astrologers, life coaches, and so many others have written book upon book about how we should approach death, "deal" with death, and live life not fearing death. Yet, so often, death consumes our thoughts. Particularly after a loved one dies, after a mass tragedy, or as our birthdays seem to come quicker and quicker on the calendar, death scares us.

Here we gather to tell the story of Christ's death, of a terrible, painful, and public death for our sins. Holy Week takes us on the journey of Jesus' last week of life. We relive and recount the gruesome way we crucified the Son of God. We recollect the disciples' experience of three days of life on earth without the Messiah. Three long days go by in which we can only imagine the depth of their grief and sorrow. Three long days take forever, it seems, as we wait for what we know is to come. Finally Sunday morning comes with the promise of a new day and a new life. Today we celebrate that the story did not end with Christ's death. Christ's crucifixion may have been a gruesome death, but what follows after three days in the grave is the most amazing sign of life, and for those who believe, eternal life. Praise be to God, Christ rose again. He came back from the grave. Christ conquered death.

The question then follows: if one has conquered death, what comes next? What follows that which we believed was impossible? What happens when the Scriptures really are fulfilled just as they were written? What do we do when God has kept God's promises? What does life after death mean?

The signs are all around us—Easter eggs, Easter lilies, children in bright new Easter clothes, the hallelujah choruses—all these and more point to new life, a sloughing away of the old ways, a celebration of beginning again. Look around you in this room; today is one of the highest-attended days for the church around the world. People come today to hear the good news, to receive a fresh start, to celebrate, if only for a day, that Christ rose from the dead to offer a new beginning. Today is all about good news: Christ has died, and Christ has risen! Hallelujah! Praise be to God!

We are empowered to live new lives, lives of confidence and assurance in the power of Christ. He has conquered death; Christ has come back from the grave. What, then, should we fear? What can stop us from living lives of absolute certainty in knowing that our God is the Lord over life and death, sin and salvation, good and evil? Our God came to us in human form, modeled a life of humility, servanthood, and unconditional love, died a humiliating and excruciating death for our sins, and then returned from the dead to prove to those who needed just a little more evidence that our God keeps promises and fulfills the Scriptures.

Today is the day we tell the story, because as believers in the resurrected Messiah, this is also our story. We too will have life after death because we believe that Jesus has life after death. We believe and we rejoice! So ring the bells, sound the trumpets, smell the lilies, hunt the eggs, and sing the uplifting songs. But let us do the same again next week and next month and in six months. We cannot forget, as our Corinthian brothers and sisters may have done, that this is of first importance: "Christ died for our sins in accordance with the scriptures" (1 Corinthians 15:3), he was buried, and he rose again. Christ has conquered death. My brothers and sisters, Christ has conquered death! Praise be to God! (Victoria Atkinson White)

Worship Aids

Call to Worship

Leader: The Lord is risen!

All: **He is risen indeed!**

Prayer of Confession

We praise and thank you, O God, for the wondrous beauty of your creation, and for the dependable cycles by which you re-create. Forgive us when we are slow to notice how you are always bringing life to what was dead. Forgive us when we are slow to believe that what you do in the natural world, you will do also with our lives after death. We want to believe. Help thou our unbelief. Amen.

Pastoral Prayer

Most Holy Lord God of all creation, we give you praise and thanks for the mystery and excitement of the meaning of this day. We have tried, so far as in us lies, to walk with you in the frustration, disappointment, sorrow, and pain of the past week. We were there on Palm Sunday, and it wasn't bad, except we had already read the rest of the story and we knew where it was all headed. We listened to the argumentation of the opposition when they wounded you with words. We were wounded too. We heard your words of assurance when you tried to comfort the disciples in preparation for your impending death and absence. We were comforted too—some. We cannot forget what happened in the Garden of Gethsemane, and when your struggle with what was to come became too much for us and we shut it out by going to sleep. Blessed Lord, how could we forget the suffering and pain of the Via Dolorosa and the ignominious Crucifixion at Golgotha? We turned away. We ran. It was a long, lonesome Saturday. Forgive us, but we thought it was all over.

How can we express our surprise and joy at the dawn of the resurrection day? We are overcome with gladness and thanksgiving that you are really alive! We are filled with new hope that because you live, we shall live also. All praise and thanksgiving to God the Father, and Jesus the Son, and the Holy Spirit. Amen. (Thomas Lane Butts)

APRIL 15, 2007

❧❧❧

Second Sunday of Easter

Readings: Acts 5:27-32; Psalm 150; Revelation 1:4-8; John 20:19-31

Hearing the Noise
Psalm 150

The scene is a children's Sunday school room. Ten or twelve children, three to seven years old, sit on the floor around the minister of music. She has handed out an array of instruments from maracas to tambourines to claves to bells. As she reads Psalm 150, she alters the words to include the instruments the children hold. When a child hears the name of his or her instrument, she (or he) plays it with silly exuberance. The reading reflects part of Psalm 150, but the sounds certainly connect with Psalm 100, "Make a joyful noise to the LORD" (v. 1).

But back to Psalm 150. While typical praise psalms call the hearers to voice their devotion and then go on to state why God deserves praise, the text of Psalm 150 is only a call to praise God. The psalm itself gives no reason why we should praise God, no concrete experience that has precipitated such a response. Praise is all you get if you maintain a myopic reading of the final psalm. If you want to know about reasons, you have to look deeper, read more, remember, and hear the noise.

You have to hear the noise of the Psalter itself. The story told by the Psalter as we have it today moves us, the readers, through the troubling history of the Israelites. Some biblical scholars believe the Psalter was written in five parts that they call "books." While book one recalls the good times of King David, by the time we get to book three, the Davidic king is gone and the covenant in tatters. We read cries of desperation and defeat. We remember the Exile. Today, we remember the Holocaust as well. Then the Psalter begins to move us in the direction of Moses and a time when the Israelites put their trust in God. By the time we get to the end of book five and the end of the Psalter, a new declaration of trust in

God is sung. The new song, however, comes only after a journey into national pain.

You also have to hear the unpleasant noise in individual lives. I do not know about you, but I am much more likely to listen to declarations of sweeping, unconditional praise from a person or a group of people I know to have experienced hardship. "Praise God!" from a twenty-something middle-class yuppie sounds different in my ears than "Praise God!" from a WWII veteran. Consider the following statement made by a member of my church family: "I am confident that God has a plan, and I have faith that God can use all things to God's glory . . . He performed miracles then, and I know God will do so again." If I did not know her story, I'd be tempted to wrinkle my nose and think to myself that she is using God to justify reality. The noise of her life, however, is that this thirty-something woman, after being in remission for ten years, has just had a third of her right lung removed due to metastasized cancer. When she sings, "Praise God!" I listen.

You have to hear the messy noise of Easter too. Last Sunday's celebration of Easter resurrection did not occur in a vacuum. It came only after we as a community of faith passed through Lent, and particularly through Maundy Thursday. During Lent, as we considered our humanity, we realized again that we are who we are, we have what we have, only by the grace of God. Even so, faced with a Jesus who lived with and for us, we are still tempted, with Peter, to disown harsh realities. We come to the cross with our eyes closed and our minds already on the empty tomb. We come forgetting that real suffering took place that night, forgetting that our sin was implicated in that suffering, closing our ears to the One who cried, "Abba, Abba!" I suggest that "He's alive!" is a miracle; but "He who begged, 'My God, my God, why have you forsaken me?' is raised from the dead!" is salvation.

I believe that individual declarations of "Praise God!" are still more descriptive than they are prescriptive. When pushed to reflect on our sentiments, few of us would simply say, "Praise God. No reason. Just praise God." Most of us would remember times when despite the unpleasantness of our lives, we knew peace, comfort, clarity, and vision. Most of us would acknowledge that even a seemingly smooth life has had its crises. We would listen to the noise in our lives and the lives of our brothers and sisters. In listening we would acknowledge the humanity and the grace around us. We would see the hungry, the lonely, the sick, and the tired. We would walk with one another and this world, and be moved. We would feed, befriend, heal, and grant rest. Lives would know resurrection, and before long, all that has breath would praise the Lord. This, my fellow listeners, is the gospel.

In a few weeks, those same children who played instruments to Psalm 150 during Sunday school will take their praise into worship. They will hand out instruments all over the congregation and invite others to join in playing as Psalm 150 is read in the sanctuary. While God in the mighty heavens hears praise, I will be hearing noise. I will hear the noise of the hurts, the triumphs, the worries, and the anticipations of all who play their instruments. In the midst of the noise, I will know that the God of grace is even now working miracles of resurrection. Praise the Lord. (Karen Hudson)

Telling the Story Again and Again

Third in a Series of Three

1 Peter 1:3-9

Did you notice anything unusual about last week's services? Folks were wearing different and new clothing. Women were more inclined to wear hats and gloves; children were in expensive tailored outfits; some families were even color-coordinated. The songs we sang had an overtly joyous ring to them, and if you listened, you heard the choir sing just a bit more jubilantly than normal. The sanctuary smelled of the Easter lily blooms that decorated the windows and stairs. After the solemn events of Holy Week, everyone was in an excited and joyous mood. Indeed, it was Easter Sunday—one of the best days in the life of the church. As a secular comparison, last Sunday was our Super Bowl—the Sunday of all Sundays. It was a day, it seemed, when everything came together; things seemed to fall into place perfectly.

Did you notice who was here last week? Our attendance was up by 40 percent. The pews seemed to be too small for our usually spacious sanctuary. Guests and family members we see only a few times a year packed this room to hear the good news of Easter. Christ is risen! Christ is risen indeed!

Should we wonder, then, why they are not here this week? Where are our guests and visitors? Certainly family members needed to return home to their own towns and states, so let us suppose they are attending their own church services at this hour. That leaves the folks who live among us who have not joined us today; where are they? Were we not inviting enough? Were our songs not uplifting enough? Was our good news of Christ's victory over death not enough to bring them back this week so they could learn what happens next in our journey with Jesus? Where are they?

Last week on Easter Sunday, we proclaimed and celebrated the greatest news in all the world. We rejoiced in the fact that Jesus Christ died for our sins so that we can have eternal life through our faith and belief in Christ. We celebrated our living in a new covenant with God through Christ's sacrifice. At our time of invitation, we offered this salvation, this covenant, to all those present at the service. So where are those who filled the pews last Sunday? The message remains the same: Jesus died for them, for us. The invitation is still open, and yet the pews are not as full.

One might think we should have even more folks in attendance this Sunday. Just think about what would happen if everyone who heard last week's glorious news of victory over death, eternal life in heaven, and salvation from sin told just one other person about this great news. If that happened, this place would have standing room only! They would be lined up out the door and down the street! So what happened? What went wrong? Where are all the people? Is one message once a year really all they need or want?

Now, this is not to discount the faithful who are here today. You know the good news, and you have come to hear it again. As the text says, we have new birth through the Resurrection. We are heirs to an imperishable inheritance. You have an amazing faith, as the text alludes; you believe and love the Lord without the evidence of having seen him in person. This speaks volumes about the depth of your faith considering the hands-on, proof-positive world in which we live. Believing without seeing in today's society is almost unheard of, which makes your faith all that much more significant.

Indeed, you are a faithful lot. You are here when others have chosen different priorities to consume their Sabbath. You have heard the good news and you are back to celebrate again. The writer of 1 Peter praised his audience for similar faithfulness as he reminded them of that which bound the church together—the everlasting power of the resurrection of Jesus Christ. The writer emphasizes the idea that the power is ongoing in the lives of those who believe, not just a warm and affirming feeling for those who fill the pews on Resurrection Sunday. This is not to excuse the fact that we should be sharing the good news after each Sunday's celebration of Christ's resurrection, for, indeed, we have good news to share.

But your faith is honorable among the masses for you have come back even without the trumpets, the lilies, and the new clothes. You are faithful to hear the good news without the pomp and circumstance of Easter Sunday. Well done, good and faithful servants. "Blessed be the God and Father of our Lord Jesus Christ!" (Victoria Atkinson White)

Worship Aids

Call to Worship (Psalm 150)

Leader: Praise the LORD! Praise God in his sanctuary;

People: Praise him in his mighty firmament!

Leader: Praise him for his mighty deeds;

People: Praise him according to his surpassing greatness!

Leader: Praise him with trumpet sound;

People: Praise him with lute and harp!

Leader: Praise him with tambourine and dance;

People: Praise him with strings and pipe!

Leader: Praise him with clanging cymbals;

People: Praise him with loud clashing cymbals!

Leader: Let everything that breathes praise the LORD!

All: Praise the LORD!

Prayer of Confession

We confess, O God, how we tend to let the reflected light of the glory of resurrection dim as we move past the occasion. We came to worship with enthusiasm and zeal on Easter Sunday, but we confess how quickly we begin to drift back into quiet indolence. Quicken our hearts and minds with the sure knowledge of how much we will still need the hope of resurrection with every day and every death that will come into our lives. In the name of Jesus, amen.

Pastoral Prayer

Most Holy Lord God, Creator and preserver of all of life, we pray to be nourished and sustained by the knowledge that your mercies are every day the same. When the clouds of doubt darken our way, and we are not quite so sure of what we once strongly believed, help us to find in Scripture, prayer, and the community of church what we need to see us through. Save us from temptation to those things and thoughts that take away what we most need, and that offer to give us what will ultimately bring us to grief. We pray for the blessed community of the church, that it may be strengthened as a witness to truth in a world where there is so much that is false. Bless our leaders that they may stand tall and steadfast. Bless all who follow, that they may find strength in others that they do not have in themselves. Grant that your love and mercy may be palpable among us today and in the week ahead. In the blessed name of Jesus, amen. (Thomas Lane Butts)

APRIL 22, 2007

❧❧❧

Third Sunday of Easter

Readings: Acts 9:1-6, (7-20); Psalm 30; Revelation 5:11-14; John 21:1-19

Heavenly Praise and Worship
Revelation 5:11-14

One of the great joys of my life is that once in a while God gives me a glimpse of heaven. Each glimpse has been an experience of great joy and wonder.

Some years ago several friends and I went to a special event, sponsored by the City of Chicago, called "The Taste of Chicago" and held on the shore of Lake Michigan during a weekend in July. It was a huge event with more than three hundred thousand people in attendance. The Taste of Chicago was simply awesome and wonderful.

During the weekend, hundreds of restaurants, large and small, famous and not so famous, set up booths and sold samples of superbly delicious food. There was a vast variety of national, international, and ethnic foods. We started at a Greek booth and tasted fine breaded veal. Then we had mouthwatering roasted corncobs. Next we went to a Hungarian food booth and ate something that was hot and spicy. On and on we went. We did not eat much at each stop; we tasted a sample. Some samples were small, most were good-sized, and once in a while we got a large sample. We tasted different kinds of luscious breads and pastries. I felt as if I were in food heaven.

The Taste of Chicago is an amazing event. We did not get to all the booths—there were too many of them. I was surprised by the variety of nationalities and ethnic groups that participated. I saw people from different countries of Central America, South America, Africa, Europe, the Middle East, the Far West, India, and the various regions of the United States. I smelled different kinds of foods; some of the smells were absolutely wonderful and others were strange. I saw people drinking various beverages including drinks I did not recognize. I heard many languages spoken.

Another surprise was the relative peace at the event. Everyone was relaxed. As big as it was, a sense of joy pervaded the entire event. I heard many kinds of music: mariachis, polkas, Caribbean music, salsa, blue grass, rock and roll, several John Sousa marches by high school bands, and music from India and Asian countries.

I had a thoroughly grand time. Later, when I thought about The Taste of Chicago, I realized God had given me a glimpse of heaven.

If you have ever wondered about what goes on in heaven, John gives us a glimpse in Revelation, chapter 5: "Then I looked, and I heard the voice of many angels surrounding the throne and the living creatures and the elders; they numbered myriads of myriads and thousands of thousands, singing with full voice" (vv. 11-12). The book of Revelation is about glimpses of heaven.

I also find frequent references to what heaven is like in cartoons or comic strips, but they are usually wrong. Most do not show praise and worship in heaven—heaven is all about praise and worship. The millions of angels and all other living beings, "every creature in heaven and on earth and under the earth and in the sea" (v. 13), praise and worship God.

When we get to heaven, we will be joyfully praising and worshiping God, and we will be doing it forever. That is why it is so important to come to worship, because when we worship with a grateful heart and an open mind, and with joy in our souls, we get a glimpse of heaven. In our worship services we are getting ready for eternity.

Another thing evident in John's vision of heaven is that heaven is for everyone, every age, every time period, every nationality, every ethnic group, every tongue or spoken language, every tribe, every country. God loves everyone and wants all of his children to be with God forever.

In John's vision, the heavenly hosts are praising and worshiping the Lamb who was slaughtered. That Lamb is Jesus Christ, who suffered, was crucified, died, and was buried. The Lamb of God was sacrificed on our behalf that we may be forgiven and have new life. On the third day, Jesus Christ was resurrected, ascended into heaven, and now sits at the right hand of God. Because of Easter, Jesus Christ is now in heaven waiting for his followers. What great assurance!

John's message is one of hope for troubled times. In Revelation, chapter 5, we get a glimpse of heaven, and we see that in heaven all creatures—above, here, and below—praise and worship God. We see a heaven where there is an eternal abundance of love, joy, and peace.

The Lord Jesus said, "I am the way, and the truth, and the life. No one comes to the Father except through me" (John 14:6). You get to heaven by having a relationship with the Lord Jesus Christ. Come to praise and worship God as often as you can, and do it with a grateful heart, with much joy, and with a sense of peace and assurance that even as you worship and praise God, God loves you and is blessing you! Come to worship and catch a glimpse of heaven! (Roberto L. Gómez)

Believe It and You Will See It

First in a Series of Three: Exploring Rocky Relationships

1 Peter 1:3-9

As with every book in the New Testament, there is controversy around the date, authorship, and details of what we know today as 1 Peter. Although there is some debate, most biblical scholars attribute this writing to the hand of the apostle Peter or to a scribe writing on his behalf. It was most probably written from Rome about 64 C.E., during a time when the early church was facing great and growing persecution under a Roman tyrant named Nero. The writing was directed at a scattered group of believers with a general word of encouragement to remain in a spirit of holiness despite the persecution.

As we begin this series on the Christian family, we read Peter's words for insights that will give us strength to overcome rocky relationships.

The first-century church was divided between two primary cultural traditions, Jews and Gentiles. From these two very different traditions, God was working to bring together a single body in Christ. At first the church was predominantly Jewish. In fact, the early believers were seen as a Jewish sect focused on the teachings of Jesus. It was a huge surprise and a great conflict when people began to discover that God was welcoming the non-Jewish or Gentile peoples. Ultimately, we discover that Peter was not writing to either the Jewish or the Gentile believers, but rather was doing his best to communicate with a more unified church that was firmly grounded in a deeply committed faith in Jesus Christ.

A key center for teaching faith is the Christian home. Family is the essential ingredient for creating a place where people can grow in faith from an early age. But we would all agree that family life is struggling.

Marriages fail, children wander off, reconciliation becomes an obstacle, and hope runs thin.

With struggle and pain on his mind, Peter writes from his cultural context and helps us find hope in the middle of struggle.

Peter uses the metaphor of gold that is cleansed of impurities through the refining fire. It is the refining fire that brings him to conversation about purity or holiness. He desperately wants the people to move beyond suffering to discover the desire of God. But you know how your vision can be limited during times of suffering and struggle!

Dewitt Jones is a photographer for *National Geographic*. Perhaps you have seen his work without noticing his name within the classic yellow covers of the magazine. But Dewitt Jones is more than a photographer. He is a philosopher and a theologian who happens to enjoy capturing images in light and dark. He uses his camera lens to help others catch a fresh vision of life. He believed for many years that if you could see something, it was real. After exploring a fresh lens, he discovered that if you first believe in something, you will see it.

We are often limited by our personal visions. What is your vision for your family? Are you praying for the day when the kids all leave home? Are you content with chaos? Could you use a fresh lens? Could your current struggle actually be an opportunity for God to apply a new teaching to your life?

When struggle and suffering capture our hearts and control the attention of our spirits, when we can see nothing but difficult days ahead, when it looks as if the sun will never shine again, we are invited to take a second look. Pick up a new lens. Look beyond the immediate so we can see the eternal. Look beyond the pain so we can see the promise. Look past the failure so we can be strengthened in our faith. Read Hebrews 11:1 and reflect on your current level of faith.

While God is working on developing your faith, take a second look at 1 Peter. This epistle offers at least two specific benefits of trials and struggles.

First, so our faith can be demonstrated as genuine, Peter uses the image of gold that is refined by fire to become pure and precious. Trials will come. Families will face times of stress. As a result of focusing on our faith, we grow stronger. We become more dependent on our faith and more Christlike in our attitudes and in our behavior. If we believe it, we will see it!

Second, the writer reminds us that trials are only temporary. The focus of our lives must be on the hope and the promise. In fact, the writer suggests that we can rejoice and celebrate in the face of our current stress because God has a fresh promise that is about to be revealed.

My friends Pete and Barbara spent ten years working in the mission field in Uganda. They worked with children who were beyond poverty. Today they serve abandoned children in Romania. While visiting Pete and Barbara in Romania, we happened to be sharing a cup of coffee when the mail arrived. Barbara opened a letter, read one line, and began to cry. With a heart overflowing with faith and eyes abundant with love, she read the first line. It said, "Dear Mom." With her voice cracking, Barbara could say only four words, "She calls me Mom."

Family is made strong by faith, and faith will lead us to believe so we can see what God has in store for us today. What is capturing your vision? Is it faith or is it frustration?

Are you predominantly committed to the way of the world that says, "Don't believe it until you can see it"? Or are you willing to focus the lens of your life on the message of Jesus Christ and the image of faith that is refined by daily life? (Randy Jessen)

Worship Aids

Call to Worship (Psalm 30:1-3, 12*b*)

Leader:	I will extol you, O LORD, for you have drawn me up, and did not let my foes rejoice over me.
People:	**O LORD my God, I cried to you for help, and you have healed me.**
Leader:	O LORD, you brought up my soul from Sheol, restored me to life from among those gone down to the Pit.
All:	**O LORD my God, I will give thanks to you forever.**

Prayer of Confession

Dear God of our lives, we confess that, like Paul, we have heard you speak to us in one of the many ways in which you communicate, but we have not listened. We know that you have tried to send us to people and places where we could be cured of our blindness, but we would not go.

Forgive us for not listening. Forgive us for choosing to continue in our blindness. Speak to us again. Show us once more. In the name of Jesus, amen.

Pastoral Prayer

Glorious God, we thank you that we are known to you, that you have carved our names on the palms of your hands. In a world where we are known by numbers, we thank you that you know us by name. We thank you for the life and death of our Lord Jesus and for the Scriptures, which are beacons of light in a dark world to turn us around when we have lost our way. Keep us ever faithful to the highest and best we know in a world that would lure us to the lowest. We pray for the needs of people around us who are no longer sure that anybody cares. Hear our prayers for the poor and the oppressed who suffer the afflictions of poverty, abuse, and neglect. Forgive us, one and all, who have offended the light of your love, and help us dare to trust in your love and mercy, which is larger than our sin. In the saving name of Jesus we pray. Amen. (Thomas Lane Butts)

APRIL 29, 2007

❧❧❧

Fourth Sunday of Easter

Readings: Acts 9:36-43; Psalm 23; Revelation 7:9-17; John 10:22-30

I Know Them
John 10:22-30

The British rock band Led Zeppelin sang a song called "Dazed and Confused." At times we may feel dazed and confused emotionally, intellectually, or spiritually. We feel dazed and confused due to many different voices that beckon us. If you want to buy a car and you are not sure what kind of car you want, you will soon be dazed and confused. If you want to build or buy a house and you are not sure what kind you want, you will soon be dazed and confused. If you are deciding what to do with your life, you might feel dazed and confused: go with the military, go to college, get married, get a job, change careers, retire?

Our religious lives can also become dazed and confused. If you were a new Christian who moved to our community, just think of all the different Christian churches in our town: United Methodist (English and Spanish), Presbyterian, Baptist (English and Spanish), Roman Catholic (English and Spanish), Nazarene, Disciples of Christ, Church of Christ (English and Spanish), Assembly of God (English and Spanish), and various independent Pentecostal churches (English and Spanish). To make things a bit more confusing, each church offers a different version of religious belief, a different type of worship, and even a different perspective of our Lord Jesus Christ. One church will emphasize tradition. Another denomination will emphasize the Bible. Another religious group will emphasize the Holy Spirit experience. Another religious body will stress the use of reason.

By contrast, some people grow up in one church and have a lifelong, constant faith experience. Then, when it's least expected, a terrible life experience shakes one up and one ends up dazed and confused about faith and life.

In today's Gospel lesson Jesus responds to people who are dazed and confused. The Gospel of John tells us that Jesus was near the Temple in Jerusalem during the Festival of Dedication of the Temple. The Festival of Dedication of the Temple is now known as Hanukkah. This Jewish festival celebrates the victory over the Seleucids, led by Antiochus IV Epiphanes.

During the Festival of Dedication of the Temple, Jews remembered the destruction and vandalizing of the Temple and Judas, called Maccabaeus, who drove out the Seleucids and restored the Temple. King Herod and an elite group of priests were in an alliance with the Romans who controlled Israel. Many Jews wondered whether a Messiah would come and change their political and religious situation. People were dazed and confused: should they continue the temple tradition? Was John the Baptist the Messiah? Was Jesus of Nazareth the Messiah? It was then that some Jews asked Jesus if he was the Messiah.

If you read John 10:22 and the following verses, you will see that Jesus does not answer. There are two reasons for his silence. First, their understanding of Messiah is different from his. Their perceptions of the Messiah include political, economic, and religious hopes and expectations that Jesus refuses to fulfill. Jesus' ministry is to proclaim the good news of forgiveness and new life in the kingdom of God.

Second, Jesus knows these Jews are not interested in hearing him. Their minds are made up; they choose to reject Jesus. Jesus attributes their rejection of him to their not belonging to his flock. They follow another shepherd. Then Jesus speaks of those who belong to him. "My sheep hear my voice. I know them, and they follow me. I give them eternal life, and they will never perish. No one will snatch them out of my hand. What my Father has given me is greater than all else, and no one can snatch it out of the Father's hand. The Father and I are one" (John 10:27-30).

I started this sermon by saying that there are moments in life when we feel dazed and confused. We feel lost and afraid. We feel alone and abandoned. We want somebody to find us, to call to us, to lovingly embrace us, and to tell us things are going to be okay.

If we belong to Jesus, if Jesus is our Shepherd, then when we get lost and are feeling dazed and confused, Jesus will look for us and find us. What a moment of grace, joy, and peace it is when we hear Jesus calling our names. You see; Jesus knows us. He told the Jews about his flock and said, "I know them."

Recently, during a hospital visit, a church member told me, "I am not in the hospital I wanted. The doctors here do not know me." That is not a good feeling. On the other hand, some church members have told me as I visit with them, "I was so glad to see my doctor. He knows me. He knows what to do with me to get me well." It is a great feeling to see someone you know who can help you. That is the way it is with the Lord Jesus. If you belong to Jesus, he knows you.

Life is rarely easy. Life has its bumps and bruises, hurts and wounds. We find ourselves lost and depressed. We feel dazed and confused. If we belong to Jesus, if Jesus is our Shepherd, Jesus will look for us, find us, recognize us, bind our wounds, and take us to still waters and green pastures. Indeed Jesus says in John 10:28, "I give them eternal life, and they will never perish. No one will snatch them out of my hand." What a great blessing!

I end my sermon by praying a collect from the *Book of Common Prayer*: "O God, whose Son Jesus is the good shepherd of thy people: Grant that when we hear his voice we may know him who calleth us each by name, and follow where he doth lead; who, with thee and the Holy Spirit, liveth and reigneth, one God, for ever and ever. *Amen*" ("Collect for the Fourth Sunday of Easter" [New York: Oxford University Press, 1990], 173). (Roberto L. Gómez)

Are You a Living Stone?

Second in a Series of Three: Exploring Rocky Relationships

1 Peter 2:4-12

I have always been drawn to the writings of Peter, but this particular time of study has caused me to fall in love with the core ideas he shares and with the person I believe Peter truly was. Peter writes from a pastoral heart. He writes to Christian leaders and believers who have been scattered and are living under the persecution of Rome and the emperor Nero. One of his primary goals is to offer encouragement and a spirit of hope to followers of Christ who have been living under threat of death. He is writing to mothers and fathers who need a word of hope.

Peter speaks to their pain. He refers often to their suffering. They don't really need to be reminded of the struggle they are living under daily. But Peter uses it as a platform for bringing them new hope. We could reflect on the writings of the apostle Paul in Romans 8:18 to capture a summary of Peter's message. Paul writes, "I consider that the sufferings of this present time are not worth comparing with the glory about to be revealed to us." From that positive viewpoint, Peter speaks about the hope that is available regardless of the current situation.

From my experience with families today, there are two great themes of Scripture that have a tremendous impact because the need for each is so great. Those two themes are forgiveness and hope. We don't live under persecution or anything close to potential death because of our faith or our families, but I discover person after person living in bondage. This is not the bondage of bars or chains, but the bondage and desperate experience of unmet needs. More than anything, people need the power of forgiveness and the joy of hope for their lives. Do you know mothers and fathers who need a word of hope? Do you know young people who long for a word of affirmation and forgiveness?

I am always moved by the reality Peter spoke, not only to meet the needs of his flock, but out of his own need. In fact, shortly after writing this message, Peter was persecuted to the point of death. When faced with crucifixion, he knew that he was not worthy to die in the same way his Lord had given his life. Peter insisted on being crucified upside down. Traditionally we believe Peter died in Rome. It is that tradition that created the Vatican in Rome, where one papal leader after another carries out the Roman Catholic understanding that on the rock of Peter, the church would be built.

In this particular section, Peter uses that image of the rock. Jesus changed this fisherman's name from Simon to Peter the Rock (John 1:42), and now the Rock teaches us about becoming living stones that are built into a temple for God. Only "living stones" will bring hope to broken families.

This past week we had some work done at our home. Over the years, our concrete patio sank away from the house so we decided to replace it with a new deck. The new deck is also concrete, but it looks like stones that have been laid together to create the space. Rubber molds are pressed in and color is added to make it look like real stone. It has the image of stone, but we all know that underneath it is still just concrete. Peter offers a warning not to just have the outer appearance of a living stone, but to allow God to use our lives as the preferred construction material of God.

This message reminds us that there is nothing about the Christian life that is to be undercover. The outer appearance must match the inner commitment. That happens when we recognize that there is one Savior. The Savior's name is Jesus.

Have you ever been to the little community of Marble, Colorado? The community itself is not much, but do you know why the town is famous? As you come to the end of the road, you arrive at the huge quarry that provides some of the finest marble in the world. Sculptors and builders come from all over the world to choose a section of pure white stone. The Tomb of the Unknown Soldier in Washington is made from Colorado marble. For the past year, the operators of the quarry have been searching for a block of stone that would exactly match the stone from the tomb. Over the years a crack has appeared, but the damaged stone will not be replaced until the perfect matching stone is located and quarried. Only the perfect stone will do.

Peter says that Jesus is the perfect cornerstone for the foundation of the Christian family—perfect—without blame or blemish.

Does that mean your family is perfect and without blame or blemish? We all know there are flaws and areas of failure. Some people point to those areas of imperfection and use that as an excuse to make judgments or even to stay away from Christ. Excuses are a wonderful tool. We have all used them from time to time to justify our behavior. Are you making excuses or are you building your family on the cornerstone of life? Are we ready to create living stones and to share the breakfast table together? (Randy Jessen)

Worship Aids

Call to Worship (Psalm 23)

Leader: The LORD is my shepherd, I shall not want. He makes me lie down in green pastures; he leads me beside still waters; he restores my soul. He leads me in right paths for his name's sake.

People: **Even though I walk through the darkest valley, I fear no evil; for you are with me; your rod and your staff—they comfort me.**

Leader: You prepare a table before me in the presence of my enemies; you anoint my head with oil; my cup overflows.

All: **Surely goodness and mercy shall follow me all the days of my life, and I shall dwell in the house of the LORD my whole life long.**

Prayer of Confession

O thou who art the Good Shepherd, the guardian of our lives in the pilgrim way, we confess how we have taken your grace for granted. In the safety of your fold, we tend to forget the source of our security, thinking that the source of all that saves us is ourselves. Forgive us and restore us to a right understanding of reality. In the name of Jesus, amen.

Pastoral Prayer

O Lord and God of all, we acknowledge you as Creator and sustainer of life. We give thanks for those saving people who have intersected our lives this past week—people who have known when and how to speak an encouraging word to those who are weak and worn.

We lift up the prayers of the lonely, the hurt, the disappointed and discouraged people among us. Help us to say or sing, preach or pray, something that will touch their lives creatively. We pray for the sick, but we pray especially for those who are caregivers for the sick, who wear their energies down to a nub trying to relieve pain and give comfort to rescue the helpless sick from the desperation of their illnesses. Teach us, O Lord, how to take care of ourselves without feeling guilty for acknowledging that we who give care must also have care. Save us from the "Jehovah complex" and the "Atlas syndrome," in which we fail to see the limitations by which we are bound as any other human being.

Bless all who participate in this service today so that we may receive some of what we have come to facilitate and offer to others. And of worry, O Lord, which creeps into our lives, soaks up our energies, dampens our spirits, and tries to inundate our very existence—teach us faith that puts us beyond useless worry. In the blessed name of Jesus, amen. (Thomas Lane Butts)

MAY 6, 2007

❧❧❧

Fifth Sunday of Easter

Readings: Acts 11:1-18; Psalm 148; Revelation 21:1-6; John 13:31-35

God Is the God of All
Acts 11:1-18

In my first year of seminary, I was required to take a course affectionately referred to as "Super Bible." On the academic quarter system of this seminary, all the way from August to May, I would be in this course, taught by two professors, studying the Bible from cover to cover. One of the most difficult aspects of this course, or so I thought, would be the "interview" with these two professors where we reviewed an assigned passage from Scripture. I was assigned chapter 10 of Acts. The interview was not the terrifying experiment in torture and excruciating pain I expected but, instead, a delightful experience forever etched into my heart and mind. These two gifted Bible scholars shared with and coaxed from me the image of a God who is the God of all. I will say that again, God who is the God of all. Say that with me: God who is the God of all. Doesn't that sound wonderful? Let's see if we are at that point in our lives today.

In today's passage Peter, the "prince of the disciples," a Jew among Jews, returns from a visit to those non-Jews who had accepted the word of God. When he arrives in Jerusalem, Peter is called upon to relate his experiences. The Jews in Jerusalem respond negatively, and take a stance that perhaps God does not intend for the message of salvation through Jesus to extend beyond Jewish racial/religious borders. Peter asserts that the visit confirmed for him what all Jews should have known and lived in the first place; God is the Creator of all. God's question becomes Peter's question as well: "How can we, as humans, judge any creation of God's as being 'profane or unclean'?" While the images on the sheet in Peter's dream, depicted in Acts 10, were primarily animals, Peter was quick to realize that God used the animals to represent humans, and no human should ever judge another as being "profane or unclean." Dietary laws, used by the Jews for centuries, had limited their social interaction with others and now threatened relations among Christian believers. The barriers between people had to come down, and God used Peter to begin the destruction of those walls.

As we continue our Easter journey of new life, there can be no greater rebirth than our acceptance of all. We must certainly embrace the view that all human beings are made in the awesome image of God. Here it is, the Easter season of 2007, and we wish we could declare the end of all "isms," especially racism, but we know this is not yet true. I invite you to look around this room and see all of God's people present with us. Do we, on this Sunday morning, reflect the whole spectrum of society today? Have we broken down the walls and barriers of race as we know we should? Have we allowed God to open our hearts to lovingly welcome all who come to join us in worship?

Peter shared what he received from God. Peter came to understand that God works in mysterious ways to help change our attitudes and perceptions of others. We cannot do it alone. Peter had been taught that Gentiles were unclean; that to interact with them was unclean. To sit down and eat at the same table with Gentiles was one of the worst things imaginable. It took a visit from God in a vision to change Peter's perception of the Gentiles. This same God visited the Gentile Cornelius with a vision, calling him to send for Peter. Perhaps both men were frightened; change of habits and customs is frightening. But the obedience of both brought great blessing to the Christian church. Peter called it the blessing of the Holy Spirit coming down as they met together in fellowship; the Holy Spirit coming as God's gift of strength and comfort for those living the new life in Christ.

On this Sunday, then, we should ask ourselves some questions about our lives. First, are we praying on a regular basis? Peter modeled a life of obedient and willing prayer to God every day, using the model taught him as a child and by the Lord. Second, are we praying in such a way that allows God to speak to us? I don't need to remind us that prayer is not a dictation to God of our "To Do" lists. It is a regular and integral part of worship. If we are praying on a regular basis, are we obedient when we hear God's leading or do we stay mired in our destructive ways? Our journey is more fruitful when we are obedient to God. In a couple of Sundays our journey of faith will lead us to the celebration of Pentecost. It is not too early to ask ourselves if we are yet aware of the power of the great gift from God that can still change attitudes, perceptions, and yes, even lives.

Let our rejoicing in the God who is the God of all be like the psalmist's in today's Psalm 148: "Wild animals and all cattle, creeping things and flying birds! Kings of the earth and all peoples, princes and all rulers of the earth! Young men and women alike, old and young together! Let them praise the name of the LORD, for his name alone is exalted; his glory is above earth and heaven" (vv. 10-13). It is my prayer that your presence in worship today has brought new wisdom, peace, and, as the psalmist says, "joy, the joy that endures"—the joy that helps spread God's love to those who need it most! Amen. (Eradio Valverde Jr.)

Have You Found Harmony?

Third in a Series of Three: Exploring Rocky Relationships

1 Peter 3:8-22

How many of you grew up in a small town? Your idea of a small town may be different from the next person's. No matter where you grew up, would you agree that small-town life is inherently different from city life? Sometimes your definition of a small town is relative to how big the next town is. My wife and I lived in a town of 350 people. That's what I call a small town. When we went to the basketball game on Friday nights, we saw three-fourths of the town folks and about half of the farm families. We missed some of them at the basketball game, but we knew we would see 90 percent of the rest of the community the next Tuesday evening at the Lions Club pancake supper.

Small towns are all about relationships. Everyone knows everyone in a small town. Many of them might actually be related, so you have to watch what you say. Small towns are about relationships. But then city life is also about relationships. In fact, everything we do, in one way or another, is about relationships. In the city setting, your neighbors may not know the intimate details of your life. It may not make the newspaper when your uncle from Chicago visits, but life is still about relationships.

I have a concern about family relationships in our world today. It seems that people don't know or care about one another the way they may have in days past. I may be wrong, but I get the feeling that people today are often connected by fairly thin threads.

For example, I discovered an interesting relational phenomenon. This may not be news to you. In fact, some of you may have even taken part in what I am going to describe as a "flash mob." Do you know what I mean? Here is an example of a flash mob. August 11, 2004, in downtown Denver, a group of people gathered to dance, laugh, and make joyful noises for three and half minutes, beginning at exactly 3:42 p.m. Now, does that sound strange? It might have been fun, but I wonder about the more than one thousand people who experienced this event whose only other connection to one another was the Internet. That's not a family.

Peter writes with a compassionate agenda to remind us that family relationships are central to our faith. He acknowledges that people sometimes suffer and struggle. We also know that the struggles of life can bring a deeper faith. Peter says we can live in a solid relationship with God and grow in our relationships by building on the perfect cornerstone of Jesus Christ. He gives us instructions about serving one another through the priesthood of all believers. We receive information about how we are to respect everyone and to have a special place in our hearts for nonbelievers. Peter even shares thoughts about marriage relationships and about respecting people in authority. And then, as if Peter were standing in front of his audience—as if he wanted to look into the eye of every listener—Peter writes, "Finally, all of you, live in harmony with one another" (1 Peter 3:8 NIV).

Like gifted musicians coming together to tune their instruments so they can move in concert to create something absolutely beautiful . . . like gifted athletes working together on the playing field in an unselfish effort to reach a common goal of a championship trophy . . . like God's design, described in Ephesians 4, a divine design that challenges every follower of Christ to grow continually in a spirit of unity, faith, and maturity . . . like the apostle Paul's prayer in Philippians 2, that his joy might be complete because believers are coming together to share a common spirit and a common purpose . . . all of you, especially in the context of a family, live in harmony with one another.

It is an extension of the Great Commandment when Jesus says we are to "love the Lord our God with heart, soul, mind, and strength . . . and our neighbor as ourselves" (see Luke 10:27). Ultimately, this is God's desire for every one of our lives. It is God's desire for every family, every relationship, and for every church. All of you live in harmony with one another.

How in the world are we going to live in harmony with one another? How will that happen for families that look for reconciliation? Aren't there too many differences of opinion that separate us?

Live in harmony. Live as one flame. Live as people who are gathered around a common purpose and united by a shared vision. Live as Easter people. All of you, Peter says, all of you, live in harmony. Then Peter shares the essential components of that unified spirit. He says living in harmony will be marked by five key relational elements:

> Be sympathetic,
> Love one another as siblings,
> Be compassionate,
> Experience humility,
> And don't repay evil with evil.

These principles apply to everyday life, but they must start within the context of the Christian home. In John 13:35 Jesus says, "By this, all men will know that you are my disciples, if you love one another" (NIV). Have you found that kind of relationship in the life of your family?

My deepest personal pain comes when I discover that people have become angry and divided within the family. Sometimes those divisions last for years. It sounds simplistic, but try a lesson from the Rock. Hear the word of Peter once again. Let it resonate within your soul and help you reset your priorities. (Randy Jessen)

Worship Aids

Call to Worship (Psalm 148:1-6)

Leader:	Praise the LORD! Praise the LORD from the heavens; praise him in the heights!
People:	**Praise him, all his angels; praise him, all his host!**
Leader:	Praise him, sun and moon; praise him, all you shining stars!
People:	**Praise him, you highest heavens, and you waters above the heavens!**
Leader:	Let them praise the name of the LORD, for he commanded and they were created.

People: **He established them forever and ever; he fixed their bounds, which cannot be passed.**

Prayer of Confession

We confess, O God, that we are a troubled people, tossed first one way and then another by forces over which we seem to have no control. In so many important matters, the center of our resolve has collapsed, leaving us without purpose and meaning. Forgive our undisciplined ways that have left us vulnerable to destructive forces. Grant us renewed resolve to find your ways and walk therein. Through Jesus Christ our Lord, amen.

Pastoral Prayer

Gracious God, whose love for us is not only greater than we know but greater than we can know, hear our prayer of praise and thanksgiving. We come to this place of worship to formally put ourselves in your presence, but we know that we are never outside your presence. We confess, to our amazement, O Lord, that you love us when we find it hard to love ourselves. We are grateful that you believe in us although you know us so well. Help us in our resolve to respond creatively to your love and trust. May our sure knowledge of your love and trust give us the motivation and strength to make love and trust the mood and manner of our relationship to others.

We pray for this church, its mission, its leaders, and its people. Bless us individually and collectively with the power of your spirit as we worship and work together. In the name and spirit of Jesus we pray. Amen. (Thomas Lane Butts)

MAY 13, 2007

❧❧❧❧

Sixth Sunday of Easter

Readings: Acts 16:9-15; Psalm 67; Revelation 21:10, 22–22:5; John 14:23-29

What Do You Do When God Calls?
Acts 16:9-15

Our God works in some wonderful and unexplainable ways. That affirmation has been the constant theme of every Easter season. A Savior nailed to a cross, then buried, comes back to life in three days as Jesus had predicted. For the disciples then, and believers now, nothing could be more wonderful or unexplainable. Indeed, the Easter story didn't end there. The risen Christ visited Saul of Tarsus and, in one of the Bible's most dramatic conversion stories, turned Paul from captain of the opposition into captain of the home team.

Today we visit a passage from the Bible that confirms this encounter. We will discover that most of what we consider blessings are visits by God. Some visits we receive and enjoy; others trouble us. Further, some visits we cannot explain and simply say it must have been the hand of the Lord. Such was the case some years ago when I was serving in a city near the U.S.-Mexico border. My congregation had several lay teams in mission work who would, on their own, gather clothing, supplies, Bibles, materials, and the like, and go to Methodist churches south of the border. Their ministry was rewarding to them and a frequent source of refreshment and inspiration for me.

One particular couple from my church loved to leave on the spur of the moment, led by God, they said, to visit pastors or members of churches along the Mexican side of the border. On one particular day they called me and invited me to come along for the ride to deliver some goods to a pastor I had met some months earlier. He served a tiny church and was a recent newlywed, full of energy for the work of the Lord in this small village, eager to spread the gospel. As we approached his home at the end of a long, dusty road, there seated on the porch was this young minister, head bent over an open Bible. He glanced up, immediately recognized the van, and began running toward us, waving and jumping with excitement. He opened my door and hugged me as he explained, "I just finished a prayer asking the Lord to send you to visit me!" I asked very innocently, "Me?" And he said yes and explained the why of his request. I talked with him about the situation he was facing in hopes that it might bring a blessing, and we enjoyed a great visit, closed our time with prayer, and I returned home. Only the Lord knows what purpose I served that day, since all I did was to say yes to an invitation to travel to Mexico, expecting only to help unload things from a van; not to help a fellow pastor with a load he was carrying.

What do you do when God visits? Paul would instruct, "Say yes" to whatever God leads us to do. Paul was visited with a vision, one night as he slept, of a man from Macedonia imploring Paul to "come over to Macedonia and help us" (Acts 16:9). Paul, convinced it was God calling him, obediently began making plans to travel to that region and fulfill this call.

God visits us regularly and, whether through dreams, visions, or recurring thoughts, plants seeds in our minds that, if followed, may result in special blessing for the work of God even today. Paul's call involved visiting a significant region of the time, to bring the good news about Christ's love. Travel was difficult, but Paul and Timothy finally reached Philippi. Once there, they ventured outside the city gates to the river, where they believed they would find a place of worship. Paul shared the good news with the women gathered there. Lydia received this salvation message and opened her home to host what became the church in Philippi. Some scholars believe that while in Philippi, Paul wrote his second letter to the Corinthians and his first epistle to Timothy. We also have the epistle to the Philippians; those encouraging words Paul shared some years later with the church he founded there. This was, indeed, a fruitful visit. What do we do when God visits? Are we open to God's leading?

Today is the perfect day to ask ourselves these questions. Have we considered that every obedient step we take may guide us to the place where a wonderful seed is planted for fruitful ministry? Dare not to limit God's power to share exactly what is needed to be faithful. Dare even to imagine that God may provide exactly what we thought we didn't need, as was the case with the disciples on that first Pentecost Day. God visited them in a mighty way and continues visiting today.

I serve in the ministry as the result of a recurring visit by God. I told God that I was not the right person, and shared hundreds of what I thought were excellent excuses to dodge this call. I placed conditions on my call; I had to overcome my shyness and I had to be more willing to stand in front of people to speak God's Word. Wouldn't you know it; God did all those things and more.

This is the last Sunday in the Easter season. Next Sunday we will celebrate Pentecost, the day when the Holy Spirit visited the disciples and empowered them to share God's good works in many languages. The disciples followed God's leading to take those steps to share the way God continues to work in all the lives that trust God and let God work in them.

Where is God leading you? (Eradio Valverde Jr.)

Breaking and Making Habits

First in a Series of Two on Character

Exodus 20:17

Like most boys who grow up in the part of the world that I'm from, I played football as a teenager. "Two-a-days"—what players and coaches call those brutal preseason practices that take place every morning and afternoon under the hot August sun—were my least favorite aspect of the sport. Removed from the lights and the fans and the cheerleaders, these practices were designed to build strength and endurance through a steady diet of sit-ups, push-ups, running, and tackling under the hot North Carolina sun. The sit-ups were the most brutal for me. We were always challenged to see who could do the most sit-ups—at the end of practice! During this portion of practice, our coach would always utter the words that have remained with me: "People—football doesn't build character. Football reveals character."

To an overly analytical adolescent, this was deeply troubling. If this doesn't build character, what does? After all, I thought "building character" was precisely what my parents wanted to occur that season, and even I hoped that it might make me "tough." Was a person born with "character"? What if I was born without it? Did I have time to build character if I didn't possess it already, or would I be labeled as one with weak character, when really I simply had weak abdominal muscles?

To be fair, I don't know if my football coach believed that some are born losers and some are born winners. Maybe he believed that a certain amount of formation had already occurred in our lives, and football would not change that but would reveal what sort of formation it was. And yet, for some of us there is much to overcome even from the beginning—a genetic predisposition toward chemical dependency or a father whose primary form of communication is screaming. The Greeks recognized early on that there is an element of "moral luck"; if you were born into a family that trained you poorly (morally or otherwise), you have habits to break and new habits that need to be formed. The Greeks claimed that certain things were nearly impossible to overcome entirely. This, combined with the claim of modern psychology that most of our habits are formed by the time we are three years old, paints a dim picture for the malformed person—even one in junior high.

The Bible offers a slightly different understanding of the way things look. Granted, we often seem to be formed in a way that makes it difficult to "do the right thing" in given situations. Yet the Bible proclaims that, through encounters with the one and living God, conversion to a new form of life is possible. It is the Son who lived out this alternative form of life in the flesh, and it is the Son who assures us that the Holy Spirit will always be there to empower us to live as Jesus lived.

Whatever one believes about conversion and the power of the Holy Spirit, history tells us that change is difficult. Again, the Greeks understood this well. Persons can't typically turn their desires on and off like a light. Moreover, it isn't easy to redirect the desires one finds already present. Add this to the fact that desires often become habits, and we see the importance of the formation of desire. Why? Habits are, by definition, easy to form and hard to change. One's habits determine one's character; they determine how one acts characteristically.

Adopting these well-established truths into the Christian tradition, Saint Thomas Aquinas called well-directed habits "virtues" and misdirected habits "vices." For Aquinas, habits are either good or bad, and we all have them, so they are crucial. The goal is to align desire and action. Being "moral," then, is not overcoming our desires, but changing them so that when we act characteristically, we act well, in a way that is faithful.

Lest we be tempted to think that the philosophers have a monopoly on the truth about acting morally, it is important to see that the Bible provides us with insight on desire. I have never understood the place of the ninth and tenth commandments, the commandments not to covet. Why was it important to tell me not to covet my neighbor's donkey or wife when I had already been commanded not to steal or commit adultery? Luther famously said that the ninth and tenth commandments make it impossible for persons not to come under the judgment of the biblical law. That is, if we think we can live without committing adultery, without stealing, without worshiping false gods or dishonoring parents, without lying or killing anyone, and without profaning the Sabbath or the name of the Lord, then "do not covet" (see Exodus 20:17) will surely trip us up (Martin Luther, *The Large Catechism* [Philadelphia: Fortress Press, 1963], 48-51).

In one sense, Luther is right. Complete faithfulness is rare, if not impossible. But the commandments not to covet, like the others, are not a contingency plan meant to trip up the most righteous persons, thereby placing them in need of justification. Rather, these commandments confront our desires. Because our desires are behind our actions, formation of those desires is crucial. The commandments not to covet tell us what not to desire, and thereby give us the gift of imagining how our lives can be different than they are, different even from what Madison Avenue depicts as "the good life." Thus, rather than habituating us into a life lived in pursuit of the things we don't have, these teach us to desire appropriately, and thereby build the specifically Christian character that will be revealed in our lives. Get these right and, adherently, the rest of the commandments will come. (Scott Bullard)

Worship Aids

Call to Worship (Psalm 67:1-5)

> Leader: May God be gracious to us and bless us and make his face to shine upon us.

> **People:** **That your way may be known upon earth, your saving power among all nations.**

> Leader: Let the peoples praise you, O God; let all the peoples praise you.

> **People:** **Let the nations be glad and sing for joy,**

> Leader: For you judge the peoples with equity and guide the nations upon earth.

All:　　　**Let the peoples praise you, O God; let all the peoples praise you.**

Prayer of Confession

God of Justice and Mercy, we confess how in our carelessness we have wandered from the path of truth and righteousness so clearly exemplified for us in Christ Jesus, our Lord. We pray your healing for the spiritual ills in our lives and your help with fractured relationships. May the sure knowledge of your forgiveness and grace give us greater resolve to live more godly lives. In the name of Jesus, amen.

Pastoral Prayer

Dear God, whose face we have not seen except in the faces of others, and whose nature lies beyond the wildest stretch of the human mind, we come today with thankful hearts for we do know of you from the life of Jesus, and from what we know and feel in our own hearts.

On this day, when thoughts of family play across the backdrop of our minds, we pray to be forgiven for our failures in family matters. Forgive us for neglecting children and spouses in order to spend more time at the workplace or on the golf course. Forgive us for giving our loved ones money and things as a substitute for love and time. May the unconditional love we know from you, O God, which we best see in Jesus and sometimes see in people, seep through our relationships to redeem the brokenness in ourselves and others.

Hear the unspoken prayers and concerns of this congregation. In the name of Jesus we pray. Amen. (Thomas Lane Butts)

MAY 20, 2007

❧❧❧

Seventh Sunday of Easter

Readings: Acts 16:16-34; Psalm 97; Revelation 22:12-14, 16-17, 20-21; John 17:20-26

Where God Works
Acts 16:16-34

As I read this passage, I considered a story I heard about Saint Thomas Aquinas. While walking with a friend in the midst of the splendors of Rome the friend said, "We Christians certainly can no longer say silver and gold have we none." Saint Thomas responded by saying, "But neither can we say to the lame man, in the name of Jesus Christ rise up and walk."

On the surface these two events in Paul's ministry seem problematic for the modern church. These dramatic stories—a slave girl with unique gifts, two advocates of the gospel and a jailer all released from their different forms of imprisonment—are a challenge. Where do we see such power emerging in and through the church? Like Saint Thomas, we may be painfully aware of the lack of life-transforming power in the modern church and its witness.

That may be precisely the reason Luke shares these events with us. Luke calls us to attentiveness to God's saving power. Perhaps Luke is inviting us to move beyond surface diagnosis of the church's limitations to a deeper reflection on God's activity that we can identify and recognize and in which we can participate.

Luke invites us to gratitude for our own salvation and freedom. Most disciples have a story of "being saved." While we may not have been in a physical prison, we do have our chains. At some point we were lost but were found. In some way, God's grace penetrated our solitary confinement and we were set free. Disciples are persons who, in the presence of hurt, guilt, and powerlessness, discover the love of a Savior present at the point of needing to be saved.

We are invited to be in touch with this portion of our personal faith history. Our stories can then resonate with the important themes of this story. Luke is firmly convinced that God's love seeks people out no matter who they are, no matter what their positions in society, no matter the circumstances in which they find themselves. The need for a Savior is a great equalizer. If we can be saved, then so can anyone else. If we can renew our gratitude for God's work in us, then we can be in touch, once again, with the power described in this story.

We can also be more attentive to the community of faith and the stories of God's healing and releasing, which we have in common with our brothers and sisters. Luke invites us to move to a deeper level of sharing within the church.

Where have you seen God at work? Where have you experienced God's freedom lately? These questions move us away from conversations about the accuracy of our theological opinions, our pessimistic worries about the state of our lives, or diagnosis of the state of other persons' lives. Freed from idle chatter, from prejudices, and unquestioned assumptions, we can be open to experiences of redemption and freedom.

One other important component of this story is the presence of those who are not free. A slave girl and a jailer are prisoners in different cells in the same fortress of fear, oppression, and hopelessness. Paul and Silas, first on the way to a prayer meeting and then singing hymns while chained to a wall, find their lives and experiences intersecting with these two for whom Christ died and rose again. In their freedom they offer the key to unlock the chains of bondage.

It happens to those who pray and worship. God provides people with whom our experiences will intersect in helpful and healing ways. Luke is not describing an event that lives only as the memory of the church. The event of God's deliverance happens over and over again for the church and through the church. Luke is saying, "Wake up, church! This could happen to you!" (Bob Holloway)

The Hard Sayings

Second in a Series of Two on Character

Matthew 5:17-48

At the end of last week's sermon, we looked at the Ten Commandments, specifically the commandments against covetousness, and saw that, through them, Christians can learn to act with a specifically Christian character. That is, upon conversion, Christians enter into a way of living that sees how our lives can be different. The Ten Commandments summarize that life for Christians. They demand a way of living that looks vastly different from the way so many persons were living then and in stark contrast to the way in which so many are living now. Behind faithfulness to these commandments is the reordering of our desires, which requires both acknowledging that the way things are is not the way things have to be and relying on the power of God to offer the world an alternative way to live. Why do we need to speak of the character of our lives in this way? Because this is how we witness—persons don't have to be locked into disordered desires, but persons do have to know that desires are, in fact, disordered to be unlocked from them. A change in our desires will result in the way we characteristically act.

When we talk about the commandments against covetousness in this way, it seems easy to make the leap to the Sermon on the Mount in the New Testament. Among other things, Jesus says, in Matthew's version of this sermon, "You have heard that it was said, 'An eye for an eye and a tooth for a tooth.' But I say to you, Do not resist an evildoer" (Matthew 5:38-39). Just as we heard the claim last week that the commandments not to covet were impossible to adhere to, the church has often taken Jesus' allegedly excessive stringency to imply the impossibility of following Jesus' teachings, calling these words from the Sermon on the Mount the "hard sayings" of Jesus. The danger here is implying that the so-called hard sayings are meant for those who find the other sayings easy, or that they are only for a small, dedicated group of fanatics. With Luther, others claim that these are meant to throw us back into our need for grace, or even that they are part of Jesus' "interim ethic."

There is something incomplete with each of these options. In the first place, it seems that Christianity ought to have little room for an "interim ethic." Is Jesus irrelevant for living well here and now? If we can't take Jesus seriously here, where can we begin to take him seriously? Second, a two-tiered ethic—saying that some teachings are generally applicable while others apply only to those set apart for a higher moral calling than the masses—isn't sufficient either. Rather, this seems more like a strategy used to "civilize" Christianity, to make it a respectable religion among other respectable religions, one that doesn't make too many unreasonable claims and will help us lead good, "balanced" lives.

The response to the "hard sayings" can never be that there's a whole lot of stuff necessary for holiness that most of us can't do. This attitude reminds me of a statement John Howard Yoder made in one of his final public lectures: "A life of suffering servanthood an impossible calling, you say? No way, we simply haven't tried it yet, because it doesn't sound like too much fun." The "hard sayings" are not hard because they're impossible. They're hard because they war against what we think we want.

This claim, that the hard sayings are hard because they war against what we think we want, implies several things. First, as we covered last week, it implies our desires aren't always aligned with the will of God. Second, and more pertinent to our discussion today, this claim implies that we don't know what we want. At the same time, saying that we're self-deceived about our own desires doesn't seem to make a lot of sense. How could we be self-deceived about our own desires? For me, it is helpful here to think about our fantasies. We usually think of fantasies as things we create, perhaps when we can't get what we really want. Yet the first thing to note about fantasies is that they do not simply trick us into thinking we have obtained something we can't have. Rather, a fantasy constitutes our desire and provides its coordinates. Fantasy literally teaches us how to desire, what to desire. And, as we began to discuss last week, this is where Madison Avenue tries to grab us—by teaching us what to desire. We are, in order to fit in, and even in order to keep the economy running, to desire things, and usually new things. Rather than "buy this," Jesus says, "If someone wants to sue you and take your tunic, let him have your cloak as well" (Matthew 5:40 NIV). More abstractly, but deeply connected to this "economy of desire," while Jesus encourages us to "turn the other cheek," we are taught early on to "stand up for yourself," or to "look out for number one."

Just as we said of the ninth and tenth commandments, the reason we feel implicated by the "hard sayings" of Jesus is not because they are meant to trip us up or to ensure that we stand in need of grace. We feel implicated because we are told who we are supposed to be. Moreover, in telling us who we are to be, these directives give us resources for naming how it is that we are not yet those people. The hard sayings give us the ability to name our lives as sinful, and that ability is a great gift! So the sayings of Jesus do not name an unavoidable aspect of our lives for which we are nevertheless judged, but tell us that even concerning our wants and our fantasies we are self-deceived. Just so, they give us the gift of imagining how our lives can be different than they currently are. (Scott Bullard)

Worship Aids

Call to Worship (Psalm 97:1-6)

Leader: The LORD is king! Let the earth rejoice;

People: Let the many coastlands be glad!

Leader: Clouds and thick darkness are all around him;

People: Righteousness and justice are the foundation of his throne.

Leader: Fire goes before him, and consumes his adversaries on every side.

People: His lightnings light up the world; the earth sees and trembles.

Leader: The mountains melt like wax before the LORD, before the Lord of all the earth.

All: The heavens proclaim his righteousness; and all the peoples behold his glory.

Prayer of Confession

We confess, O God, to the endless variations of perversity that plague our lives, corrupt our relationships, and bring out attitudes we thought we had long since conquered. Forgive us for playing god and making judgments of who is worthy and unworthy, and for assuming we have superior knowledge in matters about which we know so little. You know, O Lord, how ungodly we can be! Forgive us, restore us, and give us resolve to be more like Jesus, in whose name we pray. Amen.

Pastoral Prayer

Almighty God, whose love is beyond our comprehending, and whose care is beyond our understanding; calm our anxious and stress-ridden minds. Grant us the strength born of stillness and the wisdom born of meditation as we worship today.

We have had every intention of following Jesus, but we confess that our choice to follow at a safe distance is an integral part of our sin of rebellion. We confess to our halfhearted support of the highest and best that we know. We have betrayed the Christ with faint praise and faltering trust. Forgive us.

We pray for those in trouble everywhere, especially those held hostage by people and systems bent on evil design. Be with people who are caught up in circumstances of evil not of their own design. We pray not only for those who are ill to the point of hospitalization or incapacity, but we pray all the more for those who suffer slow-moving illnesses, and who must seek debilitating treatment and whose minds and hearts are anxious about their future.

Hear these and all unspoken prayers, which we offer in the name of Jesus. Amen. (Thomas Lane Butts)

MAY 27, 2007

❧❧❧

Pentecost

Readings: Acts 2:1-21; Psalm 104:24-34, 35*b*; Romans 8:14-17; John 14:8-17, (25-27)

What Has Gotten into These People?
Acts 2:1-21

"Go long," I said. These were my words as I launched a baked potato through the air of my elementary school cafeteria. I remember this event because it led to the first time I found myself in the principal's office. I remember this event because my usually even-tempered teacher grabbed my arm and shouted in my ear, "What has gotten into you?"

Someone observing the Day of Pentecost could have asked that same question concerning the people who had received the Holy Spirit. The spirit of God was being displayed in a dramatic, unprecedented, and multisensory way.

The instructions had been clear to the disciples. They were to wait in Jerusalem for the power from on high to come upon them. Jesus taught them about the kingdom of God. But this time was different. Jesus had become the risen Lord.

The disciples prayed in anticipation. In anticipation they added Matthias to be Judas's replacement. They waited in obedience and openness. No one knew what to expect.

Fifty days following the Feast of Passover, on the day known as the Festival of Pentecost or the Feast of the Harvest, the wind entered the room in a rush of sound and fury. It was as if the door to heaven had been left open and all the energy and power of God's presence filled the room. Divided tongues of flame appeared and danced on every head, on each and every one. From that moment on, everything for them would be different.

Fire reveals the essence of that which is valuable and desired. It destroys impurities, and what remains are essential elements in their most perfect form.

This suggests to me that the people in the room became the first evidence of the transforming power of a newly formed people of God. The circumstances and challenges outside the room were not changed so much as the people in the room were changed. They were given the freedom to be who they were created to be as daughters and sons of God. Their old ways of thinking and acting, which were life-denying, were burned away and replaced by death-defying life.

What happens next is equally a sign of the reign of God breaking into the world. These reshaped and re-created people begin to talk to one another out of this newness. What they hear is the language with which they can finally truly listen to one another. That is a miracle itself. They had talked over and past and about one another. Now, filled with the love that had suffered for all of them, they find one another and in the hearing, all of the false boundaries and barriers that separated them are swept away by the language of the Spirit, which can be spoken by every heart.

The pandemonium is more than some folks can tolerate. To some it is the sound of the well-ordered categories and classes of people splitting apart at the seams. It is the noisy chaos of love freed from the need to control or dominate, freed from the demand for reciprocity, freed by the power of forgiveness received and shared.

"What has gotten into these people?" they ask. For those who will not give up worn-out prejudices, the only explanation is the wine.

Peter gives the inaugural address for this earth-shattering appearance of God's kingdom. This is not all God has in mind for us, he declares. The best is yet to come. The old will dream dreams, and the young will see visions. Those who serve God filled with the fullness of God's love, both men and women, will speak on behalf of God's mercy and grace, and they will be vessels pouring out the spirit of God poured into them.

Here is the best part, cries Peter, now growing bolder and stronger and louder, the best part is that anyone who calls upon the Lord shall be saved. Yes, that is what I said. By the time Peter is finished telling the story of how God was present in and through Jesus, three thousand had been anointed by the same Spirit that filled the room upstairs, and all the men and women in it.

These are our spiritual ancestors. We too are the recipients of that Holy Spirit. We are the inhabitants of the kingdom community formed that day. It would be good if, because of our serving and sharing, we too could hear someone say to us, "What has gotten into you?" (Bob Holloway)

Weeding the Soul
Galatians 6:1-5

A recent interest in gardening has necessitated an increased interest in weeds. I have learned that if one wants an attractive garden, weeding is mandatory, time-consuming, tiring, and seemingly endless. Here in the desert Southwest, with the earth so dry from six years of drought, weeds seem to thrive better than my conventional plants. So, while on my knees, digging at weeds, I have learned that weeds are very good examples of how we humans deal with sin.

First, in my garden there is a plant that grows with wild abandon, up to a height of fifteen inches. A beautiful purple flower blooms atop silvery-green stems and leaves; in fact, I didn't even recognize it as a weed at first. Then it started taking over the bed where I had planted some real flowers. The outward appearance of this weed is deceiving. Some sins can be like this weed—the sin disguises itself in the beginning. Gossip is an example of this—at first, information is shared and appreciated by one's listeners. Then, motivation changes and what was once just information becomes backbiting. We may want to be seen as a person who has a wealth of information about other people, or maybe we want to discount the person we are gossiping about because of jealousy or fear. At first, gossip seems harmless, but upon closer inspection, it not only hurts other people, it undermines our own trustworthiness.

My yard also sports a weed known in New Mexico as "goat's head." It spreads out, sometimes as far as three feet! The taproot is very long and the branches reach out, very flat and close to the ground, growing new roots. The goat's heads become very hard and break off when they are mature. The weed itself, with its branches inching across the yard, reminds me of how sin can spread. Using the example of gossip again— when confronted, we may lie about our words, and another branch reaches out. Then, if we complain or feel sorry for ourselves, pride takes root.

Weeds are also examples of how we react when confronted about our sins. The purple weed's defense is little spikes. When one tries to pull this purple flowering weed, the spikes around the root prevent one from getting a good hold on the stem. Confronted about sin, a person's defense may be to answer with barbs. Out of embarrassment or shame, we want to hurt, to attack the messenger. The danger is that the sin is not acknowledged and the person never repents.

The other part of that defense system is the "quick getaway"—the weed breaks off at ground level with very little effort. If we don't like what we hear, sometimes we just leave. Have you ever talked to someone about a shortcoming, and suddenly find that your phone calls are not answered or they are always too busy to have lunch? Unfortunately, the danger still exists—no repentance and no spiritual growth.

Another weed in my garden is one that when you grab the root, the top layer just slides off, exposing a slippery, sticky mess. One can't grab the stem to remove it; there is nothing to hold on to. In human terms, this is reminiscent of the person who, when confronted about their sin, acts as if they do not hear a single word you are saying. They ignore everything. They may nod in agreement, but because they are not really listening, your words mean nothing and they respond by doing nothing! Or, they change the subject, barely acknowledging your conversation.

This brings up another point—you must excavate the entire root of the weed, or it will just get stronger and longer. Many times, we may be tempted to deal with symptoms, without getting to the root cause. Unfortunately, since the root is still there, another symptom will arise. Since we have been talking about gossip, what could be the root cause? I think it is coveting—wanting what another person has. Gossip is a way of putting yourself first while putting another down. We may desire to be popular, easy to talk to, knowledgeable about people and their circumstances. Covetousness, unchecked, manifests itself in other ways: greed, financial foolishness, robbery, even violence.

My garden has its fair share of weeds. I have learned that softening the soil around their root systems works best. After a good rain or watering, the weeds are easier to get out. When you pull the weeds out, grab the stem close to the ground, exert steady pressure and pull straight up. Too much pressure and the plant breaks off, too slight and your hand slips off, and take care not to jerk when you pull.

When it comes to confronting sin, in ourselves and in others, the first step is to determine our motivation for wanting to correct it. The Bible is clear about this: "Rebuke those who persist in sin in the presence of all" (see 1 Timothy 5:20), but then again, human nature may cloud our vision. Will the correction glorify God? Is the relationship between this other person and God strong enough, rooted in Christian love and trust, to withstand some correction?

We can apply these gardening principles to weeding sin. Since the soil should be moist around the weed before pulling, soften the soil of the human heart with love, patience, trust, and compassion. The slow, steady pressure in weeding becomes the loving, articulate explanation of the sin. The sin need be explained only once; if you do it more often, it is more like nagging than loving correction. In gardening, once the weed has been pulled out, it is discarded. I cannot think of one time when I have gone back to the garbage can to make sure the weed is still in there. It is the same in confronting sin; trust in the Holy Spirit to convict one of sin, without judgment or condemnation, then trust that change will take place.

Scripture reminds us that we all sin, but we are not always rebuked. We see and accept sin silently. May the Holy Spirit give us the courage and the gentleness to weed souls from sin, perhaps starting first with our own. (Raquel Mull)

Worship Aids

Call to Worship (Psalm 104:24, 31, 33-34)

Leader:	O LORD, how manifold are your works! In wisdom you have made them all....
People:	**May the glory of the LORD endure forever....**
Leader:	I will sing to the LORD as long as I live;
People:	**I will sing praise to my God while I have being.**
All:	**May my meditation be pleasing to him, for I rejoice in the LORD.**

Prayer of Confession

Dear Lord of our lives, forgive the suffering and pain we have caused others by thoughtless words and deeds. Forgive our spiteful attitudes of hate and our perverse wishes for revenge against our enemies. Forgive our ungodly theological formulations in which we misuse you to explain what we do not understand. Forgive us for suggesting you to be the source of trouble in our world and in ourselves instead of acknowledging you as our refuge and strength and a very present help in trouble. Amen.

Pastoral Prayer

Most Holy Lord, God of the universe, we confess that we really do not know what in the world you are up to. We confess our frustration at the imperfect and partial nature of our knowledge of who you are and what you are about; because we do see only through a glass dimly. Not only are we ignorant, we also are lonely for you. We treasure the glimpses of reality that you have given us. We are grateful that in time and history Jesus came to our world to give us a grand glimpse by which to measure all other fleeting insights that we have. We pray that the things we do and say and hear and see today will help us get a more satisfactory understanding of who you are and who we are in your scheme of things. Bless our efforts individually and collectively to serve you by serving others. Grant us release and relief from the fear and anxieties that confuse and frustrate our lives. Bless the sick, the wounded, and the frail persons among us. Bless each of us with the spiritual experience we need for our own particular situation. In the dear name of Jesus we pray. Amen. (Thomas Lane Butts)

JUNE 3, 2007

✥✥✥

First Sunday after Pentecost/Trinity Sunday

Readings: Proverbs 8:1-4, 22-31; Psalm 8; Romans 5:1-5; John 16:12-15

Peace with God
Romans 5:1-5, (6-8)

Paul writes: "Therefore, since we are justified by faith, we have peace with God through our Lord Jesus Christ" (Romans 5:1). We have peace with God. I wonder if Paul means that we *were* at war with God. Could this be why Paul tells his readers, "Therefore, since we are justified . . . we have peace"? What does it mean to be at war with God? Perhaps these questions do not occur to many people in today's modern world. But maybe they should. To be at war with God describes the struggle deep within people to find meaning and value in life.

When we consider the many ways that modern people avoid intimacy with others or try to relieve the anxiety in their lives by misuse of sexual relationships, alcohol, drugs, or inappropriate attachments to work, we begin to see how war with God occurs. Paul, although he wrote nearly two thousand years ago, speaks to us today about our need of peace with God.

Our lectionary epistle text culminates the opening section of Romans. It marks a transition from Paul's discussion of the importance of Abraham to the Christian faith, and then shifts into Paul's elaboration on a believer's life in Christ. This passage helps us understand the basis for peace with God. As sinners, elsewhere described as "ungodly," we are at war with God. Most people want to live in love and charity with their neighbors. When we are at cross-purposes in our relationships, it bothers us. How many times have we had a falling-out with someone because of something relatively minor that occurred? Because of our pride—and also because of the other person's pride—reconciliation is usually hard fought.

145

Most of the time, we simply accumulate enemies because we do not know how to initiate peace through reconciliation and forgiveness.

Perhaps the same is true of our relationship with God. We want to live in harmony and peace with God, but somehow we have an uneasy feeling that all is not well in our relationship with God. Even so, Paul clarifies how reconciliation is possible between God and God's creatures in this passage.

I want to note two of many important lessons the Romans text teaches us. The first is reasonably simple. Paul wants the readers to understand that God initiates our peace with God even before we supply anything to the relationship.

So what do I mean by this? Let me illustrate. Some time ago, I noticed our neighbor, Todd Forest (not his real name), out raking leaves in his front yard. He was busy filling five or six strategically located trash bags. Then I noticed his four-year-old son, Reagan, clutching a handful of leaves. The four-year-old dutifully helped his dad by putting a small fistful of leaves into a bag. Reagan did this several times. Do you think, in the big picture, Reagan was helpful? No, but Reagan thought he was and, for his father, that was enough. It was not Reagan's effort but his father's love that made his work meaningful. The good news is that our peace with God does not require us to initiate the terms of peace; God has already done this for us! Remember when Paul wrote, "For while we were still weak, at the right time Christ died for the ungodly.... But God proves his love for us in that while we still were sinners Christ died for us" (Romans 5:6, 8).

The second important aspect of this passage is that there is a "circular effect" in what Paul writes. Paul starts with the hope in God and continues through suffering—endurance—character—and back to hope. Just as with peace, hope begins in God and ends in God. We may go through many ages and stages, but all along our way, for believers, there is always hope.

My friend Tom Butts tells a story that helps us understand the divine gift of hope. One of the most admired, and often feared, persons in twentieth-century public life was the indomitable Winston Churchill.

Perhaps the most notable of all Churchill's characteristics was his refusal to surrender during the most adverse situations. In June 1965, only a few months before his death, he gave the commencement address at an English university. He was so unwell that he needed help to the podium. Once there, Churchill stood in silence for a long time. Then the voice that had once called Britain back from the edge of despair sounded publicly for the last time. Churchill said, "Never give up! Never give up! Never give up!" and sat down. There was a long silence, and then the listeners rose to their feet and applauded.

Pundits had pronounced Churchill's political career dead on several occasions, but he never gave up and he always came back. People saw evidence of his spirit at his funeral, celebrated at St. Paul's Cathedral. Churchill had carefully planned his funeral to the final detail.

There were some of the great hymns and, of course, the splendid liturgy of the Anglican Church. But there were two things Churchill planned that made his funeral service as unforgettable as his life. When the priest pronounced the benediction, there was a long silence. Then a bugler, high in the dome of St. Paul's, sounded the familiar notes of "Taps," the military signal of day's end. After another silence, another bugler in the dome played "Reveille," a signal of a new day. It was quintessential Churchill (Thomas Lane Butts, "People of the Second Bugle," e-mail newsletter article in *An Encouraging Word* [Monroeville, Ala.: First United Methodist Church, March 31, 2005]).

"But God proves his love for us in that while we still were sinners Christ died for us" (Romans 5:8). We are the people of the second bugle, for where there is God there is hope—even for us! Especially for us! (David N. Mosser)

Life in the Inflatable Church

First in a Series of Three on the Holy Spirit

Acts 2:1-17; John 20:19-22

Just when I think we've spent our last nights, ever, on inflatable air mattresses, Kris and I sign on for a few days in Costa Rica with our mission work team. Addicted to comfort, it won't be an easy adjustment. But we'll make it. I'll just unfold our air mattresses and preach to them, letting hot air do the rest.

Still, the value of inflatables is not debatable. Not every act of "blowing something up" is a bad act. Consider the inventive genius of England's Michael Gill, who, a few years ago, gave us the world's first inflatable church. No joke. You can put sixty people in it, which means it could effectively service 20 percent of the churches in my denomination. In addition to being forty-seven feet high, it includes a blow-up organ, altar, pulpit, pews, candles, and stained-glass windows.

No explanation was offered as to how air gets to and through it. One suspects it requires something more than pastoral huffing and puffing. Neither are we told how mobile it may be. But in a denomination where, from the days of John Wesley, preachers have been called "traveling eld-ers," I suppose we could be issued one of Michael Gill's inflatables at ordi-nation and, with the aid of a sturdy trailer hitch, lug our place of employment wherever we go.

After all, Jesus instructed his disciples to travel light. Paul viewed the entire world around the Mediterranean Sea as his parish. The book of Hebrews highlighted the early tent wanderings of our Abrahamic ances-tors. In addition, John Wesley's instructions to preachers included the admonition "to never spend any more time in any one place than is absolutely necessary." Which means that we preachers could be the new "Paladins" of the ecclesiastical landscape, freely distributing business cards that read: "Have Church, Will Travel."

Once upon a time, we Wesleyans really were light-traveling, circuit-riding people. Our preachers carried a clean white shirt in one saddlebag and a well-worn Bible in the other. My favorite Methodist circuit-rider story concerns Rev. Peter Cartwright, who was known for saying "I smell hell here." I picture him riding into a settlement at full gallop while screaming at the top of his lungs. Would that I had the guts to do that the first Sunday in my present pulpit.

But before I close these reflections, I want to move from a discussion of the church's mobility to a discussion of the church's energy. For the inflat-able church can't rise from the ground—let alone travel hither and yon—until it is first filled with something. But what?

If I were Michael Gill, I wouldn't fill it with helium, lest the church fall prey to overinflation. Too much helium, and the church will go floating off through the heavens—serene but separate—looking over it all, but much too much above it all. What earthly good is a heavenly church like that?

Nor would I count on the hot air of the preacher to push out the walls and puff up the pews. Not because preachers aren't capable of thunderous gusts of proclamation; not because truth cannot ride the wind of their rhetoric; but because preachers, like all mortals, are fallible. Worse yet, few of them come with expansive diaphragms.

Nor would I look to fortuitous winds to inflate the church. Because the church that depends on a favorable environment to rise and expand will suffer when there is no wind; and will suffer, even more, when there is cruel wind.

This means only one thing. The Spirit is going to have to infuse Michael Gill's church—inflate Michael Gill's church—inspire Michael Gill's church. But we preachers would rather talk about what we need to do, what we need to change, which currently "hot" church *we* need to visit (the better to copy everything they do as a part of our effort to resurrect this or that church from this or that sleep). Much of which is needful. Some of which is helpful. But, biblically speaking, I've got a handful of dust from Genesis 2, a valley of bleached bones from Ezekiel 37, and a room full of frightened disciples from John 20 to suggest that the Spirit can start with virtually nothing and work miracles.

So let me ask you, "How much of our success locally is our doing and how much is the work of the Spirit?" Darned if I know. "How much of what newcomers claim they feel in the first ten minutes they enter this building is our doing and how much is the work of the Spirit?" Darned if I know. But it ain't all us. That much I do know.

Does the Spirit still come to the church? Assuredly. Does it come like Pentecost in the book of Acts, with all of its visual, auditory, and linguistic pyrotechnics? Possibly. But if Acts 2 were to suddenly replicate itself in our sanctuary, it would scare me half to death. For me, the coming of the Spirit is more as John describes it midway through his twentieth chapter. For that's when Jesus came to his friends, stood among his friends, and (get this) breathed upon his friends. Whereupon he said: "Receive the Holy Spirit" (v. 22).

Do I understand that? No, not really. Although, yes, maybe a little. I know that the only way you will ever get breathed on by Jesus is if you are standing close to Jesus. Clearly, too, the only church that will ever get itself breathed on by Jesus is the church that is standing close to Jesus.

So let's assume that once or twice—maybe more—you've gotten a little cozy with Jesus in this place. And let's assume that when he exhaled, you inhaled. Meaning that you have him; or you have the Spirit; or you have his Spirit. Lines get a little blurry here (meaning I'm not entirely certain what we have). But the real question is: "Once you've got it, what do you do with it?" The Spirit, I mean.

One thing you do not do: you do not hold your breath. If you hold your breath too long, you will die. That's exactly what will happen to you. So what's the alternative? Well, I suppose you could breathe on one another.

This is pretty much how we inflate the church. Jesus breathes on us. And we breathe on one other. (William A. Ritter)

Worship Aids

Call to Worship (Psalm 8:1, 3-6, 9)

Leader: O LORD, our Sovereign, how majestic is your name in all the earth!

People: You have set your glory above the heavens....

Leader: When I look at your heavens, the work of your fingers,

People: The moon and the stars that you have established;

Leader: What are human beings that you are mindful of them,

People: Mortals that you care for them?

Leader: Yet you have made them a little lower than God,

People: And crowned them with glory and honor.

Leader: You have given them dominion over the works of your hands;

People: You have put all things under their feet....

All: **O LORD, our Sovereign, how majestic is your name in all the earth!**

Prayer of Confession

We come now, O Lord, to confess how we have sinned against the best that is in us, and we have exploited for our selfish ends the gifts and talents that you gave us as tools with which to be in ministry to others. Our sins are too numerous to name, but neither their number nor magnitude put them beyond forgiveness. We pray that when you have pronounced your forgiveness upon our sin that we will be as willing to let go as you are to forgive. Forgive us for not being willing to put as much distance between ourselves and our forgiven sin as you are willing to put—"as far as the East is from the West." Amen.

Pastoral Prayer

Almighty God, our heavenly Father, by whose hand all that is came to be; and by whose inspiration good men and women of every age have been moved to seek the common good by moving beyond the circum-scribed boundaries of their own lives to touch the lives of others; we are moved to a deep sense of gratitude for the strength to love in the midst of hostility and indifference; and we celebrate the sensitivity you have given us to hear the cries of others above the selfish bickering of our own souls.

You have promised us so many good things that we have little reason for unhappy lives all the time. Help us to grieve our losses when they happen, and then pick up our share of life's load and keep moving on.

We bless the sick. We pray for those who are having tests and surgeries this next week. We pray for the walking wounded among us, who look so good on the outside, but who are in a real mess inside. We pray for the dead, O Lord; there are so many of them. May the quality of their lives excel the best that this life ever offered.

Hear us, O Lord of the universe, and let not our words be lost between us and you. Amen. (Thomas Lane Butts)

JUNE 10, 2007

❧❧❧

Second Sunday after Pentecost

Readings: 1 Kings 17:8-24; Psalm 146 (*UMH* 858); Galatians 1:11-24; Luke 7:11-17

Who Has the Power?
1 Kings 17:8-24; Luke 7:11-17

Recently a commercial jingle asked listeners, "Who has the power?" The advertisers would be dismayed that I don't remember the answer in the ad, or even what product the song was advertising. What I do know is that this is not a new question. In fact, it is one that the early readers of our texts were asking about God in their day. The stories in 1 Kings 17 and Luke 7 answer that question in an interesting way.

If we were to step into Elijah's world this morning, we would find many things that look and sound all too familiar. As this story opens, the surrounding area is experiencing extreme drought that is creating great hardship for the people. Many of our world neighbors who have experienced deadly hurricanes, earthquakes, and tsunamis over the last few years can relate all too well. Folks then were asking the same questions we have been asking now: "Where is God in all of this?" "Who is responsible?" "Who can help us?"

In Elijah's time, King Ahab had turned from following Yahweh, God of Israel, and instead, began to favor the Canaanite god Baal, believed to be the god of rain and vegetation. The Canaanites thought that when there was rain, Baal was alive and death had been defeated. When there was drought, they believed that Baal was dead and death had won. Today's text begins with the word of the Lord coming through Elijah. "There shall be neither dew nor rain these years, except by my word" (1 Kings 17:1). In essence, the people viewed God's announcement as a challenge to Baal. When it does rain, the people hear, it will be Yahweh, the God of Israel, who sends it.

In the meantime everyone, even those faithful to God, will feel the effects of the drought. God tells Elijah to go and hide by the river where God miraculously provides food through the ravens, birds that Elijah would have considered unclean. But soon, the river dries up and God sends Elijah to a widow for food. Circumstances seem even worse here than by the river. As he approaches the city gate, he sees the widow and calls to her, asking her for water and food. This Canaanite woman finds herself in a quandary. Ancient hospitality demanded that she provide for Elijah, but the famine and the apparent death of her god Baal have left her and her son one meal away from death themselves. What is she to do? She explains her situation to Elijah, and he replies, "Do not be afraid. Thus says the Lord God of Israel, your flour and your oil will last until the Lord sends rain" (see vv. 13-14). And it happened as the Lord had said. Who has the power?

Just when it seems that the widow will be spared, her only son and sole means of support falls hopelessly ill. In her anger she rails against Elijah, "What have you against me, O man of God? You have come to me to bring my sin to remembrance, and to cause the death of my son!" (v. 18). Once again, Elijah implores God on behalf of the widow, and God restores the son to life. When the widow's son is returned to her, she proclaims, "Now I know that you are a man of God and that the word of the LORD in your mouth is the truth" (v. 24). Who has the power?

The Gospel story is remarkably similar to Elijah's story. As Jesus enters the town gates at Nain, he is stopped by a funeral procession. Jesus learns that a widow's only son has died. Walking over to the coffin, he speaks to the man and commands him to get up. Luke tells us that the young man sat up, began to talk, and was returned to his mother. The crowd responds, "A great prophet has appeared among us . . . God has come to help [God's] people" (Luke 7:16 NIV).

Although Luke does not mention the Elijah story, faithful Jewish listeners would have been quick to make the connection themselves. They knew that Elijah was a great prophet of God, and that this Jesus must be a prophet as well. But perhaps this Jesus is even greater. After all, Elijah called on God to heal the widow's son, but this Jesus gave the boy a direct command. Who has the power? God, through Elijah, fed the widow; but Jesus himself feeds the multitude. Who has the power?

This morning's texts make it clear that Yahweh, the God of Israel, has the power. But equally important is how God chooses to manifest that power. Unlike our biblical ancestors who lived in a prescientific culture, we no longer consider natural disasters, such as floods and earthquakes, to be acts of God. We now understand that changes in weather patterns or shifts deep within the earth are causal factors. But, like our ancestors, we still look for God's presence in the midst of these times.

It is significant to note that in Elijah's time, God intervened in a very unlikely place. Widows were near the bottom of the social ladder, and they were dependent on children to care for them. Widows without this support were often destitute and at the mercy of the unforgiving life on the streets. The Sidonian woman Elijah met was not even a worshiper of Yahweh (she refers to Elijah's God as "your God" not "my God"). She is not even a believer, yet she is the recipient of God's miraculous provision (*The New Interpreter's Bible*, vol. 3 [Nashville: Abingdon Press, 1999], 129). In this story, the woman becomes the first example of God's universal love that reaches beyond the human-made boundaries of citizenship, ethnicity, gender, and religious affiliation. Who has the power? (Tracy Hartman)

On Stopping the Service to Raise the Dead

Second in a Series of Three on the Holy Spirit

Matthew 10:5-8

When the Day of Pentecost had come, they were all together in one place. Suddenly there came a sound like the rush of a violent wind. Flaming tongues appeared. Strange languages were heard. We should never be surprised by anything when friends of Jesus come together in any place, at any time, for any reason. With that in mind, here's the story of Fred Jones, who once came to me, fifteen minutes before the service, with this: "I'll sit among the congregation. Midway through the service, I'll pretend to fall asleep. You stop preaching and come out and rouse me. I'll leap up—shout Hallelujah—and cry that I've been raised from the dead. Then you go back and finish your sermon." Suffice it to say, Fred didn't do his thing. I didn't do mine. And the service went on as usual—which is the way most of us expect it, and the way most of us like it. Why bring it up? Because of an observation by John Wimber. When Wimber first became a Christian and Bible reader, he went to many churches asking, "Where's the stuff," meaning the miracles that were present in the Bible. He thought if miracles happened in the Bible, they should be happening today.

"Where's the stuff?" This question wouldn't even have rippled my stream of consciousness, had not my bishop asked the same question at an opening session of our Annual Conference. The bishop asked: "Where's the stuff?" More to the point: "Where's the stuff in your churches?"

Citing texts like the one where Jesus sent his disciples out to cure the sick, cleanse the lepers, cast out demons, and raise the dead; she (the bishop) coupled Jesus' command with his reassuring promise that not only would they do "the stuff" they had seen Jesus do, but "greater stuff" to boot. Then she began to chide us, not only for not doing it, but for no longer believing we could do it. At about this point in her sermon, the bishop was really "getting it on." So she kept going until she came to this:

> I ask you, when was the last time (in any of your churches) that even a single blind person regained their sight? When was the last time (in any of your churches) you blessed and broke two of anything and fed five thousand hungry people? Or when was the last time (in any of your churches) anybody was raised from the dead as a result of your preaching? (Linda Lee, Opening Sermon of Detroit Annual Conference, June 1, 2001)

Now I have to tell you, those sentences brought the house down. Or, to be more accurate, brought about 10 percent of the house down. The rest of us applauded politely, even though we were shocked into mind-numbing disbelief. Had the bishop actually said that? Did the bishop really mean that? Was she talking figuratively? She quickly added, "I am talking literally."

My first reaction was to be defensive and angry. I wanted to ask, "When was the last time that stuff happened in a church you served, Bishop?" But I kept my mouth shut, pondering the matter a little longer. That was when I made an interesting discovery. What I was really processing was my own sense of ministerial impotence. I didn't know if I could do any of that "stuff," even if I tried. But what my bishop was trying to do was remind people like me that there is (by God) more power in me than I either know or claim. And equally so for any church I serve.

I don't know what miracles are. If I could explain one, it wouldn't be one. Truth be told, I resonate to John Claypool's observation: "A miracle may best be described as what happens when God chooses to do suddenly what God normally does slowly" (John Claypool, "What Can We Expect of God?" presented at First United Methodist Church, Birmingham, Michigan, March 3, 2001). I don't know how water becomes wine in the twinkling of an eye. But I know how water becomes wine (by God's good design) over several months of vineyard planting, rain falling, vines sprouting, grapes fattening, and juice fermenting. Most times, God works at one pace. But every once-in-a-blessed-while, it seems God speeds things up.

But that's a subject for another day. What I need to remember now is that God is a tireless worker. For those who faithfully labor in God's fields, there are often tremendous (albeit unpredictable) results. The smarter I get, the less I understand. But the longer I minister, the more I marvel. (William A. Ritter)

Worship Aids

Call to Worship (Psalm 146:5-6, 7b, 8-9)

Leader: Happy are those whose help is the God of Jacob, whose hope is in the LORD their God,

People: Who made heaven and earth, the sea, and all that is in them; who keeps faith forever; . . .

Leader: The LORD sets the prisoners free;

People: The LORD opens the eyes of the blind.

Leader: The LORD lifts up those who are bowed down; the LORD loves the righteous.

People: The LORD watches over the strangers;

Leader: He upholds the orphan and the widow,

People: But the way of the wicked he brings to ruin.

Prayer of Confession

Dear God, we confess how carelessly we have filled our lives with so many things of lesser value that we have little time left for things that really count. We rush from place to place and person to person, leaving half-finished conversations and feeling fragmented. Help us learn to be quiet, to wait, to slow down, to listen carefully to others and to listen for some word from you, O God. We do not believe you intended for us to live such fevered lives, and we don't know how things got to be this way. Help us, Lord. Amen.

Pastoral Prayer

Great God, King and Creator of the universe, we come into your presence today with praise and thanksgiving. We pray that as the exact significance of our personal lives continues to unfold, that we may wait with patience as you reveal to us the things we want to know; and that we may conscientiously use the insights that we already have in our daily lives.

Save us from vain delusions of grandeur, in which we fancy ourselves as being greater than we really are; and save us from self-deprecating thoughts and actions that make us less than you made us to be.

Save us from unreasonable fears that steal away our courage and cause us to suspect everybody and everything. Heal us from the wounds of past failures that stifle our sense of adventure and make us afraid to try new things.

Give us a firm hold on our faith in your love for us so that our guilt from the past, both imagined and real, will not pervert our relationships with others or poison our concept of ourselves.

We remember with love those who have been wounded in some way and find it hard to forgive and be forgiven. We commend to your tender care those whose brokenness is so deep, so recent, so personal, or so embarrassing that they cannot speak of it. Give us sensitive spirits toward people who act odd or seem strange as the result of wounds that are older than memory—wounds that are surrounded by so much pain, we dare not go near where we buried them, much less try to dig them up. Teach us how to give special dimensions of latitude to those who have been hurt in ways that we have not been hurt or in ways that we cannot see and understand.

Bless us as we try to be the true church to ourselves and others today and all this week. Amen. (Thomas Lane Butts)

JUNE 17, 2007

❧❧❧

Third Sunday after Pentecost

Readings: 1 Kings 21:1-21a; Psalm 5:1-8; Galatians 2:15-21; Luke 7:36–8:3

One Nation Under God
1 Kings 21:1-21a

In just over two weeks, it will be the Fourth of July. Many of us are already planning how we will spend the holiday, an extra day off work. Picnics and trips to the beach or mountains may be on the agenda for some. For others, parades, fireworks, patriotic decorations, and Uncle Sam may fill the day. However we choose to celebrate, I hope we will all include time to reflect on and appreciate the unique freedoms that we enjoy.

The founders of our nation were committed to the concepts of liberty and equality for all. Today, many of us can still quote most of the preamble to the Declaration of Independence: "We hold these Truths to be self-evident, that all Men are created equal, that they are endowed by their Creator with certain unalienable Rights, that among these are Life, Liberty and the Pursuit of Happiness."

Our early leaders were so committed to the rights of citizens that just fifteen years after they wrote the Constitution, they amended it with the Bill of Rights. Part of the purpose of these first ten amendments was "to prevent misconstruction or abuse" of powers by the federal government.

These are wonderful ideals and principles, and, thankfully, most of the time they work. However, none of us have to look far to find abuses in our systems of government or commerce. It is not uncommon to hear about federal, state, or local governments condemning privately owned land and all but taking it from citizens for use in public projects. Large corporations gobble up small businesses in hostile takeovers, and the little guy has limited recourse. Unethical CEOs and accountants siphon millions of

158

dollars out of companies, destroying the livelihood of hardworking people and bankrupting the retirement funds of those depending on that money for survival. Major insurance companies use loopholes to deny claims, leaving policyholders with insurmountable debt and limited avenues of appeal. Despite the protection our founders offered us, sometimes it seems as if the little guy just can't win.

In today's Old Testament passage, we learn that this is not a new problem. The little guy in this story is a man named Naboth, and he owned a vineyard that had been in his family for generations. King Ahab, who had a palace adjoining the property, decides that he wants the land for a vegetable garden. He makes Naboth a good offer; he will either pay him a fair price for the land, or give him a better vineyard. So far, so good—until Naboth responds.

"The LORD forbid that I should give you my ancestral inheritance," Naboth replies (1 Kings 21:3). Although his answer may sound arrogant to us, it wasn't intended that way. In Naboth's day, Israelite law stated that ancestral land should remain within the family, and this right to ownership was inalienable. When Israel took possession of the land, portions were divided among the tribes. The laws protected the integrity of these original assignments. Naboth's refusal to sell was partly the result of a religious obligation; he would have been profaning Yahweh's name and ultimately selling Yahweh's land. There was no way he could say yes.

Although Ahab was undoubtedly aware of these laws, he went home resentful and sullen, whining to his wife, Jezebel. Now Jezebel was a follower of Baal, not of Yahweh, and she had no respect for Israelite law. She decided that if Ahab wanted the land, he should have it, and she took matters into her own hands.

The narrative tells us that, using the king's name and official seal, she wrote letters to the elders in Naboth's hometown. The letters call for an elaborate setup and frame job that end with Naboth's execution for blasphemy and treason. Her scheme worked just as she had planned. When she received word that Naboth was dead, she told Ahab to go and take possession of the vineyard. Another little guy who was supposed to have inalienable rights had lost again.

Fortunately, Ahab does not get away with it. As he is going to take possession of the vineyard, he encounters the prophet Elijah. Elijah brings a condemnation to Ahab, reminding him that what he has done is evil in the sight of the Lord. Although Ahab repents and delays God's judgment for a while, eventually his family pays the consequences for his actions.

In this story, it is easy for us to relate to Naboth. We can all think of times when we've felt we have been on the short end of the deal. But, if we are to be faithful disciples in our day, we must ask ourselves some hard questions. Who are the Jezebels around us? More important, are we as the church offering the prophetic voice of Elijah against the corruption that we see? Or do we more often function as Ahab in the story, sharing in Jezebel's responsibility for corruption by standing by in permissive silence? (Richard Nelson, *First and Second Kings* [Interpretation Commentary; Louisville: Westminster John Knox, 1987], 145).

This story reminds us that offenses against the defenseless are offenses against God. The psalm for today echoes this lesson: "You are not a God who delights in wickedness; evil will not sojourn with you. The boastful will not stand before your eyes; you hate all evildoers" (5:4-5). As we prepare to celebrate our own rights and freedoms, may we make sure that we are protecting the rights and freedoms of all. Only then will we truly be one nation under God. (Tracy Hartman)

Trickle Charge

Third in a Series of Three on the Holy Spirit

Genesis 1:1-5; Acts 2:1-17; John 14:15-18

We read the story in Acts 2 because it has the feel of "fire and motion" about it, even as we understand this is not just any fire and motion, but God's fire and motion—made possible through the agency of the Holy Spirit. In effect, what we have is a room full of people, all fired up, talking at the same time, in a cacophony of languages. Some who heard it called it "babble." But others, taking time to sort out words and phrases, said: "I recognize that language." But where did these people learn these languages? Scoffers said, "Pay no attention to these people. You will find what is in them, once you check the wine supply."

Peter countered with a pair of arguments. First, he said, these people haven't been up long enough to get this high. Second, if they are drunk, it is more God's doing than the barkeep's. For what is in them is not spirits, but Spirit. Either Peter was sufficiently convincing or the Holy Spirit was not yet done for the day, because before the sun called it quits in the west, fully three thousand bystanders approached the disciples, saying, "Tell us what we need to do to get what you seem to have."

The mistake we make, some two thousand years later, is assuming that, because the Spirit came in that manner once, the Spirit will come in a similar manner every time. Persons who think this draw the erroneous conclusion that if the Spirit doesn't come in like fashion, or in a manner that is similarly spectacular, it can be logically inferred that the Spirit hasn't come at all.

I remember the first time I worshiped in a church where people were regularly "slain in the Spirit." This is a phrase that describes what happens when an individual comes to the altar and is touched on the forehead by one said to possess gifts for healing. When the touch is received, the individual is often propelled backward, as if having been struck a stunning blow. This fall is best described as a faint, although not all the same medical criteria apply. Churches that feature "slayings in the Spirit" provide assistants to stand behind the people being "touched," the better to catch them when they tumble.

Such occurrences are cited as evidence that "surely the Spirit of the Lord is in this place." It may be so. It may not be so. I know of nothing to be gained by trying to figure the "whys and wherefores" of every strange thing that happens in church. The power of the Spirit is great. So too is the power of human suggestibility. I lack the discernment that would enable me to tell one from the other.

In truth, most of us do not know how the Holy Spirit operates. Neither are we all that certain who, or what, the Holy Spirit is. Biblically, we have a host of suggestions. Early in the book of Genesis, the Spirit is associated with the creative process: "In the beginning . . . God created the heavens and the earth. . . . Darkness covered the face of the deep, while a wind from God swept over the face of the waters" (Genesis 1:1, 2b).

This is one of those places where I prefer an alternative version, wherein we read: "God's Spirit brooded like a bird above the watery abyss" (v. 2b *Message*). The word *brood* sounds beautifully gestational, as in a mother hen brooding over her nest, an artist brooding over his paints, or even a preacher brooding over blank pieces of manuscript paper.

Next, turn to Psalm 51, alleged to be David's prayer of confession after his affair with Bathsheba and his complicity in the death of Bathsheba's husband. David prays, "Create in me a clean heart, O God, and put a new and right spirit within me. Do not cast me away from your presence, and do not take your holy spirit from me" (vv. 10-11).

In this psalm, the Spirit is seen, not in a creating mode, but in a protecting and renewing mode. David is clear that if God's Spirit is removed, he (David) will have no future.

Now move from David to Jesus. Mark writes that when Jesus was baptized, the heavens opened and the Spirit descended upon him like a dove. What a beautiful image. But here, the Spirit is neither creating nor protecting; it is anointing and announcing. Later, when Jesus first speaks in the synagogue, there is an implied matter of "credentials" to settle. What (or who) gives Jesus the right to speak? Interestingly enough, Jesus produces neither a diploma nor an ordination certificate. Instead, he says: "I am here because the Spirit of the Lord is upon me." Again, the Holy Spirit anoints.

Years later, John records Jesus as saying something like this to his disciples: "I must leave you soon. It will be better for you that I go. But I will not leave you alone. I will pray to my Father. He will send you another. The one he sends will be your comforter, your instructor, and your advocate. The coming one will be with you forever. You will not be orphaned. You will not be impotent. You will receive power from on high."

And who will do all of the above? The Holy Spirit, that's who.

Over the years, I have tended to distrust the more spectacular and implausible claims made in the name of the Holy Spirit. I have waited, instead, to see the fruits. Don't tell me how high you jumped the night you got religion. Tell me how straight you walked the next morning, once you came down.

As for me, the Spirit has never bowled me over, knocked me down, blinded my eyes, stopped me in my tracks, or made me talk in a strange way. But once a week, usually on a Friday or a Saturday, the Spirit wrestles mightily with me—occasionally even speaking through me. There have been a few occasions when the Spirit has sustained and renewed me, at the very moment when I was beginning to think of myself as an orphan.

One might describe my "walk with the Spirit" as unspectacular. Somehow, the word *unspectacular* doesn't quite feel right. So let me substitute the word *steady*. Steady is not to be sneezed at. My auto mechanic tells me that a jump-start will suffice to start my car when the battery is dead. But the best way to bring a battery to full strength is by means of a trickle charge. What is a trickle charge? It is where one's battery remains connected to a power source for hours and hours.

There are some who need to be "slain in the Spirit." There are some who need to be "jump-started by the Spirit." There are some who need to be "baptized in the Spirit" (so great is the need to dramatically wash away the old and superimpose the new). There are some, and of this I have no doubt, for I am one of them, into whom the Spirit has quietly trickled for hours and hours and hours. Whatever starts your heart, my friends, whatever starts your heart. (William A. Ritter)

Worship Aids

Call to Worship (Psalm 5:1-3)

> Unison: Give ear to my words, O LORD;
>
> give heed to my sighing.
>
> Listen to the sound of my cry,
>
> my King and my God,
>
> for to you I pray.
>
> O LORD, in the morning you hear my voice;
>
> in the morning I plead my case to you, and watch.

Prayer of Confession

Dear God and Father of us all, we confess that we have not been loyal to or thoughtful of the members of your greater family. We have done things we ought not to have done, and left undone things we ought to have done. We have not bridled the impulse to be critical of people we do not understand, and we have been judgmental of those with whom we do not agree. Teach us to temper our words, sweeten our attitudes, and soften our eyes so that we will not inflict wounds we will later regret or cause pain of which we will later be ashamed. May Jesus be our guide. Amen.

Pastoral Prayer

O Holy and mysterious God, Ruler of heaven and earth, Creator of the far-flung beauties of the universe, and Author of the deep mysteries of life; as we brood over your incomparable majesty and individual care for each of us, we are filled with a sense of awe and reverence.

We acknowledge that we are here for reasons not entirely clear to us. We trust you willed us into existence. We acknowledge that any mechanism by which we came here is secondary to the mysterious fact that you willed us into existence. We confess that for all we know, we yet remain ignorant of the exact purpose of your wanting us to be here.

We come before you today deeply burdened by our ignorance concerning some important aspect of this life you have given us. Dear God, we know of no other place where we can un-shoulder burdens of such depth and magnitude than in your presence. We do not ask to see and understand everything, for we know that such knowledge is beyond us. We do not ask to see from where we are to the end of the way, but we do pray for enough knowledge and insight to set us free from anxiety, apprehension, and the recurring fear that there may not be any purpose behind our lives. And, for such as we cannot know, and will never understand, grant us an abiding faith that you see and you understand, and that you will not let our lives sink into meaninglessness and amount to nothing.

There are so many situations of illness and sorrow and unhappiness in the lives of people that we cannot name or describe them all. We know, O God, there are those around us whose lives have been shaped by sorrow, whose way has been watered with tears. You know them already! Our prayer is that you know we are on the side of health and healing. We want to be part of a faithful team that brings peace, love, and joy. Teach us, O God; and let Jesus be our guide. Amen. (Thomas Lane Butts)

JUNE 24, 2007

❧❧❧

Fourth Sunday after Pentecost

Readings: 1 Kings 19:1-15*a*; Psalm 42; Galatians 3:23-29; Luke 8:26-39

Binding the Strong Man
Luke 8:26-39

As Jesus arrived at the country of the Gerasenes, a man possessed by demons met him. An outcast, wild, untamed, and living naked among the tombs, this man was kept shackled and under guard. But no chains could hold him. Time and again, the man would break free, to be driven out into the wilderness by the demons that possessed him. Why did the townspeople seek to chain and guard this man? Luke doesn't tell us. But the account that unfolds speaks volumes about his would-be captors, and if we listen carefully, about ourselves as well.

When Jesus commanded the unclean spirits to depart, the man shouted at the top of his voice, "What have you to do with me, Jesus, Son of the Most High God?" (Luke 8:28). Afraid of being cast back into the abyss, the demons begged to be allowed to enter a nearby herd of swine. With Jesus' permission, they came out of the man and entered the pigs, causing them to rush down the bank and drown themselves in the lake. When the people living nearby heard the reports of the swineherds, and saw the man sitting with Jesus, clothed and in his right mind, they were afraid and asked Jesus to leave.

While fear in the face of the awesome and holy power of God is understandable, many nagging questions come to mind. Why was there no celebration at this miraculous exorcism? Why was there no joy that one of God's chosen people could now rejoin his family and society? From these questions, other questions arise. How would the townspeople feel about having the man live among them, knowing that they had always sought to keep him bound and chained? How would the man feel toward his

165

former captors? But the question that haunts me the most is: what value do we place on an individual life? How far would we go, or what would we risk, to save a life? In essence, how do we weigh the needs of society against the needs of individuals?

This dilemma is captured brilliantly in movies two and three of the Star Trek series. In *Star Trek II: The Wrath of Khan*, when the starship *Enterprise* is about to be destroyed, Spock sacrifices his life to save the ship and crew. As a Vulcan, Spock adheres to the utilitarian ethic: "the needs of the many outweigh the needs of the few or the one." In *Star Trek III: The Search for Spock*, meanwhile, Captain Kirk communicates the opposite ethic: "sometimes, the needs of the one or the few outweigh the needs of the many." In *Star Trek III*, Captain Kirk and crew risk court-martial and even death to return Spock's *katra* (his mind/soul/spirit) to his body.

While this latter ethic feels good to us in the abstract, it is much harder to live out when faced with actual sacrifice. How did the family members feel whose pigs had drowned? Did they feel the possessed man's liberation was worth the cost or did they feel the price was too high? Did their heirs rejoice with the man or begrudge the loss of their inheritance? Would we fare any better today? If we knew that a sizable tax increase would mean that those with mental disorders could lead normal lives, or that no one would again get Alzheimer's or Parkinson's, would we vote for it? Or would we rather keep our taxes low and keep mental patients chained by their delusions or by the numbing side effects of psychotropic drugs? If we knew that people who suffered from the demons of alcohol and drug addiction could kick their addictions once and for all, but it would mean the bankruptcy of a family business, would we embrace our personal loss for the sake of the greater good?

Further, what about the townspeople? How would they feel about the prospect of daily interaction with a man they had habitually guarded and bound with chains? Would they be able to meet his eyes? Would they resent him for what he had "made" them do to him? Is it any wonder that they were seized with great fear?

As one who majored in philosophy and religion, I enjoy the ethical dilemma of whether "the needs of the many outweigh the needs of the few or the one," or whether "the needs of the one or the few outweigh the needs of the many." But I find no evidence in Scripture, especially in Luke's Gospel, that Jesus found this to be a dilemma at all. Jesus heals people because he can do no other. Whether or not Jesus foreknew that his exorcism would result in a family losing its herd of swine, or in feelings of discomfort and shame by the townspeople, I cannot see Jesus acting any differently, or giving those considerations any weight. Are not the sons and daughters of Israel of more worth than a family's wealth or a community's comfort? Are not we? Are not the least of those in our midst?

The good news in today's Gospel story is that God seeks to free us from all that binds us. Jesus Christ comes to us to save us from our demons: whether they be drugs, alcohol, the need to be right, the need to look good in front of others, the need for social status, or other demons. The challenge in today's Gospel story is to celebrate victories of human liberation, even if they come at a high personal cost. Celebrate we must, for we are all being saved from our chains by Jesus, the Son of the Most High God. (B. J. Beu)

Humans Before God

First in a Series of Two on Forgiveness

2 Samuel 12:1-14

The Sunday school teacher's lesson for the day was forgiveness. She began with a question: "What do you have to do in order to be forgiven?" One little hand shot up. This boy was certain he had the answer. He said, "In order to be forgiven, you've got to sin!"

Sin is a word that dominates the Bible. The Bible's first eleven chapters try to explain why the world is in such a mess. These chapters of Genesis trace the trouble to sin. Sin is the common condition of humans in every age. We all do wrong and fail to do right, whether we intend it or not, and we must find a way to deal with our sin.

The story of David and Bathsheba illustrates how we humans fall into sin and how we can find our way back to God. Six steps are involved.

The first step is the sin itself. In David's case it begins as much wrongdoing does—with a single glance or desire. David desires Bathsheba. The biblical word for such desire is *covet*. Coveting has a way of evolving into action. That is why Jesus talked so much about impulses—about what goes on inside us. Desires are the springboards to actions. In Jesus' Sermon on the Mount, he links coveting and adultery. By moving from coveting to adultery, David breaks the tenth and seventh of the Ten Commandments.

But the occasion of sin is not over. Bathsheba's husband, Uriah, is still hanging around. In devising Uriah's murder, David violates the sixth commandment. Notice how one wrongdoing leads to another. The king has fallen to what has been called the "imbecile earnestness of lust."

Step two is a time of enjoying the benefits of the deed and justifying it. David and Bathsheba have a son and are happy for a while. Life feels good. David no doubt justifies his deed on several counts. He may even congratulate himself on rescuing Bathsheba from a life with a clod like Uriah (although the text hardly suggests this).

The third step is the piercing moment of discovery or the realization of guilt. In David's case, God sends the prophet Nathan to uncover David's deed and name it for what it is. In many cases this revelatory moment is less dramatic, and the messenger may be nothing more than the light of our own consciences.

Step four is a time of calculation or bargaining. The wrongdoer can respond to the situation in any of several ways: by proclaiming innocence, by trying to cover up the deed, by stonewalling, or by cutting some kind of a deal with God to contain the damage, such as making a limited confession or pleading "no contest." Maybe that would work?

The process could end at step four, and, unfortunately, sometimes it does. But in David's case there is a fifth step called confession. David quickly decides that the best thing for him to do is to confess. He says to Nathan, "I have sinned against the LORD" (2 Samuel 12:13). David's deeds were terrible. Israel felt obliged to record them in her most sacred Scriptures. But there is another thing Israel could never forget about David—his truthfulness and his decisiveness. Being a person of power and action, David understood the importance of being decisive and taking responsibility. He chose not to dissipate his energy in a cover-up or in blaming. David said boldly, "I did it. The consequences are mine."

There were consequences. There always are. Even the most complete forgiveness doesn't cancel the consequences of our wrongdoings—not for David and not for us.

If there's a fifth step in this process, then there's a sixth step—restoration—a work of God. Restoration or forgiveness generates a kind of healing that is often sudden and miraculous. Once again things are right between God and us and between our neighbors and ourselves. It is a wonderful feeling, such a cleansing feeling, and we want everyone to have it!

The good news of the gospel is that with God, forgiveness is overflowing. Forgiveness is basic to God's nature and is a mighty fountain from which all of us are invited to drink. It is a privilege for those who strive to know God and live in God's will.

But the road to God's wonderful gift of forgiveness goes through the difficult act of confession—our decision to admit our wrongdoing and seek restoration and also to confess that there are things we ought to have done but failed to do. This is the tough part. It's our part. We must unflinchingly acknowledge our sins of both commission and omission. When we humans come before God, it must always be in the spirit of the old prayer of confession: "All of us like sheep have gone astray." These are difficult words, but without them there can be no wholeness for us or for our neighbors.

Terry Anderson was kidnapped by Muslim extremists in Beirut in 1985 and held for six and a half harrowing years. During his confinement Anderson had an encounter with Father Jenco, a fellow hostage. Anderson had left the church when he was young but had recently resolved to return. Anderson had not gone to confession in many years and decided to take his first formal step back to the church by making confession with Father Jenco.

Anderson had spent months lying chained on a cot with little to do but read the Bible and examine his broken life. He poured out his heart to Jenko in a flood of emotions as both men wept. Anderson asked forgiveness for his sins in word and thought, in what he had done and not done. At the end, Jenco hugged Anderson and declared God's forgiveness.

That confession was Terry Anderson's first step back to the church. It seemed to him like the right and necessary thing to do. Its power was fed by a conviction that there is One who is always ready to forgive us, restore us, and welcome us home. (Sandy Wylie)

Worship Aids

Call to Worship (Psalm 42:1-2, 5-6a)

> Leader: As a deer longs for flowing streams, so my soul longs for you, O God.
>
> **People: My soul thirsts for God, for the living God. When shall I come and behold the face of God? . . .**
>
> Leader: Why are you cast down, O my soul,

People: And why are you disquieted within me?

All: Hope in God; for I shall again praise him, my help and
           my God.

Prayer of Confession

Dear God, we confess that our pride makes us think we can handle any-thing alone, but our experiences tell us things happen that are beyond our power to fix. Grant that when we reach the margins of our strength we may have the faith to let you teach us about the "holiness of helpless-ness," the strength that comes of weakness and the way in which the sacrament of failure can be more saving than the sweet smell of success.

We come before you, O God, not flexing our muscles, but on our knees, praying that you will transform our weakness and failure by the alchemy of your love. In the name of Jesus, amen.

Pastoral Prayer

Dear God, Father and Mother of us all, we come today with expectant hearts, hoping for some fresh insight into your will for our lives, and pray-ing to be forgiven for all those times you have tried to show us the way and we looked the other way. We thank you for the church through which we experience the support of a community of prayer. We pray for our leaders in both church and state that they may be given the gifts and graces essen-tial to those who lead. Grant us a common vision of ministry that will lift us beyond petty differences that endanger our unity in Christ.

Save us from ultimate discouragement with ourselves, our condition, and our relationships. Save us from malignant pessimism about ourselves, our friends, and our world. Lift our relationships beyond chronic criticism of those we love and with whom we live.

We confess, O God, that we cannot anticipate or articulate the inner-most needs of everybody, so today we pray for those highly specialized, sometimes secret needs of those among us who feel "left out" of the gen-eralized petitions we make. May the silent scream, the unseen tear, and the unspoken need that gets past human perception be heard and seen by him before whom the secrets of every heart are veritably known. May the grace of this hour become bread for every soul. In Jesus' name, amen. (Thomas Lane Butts)

JULY 1, 2007

❧❧❧

Fifth Sunday after Pentecost

Readings: 2 Kings 2:1-2, 6-14; Psalm 77:1-2, 11-20; Galatians 5:1, 13-25; Luke 9:51-62

A Double Share
2 Kings 2:1-2, 6-14

As we move through life, a moment of decision arises that determines the subsequent course of our lives—a moment that determines whether we remain who we were or become the people God created us to be. Elisha's moment of decision came as he journeyed with Elijah from Gilgal. Elijah, the greatest prophet since Moses, was carried up to heaven on a fiery chariot, leaving Elisha and Elijah's other followers behind. The journey would determine whether Elisha became a powerful prophet like Elijah or faltered along the road. Would Elisha have the courage to continue with Elijah until the end? Would he be bold enough to ask for a blessing before Elijah departed? Nothing was settled when they set out together, and everything depended on the answers to these questions.

Twice on their journey, Elijah tries to persuade Elisha to remain behind. Each time, however, Elisha responds, "As the LORD lives, and as you yourself live, I will not leave you" (2 Kings 2:2). Elisha's decision to stay with Elijah seems natural and easy, until we remember that a disciple was not supposed to defy his master's request. Disciples were not permitted to refuse a direct command. Was Elijah testing his resolve or did he really want to go on alone? Elisha's decision to follow Elijah took more than faithfulness to his master; it took chutzpah. And yet, Elijah may have been looking to see if his disciple possessed just this quality, for it would take great courage and nerve for Elisha to speak the Lord's judgment against the king once Elijah himself was gone.

When Elijah, Elisha, and fifty men of the company of the prophets reached the Jordan, Elijah rolled up his mantle and struck the river, parting the water. Leaving the others behind, Elijah and Elisha continued across the Jordan alone. Upon reaching the opposite shore, Elijah asked Elisha what he could do for him before he was taken away. Having proved his faithfulness and his resolve, Elisha boldly asked: "Please let me inherit a double share of your spirit" (v. 9). This was no small request from a meek disciple. This was a request from a person prepared to assume his master's place—a request from a prophet who knew he needed help, and felt worthy to receive it. It was a request that was sure to make God smile.

How many of us feel worthy of receiving God's blessings? We have been created in the image of God, and yet we often come before the Lord with the attitude that we are unworthy of God's help or of God's attention. Quite frankly, I think this self-deprecating attitude irritates God. I love that scene in the movie *Monty Python and the Holy Grail*, when God tries to talk to King Arthur.

God: "Oh, don't grovel! If there's one thing I can't stand, it's people groveling."

Arthur: "Sorry."

God: "And don't apologize. Every time I try to talk to someone it's 'sorry this, and forgive me that, and I'm not worthy.' What are you doing now?"

Arthur: "I'm averting my eyes, O Lord."

God: "Well, don't. It's like those miserable psalms—they're so depressing. Now knock it off!"

Elisha knew he was worthy of receiving a double share of Elijah's spirit. What's more, Elisha knew he needed this blessing to help him complete the tasks that lay ahead. We all need God's help to fulfill our ministries and our call to discipleship. When I was in chaplaincy training at Children's Hospital of Michigan, I worked with a fellow resident named Billie. When the stress of working with suffering children, hysterical family members, and the occasional insensitive medical provider became too much, Billie would cry out, "Lord, I need a blessing!" The fact that she did not throttle one individual in particular is strong testimony that Billie received her blessing. Billie knew, with every fiber of her being, as did Elisha, that God blesses us when we have need and when we have the confidence to ask.

Elijah knew that Elisha was worthy of the blessing he sought, but it was not up to him to bequeath it: "You have asked a hard thing; yet, if you see me as I am being taken from you, it will be granted you; if not, it will not" (v. 10). Just as it was not in Elijah's power to grant Elisha's request, it was not in Elisha's power to see the fiery chariot unless God granted him the ability to do so. Herein lies a much-overlooked spiritual truth. When God blesses us or gives us a spiritual gift from the Holy Spirit, it is a reflection on the giver of the gift, not on the one who receives it. When we ask for and receive a blessing, it is not a reflection on our holiness, faithfulness, or piety; it is a reflection of God's generous nature and gracious love. We have no reason to boast in our gifts and blessings, because we did not earn them—God through the Holy Spirit gives gifts and blessings to whomever God chooses. But we do have reason to give thanks for what we have been given.

When the whirlwind came and carried Elijah into heaven on God's fiery chariot, Elisha beheld the sight and knew his request had been granted. Picking up Elijah's mantle, Elisha went back, parted the waters of the Jordan, and assumed the role as God's prophet to Israel. Like Elisha, we too will lose people of faith on our journey. Will we ask God to bless us with a double share of their spirit, or will we keep silent? We have nothing to lose in the asking, and everything to gain. (B. J. Beu)

Humans Before Each Other

Second in a Series of Two on Forgiveness

Matthew 18:21-35

When Elizabeth Barrett Browning married Robert, her parents disapproved so strongly that they disowned her. For ten years Elizabeth wrote letters to her parents almost weekly. In the letters she expressed her love for them and asked for reconciliation. They never replied. Then one day Elizabeth received a large box in the mail. To her enormous heartbreak, it contained all of her letters. Not one of them had been opened.

Today those letters are considered to be among the most beautiful love letters in the English language. Had her parents read only a couple of them, their relationship with their daughter might very well have been mended. They missed out on one of the world's greatest treasures and never even knew it; but more tragically, they missed out on an even bigger treasure: their daughter!

In our first sermon in this series, we noted that the Bible's first eleven chapters try to explain why the world is in such a mess, why there is so much strife. The diagnosis is that we humans live in sin. Our sinful nature and behavior cause estrangement between God and us, between our neighbors and us, and between the natural order and us.

I don't need to convince you that there are big problems in the human family. There always have been. The pages of history are filled with war and strife. The number of people killed in wars in the last five centuries is enormous: 1.5 million in the sixteenth century, 6 million in the seventeenth century, 6.5 million in the eighteenth century, 40 million in the nineteenth century, and 180 million in the twentieth century. War and murder have been sad facts of life throughout history; this new century may become the most violent yet. Of course, estrangement touches us at many levels other than war; and the closer it comes to home, the more it hurts.

The writer of Matthew's Gospel is very attentive to estrangement and to the role that Jesus and the church play in overcoming it. Matthew portrays Jesus as "the Great Forgiver." In Matthew, Jesus is constantly greeting those he meets with the news, "Your sins are forgiven!" Forgiveness is a common theme in Jesus' teachings. Jesus wants us to voice forgiveness in our prayers, "and forgive us our debts, as we also have forgiven our debtors" (6:12). Jesus especially wants us to practice forgiveness in the church. Just prior to our text (18:15-20), Jesus includes a method for resolving a case in which "another member of the church sins against you" (18:15).

The church is the worldly embodiment of Jesus' ministry, and Jesus' ministry was strongly centered on forgiveness. Therefore, it is important for church people to model forgiveness for themselves and the rest of the world. God calls the church to pioneer in and witness to those virtues the world needs. Thus, for Christians, forgiveness isn't an occasional act of heroism. It's a way of life in Christ. It's how we embody our relationship with God and extend such a relationship to others. It's how we work with God to make all things new, including ourselves. It's how we restore communion with God, with our neighbors, and with the whole creation.

First-century Judaism taught that one might forgive a neighbor once or twice or perhaps three times, but four times was beyond the limit. In our text, Jesus counters this notion by removing all limits to forgiveness. In some translations Jesus tells us to forgive 77 times; in other translations it's 490 times. The exact number matters little because this is a figure of speech. Jesus is saying there should be no limit to forgiveness. Do it endlessly!

As is often the case, this parable of Jesus works by using extravagant contrasts. A slave owes his king ten thousand talents. This is such an astronomical amount of money as to be an inconceivable debt. Amazingly, the king snaps his fingers and forgives the debt completely!

That forgiven slave then refuses to forgive a very small debt that a fellow slave owes him. How small? He refuses to forgive a debt that's five hundred thousand times smaller than the amount he owed the king!

Jesus' point is clear. God is forever merciful to us. We should be grateful for that mercy, internalize it, and model it in our behavior toward others. To do less is to dishonor God's forgiveness.

I heard a story about a family that lived in the mountains of the West. The son had married a young Native American woman. His parents were against the marriage and shut out their daughter-in-law. One night during a raging blizzard the young man appears at his parents' door to say that his wife is in labor. He needs help to get her to the closest hospital. His father refuses to help.

The child dies because the mother couldn't get medical help in time. When the father of the young man hears the news, the enormity of his guilt overwhelms him. He knows that somehow he must go to the hospital to beg the forgiveness of his son's wife. Holding a little bouquet of flowers in one hand and his hat in the other, he unexpectedly appears in the doorway of the hospital room. He wants to say the right thing, but words won't come. Finally, with tears in his eyes, all he can manage to say is, "Spring is coming."

The good news of the gospel is that spring is coming! Spring is coming for God's children whenever they face one another to attend to the brokenness in their relationships. The hardest words any of us speak are the words by which we ask and grant forgiveness. But they are the most necessary words—because without them we all perish! (Sandy Wylie)

Worship Aids

Litany

> Leader: Freedom is a blessing from God.
>
> **People: Christ came into the world to offer good news that liberates both now and forever.**
>
> Leader: Christ came to set free the captive, bring liberty to the oppressed, and offer vision to the blind.
>
> **People: We celebrate God's good news. Come; let us live as people set free through Jesus Christ.**

Litany of Forgiveness (Service of the Lord's Supper)

Leader: O Lord, we come together at your table and ask of you this day: Forgive us our sin.

People: And forgive us our sins.

Leader: Make whole the brokenness of our mortal journey,

People: And make whole the wounds of our daily journey.

Leader: Bind us closer to you, O God,

People: And bind us closer to each other.

All: We make this humble bequest in the name of our Redeemer and Savior, Jesus Christ. Amen.

Benediction

Go forth to serve—give yourself away!
Go forth to save—offer grace each day!
Go forth to live—live in God's love always! (Gary G. Kindley)

JULY 8, 2007

❧❧❧

Sixth Sunday after Pentecost

Readings: 2 Kings 5:1-14; Psalm 30; Galatians 6:(1-6), 7-16; Luke 10:1-11, 16-20

The Power of the People
Luke 10:1-11, 16-20

Jesus sends seventy of his followers on a training mission, out into the villages to spread the good news of God's kingdom—a kingdom of love, forgiveness, and eternal life.

Jesus knows that our world is ripe with need, a world in which the harvest is plentiful for those who wish to share God's good news of love. "The harvest is plentiful, but the laborers are few; therefore ask the Lord of the harvest to send out laborers into his harvest" (Luke 10:2). We know that laborers are few today, just as they were in Jesus' day. We know that the harvest is plentiful, in a world where fewer than 40 percent, often as low as 15 to 20 percent of people in our neighborhoods connect their faith with a church community.

And yet, we may hesitate to labor in the fields of this world. We may be unsure of how to share our faith journey with others. We may be insecure about answering questions regarding what we believe and why. We may be nervous about associating with people who aren't in the church. Or maybe we're just so busy and overwhelmed that we don't think about inviting a neighbor to church or vacation Bible school. Maybe our schedule is so crowded that we can't find the time to talk about our faith journey with a new Christian.

Despite our objections, however, Christ calls us into the same discipleship as those first followers were called. It's safe to assume that even those seventy were not feeling prepared for what they had to face in their travels and ministries. Jesus knew that he was sending them out like lambs into the midst of wolves. No lamb is ever prepared to encounter a pack of wolves! But Jesus gave them some instructions—instructions given to us as well.

Jesus first tells them not to take any extra baggage. Do not carry a money purse, a bag, or even an extra pair of sandals. To labor in God's vineyard, we need good traveling shoes and a light load. Good traveling shoes for ministry are like good traveling shoes for hiking: well worn and well built, able to withstand the hardships of the journey. Shoes for our walk of discipleship need to be constructed of a deep and profound faith in God. The fabric of good traveling shoes needs to be durable—the very presence of Christ woven into our lives for every step of the journey.

Jesus then calls us to enter the households of strangers and proclaim God's peace. We get a taste for what that means in worship when we take a moment to greet our neighbors. This is our opportunity to share God's peace with the people around us and to share Christ's love with the new people we encounter. In doing so, we build a community of faith and love where people experience the peace that passes all understanding.

But how do we share that peace with people who do not worship with us? How do we go out into the world, into the homes of friends and neighbors and family members to share the good news of God's love? We do so by offering God's peace and hospitality in our words and actions, and by accepting the hospitality and love that strangers offer to us. This type of evangelism need not frighten us. It simply means doing what Jesus would do, sharing God's peace with all whom we meet, and teaching God's love to those who don't know about God's love. Evangelism is nothing more than sharing our Christlike passion for God's kingdom with those who are not sure what Christianity is all about.

When we evangelize, we do so with open hearts to the gifts that we will receive from the people with whom we share our faith. The sharing of God's kingdom and ministry undertaken by those seventy followers involved give-and-take, showing all people that their work and offerings were of value. When we share our faith with others, we will learn even more than we teach. When we give God's love to others, we receive back a hundredfold. As we introduce others to Christ, we will find that their hospitality to us enriches our lives.

The seventy followers returned with joy for the successes they saw in their ministry efforts. Jesus knew, because of their faith and their willingness, that even the deepest powers of evil had been defeated. Satan himself had fallen out of power because of the power of God's Holy Spirit working in the people. Nothing could stop the great work those seventy people had started. Consequently, today, we receive that same call. It is a call we are capable of answering so that Jesus can say even to us, "I watched Satan fall from heaven like a flash of lightning. See, I have given you authority to tread on ... all the power of the enemy; and nothing will hurt you" (Luke 10:18). Through Christ, God gives us the power to be God's people.

We can be the laborers who will reap God's harvest. God has called us to labor in this world until every person we encounter knows Jesus Christ, every sad soul we find experiences God's love, and every family or child or old person in our neighborhood knows that in Christ's church they can find a friendly face and a warm community. However, we cannot accomplish such a harvest without a lot of work, nor can we do so without the power and grace of the Holy Spirit.

The Holy Spirit is granting us the power and the grace. Now it's up to us to get out into the fields and start the labor. This is no time to let the fields lie fallow. This is no time to sit back and say, "I don't think we're rich enough to give anything back." This is no time to say, "I don't really have time to call on those new visitors." This is no time to say, "I don't feel like teaching Bible school this year." Now is the time to say, "Yes, Lord, we're here for you and for your world."

The harvest is plentiful. The fields are ripe for harvest. We can be the laborers who bring in that harvest. (Mary J. Scifres)

The Freedom of God

First in a Series of Three: Relation of Church and State

Psalm 2

Have you ever gone on an extended trip, and when you return, you are glad to be home? Which means, I think, that sometimes we take home for granted. It could also be that sometimes we take our citizenship for granted, sometimes we take our faith for granted, and sometimes we take freedom for granted.

We think about freedom this time of year. The signers of the Declaration of Independence helped to make many of our freedoms possible. Yet some of them were captured as traitors, others were tortured, some lost their homes, and two lost sons during the Revolutionary War. Nine of the fifty-six fought and died from wounds or hardships related to the war, while others lost livelihoods and personal property.

Many of these heroes gave up tremendous advantages because they valued freedom more. They were motivated by the simple words: "for the support of this declaration, with firm Reliance on the Protection of Divine Providence, we mutually pledge to each other our lives, our Fortunes, and our sacred Honor."

The signers took nothing for granted. There was a cost to freedom. What does freedom mean to us? There are Christians all over the world who do not have the freedom to worship. Some are meeting in house churches. Some have gone into their closets to pray, to use the language of Jesus, knowing that their Father hears them in secret. They are isolated, alone. What does freedom mean to them? They don't take freedom for granted.

A problem occurs when we begin to take our freedom for granted. We forget about the One who is the only source of our freedom, God. In today's text, the rulers of this world think they have the ultimate power, they conspire and plot; they want to put themselves in the place of God.

I remember a vivid scene on television. Cardinal O'Connor of New York had died, and the service in his memory was in Saint Patrick's Cathedral, in New York City. In attendance were some of the most powerful people in the world: the president, the vice president, the candidate for president, the mayor (then a candidate for senator), and the first lady, who was also a candidate for senator.

They were all people of power. They all looked really uncomfortable. I think I know why. That service was a reminder that the power of God is more powerful than the powers of the rulers of this world. "He who sits in the heavens laughs; the LORD has them in derision" (Psalm 2:4).

God laughs at the powers of this world. That is because God has the power, and God controls the future. We sing this in our Christmas carol: "He rules the world with truth and grace, and makes the nations prove the glories of his righteousness, and wonders of his love" (Isaac Watts, "Joy to the World," *The United Methodist Hymnal* [Nashville: The United Methodist Publishing House, 1989], 246).

The power of God is placed, not in hopes of the rulers of this world, but in the promise of the Messiah, the Son, the Anointed One. Even if others seem to have the power, even if the future seems to belong elsewhere, this is the word of the Lord. The nations will be your heritage, and the ends of the earth your possession, pointing us, I think, to the great commission to be witnesses and to make disciples, in obedience to the teaching of Jesus.

But God's idea of Messiah, we learn later in the story, means something different than we had thought. God is going to set the captives free. Jesus speaks it in Luke 4, borrowing from Isaiah 61: the Messiah would set the captives free, but there was a cost to freedom. The cost of freedom was the Cross.

The psalm ends with a warning: be wise, rulers; be warned, politicians. "Serve the LORD with fear, with trembling, ... [or] you will perish" (v. 11). This is the crux of our celebration of independence. Those who have fought, who have sacrificed in ways that many of us cannot really understand, surely did so with a faith and a trust and a hope for a nation where there would be freedom to worship, freedom to speak, freedom to gather, freedom to live. Freedom comes from God, but there is a cost of freedom, and God sometimes uses individuals to pay that cost.

We are not to squander the sacrifices of those who have gone before us. Instead, we are called to live in such a way that we honor their sacrifices; to remember the cost of freedom, to take seriously our freedom to worship God, not just as rhetoric, but as a rule of life. Surely, those who have gone before us did not risk their lives so that we could grow more affluent and less compassionate, more entertained and less holy, more cynical and less prayerful.

The God of the Bible is the God of all nations. "God shows no partiality," Peter pronounced in Acts 10:34. God does not love us more than the other nations of the earth. However, there is no doubt that we are a blessed nation. Perhaps we have become distracted from our destiny. We have been blessed with the gift of freedom, but we have not always known how to use that freedom, or even how to give thanks for it.

Psalm 2 ends with the words "Happy are all who take refuge in him." God is our freedom. God has the ultimate power. When we know this, we have freedom. Jesus taught, "If you continue in my word, you are truly my disciples ... you will know the truth, and the truth will make you free" (John 8:31-32). (Kenneth H. Carter Jr.)

Worship Aids

Invocation

Creator God, we gather to worship and praise your holy name. Today, we especially lift up in prayer those in desperate places, those in lonely places, those in broken places, and those in fearful places. Wherever we find ourselves on the journey, thank you for being there. In your name we pray. Amen.

Litany (based on Psalm 111)

Leader:	Praise the Lord!
People:	**I will give thanks to the Lord with my whole heart,**
Leader:	In the company of the upright, in the congregation. Great are the works of the Lord!
All:	**God's praise endures forever.**

Benediction

Be in the world but not of the world. Be people of light in dark places, people of salt in unsavory times, and people of love where there is hatred. Go! Be! Amen! (Gary G. Kindley)

JULY 15, 2007

❧❧❧❧

Seventh Sunday after Pentecost

Readings: Amos 7:7-17; Psalm 82; Colossians 1:1-14; Luke 10:25-37

Be a Good Samaritan! Servant Leaders Needed!
Luke 10:25-37

One spring night in college, some friends and I were in a head-on collision with a drunk driver. Everyone in our car was shaken up, in a good bit of pain, but without serious injury. Only a minute or two later, a car drove slowly to our resting place. Out stepped an older man, asking if he could help. We explained our situation, and before I knew it, we had a leader. After checking on the other driver, he drove us to a nearby farmhouse where we were given shelter until the ambulance arrived. The stranger stood nearby and kept us focused as the police questioned us. Soon after, he surprised us by showing up at the emergency room to help with the doctor's questions and to await the arrival of our parents. Then he slipped away without ever telling us his name. A few days later, we all agreed that our fearless leader had been an angel in our midst, a gift from God, a good Samaritan sent when we needed one the most—truly a servant of God.

This morning's scripture reading describes a similar person. Known affectionately as "the good Samaritan," one traveler stopped to care for a crime victim. That traveler was not the pastor or priest, the deacon or elder, the council chair or church moderator. No, the traveler who stopped was what both of the first travelers should have been: a servant leader.

The good Samaritan who stopped to care for this man knew how to take charge while serving with humility and grace. Jesus tells us this parable, this teaching story, not to condemn the priest or the Levite, not to condemn pastors or church officers, but rather to help all of us, in

183

whatever roles we fulfill on this earth, to strive to be servant leaders, to strive to be like the good Samaritan.

So often, this story is seen as a simple story about helping someone. And it is that. But the lessons go so much deeper than the simple phrase "Be a good Samaritan" would suggest. For being a good Samaritan involves servant leadership, which is a lot more complicated than simply being a helpful person. This parable helps us to see what it means to be a servant leader.

First, we need to remember that the traveler who stopped to help was not a local native. He was not even a person who was particularly welcome in that region. Samaritans were the "other Jews," the ones who weren't as smart, weren't as rich, weren't as clean, weren't as religious, just weren't quite right in the minds of Jerusalem Jews. Samaritans were often outcast, shunned, even persecuted when they left Samaria and went into Judea. So, we learn that servant leadership means serving even in places where we don't feel welcome, even in places where we're not all that comfortable, even in places where people are disrespectful and unappreciative.

Second, the helpful Samaritan cared personally and lovingly for the one robbed. You can imagine that the man must have been in pretty bad shape by the time the Samaritan came along—open and bloody wounds framed in that crusty, dirty mixture of blood and road dust. The victim was perhaps not terribly friendly, if even conscious. I suspect lifting him onto the back of a donkey was not an easy task. But servant leadership is like that. It's often dirty and icky, tiring and grueling. No wonder Christ teaches that we must humble ourselves in order to serve God!

Third, the Samaritan who cared for this robbery victim was willing to take charge, to do what one church guru calls "ministry anytime, anyplace, for anyone, no matter what." This Samaritan traveler knew he was not going to be respected by some Judean innkeeper. But he didn't give the innkeeper a chance to turn him down. He paid for the injured man's needs, told the innkeeper what to do and how to do it, and promised to return and care for any follow-up needs. The good Samaritan was willing to lead. You see, servant leadership is more proactive than simply serving when asked to serve. Servant leadership is about taking the initiative to serve, seeing a need and fulfilling that need, recognizing a problem and finding the people to help solve that problem.

And so, I say, "Be a good Samaritan!" and the world will be a better place. "Be a good Samaritan!" and the church will be a stronger institution.

"Be a good Samaritan!" and our homes, our communities, and our world will grow closer and closer to the likeness of God's kingdom—the world and homes and communities that God intends for us to build on this earth.

But remember that being a good Samaritan means being a servant leader. And servant leadership means serving anywhere there is a need, even in times and places where we are neither comfortable nor appreciated.

Servant leadership means caring, personally and lovingly, for the people we encounter—not just sending a check and hoping someone else will take care of it, not just caring for the clean, easy problems of our lives—but digging into the dirt and helping that dirt to become fertile ground for physical health and spiritual growth.

Servant leadership means taking responsibility for the ministry needs of our world, whether we think those needs are in our job descriptions or not. It means serving not just when asked, but when needed; serving not just as followers of Christ, but as leaders of Christ's people; serving not just when it's convenient, but when it's necessary; serving and leading so that others may help us in our efforts to be in ministry all the time, in any place, with anyone, no matter what.

Be a good Samaritan! The world needs more good Samaritans! The world needs our servant leadership! (Mary J. Scifres)

A Kingdom Not of This World

Second in a Series of Three: Relation of Church and State

John 18:33-38

If we follow the events of the life of Jesus, we soon discover that we are beginning to shape our lives in accordance with his life. There are anticipation and fulfillment, preparation and birth, then expansion of the light that shines in the darkness, then a movement toward a cross, and mounting conflict, and then a death, and then a resurrection, and now, exaltation. Jesus came, at the beginning of his teaching ministry, to announce that the Kingdom was at hand, and we gather to celebrate Jesus' kingdom, rule, and reign.

While this would seem to be important, it is also a little odd. We may call Jesus many things—Lord, Savior, Healer, Master, Teacher—but we rarely refer to Jesus as King. It seems so foreign even from the status Jesus would claim for himself—we think of an itinerant rabbi and healer who worked sometimes in crowds but just as often among small groups of two or three friends in out-of-the-way places.

Jesus often spoke about a kingdom, but it was the kingdom of God, and Jesus seemed to point beyond himself, to the signs of that kingdom. "The blind see, the lame walk, the lepers are cleansed, the deaf hear, the dead are raised, and the poor receive good news" (see Matthew 11:5).

In the Lord's Prayer, we ask for something like this: "Thy kingdom come. Thy will be done." Now we are getting a little closer, I think, to our real discomfort with this idea of Christ as a King. If we are honest, we may sometimes wonder, Is Jesus really in control? At Christmas we sing: "He rules the world with truth and grace, and makes the nations prove the glories of his righteousness, and wonders of his love" (Isaac Watts, "Joy to the World," *The United Methodist Hymnal* [Nashville: The United Methodist Publishing House, 1989], 246).

Perhaps you are comfortable saying at a personal level, "Jesus is the Lord of my life." But who rules the world? Who is in charge here? Think of Bosnia, Rwanda, Iraq, and yes, our own United States. Have the kingdoms of this world, in the thunderous refrain from Handel, and John's Revelation, become the kingdoms of our Lord and of his Christ? Does he rule the world? Is Jesus really King?

Well, it turns out that this is precisely the question Pilate asks of Jesus. "Are you the King of the Jews?" (John 18:33). You see, Pilate is accustomed to being in control, in charge. And so he is asking, "Are we in the same business? Are you the competition?"

Jesus responds: "My kingdom is not of this world" (v. 36 NIV). It is something different. That is what we are trying to figure out. Why is it different? What is this kingdom? What does it have to do with us?

When we say the Lord's Prayer, we pray, "Thy kingdom come. Thy will be done . . ." When we pray these words, we are praying something pretty revolutionary. We are willing to allow our sphere of influence to be God's sphere of influence. We are willing to allow God's agenda to become our agenda.

Consequently the kingdom of God pervades all of life. The greatest sign of the kingdom was Jesus' life: his preaching, his teaching, his healing. In this way, Jesus was relating the kingdom to the whole person and to all of life: preaching, to our spirits; teaching, to our minds; healing, to our bodies. The mind, body, and spirit, all within the sphere of God's influence—how we pray, what we think, what we do with our bodies, our possessions—all of it is under the judgment and mercy of that prayer: "Thy kingdom come. Thy will be done, on earth, as it is in heaven."

Pilate is focused on a particular plot of earth; we would call it "turf" these days. So Pilate asks, "Are you the King of the Jews?" meaning, "Are you the king of one of the competing tribes?" People still ask the same question about Jesus and his church. Is it one competing activity, say, with a sport or with family or with work? Are you the King of the Jews? If I can get a handle on who you are, I will know what to do with you! You know, put you in the religion section of the newspaper, let you have some property on the edge of town, have "just a little talk" with you every day, and then get on with life as usual.

What kind of King are you? Jesus says, "My kingdom is not of this world." At first Pilate must be a little relieved. "Oh, good. I was worried there for a minute." Pilate is a powerful man. For example, he could put people to death, a power that he would exercise.

"I have come into the world, to bear witness to the truth" (v. 37 RSV). Jesus will not coerce; he bears witness. If we are "of the truth," we will hear his voice. If we hear Jesus' voice, we will follow in his path. If we follow in his path, we will find that our wills are becoming meshed with his will, our plans with his plans, our purposes with his purposes. We are not coerced to accept Christ and the coming of his kingdom. But we pray for it, "Thy kingdom come. Thy will be done in earth, as it is in heaven.... For thine is the kingdom, and the power, and the glory, for ever" (Matthew 6:10, 13*b* KJV).

Our calling is to live as citizens of the kingdom of God. If it seems, from our side, to be a work in progress, the good news is that this is God's great work also: to change us, over time, to shape us and mold us, to make us more like Christ, but more than that, to create a new heaven and a new earth.

God's great intention is that something more might happen. But God's kingdom does not come by force. For this reason God's kingdom differs from the kingdoms of this world. It is marked by patience, persistence, and perseverance. It is always in the world, but never of the world. We are citizens, you and I, of the kingdom of God. Amen. (Kenneth H. Carter Jr.)

Worship Aids

Invocation

Come, Holy Spirit, and kindle in our minds the knowledge of your presence. Remind us this day that there is no place where you are absent, no soul you have abandoned, and no mercy you have withheld. We open our lives to you. Amen. (Gary G. Kindley)

Prayer of Confession

Holy God, as we worship this day, we recognize that we are not yet what you created us to be. We pray that although you perceive our shortcomings, for you see everything as it truly is, that we too might see ourselves not only as you observe us but also as others see us. Help us come to authentic and godly self-knowledge. This knowledge helps us understand that without you, we are nothing but dust. It is your spirit that animates us and gives us life. Inspire us to be excellent stewards of the most precious gift you can ever give us: a deep and abiding relationship with you. In Jesus' name we pray. Amen. (David N. Mosser)

Call to Worship

O Holy Spirit, into your midst we present ourselves for power and for wisdom. We open our hearts and surrender to your warm embrace. Amen.

Benediction

The peace of God go with you. Serve the Lord with gladness, love the Lord with abundance, and live for the Lord by serving others. Amen. (Gary G. Kindley)

JULY 22, 2007

Eighth Sunday after Pentecost

Readings: Amos 8:1-12; Psalm 52; Colossians 1:15-28; Luke 10:38-42

First Things First
Luke 10:38-42

Poor Martha; she seems to be lost in the New Testament story. Of all people, Jesus should have recognized and congratulated Martha for her servant heart. We can all put ourselves in Martha's shoes. Company has come at the last minute, details haven't been worked out; the table must be set, food prepared. One wonders if Jesus had also brought along the twelve disciples. How many tasks did Martha need to perform? She needed Mary's help. Our sympathies are not with Mary, but with Martha. Why? Because we've all had those moments when there was too much to do, too little time, and not enough help.

We've all been captured by the "tyranny of the urgent." We've been caught with lists too long and so many things that need to be accomplished yesterday. The overwhelming sense of our day is that we must keep running a frenzied pace or the whole mess will eventually catch up with us. We work longer hours than we should or need to work; we miss the most important moments of life. The watchword has become not *quantity*, but *quality*. Not quantity time with children, just quality. Not much time with friends, just make it quality. Not much time for God, just make it count.

Quality relationships, quality parenting, a high quality of personal prayer life; all require time. We cannot rush the important things of life and expect to gain real meaning or real quality. Why do we rush the important things of life? Because we have got so many ordinary things to do that we just have run short of time. One of the tragedies of the modern technological and information age is that we have created so many electronic devices to "save us time" and allow us to do more and be more efficient that we must give incredible amounts of time responding to these means of communication. On a plane recently, I overheard a man complain that he had to respond to four hundred text-mail messages every day. In the terminal he was furiously trying to respond to all those messages and finally, in frustration, just threw his cell phone to the floor. What is truly important?

The speed of computers has led us to believe that people should respond instantly or quickly to our many queries of them online. Another man said, "I need some time to think about my response, but so many people expect an immediate answer and are angry when I don't respond quickly."

The urgent often keeps us from putting first things first. As I moved from a smaller church to a larger church, one of my friends who had watched me work long hours and become frustrated with my ministry reminded me, "Protect your think time." What a concept. Time to think and perhaps write. Time to think about my response in communication. Time to think about what my family really needs. Time to think about ways to care for my neighbors and people in my circle of influence. Jesus understood that Mary was alert to the most important things.

Years ago one harried mother of three sought solace in a clean house. Her children and husband desperately sought to have her attention and time to just be together, but her passion for cleanliness and a "germ-free" environment drove her activities every day. Over the years that family drifted farther and farther apart as both husband and wife gave their attention to the minutiae of home and work and ignored the more important work of relationships and play and communication.

What was Mary doing? We can only conclude that Mary gave her attention to Jesus. We can imagine that Jesus talked to her about his travels and his teaching. Jesus may have told her about the Gerasene demoniac or his experience in the wilderness. He might have talked with her about real-life issues or the matters of the heart. Mary must have hung on every word that Jesus offered, perhaps saying what the disciples said: "You have the words of eternal life" (John 6:68). Mary's life was ordinary enough, but when Jesus came to town something extraordinary was taking place. Mary just wouldn't miss the opportunity.

Years ago, as I traveled through Nepal, I had an opportunity to drive up into the Himalayas early one morning to watch the sun rise. Our tour had been long and I was tired and feeling sick, so the morning of the early tour

I pulled the covers over my head and went back to sleep. I've always regretted that decision. I had a once-in-a-lifetime opportunity to see the sun rise over the highest mountain range in the world, and I passed it up because I was sleepy. Mary wouldn't pass up the most important thing: spending time with the Master.

I wonder what would happen to the church if we placed as much importance on spending time with the Master as Mary did? I wonder what would happen to committees and classes and teams and ministry if we sought to spend as much time in listening prayer and hearing the words of Christ as we do in getting the job done?

John paints a different picture of Martha in his Gospel. Jesus comes back to Mary and Martha's home to find that the funeral of Lazarus has already taken place. Who comes running first to Jesus? It's Martha. Running to Jesus she says, "If only you had been here sooner, Lazarus would be alive." Jesus tells her that Lazarus will live and tells her that he is the resurrection and the life.

Martha answers, "Lord, I believe that you are the Messiah." Then, running into the house, she calls Mary. (See John 11:17-26.)

In the presence of Jesus the "tyranny of the urgent" fades, and the one with an open heart catches Martha discovering the power of putting first things first. (Guy Ames)

In Him All Things Hold Together

Third in a Series of Three: Relation of Church and State

Colossians 1:11-20

Paul makes an astonishing claim about Jesus. "He is the image of the invisible God.... All things have been created through him and for him.... In him all things hold together" (Colossians 1:15-17). These are compelling words, but they seem to be at odds with the world we live in, don't they? What, in our world today, is holding together? There are red states and blue states. There is a Christian world and a Muslim world. There is the FOX Network and National Public Radio. Women are from Venus. Men are from Mars. Or vice-versa, I can't remember. Life is fragmented. We don't write one letter; we send six e-mails. We don't have a thirty-minute discussion about sports; we have fifteen two-minute conversations.

Life is fragmented. Of course, sometimes the fragments are not only out there, they are in here; they are within us. "The good that I want to do,

I do not do," Paul says (see Romans 7:19), and we know what he means. Our lives are fragmented.

We hear the affirmation of Paul, "In him all things hold together," and yet our eyes and our hearts tell a different story, don't they? What, in our world today, is holding together? We read the newspapers and watch television. I am reminded of the first of the twelve steps in the Alcoholics Anonymous tradition. "We admitted that we were powerless . . . that our lives had become unmanageable."

Because we are, most of us, people who can make our way through the obstacles and challenges of life, we are inclined to try to solve this problem of fragmentation. We have our different strategies.

One is nostalgia. A family friend watches *The Andy Griffith Show* three times a day; life was simpler when the question was whether you could trust the stranger who had come from a faraway place like Raleigh!

Another strategy is to retreat to our little corner of the world. Life happens in a ghetto of religious people who look, think, and believe like us. We are islands unto ourselves, and this world is not our home; we're just passing through. Each strategy, nostalgia, and retreat has an appeal, but none are ultimately faithful.

Another strategy is appealing. We can adapt. We can immerse ourselves in the world. Christians know how to do this. We just put it all in a blender, and when we are finished, it goes down easy. But there is a problem. This is never really good for people of faith. As Jews, Christians, or Muslims, we know that we will lose our identities if we learn to swim in a pagan world.

There is yet another strategy. It is the one that flows from our scripture. I have learned that when the Bible teaches us to be strong, to endure, to be patient, to give thanks, there must be a reason. The context must have been one in which the believers might have been tempted to give in, to quit, to despair, to become cynical, to compromise.

Instead, Paul writes, "May you be made strong with all the strength that comes from his glorious power, and may you be prepared to endure everything with patience, while joyfully giving thanks to the Father" (Colossians 1:11-12). Why be strong? Why endure? Why be patient? Why give thanks? Because God "has rescued us from the power of darkness and transferred us into the kingdom of his beloved Son" (v. 13).

There is the word *kingdom*. To the first hearers of this word, it would have made perfect sense. The strategy was and is spiritual resistance. The kingdom of God was at odds with the empire. It always is. To say Jesus is Lord is to say that Caesar is not Lord.

We sometimes assume that Jesus is narrow and parochial, and that the world is broad and inclusive. But what if the reverse is true? What if Jesus is broad and inclusive? What if all things in heaven and on earth were created through him and for him, thrones and rulers and dominions and powers? We sometimes assume that Jesus somehow belongs to us, but what if Jesus belongs not to the church but to the world, what if in him all the fullness of God was pleased to dwell?

So we confess that his name is above every name, but we do so with a corresponding humility about ourselves. If you will read the first chapter of Colossians and the second chapter of Ephesians and the second chapter of Philippians, you will note similarities. Each speaks to the power of Jesus Christ, which overcomes all obstacles, which unifies all peoples, which implies a lordship over all things. But note that each passage has a very distinct teaching about what this means for his followers.

The lordship of Jesus Christ creates people who are humble, patient, and reconciling. Even if we accept the vision of Christ as our King, we confess that as his followers we have no privileged knowledge, only a faith that we receive by grace. Even if we see the kingdom of God as a power that overcomes Caesar's rule, we remember that the meek will inherit the earth, that the peacemakers will be blessed, that the wolf and the lamb will lie down together.

The lament is that Christians have not always lived in the kingdom of God. Our arrogance has led to crusades. Our indifference has led to holocausts. Our irrelevance has led to a vacuum. Our fragmentation has led to unbelief. The divided body of Christ in the world is an outward and visible sign of an inward and spiritual disease.

And yet there is, ultimately, good news. In him all things hold together. In your life and in my life, this is possible. "Through him," Paul insists, "God was pleased to reconcile to himself all things, whether on earth or in heaven, by making peace through the blood of his cross" (Colossians 1:20).

Let the Christians of the world avoid nostalgia, retreat, and adaptation, and let us engage in the necessary disciplines of spiritual resistance: telling the truth, loving our neighbor, welcoming the stranger, bearing witness to the love of God, repenting of our sin, becoming peacemakers. (Kenneth H. Carter Jr.)

Worship Aids

Invocation

Almighty God, console us with the comfort of your warm embrace, compel us with the conviction of your all-knowing spirit, cleanse us with the power of your amazing grace. We humbly ask this in your name. Amen.

Call to Worship

Leader: Love calls us.

People: Love claims us.

Leader: Love gathers us to this place of worship, to this community of faith.

People: Love calls us to each other.

All: We answer the call, O God of love, by gathering here to worship, live, and love.
(Gary G. Kindley)

Pastoral Prayer

O Gracious God, help instill in us the spirit of compassion that dwelled in the "good Samaritan." This Samaritan took many risks and offered all he had to share his bounty and hospitality with a stranger. Each day, we as believers encounter many circumstances in which Christ offers us opportunities to live out our Christian convictions. Give us the courage and discernment to take up Jesus' cross and offer Christ's love to others. Bind us together as a community of persons who offer our lives to those for whom Christ also died. We pray this and every prayer in the name of our Messiah. Amen. (David N. Mosser)

Benediction

Blessed are the poor in spirit, for they know they need God. Go out and bless the world by sharing and showing the good news of God's love. Live in grace and peace. Amen. (Gary G. Kindley)

JULY 29, 2007

Ninth Sunday after Pentecost

Readings: Hosea 1:2-10; Psalm 85; Colossians 2:6-15, (16-19); Luke 11:1-13

Children of the Living God
Hosea 1:2-10

For those who struggle to find the message of a compassionate and restoring God in the Old Testament, I challenge them to read and absorb the prophet Hosea. What a powerful story!

The stories of families in the Bible, particularly in the Old Testament, are often the stories of brokenness. Over and over again we see the damage done to families who struggle with intimacy (David and his children); we see the hurt caused by family favoritism (Jacob and Esau; Joseph and his brothers). The Bible tells the truth about the pain that comes to us when we cannot love, cannot live honestly, do not offer faithfulness within the boundaries of families. There is nothing more relevant to our twenty-first-century society than the reality of homes that are in deep crisis because of our inability to learn how to love as God has created us to love.

The foundation of our love is found in the reality of God's love for us. John writes in his short letter, "We love because he first loved us" (1 John 4:19). The young couple who stand before a minister as they are offering their vows have a naive conviction that they have invented love. The reality is that God has made us to know intimacy, to give love, and the beginning of that love is in the heart of our Creator.

Since the beginning of creation, God has sought to let us see the love that God has for us. The unbelievable task Hosea has been given is to paint an object lesson for people who have lost the sense of God's passionate love.

Hosea loves Gomer, but Gomer doesn't love Hosea. She uses him; she betrays their marriage. Three children are born, but only one has his DNA. Two children have other fathers. Gomer has traded love for sex, and in the end, she has wounded five people. God wants us to understand the power of divine love. It is God's love that can settle the chaos of our hearts and our homes.

Our friends in 12-step groups remind us that the very first step in healing from the brokenness of addiction is to recognize that the addiction (read *sin*) has made our lives unmanageable. How in the world can we begin a road of spiritual recovery? We must stop the lies; we've got to tell the truth about our own lives—we cannot manage. The second step says simply, "Came to believe that a power greater than ourselves could restore us to sanity." Until we tell the truth about ourselves, we will maintain a defensive barrier between God and us. Hosea paints an honest picture— God's people have preferred false lovers to the true love. Times have not changed the picture much.

We couldn't imagine a father naming his child "No Mercy," nor could we imagine a mother calling her child "Not My Child." Yet we live as if we are not God's children. Most Christian folks live as though they don't really believe what they say they believe. In some ways Hosea's story reminds us of Jesus' story of the loving father and the prodigal son. The loved one does not recognize the love that is being shown. Instead of seeing the love and generosity of God, we want it all. We live as though it's "all about us."

God's love, however, won't let us go. Although the family has been broken up by abuse, shame, and betrayal, God doesn't forget us. There is nothing we can do to separate us from God's love, Paul writes to the Romans (see 8:38-39). God wants me to know—God wants you to know—there is nothing we can ever do that will set us outside of God's love.

Don't you love the concluding picture in this passage? God will redeem the broken family. God will reclaim the abandoned children and make them his own. In the places where hopelessness has been heaped upon you, God declares, "You are my child." In the families where the wounds of bitterness and unfaithfulness have left a sense of defeat, God speaks, "I love you!" In the homes where anger and addiction and despair have risen up to divide and conquer, God cries out, "Our family will survive!"

The e-mail came through with the horrifying story of a young son who is both chemically dependent and suffering from a mental disorder; Mom is desperate to save his life, while her adult daughter is fearful for her mother's life. A college son stops his mother's suicide attempt and is forced to call the police for her safety. A husband must seek solace for his broken heart over his wife's addictions. How can we live with the heartache of the brokenness of life? By hearing God's loving call, "You are my child—I love you."

Peter was thinking about this when he wrote to the struggling young church. In the face of life's storms, they wondered if following Jesus Christ was worth the price they had to pay. Peter encouraged them, "Come to him, a living stone, though rejected by mortals yet chosen and precious in God's sight, and like living stones, let yourselves be built into a spiritual house" (1 Peter 2:4-5). He also wrote, "But you are a chosen race, a royal priesthood, a holy nation, God's own people, in order that you may proclaim the mighty acts of him who called you out of darkness into his marvelous light. Once you were not a people, but now you are God's people; once you had not received mercy, but now you have received mercy" (1 Peter 2:9-10).

In Jesus Christ, you are "Children of the living God" (Hosea 1:10). Amen. (Guy Ames)

Willing to Do Some Good

First in a Series of Two: Good Works

James 1:17-18, 22-27

There's no easy way around it. We all have to work. Whether it's at home or in the office, we can't escape our work. Jobs and chores constantly chase us, but we don't all work for the same reasons. Some of us work hard because that's what our parents did; they modeled hard work for us. Others work to make ends meet; so the bills can be paid. Still others work to get ahead, to buy more stuff, to increase savings, and to be able to retire early. We want it all—now. This kind of work focuses on what we can get out of our jobs. It's a work ethic about *me*. It's about competition. How can I succeed? So it's no wonder we call work the "rat race." Work has been given a black eye.

Our work ethic is a reflection of the very attitude we hold toward what we do. It says something about our spirit. Our culture treats work as a necessary evil. This attitude has seeped into American Christianity. We are adamant that works won't save us. Grace is more than sufficient. And we give James an awfully hard time about this "faith without works" business.

If we step back from our cultural assumptions of work and faith, we see, in the person who does good works, a genuine faith in the God of all good works.

Good works begin in the heart with a spirit of generosity. James says, "Every generous act of giving, with every perfect gift, is from above" (1:17). Good deeds are an outpouring of God's spirit and love, for God has lavished mercy and compassion upon us. As if that weren't enough, God offers friendship to us, a friendship that we live out by loving our neighbors. We're to be merciful and compassionate with other people. "Love your neighbor as yourself" is the simple yet direct command. God has given us the example to follow. We should be a people willing to give, instead of a people seeking to receive. We do good works in response to God's example.

Not long after joining my church, a new member stopped by the church office and said, "Put me to work. I work well with my hands, and I want to do some good." This man knew who he was and to whom he belonged. He was a gifted groundskeeper. He noticed that there was plenty of work around the church; he desired to use his gifts for God.

Good works are less a matter of what we do and more of who we are, who God created us to be. It's our identity. It's about the kind of spirit we have. We are a relational people. Our Jewish ancestors lived with this identity. They saw themselves as God's chosen people. Because of Jesus Christ, we too see ourselves in a special light. As God in the flesh, Jesus shows us how to live, and how to treat others. Sometimes it means "to care for orphans and widows" (1:27). Other times it calls us to feed those who are hungry. Jesus was concerned with those who were in need. Our concern should be the same.

Our country is celebrating this year the four-hundredth anniversary of Jamestown, Virginia. The English settlers who came to the "New World" were a mix of gentry and craftsmen. The world they encountered was foreign to their own. Disease and starvation threatened their lives. Social status was important to them, but survival mattered more. The settlers could survive only if they worked together. A spirit of community, regardless of status, was needed now more than ever, if they had any hope of taming the wilderness of Virginia.

Communities thrive when people work together. The collective effort, not personal accomplishment, takes center stage. Communities are effective when they understand each person's role and identity. People are gifted in different ways. One person isn't more important than another.

Churches work well when they realize and use the diversity of gifts that reside within their faith communities. Jesus modeled this kind of behavior for his disciples, who sometimes were more concerned with their own interests than with following the Lord. Jesus wanted his followers to embody their beliefs. When we put our beliefs into action, remarkable things occur. People accomplish great feats when they work together, pooling their talents and resources. James encourages the faithful to live out good works in this way.

In community, a person of good works is not overly concerned with the "me." I am not looking for recognition. We, the community, are not competing with one another. We are a relational people—with both God and one another. Community is crucial, for it enables us to be a people of good works. Our spirits find renewal in this setting. We even claim that in Christ we have entered a new covenant with God. This covenant is visible when lived out in community. Our parish, therefore, helps us become a people of good works.

Sometimes in the church, we spend too much time debating the issue of faith and works, and not enough time living out what we do believe. Deep within ourselves, I think we know that our beliefs aren't worth much if we do not act upon them. James tried to make this clear to the church. As we consider our own lives, we realize that works are a good reflection of what we believe about God, the church, and ourselves. Our works show the kind of spirit we have. The hope is that we all will want to do some good, as God has done for us. (Mark White)

Worship Aids

Call to Worship

As a cool breeze on a hot summer's day, so is the love of God that refreshes, enlivens, and sustains. We gather to feel the breeze of the Holy Spirit, and to celebrate God's presence. Let us worship God. Amen.

Pastoral Prayer

Holy God, we greet you today with wonder and humility. Your amazing grace sustains us, and the wonder of creation astounds us. Thank you for sharing the gift of life with us. Thank you for offering to us the gift of your holy presence and your unconditional acceptance. Surround us with the indescribable comfort of your everlasting embrace. Catch us when we stumble, and lift us when we cannot get up. Forgive us our sins, and heal the brokenness of our spirit, which is irreparable apart from your redemption. Save us from the uncertainty of tomorrow and the emptiness of despair. Plant in us hope that surpasses doubt, faith that overcomes fear, and love that outlasts enmity. We pray these things in the name of the Redeemer, Jesus the Christ. Amen.

Benediction

Go out to serve, live, and love in the name of the Creator, Redeemer, and Sustainer. Go forth to be the church together! Amen. (Gary G. Kindley)

AUGUST 5, 2007

❧❧❧

Tenth Sunday after Pentecost

Readings: Hosea 11:1-11; Psalm 107:1-9, 43; Colossians 3:1-11; Luke 12:13-21

Divine Parenting
Hosea 11:1-11

As a pastor, some of the most difficult situations I encounter involve families in crisis. Many times, the story involves rebellious children (teenagers or adults) who have managed to wreak havoc in their own lives or the lives of those they love. The precipitating event might have been a financial crisis. The struggle might be addiction to alcohol or drugs. There might have been a moment of poor judgment or a rash action, which led to a situation with far-reaching consequences. However the problem starts, these children often come home to their parents seeking help and guidance. They stand in need of forgiveness, as well as physical and emotional support.

As I have watched these parents struggle to help their children, I have learned that there is no fiercer thing than the love of a parent for a child. Most parents will do whatever is within their power to help restore the lives of their children to wholeness.

The tragedy, however, is that not all problems can be fixed. Sometimes, after many failed attempts at restoration, human parents have to step away from their children. I have seen situations where the ending is not happy. There have been times, for the good of the parent and the child, when the most reasonable and loving thing to do is to quit doing anything at all. Our humanity dictates that there is limit to what can be done to restore a wayward child. There comes a point where our emotional and physical resources are spent, and the child has to make it on his or her own.

In this passage, the prophet Hosea tells a familiar story; that of the nation of Israel and their relationship with God. Hosea begins by reminding the people of the early years of their relationship: "When Israel was a child, I loved him, and out of Egypt I called my son" (Hosea 11:1). Yet the nation of Israel soon tried to make it on its own, with disastrous consequences. Following their deliverance from slavery in Egypt, the people strayed from their relationship with Yahweh and turned toward idols. They did not remember the blessings that God had bestowed in the years of their wilderness wanderings. Forgotten were the many times God had cared for them. Heartbroken, God cries out for them, as God remembers all those times of nurturing, feeding, and teaching his child. God repeatedly rescued them from difficulty, yet they drifted away from their divine Parent.

Israel was like a wayward and obstinate child. After many failed attempts to bring them back into the family, God had every right to give up on them. As with human parents, God would have been within rights to step away from it all. Yahweh had come to the limit of what justice required, and it seems that Yahweh could reasonably give up hope of restoration. Yet the good news is that, unlike human parents, Yahweh is indeed "God and no mortal" (v. 9). God takes inventory and realizes that in the heart of God, "compassion grows warm and tender," and God "will not execute [God's] fierce anger" (vv. 8-9). Ultimately, it is the divine nature to grant mercy over justice. Hosea reminds us of this truth about God. God demonstrates divine parenting, a parenting that is far above anything we can experience here on earth.

In our struggles to be the children of God, I think we sometimes forget that our heavenly Parent is different from our earthly parents. We project earthly attributes onto God and set limits upon God's grace. We think in terms of justice, and the limits of what we as humans can do and provide for our children. We realize that we cannot fix everything. We become frustrated after a lifetime of granting second chances. We despair that the ending is always the same. In our humanness, we eventually give up hope that we, or others, could ever really be fully restored.

Praise God that we have a divine Parent whose love knows no limit, and whose nature is to continue granting forgiveness! This is good news for a world full of sinners like us. We look at our own lives and realize that we have a long way to go in our faith journeys. Time and time again, we sin, we ask forgiveness, we repent, and we seek to live as God calls us to live—and then we sin again. Surely, we think, there is a point where God will give up on us, a point where justice will outweigh grace and mercy. Yet the divine answer is always the same: "You are my beloved." God promises, "They shall come trembling like birds from Egypt, . . . and I will return them to their homes" (v. 11). Much like the father in the parable of the prodigal son, God welcomes us with open arms.

This is the gift of Hosea's proclamation, and the gift the church can also offer to a world that is hurting. Our ministries would be transformed if we truly believed and lived the powerful good news of this story. Our churches would be revitalized and changed in radical ways if we truly began proclaiming the good news that no one is beyond the reach of God's tender mercies and compassion. The family of God is made up of all of us, especially those who, in our human way of seeing, appear to be beyond redemption. The family of God is made up of sinners: liars, cheaters, addicts, prisoners, idolaters, and all of the other folks on the margins of society. The sons and daughters of God include those who are faithful as well as those who are faithless. It is God's divine parenting that claims all of us who seek relationship after we have lost our way. It is God's love that welcomes us home, over and over and over again. (Wendy Joyner)

We Are What We Do

Second in a Series of Two: Good Works

James 2:14-26

As a child, my family always set aside the first week of August for a family vacation. Beach trips became a family tradition. As an adult, I still have a strong emotional attachment to family vacations because I enjoy time away from the routine, time for travel, and time to spend with loved ones. I thank God for vacation time. Many of us use our vacation time to kick back and relax. It even provides us with time for reflection; and we take stock of our lives. We look back on the past. We dream about the future. We consider our journeys of faith—am I doing my best at living the Christian life?

Where in the world do we begin answering this question! It depends. We first wonder where grace fits in. Then we consider if good works are a requirement. We ask ourselves, "Do my actions reflect those of Jesus?" And here lies a temptation. The temptation is to evaluate our behavior with a checklist of right actions. Did I give to the poor? Did I share food with the hungry? Did I help someone find shelter? The list goes on. We want to know if we've done the right things. A checklist seems like a helpful tool, but it indicates something else. It suggests that our faith is mechanical, lived as a set of requirements instead of a relational journey with God.

When we read James's epistle, we recognize that good works, for a person who truly follows Christ, isn't about fulfilling a quota. Checklists aren't needed. Rather, good works are grounded in who we are. We are more than hearers of the Word. We are "doers of the word" (James 1:22). Our actions are a response to God and with God. Our actions are a part of our identity.

Good works communicate the identity of a follower of Christ. It's a natural product of the Christian life. James amplifies this idea, for nearly half of this epistle is written as an imperative. The implication is that good works are urgently needed. We don't have to look far to see people's needs. Each day we receive invitations to help and give, including calls from charities and the extended hands of homeless persons. People in need are right around the corner. They even reside within our own churches. As Christians, how should we act? Life isn't lived on the sidelines. We must get out into the world and act upon the words we believe. We enact the scripture passages we hear on Sundays. This is imperative!

My wife and I enjoy dinner parties. They provide an opportunity for us to get dressed up and have a good time with other couples. We never show up empty-handed when we're invited into another person's home, even if we have not been asked to bring any food. We feel it's important that we bring a small gift, maybe some flowers. We want to express our gratitude to our friends. We think it is good manners.

Practicing faith without works is bad manners. Genuine faith doesn't show up without offering good deeds. Practicing our faith, though, goes beyond good manners, because good deeds aren't a requirement, but a sign of our faith. According to James, a faith that refuses to help people in need is a false faith. "So faith by itself, if it has no works, is dead" (2:17). Christians have found this works imperative problematic. James seems to contradict Paul's idea that we are saved by faith alone. But neither James nor Paul insists we return to a strict following of Jewish law, that is, following a checklist. Both New Testament writers affirm "faith working through love" as the expression of good works (Galatians 5:6).

People see what Christians believe by what we do. Faith and works complement and complete each other. "Faith was brought to completion by the works" (2:22). The Christian journey seeks completeness and wholeness because of a desire to be righteous. More than having the right beliefs, righteousness means practicing our faith. James argues a faith without works is corrupt. In other words, it does us no good to attend Sunday worship if we then ignore the needs before us during the rest of the week. This is a corrupt faith.

A sincere desire for a complete faith depends upon the local church. It's in this community that we can best be "doers of the word." The church community helps us understand the implications of being a people of good works. One significant implication is that good works go beyond sharing possessions. We are called to minister to those in need, but being doers of the word also includes welcoming the very people we help into the church community. Our churches are challenged to become places of both charity and acceptance. It's imperative that we move beyond slinging a few coins into the cup of a homeless person, and seek to be a community of transformation for all people.

God gives us the chance to choose transformation each new day. When we wake, our minds may run through the day's activities. We mull over all the things we have to do, all of the essentials. Are good works essential to us? Do we remind ourselves that good works are a sign of our identities? James is a straight shooter—be doers of the word. Show the world our faith is active and alive. Faith and works are good partners. Both are needed in our world now more than ever.

So as we "kick back" in this summer season, we should enjoy the much-needed rest and time off from our jobs. And keep James's reminder in view: we are what we do; we are doers of the Word. It's a statement of fact. It's the mark of a Christian. As followers of Christ, we are called to help those in need, whenever. It's imperative we do so. (Mark White)

Worship Aids

Invocation

In your holy name we gather to worship, to remember, and to celebrate. Come, Holy Spirit, and remind us of the nearness of your presence and the strength of your power. Amen.

Pastoral Prayer

Gracious God, we gather today to worship, and to reflect on our relationship with you and with others. How is it, O God, that we claim to be mindful of others, yet do so little to end the hunger in our world? How is it, O God, that we look upon poverty with disdain or indifference, yet live with impoverished spirits? How is it, O God, that we trust strangers with the care of our children, yet balk at placing our whole trust in you?

Peel away the layers of our indifference, indulgence, neglect, and denial that we might look upon your heart and lay claim to our holy calling. Through Jesus Christ our Lord we pray. Amen.

Benediction

Empowered by the Holy Spirit, leave this place with strength and courage. Remember that you never walk alone. Amen. (Gary G. Kindley)

AUGUST 12, 2007

❧❧❧

Eleventh Sunday after Pentecost

Readings: Isaiah 1:1, 10-20; Psalm 50:1-8, 22-23; Hebrews 11:1-3, 8-16; Luke 12:32-40

Farsighted Pilgrims
Hebrews 11:1-3, 8-16

I recently attended a seminar where several of us were discussing generational differences among members of a church. One man remarked that it was torture for his ten-year-old son to wait for anything at all. In an era of high-speed Internet, twenty-four-hour retail stores, e-mail, and cell phones, there were few things or individuals not instantly accessible to this young man. The speaker reflected upon the benefits of all this modern technology, but also wondered aloud about the drawbacks for society and the church as a whole.

I have contemplated this conversation many times in recent weeks, wondering what this need for instant gratification and immediate availability might mean for my life and the lives of God's people. It occurs to me as I read texts such as this one, that the life of faith is most often discussed as a pilgrimage or a journey, rather than a sprint. Faith is often about patient waiting and trusting. Faith is often about trusting God to be at work in ways that are not easily discerned. Faith is laying aside the values of society at large and seeking after the kingdom of God. Faith is not for the faint of heart, and it's not for folks who demand clear and immediate answers.

The writer of Hebrews understood a great deal about the life of faith. The writer makes use of several historical examples to illustrate the nature of Christian faith, especially speaking to the themes of hope and perseverance. In today's lesson, Abraham's life is offered as an example for other pilgrims who seek to follow God. Abraham models quiet trust in God, whose plans cannot always be discerned or understood immediately.

First, the writer reminds us that when Abraham started his journey to the land of promise, there was no clear indication of where he was headed. The future was unclear to him, but Abraham made a decision to act in obedience. As verse 8 notes, "By faith Abraham obeyed ... and he set out, not knowing where he was going." So many times, we want to know all the answers up front. We seek to have a plan in place, even when obedience to God's call is at stake. Yet, faith often requires the people of God to take risks and to act on what they do know of God's love and faithfulness. It may be, like Abraham, we are called to trust in a future that is not clear to us. The beginning of a pilgrimage with God requires great faith. We may have to set out, not knowing where we are going. Some of us will be called into a new area of service; others may be challenged to begin a new relationship or to start a new job. Change is a frightening thing, especially when the future is unknown, but sometimes God calls us to step into the unknown so that we might be blessed and surprised by the journey ahead.

Through the story of Abraham, I am also reminded that the ending is in God's hands as well. Once we are obedient to the call of God, we sometimes lose sight of the fact that we may not ever understand the complete picture. God was faithful to Abraham, and Abraham lived to see his son Isaac. He knew that the promise of descendants was being answered, even during his own lifetime. Yet there were aspects of God's promises that Abraham, and others like him, never lived to see. "All of these died in faith without having received the promises, but from a distance they saw and greeted them" (Hebrews 11:13). The farsighted pilgrim understands that ultimate success lies not in the end result, but in faithfulness throughout the journey. Therein lies the nature of Christian hope, the assurance that God's promises will be fulfilled. It includes the belief that for all of us, the ultimate fulfillment of the promise lies at the end of life, when we see the heavenly home that God has prepared for us. Faith requires a willingness to look at life through the eyes of eternity, and understand the mysteries of promises deferred.

I realized, as I read this great roll call of faith, that one of the things I desire most is to be a farsighted pilgrim. I want to be like Abraham, who trusted God at the beginning of his journey, at the end of his journey, and all the days in between. I want to be the kind of Christian who trusts in God and God's promises fully. I want to act in faith, not by calculating the possible outcomes based on what I see, but by desiring God's blessing that I cannot see. I want to be in it for the long haul, and that's a difficult thing to do when I am surrounded by the means for instant gratification.

What would it look like if we trusted God with the beginning and the ending of our journeys? What would it look like if we took more risks and worried less? What would it look like if we lived like these forebears in the faith, who were "like strangers and foreigners on the earth"? (v. 13). Perhaps our churches would be more willing to spend money in ministry, and less worried about having an emergency fund. Perhaps we would be less anxious about being successful and more concerned about being faithful. Perhaps we would spend more time seeking the things of God, not "thinking of the land . . . left behind," but with a "desire [for] a better country, that is, a heavenly one" (vv. 15-16).

My hope and prayer for myself and for the church is that we might be farsighted pilgrims; that we not be so anxious for immediate results that we miss the blessing of a glorious adventure, following the call of God in our lives. (Wendy Joyner)

A Renewing Judgment

First in a Series of Two

Isaiah 1:1, 10-20

From time to time, I think about an occupation and wonder, "Who would want to do that?" For example, anytime I've moved—which has been quite a bit as a minister—I've thought, *Few people, at age sixteen, say to themselves, "When I grow up, I'm going to become a mover."* Think about those who, under a blistering sun, roof our homes. I can't imagine myself waking up every day to climb a ladder and nail shingles to a roof, day after day, year after year. I could say the same for jobs such as pathology, water treatment engineering, morning paper route delivery, and others.

But, of course, there are many millions who could not imagine being a preacher. When I read the opening chapter of Isaiah, I remind myself that the kind of preaching I've done for more than thirty years is rather mild compared to the assignment given the prophet Isaiah in the eighth century B.C.E. In a word, Isaiah was brutally bold. He spoke out against the coarse sin of his people with razor precision. Isaiah took on both king and people with equal energy, cutting through the surface piety of their faith while filleting their crass indifference to the poor. Isaiah was bold.

Today, we have heard one of the more cutting passages from the book of Isaiah. With no economy of words, the prophet announces God's judgment against the false and empty religion practiced by his people. And what invective there is in these blistering sentences! To begin, Isaiah condemns the Temple's sacrificial system, asking for God, "What to me is the multitude of your sacrifices?... I have had enough of burnt offerings of rams and the fat of fed beasts; I do not delight in the blood of bulls, or of lambs, or of goats" (Isaiah 1:11).

Long thought to be the center of Israel's worship, Isaiah now condemns the worship around the altar as nothing but a sham; a ritual slaughter in which God takes no delight. What brought about such judgment? Where did Israel stumble? In short, the piety required by the law, a piety expressed in sacrifice, had been abandoned for the show at the altar. The reason for sacrifice was being trampled and replaced by empty ritual acts.

During Jesus' ministry, our Lord picked up on this thin expression of faith, or at least alluded to it, when he spoke of the hard work of reconciliation. In Matthew 5:23-24, Jesus demands that justice, reconciliation, and interpersonal renewal take effect prior to offering one's gifts at an altar. The sacrifices of animals or, in our day, generous gifts of money or time, can never bolster one's relationship with God if our lives are not right with our brothers and sisters or if we are ignoring the plight of the poor.

Perhaps something else is going on here though, something even more harmful than empty sacrifices. Isaiah speaks pointedly about the worship calendar, ritual, and practice of the people. Phrases such as "When you come to appear before me," "new moon and Sabbath ... assemblies," and "new moons and your appointed festivals" (vv. 12-14) speak of carefully observed obligations required by the religious establishment. Ideally, the purpose of these assemblies, gatherings, and festivals was to celebrate God's goodness among God's people. However, this was not happening. On the contrary, the prophet gives stark witness to a religion and a society that were all show, all performance, and no integrity.

Finally, God says to his confused and arrogant people that when they worship with such superficial sacrilege, "I will hide my eyes from you; even though you make many prayers, I will not listen" (v. 15). God had condoned as much ritual sham and pietistic drivel as God could abide. There had to be change.

Here we see into the great heart of God, the magnanimous outpouring of God's compassion and care. Here is a renewing judgment. Rather than announce imminent destruction or summary judgment, God offers an invitation: "Wash yourselves; make yourselves clean; remove the evil of your doings from before my eyes; cease to do evil, learn to do good; seek justice, rescue the oppressed, defend the orphan, plead for the widow" (vv. 16-17). As a parent gives guidance to a child, so God offers instruction and care. What God seeks in God's people is not more ritual or more altar fires but quite the opposite. God seeks justice, reconciliation, and restitution. Here we feel the heart of God, who defines authentic faith in earthy, practical terms.

But, sad to say, the people then, as we are today, were suspicious. Perhaps they didn't believe God's prophet. So, as one final, loving gesture, God extends hand and heart with warm invitation: "Come now, let us argue it out, ... though your sins are like scarlet, they shall be like snow; though they are red like crimson, they shall become like wool" (v. 18). Although the people have arrogantly disobeyed, God will restore the relationship and bring healing and hope. This "arguing out" is a winsome gesture to do the hard work of reconciliation.

So there we have it; but what is this to us? For one thing, we miss God's higher purposes for life when our faith's expression is showmanship in worship while ignoring the cries of the needy and the wounds of the broken. God is not impressed with religious ritual. Rather, God is honored and worshiped with renewing relationships whereby we care for God's world and serve those in need.

Isaiah reminds us, painfully so, that most of our churches would be wise to relocate worship from the church house one Sunday morning and reconvene at a soup kitchen, a shelter for battered women, or an AIDS ward at a local hospital. The sad truth is that the larger Christian church in the United States is bloated with Bible studies while, at the same time, our country's prisons are overflowing. We spend much time eating meals at the church house when so many in our country and world have no meals to eat.

"Come now, let us argue it out—let us reason together," says the Lord. The worship of God that is authentic witness to God is worship born of faithful commitment to be God's people in the world for which Christ died and rose again. Amen. (Timothy Owings)

Worship Aids

Call to Worship

We would rather be fools in the house of God, than faithless in the ship of life's journey. Therefore, let us worship God.

Pastoral Prayer (Educator Sunday)

God of all wisdom, we pray for teachers everywhere. We pray for teachers in inner-city classrooms and in one-classroom schools. We pray for teachers whose classroom is a small house or the shade of a large tree. We pray for teachers who worry about budgets and teachers who worry about bullets. We pray for teachers whose students are poor and seeking hope, or rich but needing values. We pray for teachers whose students are impoverished of resources and those impoverished of character. We pray for teachers who are willing to rejoice in the smallest victories in learning and the larger accomplishments of others. We offer a prayer of gratitude for teachers whose lives change ours forever and whose legacy is our destiny. Thank you, God, for teachers, as we acknowledge their sacred calling and their priceless task. In the name of the Master Teacher, we pray. Amen.

Benediction

May the same God who redeems the lame, the lonely, and the lost, bring hope and promise to each day you live. Be blessed in God's grace. Amen. (Gary G. Kindley)

AUGUST 19, 2007

❧❧❧

Twelfth Sunday after Pentecost

Readings: Isaiah 5:1-7; Psalm 80:1-2, 8-19; Hebrews 11:29–12:2;
Luke 12:49-56

Decision and Division
Luke 12:49-56

There is one special day each semester on a college campus: the first day of class. All of the students will be there, most of them with freshly purchased, untouched textbooks. The teacher's grade sheet is untainted by actual grades. The students are on time; their hair is combed. They begin the semester with the very same resolve as their teachers: "This semester will be different. I will not come unprepared to class, I will not give a halfhearted effort, I will finish the semester with as much enthusiasm as I begin." This resolve usually lasts until about the first quiz, and then reality sets in.

With that reality comes division. The student tries to manage his or her time and balance obligations of work, family, and school. The student feels conflicted with too many different disciplines of study and not enough unity. Questions of identity and faith are crowded out by the immediate; the "urgent" pushes out the "important." And with every decision there are choices left unmade.

So it is with the primary choices we make in our lives. When it comes to the way of Jesus, decision brings division. Jesus taught his first hearers, and he desires to teach us that the work of God inevitably brings division, because it requires commitment and decision. But let us not hide from such a call, because in the process of division, God will unite us to the spirit of life and love, the spirit that can make a life into a masterpiece.

God will, in the process of guiding our lives, take us places where we did not expect to go. I suppose every believer at one time or another learns that.

God will, after calling us, ask us to choose between friendship with the world and friendship with the Spirit. Who could hear these words that Jesus uttered: "I came to bring fire to the earth.... I have a baptism with which to be baptized.... Do you think that I have come to bring peace to the earth? No, I tell you, but rather division!" (Luke 12:49-51). Who wants that? Surely, his disciples thought they were signing on for a little peace and security. But what they got was stress, fire, and conflict. They experienced the division that is known only by those who, above all else, seek truth.

Young adults, in college and out, face that challenge from the first day they arrive on campus. It is necessary that they transcend and move beyond the inherited values of their parents. They live with divided minds. They try to find the group in which they fit just perfectly, the campus ministry, the sorority or fraternity, the student organization. At some point or another, they find that they just don't quite fit. They struggle to find their place, their identity, their direction; and someone is always asking them, "What are you majoring in?" or "What are you going to do when you graduate?" Most of these students don't even know what they are doing on Friday night, much less when they graduate.

More often than not, this kind of insecurity, division, and conflict precipitates a crisis. In our language, *crisis* has a negative connotation, but it is a venerable old word, which only means a division-point, watershed, or dividing line. Conflict is something that we all, if we are honest, live through much of the time. There are so many choices, so many decisions, so many directions. How does today's college student get it all together? Not without help.

That is the role a church can fill for young adults, as midwife to a new identity. As we see these students move from adolescent questions, such as "What group will I affiliate with?" to young adult questions, such as "Who am I really, in the mystery of human growth?" we can be there to help them through the questions.

Here is the way it must go. We do not know when it will happen, but it will happen. The student will be walking across campus someday, maybe out by the fountain, or over toward the student union, and he or she will realize that it all hangs together—the science class and the religion class, psychology and history, spirit, mind, and body—and the young adult will begin to integrate a life, rather than prepare for a career. In the midst of that life, if the church is there to offer them Christ, they may, just may, form their life in the shape of a cross. Then they will learn that in the divisions and crises of the days ahead, God will lead them through.

God will not leave us alone; God will ever be with us, to the end of our days. "What stress I am under," said Jesus, "until it is completed!" (Luke 12:50). Jesus must have known that he would be the first casualty of the conflicts of spirit and world. Simeon said in the second chapter of Luke: "This child is destined for the falling and the rising of many in Israel, and to be a sign that will be opposed so that the inner thoughts of many will be revealed—and a sword will pierce your own soul too" (vv. 34-35). Jesus would be the first casualty of division that attends the in-breaking of God's kingdom. Jesus teaches us that when we live as citizens of the kingdom, we will be at odds with the world around us.

It is not easy being a stranger in a strange land. It is not easy being out of step with your environment. What stress we are under until our days are fulfilled. But at the end of the day we have been promised that out of division and conflict will come reconciliation, peace, and wholeness. All of the misunderstandings, aloneness, and crisis will give way to the cosmic, spiritual community of God's people.

There is one other day for the college student that is as good as the first day of class: graduation day. What song could we play other than "Pomp and Circumstance"? The football stadium is full; the whole family is there to see the one on whom its hope rests. The teachers who pushed and cajoled and threatened are all dressed up in their college colors and standing in the aisles hugging their students. The divisions are healed, the crises are behind; these students, dare we say it, have grown up. A new day starts.

There is, you will recall, a peace promised beyond the stress of following a cruciform Savior; a united human family beyond any divisions that faith may have caused. There is no conflict, no division in the kingdom of God. It is our goal. Won't you, by your faith, help us get there? (Don Holladay)

Great Expectations

Second in a Series of Two

Isaiah 5:1-7

The title of Charles Dickens's enduring classic novel *Great Expectations* is so fitting for the first seven verses of the fifth chapter of Isaiah. Here we glimpse the great expectations of our God, expectations that span the length and breadth of the Bible. See God first in the Garden of Eden, creating a nourishing place for humankind to enjoy, multiply, and thrive. See God's great expectations in the call of Abram from dusty Ur of the Chaldeans, promising to make the old patriarch the father of many nations. See God pursue the shepherd David, who, in spite of his lust-fed manner and murderous ways, is the person after God's own heart. Turn to the pages of the New Testament and see God in flesh in Jesus of Nazareth gather to himself the unlikely, the unloved, the unforgiven, and the unwanted; and create with them and among them a new community of love. This is the picture of God whose great expectations for all of us never wane through the record of Holy Scripture.

In this lovely Isaiah text, the prophet uses a parable to paint a picture, once again, of God's expectations. Let's step back from the painting in the expansive gallery of God's work, and take in this masterpiece. First, see the warm colors of God's heart. The opening lines of this parable of the vineyard use endearing, tender language as God, "the beloved," speaks of Judah and Jerusalem. God sings a "love-song," crooning affection to the people whose devotion God seeks (Isaiah 5:1). See here, at the very heart of God, a love that is both spoken and sung. Like the romantic troubadours of old, God serenades God's people.

There is more: for a moment, take in the extravagant scope of God's gift, "a vineyard on a very fertile hill" (v. 1). If you have had the good fortune to visit Napa or Sonoma County in northern California, or have seen pictures or video of this beautiful part of the Golden State, then you have the image the divine painter uses here. Planting a vineyard is no overnight business endeavor. I am told that a productive winery invests many thousands of dollars, even millions, in the development of a vineyard that may not yield its best fruit for decades. Such is the care with which the eternal Vintner prepared this vineyard. God "dug it," "cleared it of stones," and "planted it with choice vines" (v. 2). No expense was spared to ensure the finest of vines yielding the most delicious fruit.

But all is not well. The music that at first was a love song now becomes a dirge. We marvel at the painting before us until God speaks, telling us of great expectations gone sour. This prize vineyard, fully invested with "choice vines," yields "wild grapes." Whereas the farmer expected sweet, robust, prolific fruit from his vineyard, hear this farmer's disappointment when the harvest produces sour, near-worthless grapes.

The painting that was so beautiful now changes before our eyes. With brutal suddenness, the glory becomes gory, as the once-magnificent canvas turns barren, empty, void; barren of color, empty of promise, void of hope. The Beloved now speaks and compares God's vineyard to God's people. They had come into being with such promise and blessing. Now they squander their birthright and frustrate their future.

Expectations. What does God expect? Isaiah's answer flies in the face of most all our answers. Last week, when we met the prophet Isaiah, we learned that religious duty or pious displays of worship never capture God's heart. God is not so impressed with our anthems, robes, organs, windows, steeples, and carpet colors as God is impressed with our doing what is right. God is not moved so much by our carefully worded theology, orthodox though it may be, as God is by our offerings of time, money, and talent thoughtfully given to others. God is not touched so much by our prayers' emotions as God is by our hearts' devotion to justice for the poor, liberty for the oppressed, and love for the forgotten.

God's good gifts of life—so beautifully painted here as a vineyard—are entrusted to us with the hope that a harvest of "justice" and "righteousness" (v. 7) may continually season our lives and all life. What is God's Word, here painted before our still-unconvinced or, worse, unbelieving eyes, saying to us?

For one thing, we may be surprised to learn that God spares no gift. Mind you, there are some among God's people who believe that God holds back giving the "good stuff," only to dole it out from time to time like a patronizing despot. Not so! This One with whom we have to do allows the rain to fall "on the just and on the unjust" (Matthew 5:45 RSV). This Beloved of the vineyard not only wills good for us, but is intentional in "digging up, removing stones, and planting" (see Isaiah 5:2) good for us. Here is a picture of God worth framing on the walls of our hearts; the God whose light and love, grace and mercy are never withheld from any one of us.

Such generosity invites us to a higher, more ennobling way of life. This begs the question from all of us who live in this affluent, well-fed, consumer-driven culture: are God's gifts and blessings given to enlarge our territory (to reference an obscure but now well-known prayer of Jabez, 1 Chronicles 4:10), thus raising our standard of living? Or, are God's gifts given to enlarge another's territory, thus raising our standard of giving? You decide. Hear the parable of the vineyard, step back, and once again look at the painting. We, the minority who have so much, who live in a world teeming with a majority who has inadequate health care, poor sanitation, and an ever-diminishing supply of nourishing food, have to answer the Beloved of the parable.

Although our text ends with God's great expectations seemingly unmet, the message of Isaiah will not end until God's heart beats anew for a people who will be "a light of the world" (Matthew 5:14). For our part, we would be wise to let the parable speak, to give it permission to haunt our house and in so doing, to call us to a justice and righteousness that are given freely to others, even as we have freely received from God. (Timothy Owings)

Worship Aids

Call to Worship

We come seeking truth. Who can offer greater truth than Jesus Christ? Lord Jesus, we come into your presence this day.

Litany

Leader: Christ showed us the Way.

People: Christ showed us God's truth.

Leader: Christ showed us eternal Life.

People: The truth of Jesus Christ is still real today and for eternity.

Leader: Live in Christ's love and be thankful.
(Gary G. Kindley)

Prayer for Gifts / Stewardship

Everlasting and ever-giving Lord, we offer ourselves and our resources to your kingdom today. We give because you have first given to us, and we cherish the chance to be of service in your sovereign realm. Bless not only us who offer these gifts but also all who may receive them—in the precious name of the One who gave us all. Amen. (David N. Mosser)

Benediction

Live large. Serve faithfully. Make sacrifices. Love generously. Be the church. Amen. (Gary G. Kindley)

AUGUST 26, 2007

❧❧❧

Thirteenth Sunday after Pentecost

Readings: Jeremiah 1:4-10; Psalm 71:1-6; Hebrews 12:18-29; Luke 13:10-17

A Consecrated Calling
Jeremiah 1:4-10

I was appointed to my first charge at midyear. The district superintendent said they were "holding it open for me." I went to visit the small church soon after I arrived. I finally convinced the custodian I was who I said I was. As we entered the church, I realized the pastor's office could use some cleaning, and some books. Finally, I sat at the back of the one-room church, in the last pew where the checkbook and balance books were. I soon learned that the treasurer used Sunday worship to pay the bills.

It was a long way from the big city seminary to Balmorhea, Texas. As I thought about my assignment, my youth, my being equipped for ministry, I could almost hear the voice of Ezekiel's God: "Mortal, can these bones live?" And I thought to reply, "O Lord GOD, you know" (Ezekiel 37:3). God knew. I certainly did not.

Who among us, laity or clergy, can see all the contours of the call when we respond? Jeremiah surely could not have imagined. Merely a youth from a priestly family gone to seed, he was called in the thirteenth year of King Josiah, whose reign was a religious success and a political disaster. Jeremiah would prophesy through the roller-coaster years ahead. The years of Jeremiah's prophecy would see personal trouble and national crisis. Yet somehow he was called—appointed—consecrated. The next forty years would involve hardship and persecution, when all except his faithful scribe, Baruch, would turn on him. Yet it was made clear from his call that he had little choice. If he was to respond to the divine call, he must rely not on human friends, but on the divine companion. The Lord God promised, "Do not be afraid … for I am with you to deliver you" (Jeremiah 1:8)

We learn from Jeremiah's call that the ones called must see the hand of God in the most mundane circumstances. A branch of an almond tree and a boiling pot tilted slightly on its side; these were the signs that came with Jeremiah's call (Jeremiah 1:11-13). But it took a "second sight" to see the watchful hand of God bringing disaster from the north. Because Jeremiah had that deeper vision, his life would be one of hardship and trouble. He had been made to understand, at the very beginning of his prophecy, that God's hand was everywhere, hidden just below the surface.

Jeremiah's perception of God's presence was not limited to his auditory sense; one could say, "Jeremiah had not only heard about God's word, he had seen it done." Simple acts of trade, human commerce, and nature's ways became "parables of presence."

Should not the believer at all times and in all places have the same sense of God's presence? The great English poet Hopkins knew that "the world is charged with the grandeur of God" ("God's Grandeur," in *Poems of Gerard Manley Hopkins* [ed. Robert Bridges; London: Humphrey Milford, 1918]). Hopkins had learned to "see" the Holy Ghost bending close over nature and human commerce. One need only to look—really look.

Jeremiah must have found the same reality. How could he have survived otherwise, in an unfriendly, warring world? Poets and prophets have that in common. They know the way to God is through the things that God has made.

We learn from Jeremiah's call that the one called must cherish divine companionship over human approval.

"But I am only a boy!" Jeremiah cries out (see 1:6). Every young person knows the importance of "belonging." The college student struggles to find a place on the campus. These are the questions youth must ask: "Where is my place? With what group may I affiliate?" Could Jeremiah's questions have been any different? His was a priestly family; we see that in his call. In the Old Testament prophets were called, but priests were consecrated. Jeremiah was called and consecrated. Did he see his role as continuing the Priestly tradition of his family? He would not maintain the traditions and rituals of his forebears' religion; he would "pluck up and pull down" (see v. 10) every sign of complacent religiosity.

Those who read Jeremiah see a personality that desired human companionship and the easy conversation of market and table. We see it as we read Jeremiah's laments. Again and again we see his desire for friendship reflected in its absence. For him to be one of the crowd was not an option; the weight of divine compulsion would lead him out alone. He and Baruch would take on the world. The world had a way of hammering back. "I did not sit in the company of merrymakers, nor did I rejoice; under the weight of your hand I sat alone, for you had filled me with indignation" (Jeremiah 15:17).

What can be harder to accept than that one must "be alone"? Yet this is the nature of maturing, and we see clearly that Jeremiah matured, growing through judgment to grace. Maybe he even grew a little less hard on himself. At the end, when all the signs seemed to fulfill his prophecy of "no hope," he acted with hope by buying a field in his old hometown of Anathoth (Jeremiah 32).

We finally learn from the call of Jeremiah that the one called must respond to the present moment, while staying in touch with eternity.

"Before I formed you in the womb I knew you" (Jeremiah 1:5). Our passage speaks clearly to the idea of election. But Jeremiah was not elected to salvation or damnation. He was elected to a vocation, a calling. Jeremiah was meant to be a prophet. His priestly background counted for little. His job was "to pluck up and to pull down, / . . . to build and to plant" (v. 10). He could do nothing else. Even if he tried to hold the good word in, "then within me there is something like a burning fire shut up in my bones; I am weary with holding it in, and I cannot" (Jeremiah 20:9). His vocation was not in doubt. He must proclaim the word.

But Jeremiah's word, while always rooted in eternity, is yet in touch with the present. He, like all good prophets, "comforts the afflicted and afflicts the comfortable." He speaks truth to power, and healing to those who hurt. How could Jeremiah know the word to speak in each changing situation? He knew that the lively word of God is eternal at the same time that it is scandalously particular. Jeremiah knew, it seems, what eternity says today!

So today's prophet seems to bring a taste of eternity into every situation. Such a prophet of God can change the tone of a meeting by his or her silence. They can elevate a conversation by compassion. One would never think of gossiping in a prophet's presence, not because the prophet would judge you, but because his or her presence would cause you to judge yourself. Prophets don't have to tell us they speak for God; we know it.

"Can these bones live?" I asked myself in that tiny stone church in Balmorhea. Well, we started a little choir, a Sunday school class or two, and people began to come around: including old Pearl, the mayor of Balmorhea. That is a position where prestige exceeds pay, because it pays nothing. Pearl used to love to come to choir practice and sit and listen. Occasionally she would step out on the church's "porch" and smoke a cigarette. At the end of one of the services there was Pearl, standing by the preacher, asking to be baptized. We had to run across the street to get some water! In that unhistorical moment, eternity reached down and claimed another friend.

These are the moments when we know that we are among the elect; called like Jeremiah to "stand alone," but never be alone. Consecrated, called, and cleaned by the pure light of God's elect—friends of Jeremiah, friends of God. (Don Holladay)

Preparation

First in a Series of Three: Living for Today

2 Corinthians 5:1-10

In today's text, Paul seeks to connect the life we live now with the life that is to come. Paul's references to an earthly tent and our being away from the Lord speak to the temporary nature of the lives we now live. Paul sought to have the temporary understood in the larger context of the eternal. Such thinking influences how one should live here and now. What drives life in the temporary is our goal of pleasing Christ. For Paul, the crux of understanding the Christian life was the realization that we shape life by our belief and trust in the life that is to follow. For Christians who were being persecuted, such an understanding would help them make some sense of their suffering. According to Paul, at the judgment seat of Christ, each person will receive that which they deserve according to the life they have lived while in her or his earthly body. Our burdens are only temporary and serve the greater cause of Christ in the world now so that in the world to come we will have our heavenly dwelling. God's Holy Spirit acts as the guarantor of this promise and the source of our strength from this time until the end.

Certainly, through this text, we get a sense of Paul's urgency—that the Parousia was soon to come. The really tough issue for the preacher today is how to convey that same sense of urgency to a culture that believes they have all the time they need to get life right. The hook, it seems to me, is to focus on the transitory nature of this life we live. The common thread for all human beings is that we have been, or will be, surprised by life. When my father committed suicide, I received a call from a minister friend of mine. He told me my whole life had prepared me for this moment. I believe this is the heart of what Paul is saying in this powerful passage. Life now is preparation for something yet to come.

The greatest temptation for us is to get caught up in the appearances of life. Paul refutes this, urging us to live not by sight but by faith. Our faith is grounded and rooted in the preparation given to us in God's Holy Spirit, even in the midst of this life. That preparation becomes the bedrock foundation for building our lives. This should not surprise us. When we look at great athletes, great musicians, great authors, great surgeons, we see commonality in their preparation for whatever challenges may come. As Christians, God uses the gift of the Holy Spirit as our preparation for that which will come in eternity. That is a guarantee we must come to know, to trust, and to follow. With the goal of pleasing Christ, we seek to live from moment to moment, aided by our undying trust in and dedication to the Holy Spirit's leading.

Again, this is a difficult passage to preach to a culture that thinks it has everything. Even death has been institutionalized to the point that people have lost touch with the finality of dying. It would be interesting to see what Paul would do with the message of this text in such a culture. The community to which Paul preached was under persecution and that reality certainly shaped his message, with its contrast between the temporary and the eternal. Today, we might want to use the example of 9/11 to remind the listeners of the unexpectedness with which life moves and works. Where were you on 9/11? How prepared was the United States for such an event? Maybe our lack of preparation was due, in part, to the belief that something like this would never happen here, to us.

How prepared are we for the unexpectedness of life and its finality? Do we live with a sense of gratitude, a sense of awe, a sense of the importance of this moment, or a sense of how God's Holy Spirit is preparing us for what is to follow? As we heard the stories of those on the doomed flights, who made phone calls in the face of their finality, we were gripped by their eloquence in expressions of love, of meaning, of gratitude. The finality of life greets each of us, whether we are prepared for it or not. How prepared we are seems to be a relevant question to ask ourselves. For Paul, the end of life, our expectation of it, and our sense of its reality is what must, in some way, shape us in the lives we live in this moment. To live without that end in mind leaves us ill-prepared for what will follow. Preparation is rarely easy, and yet preparation is essential for any life lived well. (Travis Franklin)

Worship Aids

Call to Worship

Be humble before the Lord. Serve God with humility and contrite hearts. Worship God with bowed knees and open hearts. Come to God's house and worship.

Litany (Based on Psalm 91)

Leader: The God who gave birth to life,

People: Will protect those who call.

Leader: Accept the gift of God.

People: Claim the gift of life.
(Gary G. Kindley)

Prayer of Confession

As we complete the "dog days" of August, O Lord of the universe, help us anticipate another autumn in your holy presence. We have often failed to be your people. We have done many things for which we ask your divine forgiveness, but worse yet are the many places in our lives where we might have spoken a good word or done an act of charity—but did not. We have failed to be your sovereign people. Forgive us our pasts and open us to new futures in the world you created for us to be stewards over. In the name of Jesus we pray. Amen. (David N. Mosser)

Benediction

May peace be with you. May God go with you. May love transform you. Amen. (Gary G. Kindley)

SEPTEMBER 2, 2007

❧❧❧

Fourteenth Sunday after Pentecost

Readings: Jeremiah 2:4-13; Psalm 81:1, 10-16; Hebrews 13:1-8, 15-16; Luke 14:1, 7-14

The Preferred Method of Distraction
Jeremiah 2:4-13

Like most ministers, I receive a large number of unsolicited publications in the mail, addressing every conceivable aspect of running a church. These include scriptural and spiritual resources as well as technological and business aids. Most of these are immediately tossed into my circular file. One day, however, while I stood over the trash bin, a professional journal caught my interest. It concerned church marketing, specifically church "branding"; the cover photo featured a large, newly built, and "branded" church.

As with many new church structures, this one displayed no exterior markings or iconography. There was no steeple, no "churchy" windows, no cross, not even a church designation, save what appeared to be a neon circle "brand" encompassing two letters, evidently the initials of the church's name. In this case, the brand looked very much like what might appear on cattle. In keeping with the popular non-churchy design style, one could mistake this architecture for either a store or an office. So far, nothing unusual or disturbing—certainly, authentic worship takes place in malls and office complexes.

What caught my eye on this otherwise-nondescript building was a massive American flag that overwhelmed the entryway. This was the undeniable advertisement the building offered. If I had not been looking at a church resource, I might very well have assumed this magazine came from a political or governmental organization. The fact that this particular church was featured on the cover lent a professional imprimatur.

A friend of mine returned from visiting a very successful and well-known church constructed in a similar commercial style, and reported a conversation with one of the pastors. My friend commented to him that nowhere outside or inside the space did he see any religious iconography, not even a single cross. The pastor responded in a low, conspiratorial tone, "Well, quite frankly, the cross doesn't market very well in today's culture."

I can't argue with that. Evidently, the flag does market well. That seems the inevitable conclusion from this anecdotal evidence. I have no way of knowing for certain the sort of theology found on the inside of the "flag church," but there is no question their "brand" is strategically associated with one of the most powerful cultural icons in the United States—and it's not the cross. Church and state have evidently found a common cause in that house of worship.

This entire circumstance caused me to catch my breath. I am a patriot, that is, a person who loves his country and strives for its betterment; I would even give my life for it, I imagine. But I do not worship it. I'm sure the folks at that church would say they don't worship it either, but looking at their home church, one could easily and naturally wonder about that.

This small catch of breath caused me to consider the nature of my own allegiances. After all, I have a very well-developed capacity for finger-pointing. It's a sobering discipline for ministers and congregations alike to take stock of their fealty to the God who is above all gods and who will be second to none.

This consideration is an inevitable outcome if we give serious attention to the word of the Lord as it came to Jeremiah. This prophet's principal concern is that the house of Israel has taken up with gods other than the Lord, who brought them forth from Egypt, led them through the wilderness, and presented a rich land to them—a land inhabited by other peoples who worshiped other gods. Overwhelmed by such distractions, it was easy to lose track of their principal allegiance, giving it over to "things that do not profit" (see Jeremiah 2:11).

The logic found in the phrase "Has a nation changed its gods, even though they are no gods?" (v. 11) could be twisted into a reason to advance a nationalistic agenda in the hands of those who misread the text. The point is not to elevate the nation to an exalted status, but rather to elevate authentic divinity so the nation may have its proper identity read "humility." We can never place God before us and above us too often, for secondary matters insinuate themselves into primary status with relentless regularity. How to stay constant to the fundamental allegiance, how to keep God first is the principal discipline for those who say they live by faith.

This prompts a frank assessment of the content of our worship. Our people have more than ample opportunity for bedazzlement by the cultural iconography of the day. There is a fine line to be drawn between using cultural means to attract persons into faithful relationship with the living God and worshiping the means to the end.

Our people have ample opportunity for therapeutic environments; indeed, I often recommend them. What they lack is opportunity to hear from and about the One who inflated their lungs with breath in the first place. This One is owed our principal focus and allegiance. The church is the only place that owns this obligation. We cannot deny that its voice and intent are often smothered by cultural accretions.

There are many ways this happens. It's a brave and faithful minister who will consider the preferred method of distraction in her/his own congregation. (Stephen Bauman)

Participation

Second in a Series of Three: Living for Today

2 Corinthians 5:11-15

Much of what we find in Paul's letter to the church at Corinth is a defense of his ministry to the Corinthians. Certainly we see this apologetic shaping his thought in today's passage. Although we are not privy to all of the accusations that people brought against Paul, we sense Paul's aggressive response as he articulates his theology in this letter. Paul even suggests that, if he is crazy, it is for God. Paul seeks to give the church at Corinth reason to boast about him and others who presented the gospel there. As part of his defense, we see Paul remind his listeners it is the love of Christ that controls what has been said and done there. Paul then lays down the foundation of this Christology as he reminds them of the sacrifice of Christ on their behalf and the resurrection reality of him who had died but now lives. The heart and soul of Paul's defense is his confident assertion that what has motivated all that has been done is the love of Christ. For Paul this must be the litmus test of any authentic witness of faith.

Control is and has been an issue for human beings since the origin of time. It is control that now provides fodder for Paul as he speaks to the truthfulness of his Christian witness of faith. In this passage Paul wants the church to understand that the power of a person's life is determined by what controls it. He begins by reminding the readers that the whole nature of the gospel is one of witness and persuasion. He rests his defense on the fact that he is known by God and should also be known by them. Based upon such knowledge, Paul invites those in the church to answer critics from their knowledge of his character. Since Paul cannot be there to offer his own defense, he seeks the partnership and witness of those who have known him and who willingly speak on his behalf.

Control by the love of Christ is the foundation of Christian character. Through participation in Christ's death and resurrection we are now freed to live, not for ourselves but for Christ, who has died and risen from the dead. In identifying our nature with the work of Christ, we become controlled by his nature of selflessness for the sake of others. This Christ control becomes the source of our every decision and action. Such living becomes an expression of Christ's love in a way that embodies all this love means. For Paul, nothing must get in the way of this new life. Time, energy, and work are now directed toward this lone goal. The application of Christ's love becomes a preparation for glory, which is soon to come. Paul's credentials are his own living out of the love of Christ in his witness among the Corinthians. This is the heart and soul of his apologetic to those who would question the authority of Paul's witness to the gospel of Christ.

One of the greatest contributions of Pauline theology to the church is Paul's idea that God invites persons to participate with God in the work God is doing in the world. We see this concept articulated by Paul as he encourages the Corinthians to "live no longer for themselves, but for him who died and was raised for them" (2 Corinthians 5:15).

Paul implores these new converts to allow Christ's love to so control them that they join him in living for others' salvation. This invitation is at the heart of how Paul understood the Christian's response to God's work in Christ for the world.

I offer here an idea of invitation. We receive many invitations: to parties, to church, to supper, to a new job, to do all sorts of things, and to buy all sorts of goods. Paul invites us to give ourselves to God's redemptive work in the death and resurrection of Christ by allowing the love of Christ to control who we are and what we do. Paul's passionate defense of his work among the Corinthians is founded upon this idea.

The test of our Christian life must measure up to the controlling nature of Christ's love. This love compels us to participate with Christ in his ongoing redemptive work in the world today. In God's kingdom everyone is invited to play; all are encouraged to use their God-given gifts to make a difference in the world. Controlled by the love of Christ, God calls each person to the service of others for the sake of Christ's redeeming work. Which of us has not known the anxiety of wanting to be chosen to join something we thought important? Who among us has not worried and questioned, "Will they pick me?" In the kingdom of God there is no need to worry. God is calling you and me to come and to join in the work of eternity. (Travis Franklin)

Worship Aids

Call to Worship

Leader: We open the doors of our lives to let in the Creator.

People: We open the doors of our hearts to let in the Redeemer.

Leader: We open the doors of our minds to let in the Sustainer.

All: We come together with lives, hearts, and minds open to what God might be doing and what God may yet do. Let us listen and look for God together.

Pastoral Prayer (Labor Day Weekend)

Creator God, who both labored and rested at the dawn of our being, on this Labor Day weekend, we pause from our tasks and obligations and gather for worship. We know that we cannot undertake life's journey alone—we truly need you and one another. On this day, as a people of faith, we acknowledge our need. Work through our lives that blessings may be born from our existence. Work through our efforts that grace may come from our deeds. Give us rest from our weariness and give us strength for each new day as we live as disciples who are leaders for Jesus the Christ. Amen.

Benediction

Be laborers in the world for the service of Christ. Go and make disciples! Amen. (Gary G. Kindley)

SEPTEMBER 9, 2007

❧❧❧

Fifteenth Sunday after Pentecost

Readings: Jeremiah 18:1-11; Psalm 139:1-6, 13-18; Philemon 1-21;
Luke 14:25-33

The Real Deal
Jeremiah 18:1-11; Luke 14:25-33

Coming right off vacation, these are not the texts I would choose for
this Sunday. But that's what happens sometimes when following the discipline of the church's scriptural calendar. I would be more in the frame
of mind to share some stories from the golf course, even report how my
game improved over the summer, or perhaps relate some lovely life lesson
gleaned from travels or sailing.

But I surely cannot do that after hearing Jeremiah announce that Israel
is like a clay pot forming in the hands of God, who is about to decide
whether or not he should break it down and start again; and hearing Jesus
proclaim that I should hate my father, mother, wife and children, brothers and sisters, even life itself. Even if I might twist this into a snappy and
cynically appealing message, it wouldn't blend well with small talk, or
spiritually clever but finally inconsequential reflections from my summer
meanderings and musings.

No, these texts are about tough talk. They feel like too much, too soon,
so early in the new program year. They seem more appropriate for a study
during Lent, but then only if deemed absolutely necessary. If the church
is to reach people where they are, I imagine they are still in summer
mode, still wanting to wring out a few more days or weeks of diverting
activity, still desiring to consider nothing more demanding than whether
to indulge in a mint-chip or butter-pecan ice-cream cone.

Yet here we find ourselves pondering what theologians refer to as
"the cost of discipleship," and that sounds the opposite of "summertime
sentimental."

I am intrigued that the Gospel lesson starts this way: "Now large crowds were traveling with him" (Luke 14:25). I take this to mean, by this point in his sojourn, Jesus had developed quite a following. He had made a name for himself and had gained in popularity. Jesus must have had an appealing, even comforting message.

That's how it works today, after all. Marketing experts surely counsel clients that in the sale of their products it is important to give the people what they want. Figure that out, and you are three-quarters of the way to a successful sale. Find just the right set of words, with just the right tone that meets the people right where they are, and a clever person could sell just about anything—that's what we are led to believe. In addition, we have seen enough bald success with flimsy products to know there is truth in this advice. Politicians have certainly discovered the power of modern marketing in pitching their personalities, for instance.

The American church has caught on to this postmodern mode of thinking and selling, or should I say, evangelizing. Perhaps like you, I struggle with these issues. They are wrapped up in the mottled skin of relevancy, generational preferences, and outright pandering—but back to Jesus.

As the storyteller has it, Jesus seems at the height of his popularity. It won't be long before he passes through the gates of Jerusalem for the fateful Passover celebration that will lead him to ignominy and death as a traitor to the state. Right here, as he is reaching his peak popularity with his biggest crowd in tow, he pulls this cockamamy statement out of rather thin air. Where is his copy editor or speechwriter? Jesus is a smart guy, so doesn't he know enough to give the people what they want? And he follows that one up by saying whoever does not carry a cross and follow him cannot be his disciple. I guess Jesus really doesn't want that many disciples as it turns out.

Surely what the people think they want doesn't have anything to do with hating every important person in their lives. The same could be said of every subsequent generation up to the present one. It forces the conclusion that just this sort of statement twisted his popularity into its opposite during the last week of his life. Up to a point he was compelling, but then Jesus managed to go and wreck his advantage by saying things that just went too far.

Here, we should clear up a problem associated with translating an ancient language into the modern. The word *hate* in this passage is not our emotionally laden word for personal disgust but, rather, a Semitic idiom expressing a kind of detachment. The phrase concerns relative allegiances, not aggressive loathing.

Shortly after Jesus' death and continuing year after year, attentive, thoughtful people discovered something crucial about Jesus' witness; he was never motivated by a desire for personal advantage. Jesus seemed genuinely motivated by the needs of those around him; by the profoundest needs even they had not yet recognized lurking in the dark depths. From start to finish, Jesus relentlessly advanced the things that matter most. Like the prophet Jeremiah, Jesus too yanked people out of their complacency. He was on a mission to awaken the better angels of their nature, and more, to literally turn them into something different, something closer to the heart of God, something like a perfect specimen from a potter's wheel. Evidently Jesus knew instinctively this would not be easy and might very well cost him his own life.

Jesus walked the razor's edge and spoke the truth. Above all other commitments, one was paramount. If God is, then, logically, nothing else can supplant God. That is so even if we wish it were not. If I were to say the moon is made of green cheese, even believing that with all my heart would not change the facts. Jesus lays bare the facts. In this case he says to his admirers that if they wish to follow along his path, they better know the real deal. It was going to cost them something—something very, very important. (Stephen Bauman)

Perspective

Third in a Series of Three: Living for Today

2 Corinthians 5:16-21

In today's text Paul clearly identifies what God's saving work in Christ does in the lives of God's people. Christ's death for all people not only requires a change of lifestyle but, more important, a change of perspective. Through the redemptive work of Christ, a new perspective becomes the source of how to live life. Once a person is "in Christ," everything changes. Because Christ has died for all, and has been resurrected for all, nothing in life will ever be the same again. That which is old has passed, and this new thing God has done and is doing in Christ creates a new way of seeing and doing. A new perspective has radically replaced the former perspective.

Paul's images are vibrant and alive as they describe in detail this radical re-creation of life. Paul relates that the fate of the world hinges on the fulcrum of Christ's death and resurrection. History will never be the same again. Paul wants his listeners to understand that God's work in Christ, while begun on the cross and the empty tomb, continues as an ongoing reordering of life and the world. Paul also invites people in this new order to join God in God's ongoing work of reconciling the world to himself. Make no mistake about it; the new perspective is from God. We can sense Paul building upon the foundation he laid earlier in his discussion of eternal life. Our participation with God in this work is controlled by the love of Christ throughout. Paul then fleshes out the nature of this ministry God calls us to do.

This new perspective is grounded in God's reconciling work in Christ, through his death and resurrection. Once a person is "in Christ," they no longer see in the same way, they no longer act in the same way, for they have been reconciled to God. They are now committed to being Christ's representatives in the world.

Paul identifies two ways in which the death and resurrection of Christ affect people. First, people who have been reconciled to God are new creations; the old is gone forever. This redemption means they no longer see in the same way. Human beings have a new perspective with the ongoing reconciling work of God as the new source of that perspective. Second, as a new creation, the redeemed now join God in the reconciling work of Christ. These people become Christ's representatives to a hurting world in desperate need of God's salvation. The redeemed now are participants with God in sharing the message of reconciliation with all the world. Controlled by the love of Christ and preparing for what is to come, they now join in God's saving work in the world.

We should think about this idea of perspective. Can we understand the importance of the interdependent relationship between seeing and behavior? How one sees often determines how one behaves. How many times have we based our actions upon false assumptions? I remember watching a fight between two of my junior high teammates after football practice. One of the kids had a reputation for being tough. I assumed he was a bad kid, into the wrong kind of behavior. It was within the character I had imposed on him to be in a fight—after all, that is what "those types of kids" do. In my freshman year in high school, I played basketball and, once again, this same student was on the team. After one of our games, he and I began to talk; I discovered that he was a devoted Christian. After a while we started to hang out at school together; we soon became best friends, and he became a powerful influence on my life. Many times, our perspectives are in great need of change.

Paul wants us to reorient our perspectives to the viewpoint of Christ. The human point of view is in great need of such reorientation.

For example, would anyone who walked through the door of our church be welcome? I work with at-risk youth in a chaplaincy setting. A student showed me his seventh-grade transcript, where a teacher had written that he would not graduate from high school. Not only did this student graduate from high school, he received a full scholarship to college. Paul is right. It is time we stopped thinking from a human point of view. Perspective determines who we are and how we live. What is your perspective? (Travis Franklin)

Worship Aids

Call to Worship

Now is the time. Here is the place. Love is the reason. Great is the need. Worship God with hearts of praise and gratitude.

Invocation

Heavenly and eternal God, your transcendent power is what we invoke this day. Lift us up to rise above the trials and tragedies of human existence. Remind us that we are spiritual beings on a physical journey. Open our eyes to see the transcendence of your grace. Amen.

Pastoral Prayer

For the beauty and freshness of each new dawn, we give thanks to you, Creator God. For the food on our tables, the clothes in our closets, and a place to call home, we give thanks to you, sustaining God. For your redeeming presence in times of joy and times of tears, in days of youth and years of maturity, in moments of ease and hours of challenge, in good times and bad times, in sickness and in health, we give thanks to you, Redeemer God.

Forgive us when we ignore you, deny you, forget you, or disobey you. Constrain us when we are headstrong, enlighten us in times of ignorance, and redeem us when our journeys yield hopelessness and despair.

We pray for others who are on our hearts *[pray in silence]*, and we pray for those whose names we do not know, whose plights we do not share, but whose needs are genuine and desperate.

Thank you, listening God, for hearing our prayer, offering your grace, and blessing our lives. In Christ's name we offer this prayer. Amen. (Gary G. Kindley)

SEPTEMBER 16, 2007

❧❧❧

Sixteenth Sunday after Pentecost

Readings: Jeremiah 4:11-12, 22-28; Psalm 14; 1 Timothy 1:12-17;
Luke 15:1-10

The Flicker of Hope
Jeremiah 4:11-12, 22-28

I just knew I was hopelessly lost that day. As a young boy, I sometimes
would find myself separated from my mother when we were out shopping,
but this was different. We were in a department store in Dallas, Texas,
and I wandered away from my mother's side. Just when I realized I was lost
and began looking for my mother, suddenly the lights went out in the
store. Little did we know that a storm had come upon the area, and in a
sudden flash of lightning and thunder, everyone was in the dark.

I began to panic as I called for my mom from beneath a flood of tears.
Just then I saw it at the end of the aisle. It was the tiny flicker from a small
flashlight. It was almost indiscernible, but it was a light nonetheless. I
walked and then began running for that light. Holding the light was a
woman who worked in the store, and she had heard my cry of distress.
She had also heard my mother calling my name, and with her little light
she was able to bring me to my mother. Tiny as the light was, it was a beacon of hope amid my hopeless despair.

Jeremiah is talking to the people about their sin. His proclamation is of
desolation that comes from the ruinous sin of the people. His point is
clear: the people are corrupt; even the wisdom given them by God is corrupt. In Jeremiah 4:22, the prophet tells the people that they are without
understanding; they are stupid and foolish. Jeremiah acknowledges that
the people have some wisdom, but it is not the wisdom of God. In a clever
play on words, he writes that they have wisdom or skill in doing evil even
when they lack the wisdom or skill to do good.

Jeremiah paints the picture of desolation that is before the people. In an image that reminds us of the creation account in Genesis 1, we see a world that is "waste and void" (Jeremiah 4:23). The mountains and hills are rocking back and forth as if they have no foundation. The people are all gone, there are no animals, and everything looks like a desert. Everything is desolate and hopeless.

This is a difficult message to preach. We are people who look for the good news in everything. Even over the years as I have told my story of being lost, people know, as the story begins, that everything will turn out all right at the end. Surely there is a message of hope, yet we read of the earth mourning and the heavens growing black. There is no escape from judgment.

Just as we give up hope, however, there it is; a tiny flicker of hope nestled among the verses. It is not the last verse in this pericope; it is hidden at the end of verse 27: "The whole land shall be a desolation; yet I will not make a full end." It isn't much, but it is hope.

Jeremiah's message speaks strongly to my experience of the world. Ours is a world where people do not practice the kind of wisdom that leads us to God. Instead, we are busy using our wisdom and skill for sin and corruption. We create advanced technologies for war and destruction, and the creativity and wisdom put toward those ends seem to outweigh the creativity and wisdom put toward ending worldwide hunger and disease.

We ingeniously discover ways to have more things for ourselves, yet we seem to lack the creativity and skill to deal with societal issues such as chronic unemployment or homelessness. Ours is a world that seems bent on destruction.

The good news is that the compassion and love of God for the children of God cannot ultimately be thwarted. In the Gospel lesson accompanying this text from Jeremiah, Jesus' parables of the lost sheep and the lost coin confront us. In those stories, the one who is lost is the one who gets the full attention of God. A careful reading of those stories will help us see that, no matter how cut off or hopeless we may be, God will never give up on us.

It is fitting that, while God's judgment must be carried out against our world of sin, ultimately, it is the creative power of God that will not give up on us. When the world was "a formless void" (Genesis 1:2) without much hope, God acted, and creation unfolded bearing the mark and the image of the divine. Likewise, when our world comes to that same place of chaotic hopelessness with the pall of judgment cast over us, we are reminded that God will not, finally, forsake us.

The lesson I learned from being lost was that I was not capable of getting out of trouble on my own. I was still dependent upon my mother and the kind lady with the little flashlight. Likewise, it seems that our encounters with God's judgment serve as a reminder that our own wisdom is not sufficient. We cannot save ourselves; we are ultimately dependent upon God to bring us to the fullness of life.

In a strange way, judgment comes as a gift. It is a gift that reminds us we are dependent upon God. It is a gift that reminds us to look for the small flicker of hope that God will use to lead us out of the darkness. (Jeffrey Smith)

Leadership without Fear

First in a Series of Three: Biblical Leadership

2 Samuel 5:1-5

Max DePree begins his book *Leadership Jazz* with a story about his granddaughter. Zoe was born prematurely, weighing one pound seven ounces, and was placed in neonatal intensive care. Since her biological father was not around, the nurse asked Depree to visit Zoe each day, for several months. "And when you come I would like you to rub her body and her legs and arms with the tip of your finger. While you're caressing her, you should tell her over and over how much you love her, because she has to be able to connect your voice to your touch" (Max DePree, *Leadership Jazz* [New York: Dell Publishing, 1992], 2).

Leadership is about making connections and influencing people. Good leadership requires the ability to connect with another's soul.

The literature on leadership is voluminous and inexact. No list of leadership characteristics is exhaustive. Some of the most common characteristics include integrity, courage, a powerful presence, adaptability, and discernment. Some characteristics seem to be innate while others can be learned.

This sermon series is born from the question of whether faith has a relationship to leadership ability. Certainly, people of faith have been strong leaders, such as Martin Luther King Jr. What does our faith tradition teach us about leadership, and is there something from our faith tradition that could help us become better leaders?

We begin with what Hebrew tradition teaches us about leadership, focusing primarily on King David. Next, because leadership has a selfless, futuristic quality to it, we focus on the evangelistic efforts of the apostles Paul and Peter. Finally, Jesus himself can teach us much about leadership.

A universally accepted quality of leadership is the leader's ability to articulate a vision. The shared vision of the nation of Israel begins with God's covenant with Abraham, leading to the promised land. All leadership in Hebrew literature is spiritually based. Leaders are called by God to fulfill the overall vision for God's people. God proclaims to Moses and to Pharaoh, "Israel is my firstborn son" (Exodus 4:22). And, while Abraham, Moses, and the prophets are important instruments in fulfilling the covenant, Israel's leadership history centers on King David. The Gospel writers recognize the importance of King David and are intentional about connecting Jesus to that tradition.

What characteristics of leadership do we find in King David? How can they inform our own leadership style?

It has been said that leaders are visionaries with a poorly developed sense of fear. From an early age, David displayed courage.

When faced with the giant Goliath of Gath, all Israel, except David, was afraid. David made his way to the battlefield, against his family's will, and convinced King Saul that he could defeat the Philistine. David prevailed over the Philistine with only a sling and a stone.

David's courage brought great respect from the people of Israel and jealousy from Saul. Saul sought to kill David. David was compassionate, however, and spared Saul's life more than once. Throughout the story, David displays great respect for tradition, especially respect for the office of king.

His respect for tradition helped David build coalitions. David was able to unify Israel, north and south, because of his leadership ability and because he helped Israel recognize its commonality. "For some time, while Saul was king over us, it was you who led out Israel and brought it in" (2 Samuel 5:2). At Hebron, all the elders of Israel made covenant with David to be their king.

David was also able to develop other leaders. He gave Joab responsibility for the army, made Jehoshaphat a recorder, and several others he made priests. Those who lead without fear are able to share responsibilities and power; David was fearless.

David's compassion and loyalty are also celebrated in Hebrew literature. He remembered his covenant with Saul to not cut off Saul's family, and he remembered his friendship with Saul's son Jonathan. David gave Saul's land to Jonathan's son and extended hospitality to him. David was a servant leader, a concept we will develop later in the series.

From his confrontation with Goliath through his reign as king, David was driven by his relationship with God. David's service to Israel was faith-based.

While David is held in high esteem in Hebrew tradition, his human vulnerability is also recognized. In the middle of David's reign is the story of his encounter with Bathsheba. David not only committed adultery but made the leader of his army, Joab, complicit in the murder of Bathsheba's husband, Uriah. The prophet Nathan calls David to account for his sin, and David seeks and finds forgiveness in God.

Leaders are not perfect. David's sin, Moses' inability to speak clearly, and each prophet's shortcomings indicate that leaders in the faith are able to transcend human weaknesses.

Without fear, David accepts God's call to leadership. He is grounded in a relationship with God and performs his leadership responsibilities with integrity. Just as Max DePree helps his newborn granddaughter connect his voice with his touch, the nation of Israel finds integrity in David's leadership. Grounded in the faith, this servant of God works for justice and equity for all Israel. The uniqueness of David's leadership is his lack of fear and his reliance on faith.

From David we learn that leaders are courageous and grounded. He was more than an embodiment of the shared vision of Israel. David helped shape the community through building covenant and developing other leaders. David is a model of fearless leadership because he was able to bring Israel together in order to achieve God's vision for Israel. (Dan L. Flanagan)

Worship Aids

Invocation

Eternal Sovereign, the very nature of your existence requires faith to accept. There is an enormous chasm of doubt that often stands between you and your children. Help us to bridge that gap. Reconnect us to your power, love, and mercy that we might walk beside you. At those times when the burden of our human journey is unbearable, carry us onward, we pray. In the name of the One who is divine love, amen. (Gary G. Kindley)

Prayer for Enlightenment

Gracious God, you who are more willing to listen than we are to pray, listen to the heartfelt cries of our lives before you. Give us the wisdom and discernment to hear your fresh word spoken to us today in the prayers, hymns, special choir music, and sermon on this Sabbath day. Speak to us once again the words of life. In the name of Jesus we pray. Amen. (David N. Mosser)

Words of Assurance

The God of redemptive love hears those who ask forgiveness. Claim God's grace. Live in God's mercy. Forgive yourself and others. Amen.

Benediction

You have a mission. You have a purpose. You have the power. You have the gifts. Get busy! Amen. (Gary G. Kindley)

SEPTEMBER 23, 2007

❧❧❧

Seventeenth Sunday after Pentecost

Readings: Jeremiah 8:18–9:1; Psalm 79:1-9; 1 Timothy 2:1-7; Luke 16:1-13

A Compassionate God
Jeremiah 8:18–9:1

Israel was experiencing a drought. It was a drought unlike any that had come before. Ancient Israel, like most cultures of the ancient world, was an agrarian society that relied heavily upon the weather for survival. This year, when it came time for the rains to water their crops, the rains did not come. The people were "not saved" (Jeremiah 8:20); they were left hopeless.

In truth, the drought is a symbol of the total alienation and despair experienced by the people. The drought is nothing less than the absence of God. The prophet weeps for the people in their despair. The prophet experiences the same isolation and alienation as the people do. The prophet desires nothing more than to see the people restored and brought to a place of hope.

I can remember times in my life when I experienced such drought and felt the utter absence of God. One such time came during a very low period in my ministry when I realized that the church I was serving and I were quickly coming to a place where we could not continue in our relationship. I was a young, inexperienced pastor, and the church had major issues that turned out to be more than I could handle.

In an effort to deal with the situation, I turned to others I thought would help me. I found little help. I was losing my self-confidence, and I was seriously beginning to doubt whether I was really called to the ministry of the ordained. One critical night, I was feeling despondent. I felt as if God had completely abandoned me. I wrote in my journal about the emptiness I was experiencing and about how it felt as if I were completely surrounded by evil. It was as if God had unleashed evil completely in the world and then left me alone and hopeless amid it all. Ironically, that night was Halloween.

What I did not know until much later was that God had never left me. On the night that God seemed so absent, I fell asleep on the couch only to be awakened by a ringing telephone. It was my wife and son, who had traveled to be with family for the weekend. I distinctly remember the comforting words of my wife, and the gently spoken "I love you" of our eighteen-month-old son. God was there, speaking to me through those who loved me even though I was unable to hear it at the time.

When we read this passage from Jeremiah, it is easy to assume that we are hearing the prophet's own words. Jeremiah has lost his joy. Grief encompasses him as he hears the cries of the people. It is Jeremiah who is hurt because the people are hurt. He only desires to cure the people of their suffering. Jeremiah is the one who wishes that his "head were a spring of water" and his "eyes a fountain of tears" (9:1) so that the drought might end. Jeremiah, we think, is the one who responds compassionately to the plight of the people. But is it really Jeremiah whose voice we hear in this story?

In truth, a very strong case can be made that this is the voice of God resounding through the voice of the prophet. The God we encountered last week bringing judgment upon the people is the same God who weeps for the people in the midst of judgment.

I can remember a time as an adolescent when I made a very poor decision and found myself in a lot of trouble. My parents determined the consequences and carried out the sentence. During the time I was grounded, I missed an important ball game and band contest. My parents were sad about it. At one point, my mother cried as we talked about what this had cost me. The thought occurred to me more than once that if they would just reverse the sentence and take away the consequences, all of us would be a lot happier. For some reason, however, they were simply unwilling to consider that option.

The truth was, even though my parents were unwilling to alter the consequences of my actions, they did not abandon me. They stayed with me and cared for me and cried for me and loved me. Through it all, I learned the true value of parental love.

It is that same love God has for the children of Israel, expressed through Jeremiah's words of compassion. It is the same love God expressed in the person of Jesus. I am always moved by the passage in

Matthew and Luke where Jesus is looking over the city of Jerusalem and saying, "Jerusalem, Jerusalem, the city that kills the prophets and stones those who are sent to it! How often have I desired to gather your children together as a hen gathers her brood under her wings, and you were not willing!" (Matthew 23:37; Luke 13:34).

God's care and compassion are like that of a mother hen who seeks to gather her chicks beneath her wings in the midst of a storm or other violent threat. This is the God who is present with Israel and Jeremiah, and present with us even now.

As we experience a world where bad things happen, the gospel message for us is that God is here. When we hurt, God hurts with us. When we grieve, God grieves with us. It is God who sustains us, and it is God who sees us through the most desperate times. That is why God's name, Immanuel, is so full of meaning for us. God is with us, offering compassion and love. Thanks be to God! (Jeffrey Smith)

Franchising Leadership

Second in a Series of Three: Biblical Leadership

Acts 15:2-12

Our success as leaders has something to do with the roles we play. In the original casting of *Butch Cassidy and the Sundance Kid*, Paul Newman was to play Sundance and Robert Redford, Butch. The director's reversal of their roles points to an important aspect of leadership.

Church history tells us that Peter and Paul played the most significant roles in its early postresurrection development. They were responsible for the church's growth.

If all we had was the Gospel characterization of Peter, we would be asking how this man ever became a leader in the church. Jesus saw qualities in Peter that led him to say, "And I tell you, you are Peter, and on this rock I will build my church" (Matthew 16:18).

The Gospel picture of Peter is of an impetuous man. Jesus questioned Peter's faith when Peter failed to walk on water. When Peter rebuked Jesus, Jesus referred to him as Satan. Peter boldly claimed he would never desert Jesus, then proceeded to deny Jesus three times. Peter cut off a soldier's ear in a moment of anger.

By contrast, there are glimpses of the future Peter in the Gospels. It is Peter who proclaims Jesus to be the Messiah, the Son of the living God. Peter speaks for the disciples at the Transfiguration, in awe and reverence.

Peter and John are the first of the twelve disciples to reach the empty tomb.

In the book of Acts we see the Peter with leadership ability whom Jesus saw. Still impetuous, the Peter of Acts is the rock, the leader who, transformed by the Holy Spirit, proves to be a faithful and passionate evangelist.

At Pentecost, it is Peter who steps forth to proclaim the gospel, leading to the conversion of three thousand people in one day. He heals a lame man and raises Dorcas from the dead. After some hesitation, Peter champions the cause of Gentiles within the Christian faith. Roman and Jewish authorities were "amazed" (Acts 4:13) when they witnessed the boldness of this uneducated and ordinary man.

Peter, like King David, was fearless as a leader. The Holy Spirit was the motivating factor in Peter's becoming the foundation of the church. Peter was respected, and his leadership led to thousands of conversions.

The apostle Paul was an itinerant minister who identified and supported leaders in outposts throughout the Mediterranean. He unabashedly challenged Hebrews and Gentiles, and relied on his own Hebrew and Roman connections. As did David and Peter, Paul seemed fearless, both as a persecutor of Christians and as a Christian evangelist.

Before his conversion, Paul (or Saul, as he was called then) carried the authority of Jewish law as a Pharisee against Christians, persecuting the church. He was passionate in his persecutions, and greatly feared by the Christian community.

While Saul was "still breathing threats and murder against the disciples of the Lord" (Acts 9:1), he met Jesus in a vision while on the road to Damascus. The blinding light and voice of Jesus redirected Saul's passion. The same Pharisaic fire existed—the same fearless pursuit of his passion—but now as one who proclaimed the gospel of Jesus Christ. He immediately began to proclaim the gospel in synagogues, and "all who heard him were amazed" (Acts 9:21). They were also afraid; the disciples were slow to accept this Pharisee who had persecuted them.

Meanwhile, Paul's power within the Christian movement increased. He would enter the synagogue of each community and challenge the Jews with the gospel. While gaining converts, Paul also gained enemies within the Jewish community. He was imprisoned and threatened, and sometimes stealthily removed for his safety. Paul was skilled in rhetoric and delighted in challenging nonbelievers in the gospel. He had a great vision of spreading the gospel even into Spain (see Romans 15:24, 28).

Paul's greatest contribution to biblical leadership was in developing other leaders. His traveling companions included early church leaders such as Barnabas, Timothy, Silas, and Apollos. Within each church, named leaders were always left behind, with whom Paul maintained communication. He franchised the church.

Given the geography Paul covered, the multitude of cultures he encountered, and his skill in working with many different personalities, Paul displayed tremendous adaptability. He used everything at his disposal to spread the gospel, including his Roman citizenship and his standing as a Pharisee.

Early on, Paul and Peter found themselves on opposite sides of the Gentile debate. Should Gentiles be circumcised before they could become Christians? When Paul found resistance in the synagogues, he quickly moved outside to the Gentiles, which created controversy within the Christian community in Jerusalem. It was Peter who brought the church together in its ministry to Gentiles, assuring the Jerusalem summit that "God, who knows the human heart, testified to them by giving them the Holy Spirit, just as he did to us; and in cleansing their hearts by faith he has made no distinction between them and us" (Acts 15:8-9).

Peter and Paul were key leaders in the early church, each powerful in his own way. Peter's leadership developed through mentoring by Jesus. The postresurrection Jesus chose Paul because of his authority and innate ability of persuasion.

We might have missed their potential as leaders. Jesus simply drew from them what they had to offer. Leaders are able to identify leadership potential in others and develop it, to place people in appropriate roles.

Leadership is often more primitive than scientific. How could an ordinary fisherman and a murdering Pharisee become the seed by which the church of Jesus Christ sprouts? Peter brings his fierce loyalty and boyish emotion to his ministry. Paul brings authority, the skill of disciple-making, and his rhetorical skill. God was able to cast them well, and to motivate them through the Holy Spirit. (Dan L. Flanagan)

Worship Aids

Invocation

On this Sabbath, we approach God's table and altar out of prayerful penitence rather than public piety. Forgive us, Lord, when we care more about how others perceive us than how you receive us. In your holy name we pray. Amen.

Words of Assurance (Based on Luke 18:14)

People of God, claim and live the words of Christ. All who exalt themselves will be humbled, but all who humble themselves will be exalted. Amen.

Litany (Based on Joel 2:23-32)

Leader: In humility and holiness we are called to live.

People: **Celebrating with confidence our gifts and graces, but serving God and others with love and compassion.**

Leader: God's promise to human faithfulness is power.

People: **God pours out the Spirit upon those who believe.**

Leader: Receive the Holy Spirit and claim God's gifts,

People: **That our sons, daughters, and all God's people might prophesy, dream, and vision.**

(Gary G. Kindley)

SEPTEMBER 30, 2007

❧❧❧

Eighteenth Sunday after Pentecost

Readings: Jeremiah 32:1-3a, 6-15; Psalm 91:1-6, 14-16; 1 Timothy 6:6-19; Luke 16:19-31

Ordinary Life
Jeremiah 32:1-3a, 6-15

I hated the daily grind. You know what I mean. I am talking about the day-to-day routine that seems such an intrinsic part of our lives. There have been days when I decided to spend the afternoon in the park or just drive along a country road. Yes, I hated the daily routine, that is, until the time in my life when every day was completely unpredictable.

It was a time when a loved one was diagnosed with a horrible combination of Parkinson's and Alzheimer's diseases. It was a time when our family went through a tumultuous, internal struggle. It was time when evil besieged us at every corner. It was a time when we became afraid of what each new day might bring. I had always thrived on new adventures and uncertain futures. Soon, however, I desired nothing more than routine. I was looking for an ordinary life.

Jeremiah is seeking an ordinary life; however, he seeks something that will do much more than calm his own soul. He seeks the thing that will stand as a symbol for a bright new future. Jeremiah seeks something ordinary that will bring an extraordinary message of hope. So what does he do? He buys land! Jerusalem is undergoing a horrible siege by the Babylonians. There is no certain future, and Jeremiah himself is under house arrest. Then, almost inexplicably, Jeremiah buys land.

At that time the custom in Israel was that the eldest male member of the family, or clan, was responsible for ensuring the retention of family property. This communal understanding of redemption had its roots in Levitical law. According to that custom, Jeremiah's cousin, Hanamel, came to offer Jeremiah a piece of land. The land, just beyond the walls of

Jerusalem, was all but worthless because it lay in the hands of the Babylonians. Hanamel was facing financial devastation.

The irony is that financial ruin was the least of their worries. This was the second Babylonian conquest, and they were much more vicious than in the previous assault. When dispersion throughout the Babylonian Empire seemed the best alternative to death itself, why would anyone worry about buying and selling land?

Jeremiah, however, was not just anyone. He was the prophet, bringing the word of God to the people. His prophecy had foretold the great siege that was now taking place. His prophecy had promised punishment for Israel's unfaithfulness. His prophecy had placed him in jeopardy with his own people, especially now that it was coming to fulfillment.

A careful look at Jeremiah, however, reminds us that his prophecy was not without hope. That is why he bought the land. God told Jeremiah to buy the land and to use the deed as a symbol for the people; "Houses and fields and vineyards shall again be bought in this land" (32:15).

Amid the chaos and besieged by evil, Jeremiah did something very ordinary. It was the ordinariness of his action that brought hope. His action signaled that a day would come when life would again be ordinary. On that day the blessings of God would again be as familiar as the brush of a gentle breeze.

There are times in our lives when we need to see the ordinariness of life as a symbol of hope. I once visited with parents of a little boy who was living with cancer. The prognosis was uncertain, and the parents were experiencing the roller-coaster ride that comes with each bit of news from the physicians. At one point in our conversation, I asked the couple what they needed, and their response was unique. They said, "We need things to be ordinary. We don't need people doting on us and treating us differently. Tim needs his playmates to treat him just as they did before he had the cancer. We need our friends to socialize with us just as we did before we found out. We think we can go on if there is a chance that we can just get back to the routine of everyday living."

This is similar to the message in 1 Timothy 6, which accompanies our passage from Jeremiah. The message to Timothy is, "There is great gain in godliness combined with contentment" (v. 6). The writer challenges us to let go of things, such as wealth and power, which we think will bring us happiness. We are challenged to "pursue righteousness, godliness, faith, love, endurance, gentleness" (v. 11). In the writer's mind, these things happen in the ordinariness of life. They are found in simple acts of kindness, in everyday generosity. Those who live this kind of ordinary life will "take hold of the life that really is life" (1 Timothy 6:19).

We are people under siege. Some are under siege by evil forces. Some are under siege by greed. The good news is that, no matter how we are besieged, there is a message of hope in everyday living.

Yes, I used to hate the ordinariness of life, but now I cherish it. The life I now seek is the simple life—the life of faith—the ordinary life that puts me in touch with an extraordinary God. (Jeffrey Smith)

Leaders in the Kingdom Are Like . . .

Third in a Series of Three: Biblical Leadership

Matthew 13:24-33

It is clear the Christian church in America is struggling; without new leadership and direction, the church will continue to struggle. The institutional church today has become socially irrelevant. While the industrial revolution changed America's social structure, the church has often been a reluctant social witness. Today, Americans consider themselves religious while they ignore the institutional church. For the church to become relevant and vibrant, new leadership must radically transform the church, or create an entirely new Christian organization.

Facing similar irrelevancy, Jesus chose reform. He challenged the very core of the Hebrew faith to become less legalistic and more faith- and person-centered. The Gospels consider Jesus the fulfillment of Hebrew prophecy. At the core of Jesus' leadership was his ability to define reality. He distilled the Mosaic laws to loving God and loving neighbor. He healed on the Sabbath and ate with sinners. And through parable, Jesus described the kingdom of God.

"The kingdom of heaven is like yeast that a woman took and mixed in with three measures of flour until all of it was leavened" (Matthew 13:33). Artistically, Jesus painted a picture of what was to come, and invited people to live within that vision, inviting them to live as he lived.

One of the strengths of Jesus' leadership style was that he modeled his vision. The Gospels, particularly Luke, defined Jesus as a servant leader. He washed his disciples' feet. His ministry was one of caring for the sick, feeding the hungry, and relating to outcasts.

Servant leadership responds to opportunities. Servant leaders are attuned to human needs and organize people and other resources to meet those needs.

While everyone is called to mission, some are called to special tasks of leadership. It is clear that Jesus felt called by God to lead a reformation. He experienced validation of the call at his baptism, and again at the Transfiguration. Jesus' response to his call led Peter to declare that Jesus was the Son of the living God.

Jesus' leadership was grounded in his relationship with God. His vision for the church and its future drew some people to him and threatened others. To the established Jewish leadership, Jesus' message was radical, even revolutionary. To those who followed Jesus, his message was hopeful and bold. Whether out of curiosity or a thirst for something better, people were attracted to Jesus' message and found him charismatic.

Jesus also called others, and was always shaping a few to special tasks of leadership. The first to be called were his disciples, who were fishermen and common people. Jesus' attraction came from his compassion, his ability to peer into one's soul, and his ability to lift a person's self-worth to new heights.

In his book *The 8th Habit*, Stephen Covey defines leadership as "communicating to people their worth and potential so clearly that they come to see it in themselves" (Stephen R. Covey, *The 8th Habit: From Effectiveness to Greatness* [New York: Free Press, 2004], 98). Jesus seemed able to move people toward their greatest potential. He held a mirror before them, along with a vision of their worth as God saw them. Jesus was able to define a new reality.

Jesus lived and shared his vision, but the future of the church would depend on his ability to develop leadership. While his ministry was universal, Jesus' development of future leadership was very specific. In Peter, for example, Jesus found qualities of leadership that would serve as the foundation of the future church. Peter, and later Paul, became the pastor-developers of the reformed church, the church of Jesus Christ.

We found many of the same leadership qualities in King David. David displayed great courage; he was able to develop relationships and future leaders; his respect for tradition and his own response to leadership were grounded in his relationship with God.

The leadership abilities of Peter and Paul were less obvious. In Peter, Jesus saw passion. When motivated by the Holy Spirit, this impetuous disciple became a passionate evangelist.

Paul was authoritative and skilled in rhetoric. His passion in persecution became the foundation of his success in franchising the early church.

Because of his background, Paul was able to relate to a variety of cultures and broaden the reach of the early Christian church.

Jesus gave us the model of servant leadership. Grounded in his spiritual nature, Jesus was skilled in defining reality, helping people see their worth in relationship to God, and moving them toward a new vision. He also developed strong leadership for the new church.

The postmodern church is desperate for these leadership characteristics found in our faith tradition. The church needs Spirit-led risk-takers, visionary servant leaders. The church thirsts for leaders who will respond to God's call and to the opportunity before us. That is relevancy! The church's future is at stake. Leaders must come forth who, like David, Peter, Paul, and Jesus, are willing to risk for the vision of the kingdom of God.

The kingdom is like yeast, which, when added to flour, will leaven. Like Max DePree with Zoe (see sermon: "Leadership Without Fear," September 16), leadership is about helping people connect with their potential. Grounded in faith, we are called to be servant leaders and to seek new leadership for the church that will be the leaven for God's kingdom. If such leadership arises within the church, the church of the future will be the catalyst toward the kingdom of God. (Dan L. Flanagan)

Worship Aids

Invocation

Come, Holy Spirit, and rekindle in our hearts that which we know in our heads. Today, may our faith be not only an intellectual experience but also an experience of the heart. Amen.

Pastoral Prayer

Eternal God, there is still much that has not changed since your Son walked among us. Tax collectors are still disliked, women are still subjugated, and people who sin differently than do we are still ridiculed.

Still, too, you treasure the one who is lost as much as the ninety-nine at your bosom. That is a constant that testifies to your immeasurable grace. Free us, we pray, from our obstinacy. Liberate us, we plead, from our rigid thinking. Prod us to act, to change, and to grow. Equip us so that we have the capacity to move out of the ruts of our routines.

We pray this prayer with contrite hearts, genuine hope, and committed conviction. Through Christ, our Lord, amen.

Benediction

Change us and challenge us as we go forth into the world. May we leave different, and return next Sabbath ready for another encounter with your Spirit. Amen. (Gary G. Kindley)

OCTOBER 7, 2007

❧❧❧

*Nineteenth Sunday after Pentecost/
World Communion Sunday*

Readings: Lamentations 1:1-6; Psalm 137; 2 Timothy 1:1-14; Luke 17:5-10

More Than a Coach
2 Timothy 1:1-14

My husband is a huge college basketball fan, spending most of his free time in the winter watching as many games as possible. Needless to say, over the years, I have found myself watching quite a bit of basketball as well. I particularly enjoy attending games. There is something very exciting about a packed coliseum of thousands of fans united in support of their team. I especially enjoy watching the coaching staff during the games. They passionately instruct their players on the right moves and plays, as invested in their every move as I imagine they would be if they were playing themselves. The players, college students who probably would struggle with being instructed by an adult outside of the arena, watch the coach, listening to his every word. They realize, no doubt, that without a good coach, their God-given skills and love for the game would not reach its full potential. I imagine Paul as a kind of coach for Timothy. Paul apparently met Timothy as a young man, and was instrumental in Timothy's future as a missionary. Whereas 1 Timothy gives instruction on ecclesiastical life, 2 Timothy is more of a personal letter from Paul, the coach, to Timothy, who is in the thick of the game of his life.

Although scholarship varies on the authenticity of Paul as the author of the Pastoral Epistles, there is something very personal in 2 Timothy. Some scholars suggest that, although Paul may not actually have written 1 Timothy and Titus, he was indeed the author of 2 Timothy. It is from that perspective I write. Paul was invested in Timothy's calling and ministry. He seemed to care deeply for him as a son in the faith. As Paul approached the end of his own ministry, he was no doubt more passionate than ever about encouraging and instructing Timothy. Paul's story was well known to Timothy. He probably heard it many times. Timothy knew of Paul's conversion and transformation from a hater of Christians to a believer who suffered the rest of his life for his faith in Christ. Timothy no doubt knew that, even as he received these words of encouragement from Paul, Paul's own days were numbered. I can imagine that Timothy treasured them throughout his life.

As Christians we believe these words are instructive for us as well. They are more than words from a mentor to a student, a coach to a player. In a very real way, we are on Timothy's team. We all are called to share the gospel, to carry on the call of Christ. We too have excellent examples of faith, but carry the personal responsibility to find in ourselves the courage to share the good news.

The crux of 2 Timothy 1 is Paul's encouragement to remain faithful. The threat of persecution of Christians in Timothy's world was authentic. Additionally, Paul may have been concerned that his own death would discourage Timothy. Paul encourages Timothy to be bold and not ashamed to share the gospel. He encourages him that God is with him, and has given him the power he needs to withstand all that is ahead. He further shares that, even in his own suffering, Paul is not ashamed because he believes that God is able to deliver him from his difficulty.

We do not live in Timothy's world. For that, I am thankful. Yet, I think we can use these encouraging words in 2 Timothy. As believers, we are daily challenged to live lives of boldness and faith. No doubt, it is much simpler to allow our faith to remain private, something we observe at home or at church with other like-minded persons. This is not our calling, however. Our lives are to be living witnesses to Christ. Our faith should be naturally evident in all that we do. When we fail to live our lives as persons of faith, by our very omission, we communicate fear, doubt, and even shame of our Christ.

Hear my message clearly. I do not believe that we are intended to live our lives beating people over the heads with the gospel. (The Crusades did not prove to be an effective missionary tool, after all.) Likewise, I do not believe that equipping ourselves with Christian bumper stickers, bracelets, T-shirts, and the like is the answer. I think our most effective witness is in our evident lives of faith. It is evident in the way we treat others. It is evident in the way we do business. It is evident in the way we behave behind closed doors, the persons we are with our children and spouses. It is sometimes easier to just stick a Christian fish on your bumper or hand out a tract.

I think Paul knew that authentic ministry is difficult. Second Timothy offers some great news! God is with us. God has given us the power we need to do what God has called us to do. God is able when we are not. This is a hugely important message! When it would have been easier for Timothy to give up and run for the hills, God gave him the power he needed. When Timothy mourned the loss of his coach, God was there, equipping him to be the person of God he was called to be. When it would be easier for us to lie, cheat, and steal, God is there, giving us strength to do the right thing. When it is tempting to leave Christ at church each Sunday, God is there, empowering us to be persons of faith in every place that life takes us. Whatever our circumstances, God is able when we are not. I imagine Timothy relied on that strength over and over, probably repeating those words in moments of doubt and weakness. We too have this great message of hope. We cannot do this alone, but it is not a coach we need, it is God. God is able and powerful. Praise be to God! (Tracey Allred)

Pentecost and the Language of the Holy Spirit

First in a Series of Three: Acts—The Story of the Church

Acts 2:1-21

In the second grade, my mother thought it would be a good idea for me to learn Spanish. My follow-up, however, was not as good as her idea. In high school, my counselor thought it would be a good idea for me to take French. My follow-up, however, was not as good as his idea. When I was in college, my adviser told me I had to take a language or I would not graduate. It was my idea to take Russian. I'm still not certain whether or not my follow-up was better or worse than the original notion to take Russian.

In seminary I knew at least some of the Greek language from my encounter with Russian. Fortunately, many of the characters are identical. I'm ashamed to admit it, but I prospered no better at Greek than I did in my other frustrated attempts at Spanish, French, or Russian. Recently, I have learned more Greek than I ever expected, thanks to Aristotle and Luke. Perhaps one of the reasons I failed to thrive in language study is that language study is incremental. By this I mean that Wednesday's lesson builds on Tuesday's lesson, and Thursday's lesson, in turn, builds on Wednesday's lesson, and so on. Language and mathematics are disciplines that take no longer to master than other kinds of knowledge, but they must be done in a process of knowledge-building. Every day's learning builds on the preceding day's, and every week's learning builds on the preceding week's.

Each of us has heard the Acts story of Pentecost many times. We know that one of its major contributions is a pentecostal language of faith. You remember the contours of the story: "As they were all together in one place, divided by nationality and race, suddenly they were all able to understand numerous other languages" (see Acts 2:1-4). It was the spirit sent by God that made the Pentecost event happen. This Holy Spirit not only appeared to the eyes as flames of fire, but the Spirit also sounded like the rush of a mighty wind to the ears. The whole place was filled with the sounds of many people speaking many "known" languages of the mighty works of God. God's power and Christ's spirit reversed the linguistic undoing of human language as seen in the Tower of Babel story (see Genesis 9). [Read: Acts 2:1-21.]

Learning the pentecostal language is the major task of the church. Teaching the young and the old, the lettered and the unlettered, the language of love should be a part of every church's weekly regimen. There is, however, great difficulty in doing this. Learning a language takes an ample amount of daily devotion for its mastery. Learning the pentecostal language of love is a matter of constant discipline. Although the word *discipline* is not popular in our contemporary vocabulary, it is discipline that makes disciples. If we likened the learning of the language of God's love to the learning of a foreign tongue, then we might say that it takes constant attention to learn it fluently. In some ways, this language God gave Christians at Pentecost is more foreign than any human language we ever encounter. Our language of faith seems to turn the values of the world upside down, as Luke later comments: "These people who have been turning the world upside down have come here also" (Acts 17:6).

Most of us are hit-or-miss in our learning disciplines. Perhaps many of us attempt to learn the language of Pentecost as I tried to learn Spanish, French, Russian, and Greek. After a rousing religious experience, we may feel inspired as we sense God's Spirit filling us. This is literally what it means to be "enthused." For a time, perhaps, we are caught up in the emotion of the religious experience and throw ourselves completely into the task of learning the pentecostal language of discipleship. Learning a new language soon proves to be an arduous task. We tire rather quickly.

No one told us the learning of the pentecostal language of discipleship would prove to be so much work.

Of course the real language of faith, with a complete vocabulary, uses a multitude of terms like "suffering," "sacrifice," "crucifixion," and "unconditional love." These are foreign words to a wholly self-absorbed culture of autonomous individuals who think that life is their domain and they are in charge. Holy Creator and wholly creature—and their respective roles—have been badly confused.

The task of learning the whole language of faith, both in its joy and in its sorrow, is difficult. There should be no argument about this difficulty! The Day of Pentecost, however, reminds us that it is God who sends the Spirit upon the people. Speaking the language of faith, or even the ability to accomplish other acts of faithfulness, is not dependent upon our own strength and wisdom, but rather our faith language is given to us as a precious gift—a gift given, received, and used by people in the community of faith—for the whole people of God.

During World War II several young men, Navajo by birth, had been on a special assignment for the United States government. The Japanese had broken most of the code systems of U.S. Intelligence. Something had to be done to protect the essential secrecy of the war effort. The solution that emerged was the Navajo language. It is a difficult language. Learning it takes at least ten years for an outsider. So the War Department selected several young Navajo men. Stationed at opposite ends of several communications stations, they spoke Navajo to each other. Their language became a secret code, the code the Japanese could not decipher. They were called "code-speakers," but they merely spoke their native tongue (Richard Wentz, "The Code-Speaker," *Christian Century* XCVIII, no. 3 [January 28, 1981]: 70).

Christians are called by God to speak the special pentecostal language of the Spirit of Christ. This language is not only given as a gift, but its vocabulary is enhanced by personal experience. Just think, if we could all speak the pentecostal language of faith, then what great things God could do for us and through us. Amen. (David N. Mosser)

Worship Aids

Words of Assurance for World Communion Sunday (For dismissal at the table of the Lord's Supper)

Arise and go in peace, take from this table the taste of grace and live as gracious people. Amen.

Arise to serve the Lord, go forth with courage, character, and conviction. Amen.

Prayer of Confession

Creator of all humankind, we confess our lack of vision in seeing human need around us. We pass people on the street and look past them. We see people different in color, status, or creed, and fail to see through that which is on the outside to the human need that lies within. Forgive us, we pray, and grant us the spiritual X-ray vision to see the ache of human need and the courage to alleviate it. We pray in the name of the One who always looks upon the heart, Jesus Christ our Lord. Amen.

Benediction

Lord, give us X-ray vision to see to the heart of people's pain and give us the courage to help them overcome it. Amen. (Gary G. Kindley)

OCTOBER 14, 2007

Twentieth Sunday after Pentecost

Readings: Jeremiah 29:1, 4-7; Psalm 66:1-12; 2 Timothy 2:8-15; Luke 17:11-19

Not Bad News at All
Jeremiah 29:1, 4-7

Jeremiah was known as the Weeping Prophet, probably a direct result of the bad news that was his most frequent message. His prophetic message rarely reflected any type of good news. God chose him to be a prophet in one of the most difficult chapters of Israelite history. And, if it were not bad enough that Jeremiah spent most of his ministry delivering the bad news, he was often surrounded by false prophets who shared great news. Yet in the midst of the story of this weeping, sackcloth-wearing, yoke-of-the-Lord-laden prophet, there is a powerful, unmistakable life message of hope and faith in the midst of adversity.

Historically, life in Judah had been difficult for the generations preceding Jeremiah. Corrupt leadership and military failures had left the southern part of the former great kingdom of David vulnerable and weak. The ray of hope that Judah experienced during the reign of Josiah, which led to a brief period of revival, was dashed with Josiah's death in 609 B.C.E. Jeremiah was called as a prophet to God's people during a time of both national and spiritual weakness for Judah. As often happened in Israel's history, the people of Judah had become callous and neglectful of their relationship with God. As life became more difficult, many abandoned their faith for other types of religious practice, losing sight of their covenant relationship with God. When faith is abandoned, sin becomes rampant, and the natural consequence of sin was certainly evident in the plight of Judah.

One of the difficulties of Jeremiah for us is, at precisely these moments in history, we expect to see grace and mercy from God. For Judah during this period, God's mercy and love did not exempt them from facing God's wrath and having to accept the consequences of their own lack of faith. That wrath and those consequences came in the form of exile. Forced out of their own land and away from their homes and families, the children of Israel were compelled to live in Babylon. For a people whose identity and future were so closely tied to David's city and the familial experience, exile must have been devastating.

It is no wonder that the only word from God the exiles desired was the word of their deliverance from exile and the return to their homes. Jeremiah 29 speaks from the midst of that very struggle. The exiles were desperate for deliverance and searching for good news. There were false prophets who offered the very message so desired by the exiles, but this was not the word from God. Jeremiah, who was displaced but still in Jerusalem, wrote a letter to the exiles to dispute the false prophets and deliver the message of God's will for them. God's word, delivered by Jeremiah, was not about a quick fix for their problems or even immediate salvation. It was a different kind of message, one that is often difficult, but necessary to hear. God's word for the exiles was about acceptance, perseverance, and hope.

In Jeremiah 29, Jeremiah encourages the exiles to live life. What the exiles wanted from God was an end to their suffering. They wanted their situation to be corrected and their difficulties to miraculously improve. At the very least, they wanted their sentence in Babylon to be short-lived and to be assured of the fall of their enemies. Instead, Jeremiah writes to encourage them to build houses, settle down, live from the land, get married, have families, and pray for the prosperity of the Babylonian land they inhabit. God's will for them is to continue living life and to accept their plight. God wanted them to live in prosperity and peace even in their exile. These were not the prophetic words the exiles wanted to hear, and their initial reception to the message probably did not resound with hope. Yet the message is powerful and meaningful even to the twenty-first-century reader.

Life is not always easy. As a matter of fact, the average life is full of difficulty. Whether from the result of our own sin, someone else's, or just the natural rhythm of life, suffering will touch all of us in one way or another. While this realization can make us feel depressed or even encourage a kind of "kicking and screaming" embrace of fate, accepting life with its ups and downs is a major step toward emotional and spiritual maturity.

The exiles did not want to suffer in Babylon. They did not want to accept their predicament. They wanted God to fix it. This was not what God desired for them at that time, however. God had already demonstrated to the children of Israel that God could deliver them from difficulty and miraculously heal their hurts. I think God was teaching the exiles, through Jeremiah, how to handle life when there is no quick fix or miraculous solution. God wanted the exiles to accept their situation and live as people of faith and peace in spite of difficulty.

More often than not, we are like the exiles. When there is difficulty, we scream for relief and deliverance. When God doesn't intervene in the way we think God should, we look for something or someone else who will. Instead of accepting life's scrapes and turns, we wallow in self-pity and anger, shaking our fists at God for not doing what we think God ought to do. All the while, this message from Jeremiah is ringing loud and clear. Make the best of your circumstances. Live your lives fully. Be faithful and peaceful, even in the midst of hard times.

Having spent my adult life in church ministry, I have observed many people of faith struggling through the difficulties of life. Even the most faithful do not always land on their spiritual feet in the face of great suffering. The ones who do, however, are often glowing on the other side of their difficulties. A woman in our church, Betsy (not her real name), recently died of cancer. She was a sweet, gentle woman who always had a big smile on her face and an encouraging word on her lips. After her death, I met most of her family for the first time and heard the sad story of her life, which was full of tragedy, abuse, and suffering. In her eulogy, I mentioned the power of her persistent smile and incredible faith in the face of so much difficulty. I think Betsy personified the message of Jeremiah 29. One of the great tests of life is how we handle the hard times. It is clear that God intends us to handle them the "Betsy" way! (Tracey Allred)

A Miraculous Community

Second in a Series of Three: Acts—The Story of the Church

Acts 2:42-47

People today, just as those in the early days of the church, just don't get what the business of the church is. They confuse the ministry of the church with a bunch of "shoulds and oughts." Rather, the ministries of the church are attributed to the power of God, whose main locus in society is in the church of Jesus Christ. A confused critic of the church was

H. L. Mencken, who once quipped: "A church is a place in which gentlemen who have never been to heaven brag about it to persons who will never get there." This total misunderstanding of the church's mission ranks with Othal Brand's remark, who said concerning the pesticide chlordane: "Sure, it's going to kill a lot of people, but they may be dying of something else anyway."

Eva Braun, Adolf Hitler's mistress, writing to a friend during the siege and bombing of Berlin in 1945, wrote: "I can't understand how all this can happen. It's enough to make one lose one's faith in God." The capper for ridiculous things people say or think is found on the tombstone inscription of a British soldier found in the northwestern frontier of Pakistan. It reads, "Here lies Captain Ernest Bloomfield. Accidentally shot by his orderly, March 2nd, 1879. Well done, good and faithful servant." (The preceding quotes were found in Ross and Kathryn Petras's book, *The 776 Stupidest Things Ever Said* [New York: Doubleday, 1993], 81, 56, respectively.)

The humor in these quotations is in the fact that the "big picture" is missed by those who are involved in the smaller parts of the picture. Obviously, pesticides are used to kill insects and not people, and one wonders how much of the German policy of genocide against Jews, Poles, Gypsies, and others was actually known by Hitler's naive girlfriend. Mencken's understanding of the church as a bunch of "holier-than-thous," gathering to point fingers at others with an air of self-congratulation is obviously not founded in any authentic Christian theology. The best biblical models for the church always include images of the servant church. The church would do well to remember that when it ceases to be a servant to the world God created, it ceases to follow the Lord, the Redeemer of God's world.

Many examples from Jesus' own ministry with the disciples bear out this theme of service to others. The disciple John once said to Jesus, concerning a man who was casting out demons: "We tried to stop him, because he does not follow with us" (Luke 9:49). But Jesus told John, "Do not stop him; for whoever is not against you is for you" (v. 50). The disciples' reaction may have been one of jealousy. John and the others may have had difficulty being disciples and also inviting others to follow Jesus. They were, perhaps, more concerned about preserving Jesus for themselves alone.

Two men went crabbing one day, one of whom had been crabbing all of his life, the other going for his first time. When they had caught a few, the newcomer suggested they should put a lid on the first bucket and get another bucket. The first bucket was becoming full. "Look for yourself," said the newcomer, "you can see that the crabs are about to crawl out of the bucket."

"Oh, we've got lots more room left for crabs before we have to get a second bucket," said the experienced crabber. "You see, when one of those crabs is about to escape, one or two of the other crabs will reach up and pull it back down."

When churches pull their own members down, then the church looks like, well—it looks like a bunch of crabs. This attitude misses what the church is to do in the world. Most of us are guilty of never quite seeing the big picture. For example, why do we come to worship together? Some come to hear the music program of the church, while others come to see their friends. Some of our numbers are here because they think it will help their children. Believe it or not, some people come to church, hoping against hope they will hear something from the pulpit that will help them make sense out of this tangled ball of twine we call life.

All these reasons are perhaps noble, but they each miss the "bigger picture." According to the message about worship in the book of Hebrews, we come together to worship God in order to encourage one another in faith. "And let us consider how to provoke one another to love and good deeds, not neglecting to meet together, as is the habit of some, but encouraging one another, and all the more as you see the Day approaching" (Hebrews 10:24-25). This means that the chief function of worship is to encourage one another in the faith.

One of the great miracles of our time is to create a community of people who love one another so much that they put their private desires and wishes aside and do things for one another out of a common devotion to the Lord Jesus Christ. To have a truly great church, blessed of and by God, is a precious thing indeed. To be part of that kind of fellowship is one of God's greatest blessings bestowed upon God's people. Please, let none of us take it for granted.

When you are discouraged about the church, always remember what the early church faced. They were seen as resident aliens and oddballs who were setting out on a journey that was not only foolhardy but also unknown. About the best thing they had going for them was the promise of Jesus that this Christ of God would always be with them. With that promise alone they set their course. When you are discouraged about your church or you want to be reassured about what the big picture looks like, remember this portrait of the church in its earliest days painted for us by Luke in Acts. *[Read Acts 2:42-47.]*

Even today, the church continues to guard its authority. A story is told of an American soldier who was killed while serving in France during the Second World War. Some of his friends noticed a small cemetery beside a little church nearby. They asked the pastor for permission to bury their comrade in the cemetery. They were told that only church members were allowed to be buried there. The soldiers then dug their friend's grave outside of the cemetery.

It was late in the evening, so the soldiers camped near the French village. Early the next morning they decided to visit the grave of their friend one last time. They were surprised to find that the cemetery fence had been moved to include the grave of their departed friend. What the church excluded, the caretaker and God's grace included (Hal Brady, from an unpublished sermon, FUMC, Dallas, Texas, May 31, 1992, used by permission). This is a model to emulate as we strive to be in that number—the number of those who are counted worthy to be called the church of Jesus—the body of Christ. (David N. Mosser)

Worship Aids

Call to Worship

Come stand on the rock when all is sinking around you. We gather on holy ground. It is a foundation that shall not be moved for all eternity, yet a Spirit that moves constantly, bringing new life and fresh beginnings to all who will listen.

Invocation

The holy mountain of God is immovable, yet the wind of the Spirit is ever changing. The love of God is everlasting, but the presence of God is fresh and new each day. The Word of God stands forever, but the Spirit breathes new insight when we seek God's Word for today. Let us worship God in Spirit and in truth. Amen. (Gary G. Kindley)

Offertory Prayer

For these gifts that we are about to receive at your holy altar, O Lord, we thank you. First they were created by you, and then loaned to us. Help us return these good things of creation and be thankful for the relation-ship with you that these offerings represent. May they bless both those who give and also those who receive. In Christ's name we pray. Amen. (David N. Mosser)

Benediction

Stand firm. Live free. Anchor to the rock of faith. Go with the move-ment of the Spirit. Be blessed. Amen. (Gary G. Kindley)

OCTOBER 21, 2007

✺✺✺

Twenty-first Sunday after Pentecost

Readings: Jeremiah 31:27-34; Psalm 119:97-104; 2 Timothy 3:14–4:5; Luke 18:1-8

How Are Your Knees?
Luke 18:1-8

My grandparents recently got a cellular telephone. It was my sister's idea. She was worried for their safety, as they often drive the eighty miles between their home and the home of their youngest daughter in the next state. In the pre–cell phone days, my communication with my grandparents was probably pretty typical. There were monthly calls and occasional visits. Even with family that lived much closer than I do, telephone calls were brief and occasional; my grandparents were not big conversationalists. Since the cellular telephone entered their lives, however, my grandparents have been calling me (and the rest of the family) at least every other day! Whether it is the novelty of their new toy or the attractive nature of "free" minutes to my Depression-era grandparents, their communication has increased tenfold. I will admit that it took me a while to grow accustomed to receiving such frequent, and sometimes ill-timed, calls from my grandparents, but I must also admit that I feel closer to them than I have felt in years! There is something about persistent communication that cements a good relationship. It is clear throughout Scripture that God desires that same type of persistent communication with us.

Although the Bible is full of verses exalting the importance of prayer, the well-placed, often-overlooked parable of the persistent widow gives an additional perspective. The parable is found in Luke 18, the chapter preceding Jesus' triumphal entry into Jerusalem. The time in Jesus' life is fast approaching when he will need the support and faithfulness of his twelve closest friends. Chapter 18 suggests, however, that the disciples have not completely understood Jesus, and as seen throughout the Gospels, Jesus is working "overtime" to prepare the disciples for what is to come.

The main characters in the parable are the wicked judge and the widow. Although the judge is uncaring and unrighteous, he is eventually merciful to the widow in her tireless pleas for justice. The widow, a favorite character type in Jesus' parables, displays the kind of faith and perseverance that you would expect in a great religious leader. Instead, it is found in a simple widow, part of the most-overlooked element of society. (In just a few verses, Jesus will also exalt the faith of children, another ignored social group.) Because of the judge's evil character, the widow has no reason to expect mercy, and yet she persistently comes with her plea. Jesus' point seems to be that if an evil judge shows mercy on the persistent widow, how much more will our loving God hear our pleas and answer our cries for justice? That *seems* to be the logical end of this concise little parable, but verse 8 contains an additional thought from Jesus: "When the Son of Man comes, will he find faith on the earth?"

For centuries, theologians have sparred over the humanness and divinity of Jesus. It is clear to me that in the last few weeks of his life, Jesus himself faced inner conflict between his humanness and divinity. On the one hand, he seemed prepared for his incredible calling in a way no human could be. On the other hand, however, I think Jesus was growing nervous over what would occur after his death. He saw glimpses of potential greatness and potential failure in the disciples. In the last chapters of Luke, there are consistent examples of faithfulness in people such as the widow, the children, the tax collectors, and the disabled. Jesus seems to challenge his disciples, who continually struggle with faithfulness. "If these unlikely persons of faith believe, how can you not?" he seems to ask them. Jesus realizes that without persistent faithfulness like the widow's, the disciples will not make the kingdom difference required of them.

We will not be faced with the challenge that confronted the disciples. We will probably never be called upon to actually lay our lives down for the sake of Christ. Most of us are not faced with a hostile world that is completely unfamiliar with Jesus Christ. Yet the question of Luke 18 is for us as well. When the Son of Man comes, will he find faith on the earth? Here's an even harder question: when the Son of Man comes, will he find faith in our church? Have we become complacent? Have we grown tired of persistently crying out to God like the widow? Are we more comfortable participating in programs, studies, and meetings than we are on our knees?

My initial response when I reread this parable was "I think I know that widow!" She is a woman in our church whom I sometimes avoid because she is a little unusual and socially awkward. At least once a week, she mentions her husband and son to me, who do not know the Lord. Every week at our prayer meeting, she asks to pray for the shut-ins and unsaved. She is intensely faithful, and I imagine that her knees are nearly worn out from praying. She is not like most of the members of our church, and I think that must make Jesus sad.

I am convicted by this story. I imagine the disciples were too. After all, they were very busy. They were the chosen Twelve of the Christ. They had important jobs to do. Yet Jesus was clear on what was most important—persistent, exhausting faith—the kind of faith that brings a widow's request for justice every day—the kind of faith that leads a woman to pray for her husband for fifty years—the kind of faith that is required and expected to be a child of God. May you be persistently connected to the God of your past, present, and future, and may you feel closer than you have in years! (Tracey Allred)

As He Was Going Along and Approaching Damascus

Third in a Series of Three: Acts—The Story of the Church

Acts 9:1-20

Change is both overrated and underrated. Those who blow the trumpet of change, extolling a constant state of flux, never seem quite satisfied. Generally, however, most people do not consider change to be the cure-all some persons crack it up to be. Rather, some of us get so comfortable with the way things are that we would rather endure the pain of constancy than the anticipation of new pain that may or may not come with change. Our lesson is Luke's account of a remarkable change. Some devoted Christians recognize that if it had not been for the almost neurotic mission drive of Paul, we might not have the church we have today. Certainly, Jesus provided the content of the church's witness, but it was Paul who helped organize the church and spread its influence to the ends of the known world. [Read: Acts 9:1-20.]

In Acts 8:3, Luke told us that in Jerusalem, "Saul was ravaging the church by entering house after house; dragging off both men and women, he committed them to prison." Now we see his great transformation: from persecutor to evangelist. At the time, Jews often had two names: a Semitic one, Saul; and a Roman or Greek one, Paul. Some scholars suggest that the Roman Empire granted Jews the right to extradite their own from beyond Palestine. In early days, Christianity was known as "the

Way." Those who belonged to the Way were Jewish Christians; they worshiped in synagogues. In verses 4-5, Luke makes it clear that in persecuting members of the Christian flock, Paul persecuted Christ. Paul's destination, Damascus, is on the western edge of the Syrian Desert. It was at the intersection of important caravan routes. A contemporary historian of Paul's, Josephus, wrote that there were between ten thousand and eighteen thousand Jews living in Damascus.

This story, often entitled "The Conversion of Saul," is one of the most familiar among Christians and often used as a model for conversion. The story challenges Christians who think that growing up in the church is the same as maturing in the faith. Mature Christian faith requires an adult commitment to Christ. Saul's (or Paul's) experience reminds us that a transition or a change can knock you off your feet and challenge the way you have been living (Mark Trotter, "Acts in Easter," *Quarterly Review* [Winter 1994–1995]: 438).

Paul certainly changed his tune, according to Luke. He had obtained letters to the synagogues in Damascus in order to bind members of "the Way" and take them to Jerusalem. Followers of Jesus were not separate from Judaism in Paul's time. Rather, Paul saw them as dissidents within Judaism and an evil threat to Jewish law. Paul wanted to protect his Hebrew tradition, and followers of Christ threatened the values Paul had cherished from his youth.

Jesus, of course, was Jewish. He knew the Torah, and lived the law and taught the law. But he practiced an interpretation of the law unlike the Pharisees. His rule of "love" broadened the law or, as Jesus himself said, love "fulfilled the law." Jesus' approach to faith and life angered the Jewish establishment, and Paul was on his way to Damascus to protect the vested interests of Judaism. Perhaps for a personality like Paul's, a knock on the head or a beam of laserlike light was necessary to get his attention, but each one of us has our blind spots in life.

In every life that eventually makes a mature commitment to Christ, there comes a moment of truth. Whether it is a flash of light, an extraordinarily painful moment, or simply the realization that we are not alone, each of us comes to the truth for which we stake our lives. For me it was not an instantaneous moment as it was for Paul or perhaps even you. My conversion experience happened over time, but was tied in a vital way to Father Tom Waterman, who helped me understand what Christian commitment was all about. He, as a human being, helped me see the light of a grace-filled life. For some of you this experience happened at church camp or during confirmation, or perhaps at a revival meeting. Whenever or wherever it happened, we were ready to embrace the gospel as a way to define who we were to become.

John Wesley had his heart strangely warmed, and Martin Luther realized something new and powerful about grace in his study of the book of Romans. Those who are fortunate to be touched by God, or knocked to their knees, understand the profound implications of a life-changing call from God. I want to share the account of Augustine's conversion from his classic *Confessions*:

> I was saying these things and weeping in the most bitter contrition of my heart, when suddenly I heard the voice of a boy or a girl I know not which—coming from the neighboring house, chanting over and over again, "Pick it up, read it; pick it up, read it." Immediately I ceased weeping and began most earnestly to think whether it was usual for children in some kind of game to sing such a song, but I could not remember ever having heard the like. So damming the torrent of my tears, I got to my feet, for I could not but think that this was a divine command to open the Bible and read the first passage I should light upon....
>
> So I quickly returned to the bench where Alypius was sitting, for there I had put down the apostle's book when I had left there. I snatched it up, opened it, and in silence read the paragraph on which my eyes first fell: "Not in rioting and drunkenness, not in chambering and wantonness, not in strife and envying, but put on the Lord Jesus Christ, and make no provision for the flesh to fulfill the lusts thereof." I wanted to read no further, nor did I need to. For instantly, as the sentence ended, there was infused in my heart something like the light of full certainty and all the gloom of doubt vanished away.
> (Albert C. Outler, ed. and trans., *Augustine: Confessions*. Book 8, section 29. Online: http://www.ccel.org/a/augustine/confessions/confessions.html)

Each of us, if we are the least bit reflective about our lives before God and with our brothers and sisters in the faith, will come to a moment when we have to decide the course of our lives—with God or on our own. The decision, however, is never easy, and many of the things we have held dear may be threatened.

My prayer is that when we come to a moment of truth about our lives and faith, we will at least think and pray hard about who is giving us an opportunity to find real meaning and worth in the life God has given us as a precious gift. It may be October, but we are nonetheless Easter people. After all, Easter is a season and not simply a day. Easter is about resurrection—our resurrection to life in God. Amen. (David N. Mosser)

Worship Aids

Call to Worship

Now is the time called Sabbath. Sabbath is for worship and for reverence, for rest and for renewal. Now is the time to stand in the presence of God, who is constantly with us. Come, Holy God—Creator, Redeemer, and Sustainer. We gather to worship you.

Pastoral Prayer

Holy and gentle God, you are God of all the ages. From everlasting to everlasting, you have been and you shall be. We are grateful that you have seen fit to bless us with your presence. You have literally given birth to life itself. With life come joy and fulfillment, and the wonder of human relationships.

We give thanks for the people in this place today. People who have given of themselves and who have blessed the lives of others. What joy it brings to discover the life of Christ revealed through the dedicated service and gracious lives of others.

Thank you for the ministry that we share through Christ's holy church. We acknowledge this day the lives touched by our ministry together. Keep us mindful on this day, and in the days ahead, that you are a God who is constant and yet ever-changing. Keep us from getting too stuck in our routines or bogged down in our traditions. Keep us refreshed and challenged with the surprising opportunities of each new day.

Bless us, forgive us, console us, redeem us, direct us, uplift us, surprise us, empower us, equip us, and release us. In the name of the Christ we ask these things. Amen.

Benediction

Go forth with thanksgiving for service to the Christ. Go out and be Christ's servants in the world. Amen. (Gary G. Kindley)

OCTOBER 28, 2007

❧❧❧

Twenty-second Sunday after Pentecost/Reformation Sunday

Readings: Joel 2:23-32; Psalm 65; 2 Timothy 4:6-8, 16-18; Luke 18:9-14

A Lesson in Humility
Luke 18:9-14

On a windswept fall afternoon, two individuals approached the sanctuary of an impressive church. The first was well dressed and carried himself with assurance. His clothes and manner said "clergy." The second wore flashy clothes that advertised "drug pusher" to those who knew the neighborhood. The clergyman approached the altar rail with quiet confidence. He knelt in position to pray and did so quietly, yet with a stately voice that carried through the empty sanctuary. "Lord, I have come to give thanks to you that I am not like those who say they believe but fail to worship; I thank you that I am not an adulterer or a crook or even someone who takes the Christian faith casually. You know me, Lord. I have served you faithfully all these many years. Your law is written in my heart, and your Holy Scripture is my constant delight. Lord, I've done my best for you, not only giving a tenth of my income but also honoring many extra, second-mile, causes."

The drug pusher, upon entering the sanctuary, did not seek out the altar area. He slipped into a pew near the rear, off to the side. He gazed for a moment in quiet despair at the cross hanging above the altar. Then, as if rent internally, he cried out, "Lord, have mercy upon me, for I have made a mess of my life."

It was this second man who left with God's blessings.

I have retold, in a more modern form, the parable that Jesus shared in Luke 18:9-14. Scholars note that the first telling of this story must have left its hearers in stunned incomprehension, probably tainted by outrage. It is all too easy to slide by the offensive impact of this story.

The Pharisee comes to pray in the Temple, as is, no doubt, his custom. Properly he moves to a position of respect before God and lifts his hands in prayer. (In those times, prayers were given standing up, in respect, with hands lifted.) His prayer, carefully examined, is a prayer of thanks. It contains no personal petitions. It is based upon a sound scriptural model for prayer; the first five verses of Psalm 17 contain a similar prayer. Furthermore, rabbinic law taught that one properly prayed in thanks that you were not like others who were unfaithful. The faithfulness of the Pharisee is noted in that he mentions two works he is not really obligated to do. He fasts twice a week (in an arid climate where fasting is a real sacrifice); the law calls for only one yearly fast on the Day of Atonement. Not only does he tithe (gives 10 percent), but he also gives a tithe on items not even required—"all that I get." Here before us is a genuinely righteous man who ought, at first glance, to be a religious model for our children.

Now the other man Jesus tells of is a tax collector. To so name him is to label him as a bad person. Tax collectors not only collaborated with the Roman invaders; they made their profits by overcharging, that is cheating, the common populace. They were, by definition, a scourge on society. Scholars note that they were to be shunned by all respectable people and considered on a level with common robbers.

This man's prayer is not done properly, at the front in the prescribed manner. He stands, the text notes, "at a distance" (Luke 18:13 NIV) and is so contrite that he cannot even lift his eyes and hands to God. Jesus tells of an outburst of despair more than a common prayer. We grasp how distant the man feels from God and his sense of utter unworthiness. Furthermore, restitution appears beyond reach. He would not only have to abandon his work (how would he care for his family?) but also give back what he has taken plus an added fifth. It would be close to impossible to even identify everyone he needs to repay. Thus, not only is his situation hopeless, his inability to make proper restitution renders even his cry for mercy hopeless.

In a stunning reversal of expectation, Jesus says, "I tell you, this man went down to his home justified rather than the other" (v. 14). The most repulsive element of society forgiven! The best witness of faithfulness not forgiven! Heard rightly, this passage is an assault on common sensibilities.

Perhaps the first key to understanding the passage lies in its opening verse and closing phrase. This is a difficult passage to hear precisely because Jesus is directing it to believers. We must approach the text in confession. We are challenged to reflect on the issue of true humility.

Second, the text challenges our understanding of the nature of God. God's forgiveness is not for those we consider righteous, but rather for those who are truly repentant. There is both good news and bad news in this tale. Mercy from the Lord abounds, but only to those who give up any false notions of saving themselves. It is akin to the old story about the fellow who proclaimed, with evident pride, that he was a self-made man. People who knew him said that explained a lot of things. If he had called out for help, he might have done a better job!

The rhythm of text starts with identification, moves to confession, and engages us in repentance. Then, and only then, does the good news of God's abundant mercy become apparent. In the words of the Master, "all who exalt themselves will be humbled, but all who humble themselves will be exalted" (v. 14). (Mike Lowry)

Beyond Duty

First in a Series of Four

Matthew 5:38-42

The teenage boy was tapped on the shoulder by the flat blade of a sword. Turning around, he looked into the face of a despised Roman soldier who said, "Here, boy, take my bag—and none of your lip, or I'll give you the boot!" Under the Roman right of impressment, the soldier had the right to ask the boy to carry his bag for a mile, to run an errand for a mile, or to guide him for a mile. The boy picked up the bag, carrying it exactly one mile and no more. He then threw it down in the dust, muttered something under his breath, and returned home. Everyone in Jesus' audience understood the illustration Jesus was using in Matthew 5:41. But how did they react to these sayings of Jesus? "Do more than is demanded. Go two miles!" I feel their reaction was very similar to what ours would be. Perhaps they murmured, "No way!"

In the Sermon on the Mount, Jesus sought to help the disciples understand the nature and demand of the gospel. This was not only a gift to be enjoyed or a doctrine to be defended but also a life to be lived. Jesus' entire sermon is a challenge to perfection; however, it is also an ideal toward which all Christians must strive. Few passages in the New Testament have more of the essence of the Christian ethic than this one.

In verses 38 and 39, Jesus quotes from the oldest known law in the world, the Code of Hammurabi (2285 to 2242 B.C.E.), which is based on the principle known as *lex talionis*—what we describe as "tit for tat." We can find it in the Old Testament three times (Exodus 21:23-25; Leviticus 24:19-20; Deuteronomy 19:21). Jesus' interpretation is instructive. He says we are not to resist, that is, "fight against," or "stand against" evil. In other words, we are not to govern our actions toward others by their reactions to us.

The "slap on the face" or the "turning of the other cheek" is our Lord's way of saying that we are to live above the desire for revenge and the spirit of retaliation so characteristic of our society. The idea of "the tunic and the cloak" teaches us we are to go beyond what is demanded of us. Finally, the matter of giving is related to the totality of stewardship and must be understood both as privilege and as obligation. All giving, according to the Lord, is nothing less than giving to God. Jesus pointed this out by saying that feeding the hungry, clothing the naked, taking in the stranger, visiting the sick, and visiting the prisoners were all services unto God (Matthew 25:31-46).

All these ideas are summed up in verse 41. Obviously Jesus was laying down an eternal principle: "Do more than is demanded of you in life." We are told that Jewish boys living under Roman rule staked off exactly a mile down the road from their houses and never went beyond the stake. Let's be honest! Sometimes the demands of duty are a load in themselves. When we have to do something that we resent, we, like these Jewish boys, do it grudgingly. We look for the minimum we can do and seek to do no more. Tell a child to make his bed, and he wants to know if he has to put on the bedspread. Assign a paper to a class in school and you will hear, "How long does it have to be?" The legalism of the Pharisees is not dead! The rich young ruler mentioned by the Lord in Luke, chapter 18, is a good illustration. This individual wanted religion on his own terms. He even told the Lord he lived by the rules and the regulations. He was as straight as a gun barrel doctrinally but just as empty spiritually. He never got beyond the mile marker!

Now take another look at that young Jewish lad. What if he had taken the bag and gone past the mile marker? Did he hear Jesus preach this very sermon? Do you think this made a difference?

Actually, the entire plan of redemption is second-mile stuff. The law demanded nothing of God. People knew the law and deliberately disobeyed. God gave humankind a second chance by going beyond the mile marker. God did this because of God's great love for us. When you get right down to it, the second mile is one of consecration not compulsion, of opportunity not regulation.

Thinking of stewardship in terms not of law but of grace brings us to a new concept. Unlike the rich young ruler whose possessions possessed him, we now begin to think in terms of maximums not minimums; and rather than how little we can give, we consider how much we might be able to give. This involves the totality of our being—our talents, our treasures, and our time. When we think about our salvation, we know we cannot out-give God.

If we go beyond duty, three things will inevitably happen. We all know we have kingdom responsibilities. When we accept this and do more than the minimum, we can say we did something and sleep with a free conscience. That's first. Second, we can live in the company of the committed. We read of many in the New Testament who walked the second mile. Mary with her alabaster box and the widow in the Temple giving out of her poverty, as well as those first apostles, all living beyond the demands of duty. Third, we can live in the companionship of Christ, the One who said, "Follow me." If we do, I assure you, it will be beyond the mile marker. Then we will know the real joy of stewardship, and the church worldwide will be blessed immeasurably. (Drew J. Gunnells Jr.)

Worship Aids

Invocation

Loving God, we pause to remind ourselves of your presence. We need not invoke it in order to bring you before us, but rather to bring our lives before you. We stand in your presence and are thankful. Amen.

Call to Worship

Leader: God is with us.

People: God is with us where we work and where we play.

Leader: God is with us in times of joy and times of heartache.

People: God is in this place. Let us worship and give thanks.
(Gary G. Kindley)

Stewardship Prayer

Help us this day, O Holy God, turn our hands loose from these things of the earth—our gifts and resources—that have been advanced to us by your gracious hand. Make us ever mindful that these resources were never really ours, but only a sacred trust that you offered us to manage for a time. May we use and choose wisely as we administer the things in the household of God. Let these gifts bless the lives of others and the life of your church. Amen. (David N. Mosser)

Benediction

May we accompany you into the world on this journey of life, merciful God. May we, like the Christ, be a daily incarnation of your love and your peace. Amen. (Gary G. Kindley)

NOVEMBER 4, 2007

❧❧❧

Twenty-third Sunday after Pentecost

Readings: Habakkuk 1:1-4; 2:1-4; Psalm 119:137-144; 2 Thessalonians 1:1-4, 11-12; Luke 19:1-10

Wait!
Habakkuk 1:1-4; 2:1-4

There is something utterly human about the cry of the prophet that opens this brief book. "O LORD, how long shall I cry for help, and you will not listen? Or cry to you 'Violence!' and you will not save?" (Habakkuk 1:2). In a profound sense, this is the cry of all people of faith. The problem of theodicy (evil) in our world confronts us daily. The tsunami of December 2004 raised the issue of God's justice worldwide. Continuing war and conflict with terrorism evoke the cry around us. For many, violence in our own cities and neighborhoods invests the cry of Habakkuk with deeply personal meaning. Even a casual reading of the morning paper or halfhearted attention to the evening news beckons the cry of Habakkuk. Few issues challenge Christian faith as deeply or as personally as this question of the justice of God.

Habakkuk probably writes near the end of the seventh century B.C.E. The first two chapters are a dialogue between the prophet and God. These opening verses are directed to God as a challenge. The prophet experiences devastation and ruin, which challenge his faith. It is important to grasp that Habakkuk does not ask his question as an academic question. He is living the theological struggle expressed in the passage.

To understand this text, one must not shy away from the challenge. The prophet doesn't mince words, nor should we. What are we to think and do as a people of faith when we see evil apparently triumphant around us? Where is God when disaster and tragedy strike us?

Many a well-intended Christian gets caught in the trap of trying to excuse God or deny doubts and struggles over the issue of evil. The prophet models faithfulness in his willingness to take his struggles to the Lord. (The idea "take it to the Lord in prayer" is often sung but too often ignored.) Habakkuk does the opposite. He models faithful integrity by placing the heart-wrenching issues of his life before God. We should do the same.

The second half of the lectionary text jumps to the opening of the second chapter. The questions posed in the first chapter are now answered. What should we do when disaster and tragedy strike? We are to remain faithful. The image in verse 1 is of a soldier on guard. To stand watch does not mean to wait passively but to be expectantly on duty. There is a clearly implied trust of the superior officer for whom one is on guard. There is confidence that God will answer.

What lies behind the image of a guard on duty, of working the ramparts, is an abiding trust and confidence in God. The first response to tragedy is to be that of trusting God even in our complaint! The soldier on duty knows that he or she has not been abandoned. So too the second element of this sermon might focus on active, expectant trust. It may appear that God has abandoned us. It may seem that evil has triumphed, but the faithful will remain strong in their trust. They will stay at their posts.

Verses 2 through 4 of the second chapter provide God's answer: "There is still a vision for the appointed time." Let all see that God has not forsaken or forgotten you. The "runner" may be a reference to a herald. In ancient times, heralds would bring news if the battle was lost or won. Anxiously, people would await the news. To "make it plain on tablets" was to make it clear to all that God will ultimately be victorious, regardless of how dire the present circumstances are. In writing in large letters on a tablet, even someone running by could read the words.

The passage then moves us to embrace patience as an active form of trust and faithfulness. We can wait impatiently or rebelliously. We can wait in resignation and hopelessness, but the Lord calls us to wait actively with expectant faith. It may be delayed, but God's vindication will come. This passage probably represents a period of late Judaism, which waits for the Messiah. The application for our time is just as clear. Whether or not it is clear to us at the moment, God will come. The Lord does and will reign triumphant. Within the text, there is a deep sense of hope and encouragement given from God.

This is a hard word for us to hear from God. We live in an age of instant gratification. All too often our prayer is, "Lord, grant me patience, and I want it right now!" Yet biblically, active waiting, expectant waiting, trust-filled waiting is a crucial component of faithfulness. Isaiah's words apply here as well: "Those who wait for the LORD shall renew their strength" (Isaiah 40:31). It is important to spell out what such waiting looks like in our day.

The fourth verse adds a pointed closing. It warns us to not rely on ourselves but to fully trust God. The spirit is not right in the proud, but the right Spirit is in the righteous, because they live by faith. The faithful proclamation of this passage closes with a challenge to live faithfully in expectant, hope-filled trust. It is not a big thing to believe in God when life is fine. It is a whole (and holy) greater step to live in faithful trust and obedience when the way ahead appears clouded by despair. Perhaps the best closing to this sermon might well be a story from someone who has done so. Do you know such a person? (Mike Lowry)

Double or Nothing

Second in a Series of Four

Matthew 25:14-30

On Tuesday of the last week of Jesus' earthly life, he was involved in keen debate and bitter controversy with Jewish leaders irrevocably committed to killing him. To this day, scholars refer to Tuesday of Passion Week as the "Day of Controversy." When the leaders resisted all of Jesus' overtures and teaching, Jesus realized the hardness of their hearts and retreated to the Mount of Olives to teach. Deeply conscious of his coming departure, Jesus earnestly prepared the disciples for the time when they would have to work without him. To be effective, they must be good stewards of that which Jesus had committed to them.

With this in mind, Jesus told the parable of the talents. A wealthy man departing on a trip gave his servants money to use as capital in making business investments. The master's absence gave the servants time to prove their faithfulness in the use of the money. Obviously the master expected the servants to make some profit for him in this business transaction. The money was distributed in varying amounts according to the abilities of the servants. In modern equivalents we would say one servant received $5,000; another, $2,000; and the third, $1,000. This was a lot of money in a society in which a working man's yearly wage amounted to about $50!

The result is interesting. Two of the servants put their money to work immediately and realized 100 percent profit for their master. They did not know how long the master would be away, but they did understand the importance of being prompt in utilizing their abilities. The master commended these two servants. On the other hand, the man with one talent simply buried his talent. The master had nothing but contempt and anger for him.

In this story we often emphasize the individual with either five talents or one talent. We usually overlook the servant with the two talents. There is no real difference in the one given five talents and the one given two. Both doubled their investment; both received identical praise from the master. These two who were found faithful were rewarded with additional opportunity. The reward for faithfulness is not rest, but increased possibility for success.

The spotlight of the text, however, shines on the servant who refused to employ the gifts he had. The master gave him what he thought he was capable of managing, but the servant failed even with that. He was not criticized because he did not make two or five additional talents. He was criticized because he failed to produce anything! Notice how long it takes this servant to explain his failure. His failure was not in being dishonest or in squandering his money. He was neither bad nor wasteful. He simply did not use the talent he was given. Obviously he expected commendation but, rather than being called "good and faithful," he was called "wicked and slothful" (Matthew 25:26 RSV). Simply put, he was lazy. His punishment for neglecting opportunity was the denial of further opportunity. He lost even what he had.

In this parable several truths about stewardship emerge. The earth is the Lord's to do with as God wishes. Whatever talents we have are gifts—gifts of grace to be used for kingdom-building. At this point, we have security in knowing that we are accountable to God, not people. Furthermore, we know God is trustworthy. God's expectations are according to our abilities. Although sometimes overlooked, God's standard is dedication or faithfulness with what we have. We are not responsible for what others might have. Instead, our responsibility brings attending accountability.

Finally, faithfulness always involves some risk. This should come as no surprise! Risks are evident in every great adventure of life—friendship, love, marriage, or parenthood. Jesus cautioned us against an unwillingness to take these risks. He is forever saying, "Launch out into the deep." He knows that we cannot "find life" by "saving it" but by "losing it" in a noble, worthy cause. Any study of the Bible will lead us to discover that the faithful, the greatest servants of God, were the risk-takers.

Are modern church members guilty of hiding their talents rather than utilizing them? Do we bury our uniqueness in the sands of legalism lest we offend someone, rather than risk new approaches or innovative methods? We often say the message does not change, but the methods of sharing that message do. The churches I see growing are willing to risk, to invest, and to utilize their talents fully.

In a nutshell, we know that God created everything. God decided to share God's gifts with the likes of us—not equally but according to our abilities. God's expectation is that we will be faithful stewards of that which God has given us. Finally and ultimately, God declares our success in terms of faithfulness with that which has been entrusted to us. If we do not use what God has given us, we will lose it. If we use these things wisely, God will give us more opportunity.

Does this all relate to stewardship? I think so! Not in a legalistic way that some might indicate, but rather in the sense that those who have been blessed are to be a blessing. God's gifts are tools for service, not rewards for super-spirituality or personal pride! Although I cannot speak for all, I can testify that things always go better in my life when I remember my debts to God and to others. God has given so much to me that I want to give something back. For me and mine, there is truth in the title of this sermon. If we use wisely what God has given us, God will bless us additionally. If we bury our talents, we will lose even what we have. It really is a case of "Double or Nothing!" (Drew J. Gunnells Jr.)

Worship Aids

Call to Worship

Saints are fellow-strugglers who look beyond to see that which is true and transcendent. Today, we honor and we remember the saints whose lives have blessed our lives. Today, at God's table, we will leave an empty chair in remembrance of those who have gone before us. We remember those for whom suffering and crying and pain are no more. Today we worship, and feast, and remember.

Words of Assurance for All Saints' Observance (For dismissal at the table of the Lord's Supper)

Arise and go forth. Serve God, love others, be the saints of the church in the world each day. Amen. (Gary G. Kindley)

Prayer of Confession

When we come to you, O God, we do so upon bended knee. We know that when we measure our lives against the perfect righteousness of Jesus Christ our Lord and Savior, we recognize how we have missed the mark and fallen short of what disciples are to be. You offer us the Holy Spirit to guide and counsel us, yet we have failed to take full advantage of this precious gift for the living of true, full, and meaningful lives. Guide us into all righteousness and once again make us your people. We pray this confession and plea for mercy in the name of the One who offers all the forgiveness that passes all human understanding, Jesus, our Christ. Amen. (David N. Mosser)

Benediction for All Saints' Observance

Go forth to live as saints of the faith. Serve God. Love all. Show mercy. Forgive abundantly. Amen. (Gary G. Kindley)

NOVEMBER 11, 2007

❧❧❧

Twenty-fourth Sunday after Pentecost

Readings: Haggai 1:15b–2:9; Psalm 145:1-5, 17-21; 2 Thessalonians 2:1-5, 13-17; Luke 20:27-38

Take Courage and Get to Work!
Haggai 1:15b–2:9

You and I know what it is like to start something and then, in the middle of things, to get bogged down or hit a wall. We encounter problems, get tired, become discouraged. We cannot remember what the purpose is and lose energy for the task at hand. Some days, it is all we can do to make it to the office and get our kids where they need to go and buy the groceries and get them into the house. Given the state of the world with its running bad news of violence, war, and starvation; and the state of our culture with its pressures and temptations, it is no wonder that we feel anxious and want to go and hide somewhere and even quit. In times like these, it is easy to become like the people in Haggai's neighborhood and hurry to our houses, pull down the shades, and lose ourselves in some "reality-that-really-isn't-reality" television show.

The people of Haggai's neighborhood had hit a wall. But it did not start out that way. After the long years of the exile, they had finally returned home to Jerusalem, to find a city left in ruins and their beloved Temple reduced to a pile of rubble. At first, the people had high hopes and determination to rebuild. During captivity, the people had kept alive the memory of their vast and beautiful house of God on the holy hill. Building a new Temple would be a physical sign of their commitment to the God who had made a way out of Babylon and who now dwelled in their midst. So, only seven months after their return, an altar was constructed and the feast days were reinstated. In modern terminology, an architect was hired and construction bids were taken.

But the bulldozers and diggers came to a standstill. The temple build-ing never got beyond blueprints, for a variety of valid reasons. There was the political situation, for one. Little Judah was caught in the cross fire of surrounding kingdoms in revolt against the Persian Empire. Also, the economy was in trouble; after years of decline, of drought and famine, cash flow was a problem. Finally, Judah's "culture wars," between the returning righteous remnant and the Samaritans who were already living and working the land, had broken old tensions wide open.

Into this work stoppage came Haggai, trying to coax the tired and anx-ious workers to get back on the job. But really, Haggai! Given the state of their world at home and abroad, with enemies prowling at the borders, money going out as fast as it came in, and intercultural politics, it was not the right time to launch a building campaign. Give the people a break! Who could blame them for concentrating on their own survival and building good, safe houses and letting the religious duties take a backseat? Who could blame them for taking care of their families first and waiting to see if things got better in the next term?

Well, God could, that's who! Haggai told the people that God was tired of seeing the rubble and was ready to see some walls. The people had neg-lected their true business and run off from the work at hand. Haggai called the people to remember that their service to God was all about building the Temple—the nitty-gritty labor of hauling wood and stone, hammering and sawing, laying the foundation, and all of that—because building a new Temple would signify their recommitment to God's wor-ship and service.

For Haggai, the work stoppage was a signal that somewhere in the mid-dle their preoccupation with national security, personal financial stabil-ity, and power jostling, God's people had lost their sense of purpose. John Calvin got to the bottom of why this happened: "every one studied his own domestic interest, and had no concern for the building of the Temple" (John Calvin, *Commentary on Habakkuk, Zephaniah, and Haggai* [vol. 4 of *Commentaries of the Twelve Minor Prophets*; trans. John Owen; Grand Rapids: Eerdmans, 1950], 316). Calvin continues: they "were neg-ligent, because they were too much devoted to their own private advan-tages" (321). Calvin describes the spiritual condition of the people as one of ungrateful indifference allied with ungodliness and even accuses the people of a "sloth" (330), which has offended God and provoked God's wrath. For Calvin, *sloth* does not mean simply "laziness." Sloth is a spiri-tual condition. It is being asleep to the call of God to get to work. There is a "zoning-out" of our souls, a paralysis of action; temple-building comes to a standstill.

Haggai called the people to get back to God's work, to pick up the pieces in the middle of the ruins and add some new ones, to get to the tasks of measuring and visioning the end result. In so doing they would make a statement about where they put their ultimate trust and found their strength.

As Christians, we profess that Jesus is the manifestation of God's rule and grace. Our temple is now a spiritual temple, with Jesus Christ God's own precious cornerstone. Our temple has walls; and it goes way beyond walls. It is where the gospel is proclaimed, where the lost are found, where the captives are set free. God calls us to build a spiritual and physical temple in our time and place, in the midst of our own rubble, and to be the sign of the One who came to seek and save. But our building plans get sidetracked too.

Perhaps we have also lost a sense of purpose. Paralysis often stems from discouragement, not so much about doing the work, but from the lack of immediate and impressive results. The talk about the temple today might sound like this: "Have you seen the blueprints? The plans for this temple look pretty measly compared to the big, beautiful, and important Temple that once stood on Zion. What are we building here—a shed? This temple won't ever be as magnificent as before." Our vision is too small, and so we give up and begin to languish in discouragement and resignation.

Just as we pull down the shades and settle back to "zone out," God speaks and starts to shake us out of it: "See where you have grown coldly ungrateful and indifferent to me. Take stock of how you have become preoccupied with private interests and neglected your calling." Just when we have crumpled the blueprints and given in to discouragement, God encourages us, calling us to enlarge our vision. "The house I call you to build is not just what you can see at this moment. I will not disappoint you. For my glory will be greater than ever before and will fill this place in a way you cannot yet imagine." Haggai's message is for us as well.

Somewhere in the rubble, somewhere in our dangerous world, somewhere amid the feeling to chuck it all and hurry away to build our own houses and attend to our own problems, somewhere in our retreating slumber, the voice of God is calling to us: "Wake up, take courage, and start building my house!" May we hear, roll up our sleeves, and get back to work. (Laura Hollandsworth Jernigan)

Your Giving Gives You Away

Third in a Series of Four

Mark 12:38-44

Once again it is the Tuesday before the Crucifixion, and once again we find that stewardship is vital in the acts and teachings of Jesus. This time, Jesus' praise for a widow and her giving is set alongside condemnation of the Scribes and Pharisees. In addition to the scathing attack on their vanity in verses 38-39—their dress, fondness for attention, and places of honor in the synagogue and at feasts—the Lord declares, in verse 40, that their vanity is matched by their greed. Under the pretense of guiding widows to donate their houses to the Temple, these Scribes and Pharisees have taken control of the real estate for their own personal profit. In this pronouncement, the Lord hangs their hypocrisy on a line for all to see! Against this backdrop, Jesus praises the widow for her stewardship. The religious leaders are denounced, their poverty of spirit exposed; the widow's devotion is exalted, despite her poverty of material things. This is an assault on accepted judgment!

Picture the scene. Jesus walks into the Temple and into the Court of the Women. Between the Court of the Gentiles and the Court of the Women was a marble wall with nine gateways. Each had a sign overhead that read: "No foreigner may enter within the balustrade and enclosure around the sanctuary. Whoever is caught will render himself liable to the death penalty which will inevitably follow" (Leon Morris, *The Atonement: Its Meaning and Significance* [Downers Grove, Ill.: InterVarsity Press, 1983], 143). Thus Jews alone, both men and women, could walk this path.

Thirteen large brass receptacles, known as the "treasury," were placed here. Called trumpets because of the trumpet-shaped openings, nine of these were for the temple tax and four were for offerings—the purchase of wood, incense, temple decorations, and burnt offerings. Priests probably stood nearby to supervise the giving. Here Jesus sat down and silently watched the crowd as each person put money into the receptacles.

The rich were casting in many coins. Perhaps they had a knack for throwing them into the trumpet so that the coins rang all the way to the bottom of the container! Jesus notices a Jewish woman, a widow, who puts in two copper coins. She is not called by name but is another of the anonymous biblical characters known only by their faith. Mark mentions that she gave two lepta. This would equal one quadrans, a Roman coin worth about half an American penny. The contrast between the wealth of the rich and the poverty of this woman is undeniable and unforgettable. Jesus calls the disciples and gives them a lesson on giving: "This poor widow hath cast more in than all they which have cast into the treasury."

How do you measure a gift? Jesus measures our giving not by how much we give but by the depth of the giving. Verse 44 sums it all up clearly and pointedly: "They [speaking of the wealthy] all gave out of their wealth; but she, out of her poverty, put in everything—all she had to live on" (NIV).

The widow gave more than the others in two ways: (1) in proportion to what she had and, (2) in the spirit she displayed. God is not impressed with a large amount but with a sacrificial spirit. The gift of the widow weighed more on God's scales than that of the wealthy because it represented a sacrificial, loving spirit. Maybe it would be a divine assessment to say the widow's gift, although copper, was pure gold in the eyes of the Lord.

All of this leads to some significant conclusions. First, there is an undeniable relationship between genuine spirituality and sacrificial giving. Seldom in my ministry have I found a liberal giver who is not genuinely committed to Christ. Second, the spirit of the giver *can* be reflected in the size of the gift. The measure must never be a comparison with others but rather in the ability one possesses. The reason the rich man's offering was not acceptable is illustrated in different translations of the text. The KJV says they gave "of their abundance." Another says, "what they didn't need" (CEV). Third, real giving has a certain recklessness about it. This kind of giving exhibits a leap of faith, trusting God with everything.

Is it fair to say that Jesus still sits over by the treasury? Is how we give as important as what we give? Is stewardship a barometer of the spiritual climate within? We only fool ourselves if we think we can be good Christians and not be concerned with stewardship.

When my father died I was living in another state. I traveled home and, after the funeral, spent some time helping my mother with business affairs. I found my father's checkbook in the bedroom; the last check he had written was to his church. In more ways than one, our giving does give us away.

Your commitment to Christ, your love of the church, your burden for the lost, your concern about the needy in the world—all these are reflected in your total sense of stewardship. What others may think about it is not important. As the Lord sits by the treasury he sees your gift, and, more important, he sees your heart. Only Jesus is qualified to judge, and what Jesus thinks is eternally important. What does your giving say? (Drew J. Gunnells Jr.)

Worship Aids

Call to Worship

Heroes and heroines are persons whose lives reflect character and conviction. They are people who overcome, people who persevere, and people who press on. Today, we worship God, we remember the heroes and heroines of our world, and we remember the sacrifices paid for liberty everywhere. In the name of the Prince of Peace, we remember. Amen.

Invocation

God, grant us peace. May we never take for granted the liberty that is ours, nor the price that has been paid for such a gift. We give thanks for the liberation of our souls through Christ, and the liberty of our nation through service. We gather to give thanks, to worship, and to remember. Amen.

Benediction

We leave now to serve. We serve now to live. We live now to love. Thanks be to God! Amen. (Gary G. Kindley)

NOVEMBER 18, 2007

❧❧❧

Twenty-fifth Sunday after Pentecost

Readings: Isaiah 65:17-25; Psalm 98; 2 Thessalonians 3:6-13; Luke 21:5-19

Rejoice in What God Is Creating
Isaiah 65:17-25

We have a problem in our house. It is a problem with dirty clothes left on the floor—nowhere near the laundry chute. I am guilty, my husband is guilty, and my three boys are very guilty. When I make a request of my children or give a gentle reminder to pick up their clothes and throw them down the chute, I usually get no response. When I make a demand, as in "Pick up your dirty clothes!" I might hear someone mumble, "In a minute," but nothing happens. When I start yelling and threatening loss of privileges, the response is often different: "Okay, okay, I'm doing it!"

There's an important distinction between "I will do it" and "I am doing it now!" When I hear someone say in my house, "I will do it," I am not sure, based on previous experience, whether the act will ever be accomplished and am fairly certain that I will end up picking up the dirty clothes and throwing them down the chute. But when I see someone actually putting clothes down the laundry chute, I am helped with the housework. Doing it, present tense, makes all the difference.

The NRSV translation of Isaiah 65:17 is: "I am about to create new heavens and a new earth." An alternate translation of the Hebrew verb tense is: "See, I am creating a new heaven and a new earth." Similarly, in verse 18, we can read, "Be glad and rejoice forever in what I am creating." Notice the present tense. The difference is crucial for our faith, for when we can see that God is actually creating something new, we are helped in the here and now.

Isaiah wants us to get the difference, to see God actually taking charge and doing a new thing. According to the prophet, God has had it with "the dirty socks" lying on the floor, with the corruption and the playing around with lesser gods and the church politics and the injustice in society. God is heartsick at the bitter fortunes and wrong choices of God's people. "Therefore," says the Lord, "I am turning my head away from your former ways and the tragic past. I am making something new. I am shaping a new Jerusalem which is much better; it gives me such delight that I want you to delight in it with me!"

Isaiah proclaims good news, to be seen and experienced in the now. Before, there was war in which enemies trampled farms and occupied houses. Now, God is creating a new Jerusalem in which people live securely in their homes and enjoy the fruits of their labors. Before, mothers feared to give birth to their children in a dangerous world. Now, God is creating a world where parents anticipate the blessing of children and are confident of their futures. Before, the people wondered if God even heard their cries. Now, God is creating a relationship in which God will hear before they even speak. Before, conflict tore communities apart. Now, God is creating a peaceful reign where longtime enemies, even the wolf and the lamb, will dwell together side by side. "Behold! See what God is creating!"

Do we see it here and now? Are we in the present tense with God? Maybe—maybe not. To be honest, we might be living in the past tense, in the old Jerusalem. Much would hold us there: ugly laundry is spilling in and out of homes, neighborhoods, cities, and planet Earth; and we cannot see God doing anything about it. After all, we are the post–9/11 people, the ones dealing with the terrible realities of burying our war dead, watching the poor get poorer while the rich get richer, seeing the present-day residents of Jerusalem bombed and retaliating with bombs. It is indeed difficult to behold what God is up to in this present tense. But that is exactly what Isaiah invites us to do.

Let's be clear: Isaiah is not pushing a "grin and bear it" attitude, nor a "Just get through it and move on" philosophy. Neither is Isaiah espousing a theology that says, "Never mind about all you have to suffer today. Just wait until you get to heaven, and then you can forget all of this stuff!" Isaiah invites us to glimpse the new Jerusalem, to see signs of the new heaven and new earth, to look for evidence of God's purposeful activity before us and beyond our periphery, to look for ways God is casting away sorrow and pain, making peace and love the order of the day, to delight in that with God. It takes a leap of faith to live in this present sense, but when we do, we start to see what God is doing.

I catch a glimpse when a young man, bright and capable but caught in the downward spiral of drugs, goes out to get a gun to kill himself; but something drives him to pray and he gets on his knees. Help comes, and his life is turned around. "Rejoice with me!"

We catch a glimpse when a retired woman begins to tutor an immigrant child at the neighborhood school, and the child begins to speak English less timidly and starts to learn to read. "Delight in what I am doing!"

We catch a glimpse when a conversation between a visiting server and a homeless guest at a soup kitchen leads to shared stories and a commitment to prayer. "Be glad!"

We catch a glimpse when a group of African church youth, poor and facing hardship, gather in a field and sing and dance their praise, and testify to Jesus Christ. "Behold, I am doing a new thing!"

Be assured. God is creating a new creation. God is not waiting around to do it. God is doing it, present tense. God invites us to join and celebrate. May we catch a glimpse, and delight in the present tense with our God. (Laura Hollandsworth Jernigan)

Concerning the Collection

Fourth in a Series of Four

1 Corinthians 16:1-4

From the lofty reaches of Paul's incomparable discussion of the Resurrection, he immediately plunges into the pointed matter of the offering for the saints in Jerusalem. This particular offering is also mentioned in four other passages of the New Testament: Galatians 2:10; Romans 15:25-29; 2 Corinthians 8–9; and Acts 24:17. This gifted apostle had no difficulty making the transition from the highly theological to the essentially practical. For Paul and for us, this is not just a good approach; it is an absolute necessity. The everyday life and administration of the church are essential if the gospel is to be preached to the ends of the earth. The effectiveness of ministers is determined by their ability to deal with both the theory and the practice of the gospel.

Evidently the Christians at Corinth had asked Paul about this collection. A year prior to this, the church had promised to contribute. They began the collection, but failed to complete the task (2 Corinthians 8:10). Paul says to them, "You made a commitment to do this and you should do it." The churches of Macedonia, especially the church at

Philippi, had responded well to the offering, but the church at Corinth lagged behind. The Corinthian church was preoccupied with petty problems and blind to a needy world. Strife in any church stifles stewardship—any strife and every time!

Why did Paul emphasize this offering? Paul had promised to remember the poor (Galatians 2:10). The Jewish Christians had a plan to help the poor, and Paul thought the Gentile Christians should as well. Paul also might have thought this offering would demonstrate the essential unity of the church. Perhaps he thought the offering would allay suspicion of his work among the Gentiles. Some of the Jewish brethren who had been so critical of Paul's work among the Gentiles might be more open to validate a missionary enterprise.

In our text Paul calls this offering a *logia*, which means an "extra collection." This is the very opposite of a religious tax. We must learn we never satisfy our duty by simply discharging a legal obligation. Grace demands more! This kind of gift is not extracted, but rather results from the overflowing love of God in one's heart. As a youngster I often heard my preacher speak of God's tithe and our offering. That's what a *logia* is!

Paul is very specific in his exhortation. These Corinthian Christians were to do this on the "first day of every week" (1 Corinthians 16:2), the Lord's Day, our Sunday. Of course, this day commemorated the resurrection of our Lord and indicated the importance early Christians placed on this day. In addition, everyone was to participate. No one was to be excluded. No matter how poor or how wealthy, each person in the entire church was to be involved.

"To lay by him in store" (KJV) implies "storehouse giving," bringing the offerings to the church each week. There were to be "no gatherings" (i.e., no gathering of money) when Paul arrived. Although the timing of his visit might have been uncertain, the timing of the collection was not. Here, "lay" has an imperative meaning; this is a command, not a suggestion. When we come to worship we should give both our offerings and ourselves. The ultimate destination for all our gifts should be Christ's church, the only institution Jesus established for the extension of his kingdom.

"As God hath prospered him" (KJV) means that our giving should be in direct proportion to the way we are prospering. Paul does not rely on the Jewish system of levying a tax on all males over twenty years of age. This collection seems to be a voluntary act without any definite amount and no exact proportion. Being a Jewish Christian, Paul no doubt tithed;

however, in this text Paul lifted giving far beyond a legal system to a much higher plane.

The offering was to be taken to Jerusalem by individuals approved by the church. Perhaps some of Paul's enemies had accused him of being mercenary and Paul wanted no suspicion on this point. Early in my ministry, an older preacher counseled me not to count any money, not to have a key to any place money was kept, and not to sign or countersign any check. In other words, a pastor should avoid even the appearance of being mercenary. Paul arranged the collection, but he did not plan to take it to Jerusalem personally.

The collection is a valid, scriptural part of any worship experience. Like any other business, the church must have strong financial undergirding. God has a plan for the support of divine work, and we are advised to work God's plan. With apology to none and adherence to the Bible, let us encourage God's people to support God's work. Every missionary depends upon our faithfulness, every Christian school depends upon our faithfulness, every social ministry depends upon our faithfulness, and every evangelistic outreach depends upon our faithfulness.

The collection is to be inclusive—everyone participates; systematic—done on the first day of each week; proportionate—as God has prospered us; and voluntary, not a tax—giving from the joy of our abundance. This is a sound program for any church! (Drew J. Gunnells Jr.)

Worship Aids

Call to Worship

Joining together, we unite in service. Grasping hands, we embrace in fellowship. Linking arms, we can do anything in the name of Jesus the Christ.

Pastoral Prayer

Thank you, Creator God, heavenly Father and Mother of us all, for the abundant blessings of life. We give thanks for holy moments and sacred memories that make life so cherished. These sacred times serve as reminders that life itself is a gift of grace.

We pray this day for those whose plight is desperate. We pray for children whose lives have been robbed of innocence by war, violence, poverty, or oppression. We pray for those who are wrongfully imprisoned because of politics or faith. We pray for those whose lives are oppressed by governments who demand obedience rather than affording liberty.

We confess, Creator God, we are slow in serving, begrudging in giving, and lacking in mercy. We are not the first to step forward when answering your call, and we balk at what you might expect from us. Grant us the courage of our convictions, so that our faith might be in deeds and not just words. Empower us to be bold in our living and brave in our service. Through Christ we pray. Amen.

Benediction

May the God of assurance, comfort, consolation, and hope embrace you in times of fearfulness, and lift you up in times of weariness. Go out in peace. Amen. (Gary G. Kindley)

NOVEMBER 22, 2007

❧❧❧❧

Thanksgiving Day

Readings: Deuteronomy 26:1-11; Psalm 100; Philippians 4:4-9; John 6:25-35

Say "Thank You" to the Nice Lady
Deuteronomy 26:1-11

There are some hymns that I think we need to sing more often. Among these, the ones that reflect Thanksgiving and its themes are those we simply do not sing enough, in my estimation. What adds to this particular problem is that few churches actually worship on Thanksgiving Day. If we did, I would get a "double portion" of the hymns I love, including: "We Gather Together to Ask the Lord's Blessing," "Now Thank We All Our God," and "What Gift Can We Bring?" Clearly there are other thanksgiving-type hymns, but if we sang these three more than once a year then, in the words of Simeon, I could let God dismiss "your servant in peace, according to your word" (Luke 2:29). Is this attitude too sentimental?

Perhaps, but if there is one thing we Christian believers need help in expressing more thoroughly and more earnestly, it is the attitude of thanksgiving. It seems God has blessed us to such a great extent and for so long that we accept God's blessings, not as acts of divine grace, but rather as some sort of human entitlement. My father used to say that there was nothing worse than an "ingrate." Have we become a society— or worse, a church—of ingrates?

One of the Bible's greatest history lessons is that Yahweh, when the divine constituted the people of God, made certain that particular rituals were woven into the fabric of the community. One example is the ritual preparation for Passover (see Exodus 12). There we find detailed instructions on how, when, and where to eat the Passover meal. Moreover, these instructions yield theological meaning. Likewise, in our lesson for

Thanksgiving Day, the people of Israel are instructed concerning rituals that will continue to remind them that they are not like other people. They are a people, formed by God, to be a just society that bears in mind the less fortunate and a community that offers its thanksgiving to God. *[Read Deuteronomy 26:1-11.]*

Moses reminds the people of what they are to do when they have entered the land of promise. Not only will they possess it and settle it; they are also to offer "the first of all the fruit of the ground" (Deuteronomy 26:2). Why? Because, by offering their firstfruits to God, they remind themselves that they have not possessed and settled the land by their own doing. It is a gift from Yahweh. It is a divine expression of the grace in which they dwell. Nothing they do, nothing they can do, will alter the unearned nature of God's gift to them. The proper response of the people is clearly not self-congratulation—the appropriate response is nothing other than a human expression of thanksgiving to God Almighty. In fact, the text tells us that Yahweh and Moses leave nothing to chance. The manner of the collection and the persons who are responsible for the gathering of the gifts are quite explicit. The offering commemorates "that I [or we] have come into the land that the LORD swore to our ancestors to give us" (v. 3).

Along with the gift, a response is offered that is a reminder of why this gift and this land are important: "A wandering Aramean was my ancestor; he went down into Egypt and lived there as an alien, few in number, and there he became a great nation, mighty and populous" (v. 5). The response ends appropriately enough with these words: "The LORD brought us out of Egypt with a mighty hand and an outstretched arm ... and he brought us into this place and gave us this land, a land flowing with milk and honey" (vv. 8-9).

When the people bring their firstfruits to the Lord, they do so as a token sign and symbol of the lavish gifts that God has poured out on their community. The Hebrews worship a generous and benevolent God. And this same God expects them to live lives that reflect the generous and benevolent God they worship. In other words, Yahweh, through Moses, teaches the people the fine art of generosity toward others.

Now that I am a grandfather, I recognize that children are not born grateful—not even the best of children. Before I was blessed with a granddaughter, it was relatively simple to avoid, or at least ignore, all of the world's rude, ungrateful children. However, I have repeatedly watched my daughter and her husband remind their three-year-old daughter to "say

'Thank you' to the nice lady." My granddaughter is to say this to a stranger who has shown her some kindness or another. This scene, played out in numerous ways and places, has taught me a great truth—none of us are born grateful. Of course, it is easier to observe ingratitude in others, especially small children, than to see it in our own lives. Yet the lesson from Deuteronomy is another way that God reminds all of us, three-year-olds and grandfathers, that gratitude is a characteristic we need to learn and cultivate. We are not born grateful or thankful—we need to learn and learn, again and again.

In God's wisdom, reflected in the wisdom of the Hebrew people, a necessary means of helping us offer thanks has been provided. This means is worship. Worship offers believers a chance to say "Thank you" to the nice lady, in a manner of speaking. Worship is where we consider God's goodness and respond in a manner that reflects gratitude for the great many things we cannot do for ourselves.

So the next time you are feeling a bit cheery about your good fortune, remember that God has provided for you and give thanks. God may not be exactly a "nice lady," but it is not a bad place to begin. Amen. (David N. Mosser)

A Lesson in Praise and Thanksgiving
Luke 17:11-19

In a few short verses, Luke tells a wonderful story of how Jesus healed ten "lepers."* It is obvious from the setting that the disciples are present when this happens, although they are not involved in the process.

Jesus is traveling along the border between Samaria and Galilee, on his way to Jerusalem. As he enters a village, ten "lepers" are standing "far off." The law specified that if the wind was blowing from the direction of such people, they must remain at a distance of fifty yards from healthy people. The sufferers recognize Jesus. We do not know how they know who Jesus is, but they seem to know. They cry out in a loud voice, "Jesus, Master, have mercy on us!" (Luke 17:13). Jesus comes to where they are. He does not "cry out" to them but is near enough to converse with them, which is dangerous given the seriousness of this contagious disease. He simply says, "Go and show yourselves to the priests" (v. 14). The priests of that time were the ones to diagnose illness, and only the priests could pronounce them well. Here Jesus is functioning within the framework of the religious and social establishments. He wants them to be "officially" well so they can go back to the lives from which they have been banished by their illness.

On their way to do as Jesus had instructed, they were healed. One of them, when he saw that he had been healed, came back, "praising God in a loud voice. He prostrated himself at Jesus' feet and thanked him" (vv. 15-16). Now comes the "stinger" for the Jews. Luke reports that the one who came back was a Samaritan. This is not the first time Luke makes a hated Samaritan the "good guy" in a story. Remember the story of the "good Samaritan" (Luke 10:30-37)? Luke underscores this salient point as he has Jesus ask: "Were not ten made clean? But the other nine, where are they? Was none of them found to return and give praise to God except this foreigner?" (vv. 17-18). Jesus is sad and hurt that the Jews, who should have readily recognized him as the Messiah, have been blind to his identity. Now insult is added to injury. The Jews who have been healed walk away without so much as a "Thank you" while the hated enemy, a Samaritan, returns to praise God and give thanks. You may be sure that the subsequent Jewish readers (and leaders) were not blind to the point made.

Jesus' benediction on the life of the grateful foreigner makes one wonder about the relationship of gratitude to faith. Was there some species or degree of healing given the grateful Samaritan that the negligent nine missed? "Then he said to him, 'Get up and go on your way; your faith has made you well'" (v. 19). His faith was expressed in his gratitude. The nine had been healed, but this man seemed to have received something they missed. They received the gift for which they asked, but this grateful foreigner got more than he asked for—much more.

This thanksgiving story reminds us that gratitude is much more for the benefit of the grateful than it is for the benefit of the one to whom it is expressed. There is something transforming (saving) about genuine gratitude.

What has this to say to those who give help to people in the name of Jesus?

The absence of gratitude comes as no surprise to people who help people. It happens all the time. Some days it stings. In most cases you never really know why a person is grateful or ungrateful. The attitude of gratitude (or the absence thereof) arises from such unfathomable depths of the human psyche that we seldom, if ever, know "why," even if we take time to inquire and search. It happens.

People who are in the business of helping people for God's sake learn to rise above the compulsive need to receive gratitude from everybody they help, or they will soon leave the helping business. This does not mean we can or should be impervious to the attitudes of people we help. A word of genuine appreciation is always a source of encouragement. It does mean, when we are acting from the highest motivation, expressed gratitude will not be a condition for help.

Let's face it, the people in the greatest need of help are not always "nice" people. Many of them were not trained in the niceties of politeness. When you take food and clothing to homeless people, do not expect a thank-you note—perhaps not even a "Thank you" upon delivery. If we help people because our egos need to be boosted with praise for our acts of charity, then we will soon be sorely disappointed.

The sensitivity to "see" is essential in ministry to human need. It is easy to "turn a blind eye" to the kind of human need that, if we reach out and touch, will bring us no emotional rewards. Our spiritual maturity can be measured in direct proportion to our capacity to give to those in need without receiving the rewards of recognition, recompense, or gratitude. Jesus did not sit down and pout when only one of ten bothered to praise God for their healing and to thank Jesus as the emissary of God who brought the gift. He noted that the nine had missed something in the transaction. He affirmed the one whose gratitude and faith brought the wholeness he wanted for all of them. Then he went on his way. Can you hear what that means for ministry in our time? I hope so. It begs to be heard!

A Footnote for Creative Preachers:

After I finished this sermon brief, I remembered a book that contains a very creative homiletical approach to the question: "Where are the nine?" You may wish to find a copy and fashion a sermon around that format, adding your own prayerful imagination. The book is *The Way of the Wolf: The Gospel in New Images*, by Martin Bell. My edition is a Crossroad Book published by Seabury Press in 1968 (pages 47-52). The author speculates on why each of the nine failed to return to praise God and give thanks to Jesus. It is very good material worth reading. (Thomas Lane Butts)

*[Editor's Note: The disease labeled "leprosy" in the biblical texts is now known as Hansen's disease. Some may be sensitive to use of the term *leper* because of the stigma that has attached to that term through time.]

Worship Aids

Invocation

Dear God, we invoke your blessings upon our gathering today. Grant that our hearts and minds may be open to all the ways in which you wish to speak to us. May we shut out all thoughts that may block clear communication with you. In the name of Jesus, amen.

Pastoral Prayer

We come before you, O God, in praise and thanksgiving for all the blessings of which we are consciously aware: the joy of good health, the sight of friendly faces, the laughter of children; for food, clothing, shelter, and the beauty of nature.

We give thanks to you, O God, for unseen blessings that give meaning to our lives: peace in our hearts, courage to resist evil and affirm good, courage to be open and vulnerable, and a sense of security as we live our daily lives.

Forgive the sin that we have sense to see, which we have allowed to occur in our lives; and lead us not into temptation by the sin that lurks at the margins of life. Forgive us when our gratitude to you is not actively expressed in care and concern for others.

Help us, O God, to see our time in life as the precious gift that it is. Help us, O Lord, when our personal idiosyncrasies and unhealthy lifestyles impede us during the sacred journeys on which you have sent us. Help us when we are too proud to cry, too serious-minded to laugh, too sophisticated to enjoy, and too burdened to repent. Hear our prayer, in the name of Jesus. Amen.

Benediction

We give you thanks, O Lord, for your palpable presence in our worship in this place today, and we pray that this experience will make us more sensitive to your presence in the wide world into which we are about to walk. Amen.

NOVEMBER 25, 2007

❧❧❧

Reign of Christ/Christ the King

Readings: Jeremiah 23:1-6; Luke 1:68-79; Colossians 1:11-20; Luke 23:33-43

King of the Jews
Luke 23:33-43

Another liturgical year is almost in the books. Advent begins next week, signaling the beginning of a new liturgical year. On this last Sunday of the Christian year, the lectionary provides us with something of a capstone for "Year C," of which Luke has been the chief Gospel.

Much time has passed since we pondered Jesus' crucifixion. Luke 23:33-43 almost seems out of place today. As we anticipate what many people consider the best time of the year—the period between Thanksgiving and Christmas—we have a story that seems as if we should read it during Holy Week. Indeed, the Revised Common Lectionary places this text within the Liturgy of the Passion reading of Luke 23:1-49. I rest my case.

Why would the lectionary creators choose this text for the last Sunday of the year? Before attending to this central question, let us put the passage in context. Preceding today's lesson, Judas betrays Jesus (Luke 22:47-53) and Peter denies Jesus (Luke 22:62). Then, Jesus is not only mocked, but his accusers drag him before the religious authorities. Not wanting to be liable, the religious authorities drag Jesus before both Pilate and Herod. Jesus finally receives a death sentence (Luke 23:1-25).

It is at this point that today's lesson picks up the story. Jesus is crucified at the place that Luke calls "the Skull," although the other Gospels each use the term "Golgotha" (Matthew 27:33; Mark 15:22; John 19:17). Jesus is, of course, crucified between two criminals. In "The Seven Last Words" (see: *The United Methodist Book of Worship* [Nashville: The United Methodist Publishing House, 1992], 365), we read two of Jesus' seven utterances on Good Friday. The first of these seven words is, "Father, forgive them; for they do not know what they are doing" (Luke 23:34). The other last word in this text occurs when Jesus says to the "good" criminal, "Truly I tell you, today you will be with me in Paradise" (Luke 23:43). In addition, the text provides details of how soldiers divided Jesus' clothing and how the leaders jeered, "He saved others; let him save himself if he is the Messiah of God, his chosen one!" (Luke 23:35).

Perhaps most momentous is when some soldiers exclaim, "If you are the King of the Jews, save yourself!" (v. 37). Then Luke adds a telling detail: "There was also an inscription over him, 'This is the King of the Jews'" (v. 38).

Now we can address our earlier question: why would the lectionary creators select this text for the last Sunday of the year? Clearly, as we have followed Luke's story of Jesus through the liturgical year, we have learned many things about Jesus, and most important, from Jesus. Not only have we witnessed, through our reading and hearing of the Jesus story, miracle cures and splendid parables; we have also seen Jesus function as God's Messiah. There are so many things we have learned from and about Jesus since Holy Week that we might forget the true purpose of the Messiah.

Despite all that Luke offers us, the lectionary wants to make certain we do not neglect the central affirmation of the Christian faith as we end an old year. What the lectionary wants us to remember is that Jesus is "the King of the Jews" (Luke 23:38). Because Jesus is King of the Jews, he is also our Messiah, the Son of God, as Luke's Gospel reminds us (Luke 4:3, 9, 41; 22:70). This is the one truth we cannot forget. We may learn much on our journey with Jesus, but we must never forget that he is the Messiah, the Son of God, the Christ. Our lectionary today reinforces this vital gospel truth. The Christian faith's central vow is that Jesus is Lord and King.

When I was a small child, I watched a television show called *Queen for a Day* with my mother. As I remember the program, the intent was to make a housewife from Middle America a queen, if only for a day. The audience's applause decided which of the contestants was the most deserving of a new washing machine or vacuum cleaner or whatever household appliance was in vogue. I also remember that my mother really prized the show, although my sense of irony was well developed enough at five years of age to regard the program as a big joke.

Modern Americans may view royalty as a kind of joke, at least from our democratic perspective. Whether we remember our colonies defeating mighty King George or shake our heads over the latest scandal at Buckingham Palace, we do not tend to take the idea of monarchy seriously. Still, the Roman soldiers nailed an ironic title, "This is the King of the Jews," above Jesus' head. Perhaps, inadvertently, the crucifiers posed the eternal question to us: is Jesus really Lord and King?

I don't know how you might answer this question, but I suspect I know how Luke might answer. Luke might say to us, using the same words he put into the mouths of Jesus' companions and the eleven, "The Lord has risen indeed!" (Luke 24:33-34).

That old question remains our question for today. Is Jesus really King or is he not? If we need to dispense with the archaic language of monarchy, then our question becomes: is Jesus the controlling image of our lives with God and with other people or do other images govern our lives?

Whether or not you have a soft spot for kings in your philosophy of life, Jesus as Lord and King has a soft spot for you. The church calls it grace. (David N. Mosser)

Do You Hear What I Hear?
Luke 9:57-62

We have all heard the parables of the fox, the funeral, and the furrow many times, but do you hear what I hear?

In these parables, two persons volunteer to be disciples, and Jesus calls another. In the first dialogue, the would-be disciple may not understand that to follow Jesus means to follow him to Gethsemane, to Golgotha, and to the tomb. To follow Jesus means that, like Jesus, we really have no place to roost—we are to be like birds who "nest" only at certain times of the year. Are we prepared to pay the cost? (Remind you of the itinerant system?)

In the second dialogue, Jesus gives four commands, "Follow. Leave. Go. Proclaim."

This would-be follower wants to bury his father. Some would assume that the father is dead and needs burying. Scripture doesn't offer that much information.

Do you hear what I hear?

A first-century Jew or a Native American hears the would-be disciple asking, "Let me go and serve my father while he is alive and after he dies, I will bury him and then come." The Diné (Navajo), for example, have great respect for the family and community. Taking care of the parent is

of supreme importance, especially in their old age. Not only is the tradition of the family at stake, the dignity of the entire clan is affected. Jesus
is ordering this person to abandon his obligations to his family. Are we
prepared to pay the cost?

Look at the last dialogue. The volunteer adds a condition, "I will follow you *but* first let me go and bid my farewell to those who are at home"
(see Luke 9:61).

Do you hear what I hear?

Again, it would be easy to assume that this person, who seems to want
to follow Jesus, merely wishes to say good-bye to his parents. In the Old
Testament, Elisha wanted to kiss his father and mother good-bye before
he went off with Elijah. Elisha even took time to butcher and roast a pair
of oxen. Surely this is not an unreasonable request! For those of us who
are parents, wouldn't we be angry and hurt if one of our children called
from basic training camp and said, "I didn't have time to come say good-
bye, but you'll never guess where I am and where I'm going"?

In some modern cultures, there is even more to hear. For the Diné and
some in the Middle East, the person leaving must request permission from
those who are staying. To leave without permission is an insult to the elders, the family, the clan, and the tribe. In some cases, leaving without the
parents' knowledge may legally label one a runaway. In our Western independence and rebelliousness, we say, "I would never ask permission. I am of
age; I don't have to ask permission." Yet for many of us, whether ritualized
or not, having the family's blessing for our journey is of utmost importance.

Honestly, what would any sensible, levelheaded, rational, loving parent say to a child who wants to run all over the country with someone the
parents had never met, who doesn't have a real job, and who seems to
make enemies wherever he goes? This would-be follower is saying, "I must
ask permission from my family. I must ask and submit to my family's
authority." And Jesus says, "No, I have more authority than your family!"

These parables illustrate the tension between loyalty to culture and
family tradition and loyalty to Jesus as the inaugurator of the kingdom of
God and all of its demands. The person who cannot resolve the tension
of conflicting loyalties, who keeps turning back to look over her shoulder
to see what the family thinks, is judged "useless" for the kingdom of God.

The farmer and the plow is an apt illustration to sum up these lessons
on the cost of discipleship. The plowman, if distracted, may catch the
blade on a rock, or break the blade, or the plow will cut into another furrow. The furrows carry the water, so they need to be straight. To cut

another furrow directs the water away from the plants that need nurture. The farmer must guide the plow with one hand, determining the depth of the furrow, and guide the oxen the entire time. He labors in harmony with what is already done, what is being done now, and what lies ahead. The farmer is in harmony with the past, present, and future.

Navajos have a term for this: *hozho*. No one word will translate this; it means beauty, peace, harmony, balance. It is not just peace within one's self, it is harmony with others, with creation, with Creator. We are called to balance our lives in loving obedience to the Creator's purpose. Discipleship is strenuous, creative, and consuming, like putting one's hand to a plow and focusing on God only. It means a radical redefinition of *hozho* in our lives.

Jesus' commands are: follow, leave, go, and proclaim. Most of us have difficulty with that leave part. Leave behind family, previous assumptions, stereotypes, and behaviors. Perhaps leave behind that which society has named most valuable: affluence, prestige, a value system.

Discipleship is a calling, a lifestyle that demands integrity, honesty, and sacrifice.

Follow. Leave. Go. Proclaim. Do you hear what I hear?

Do you hear "me" or community?

Do you hear "job" or servanthood?

Do you hear "position" or discipleship?

We are not told if the three persons ever became disciples. These three short parables of the fox, the funeral, and the furrow have no ending. They are our stories too. Jesus commands: Follow. Leave. Go. Proclaim. Do you hear what I hear? (Raquel Mull)

Worship Aids

Call to Worship

We can embrace the promise of tomorrow and live with confidence for today. Christ, our Sovereign, has promised. Christ, our Sovereign, is faithful. Let us celebrate Christ the King!

Words of Assurance

Christ has the power to heal, comfort, redeem, and resurrect. Claim Christ's power. Live as Christ's people. You are forgiven. You are loved. You are redeemed! (Gary G. Kindley)

Pastoral Prayer

On this sacred Sabbath day, O God of grace and glory, we celebrate that Christ is indeed King. Jesus as our Christ has opened the door of salvation and offered us the rewards of a life lived in faith. Help us to recognize the precious gift that Christ offers us through his life, death, and resurrection. Let us take hold of the mercy offered in Jesus' cross and embrace the life he makes possible for us today. Help us become more hospitable to the guests among us and treat these persons of sacred worth with the compassion Christ first offered us. Bind us together as a congregation that calls itself the "body of Christ." In Jesus' name we pray. Amen. (David N. Mosser)

Benediction

Christ is not an earthly king but an eternal Redeemer. Go forth with the power and love of Christ. Be bold as you serve with gladness and joy. Amen. (Gary G. Kindley)

DECEMBER 2, 2007

❧❧❧

First Sunday of Advent

Readings: Isaiah 2:1-5; Psalm 122; Romans 13:11-14; Matthew 24:36-44

Ascending the Mountain of the Lord
Isaiah 2:1-5

What price does a nation pay in conducting war? Certainly we can gauge economic costs: dollars spent on recruiting, equipping, and training soldiers to fight; monies for assisting war-torn countries in returning to social stability; funds needed to help families of wounded and dead service members in living life after combat. Yet the cost in waging war is greater than mere figures indicate. What price does a nation pay in conducting war? We pay in national values, with beliefs gained or lost through the necessary cultural debate. We pay in national resolve, with the ebb and flow of support in response to battlefield dispatches. Perhaps most important, we pay in national will, with the cultural numbing that accompanies news of wounded, dead, and missing soldiers and civilians. Often, these costs exact a far greater price on us than we first anticipate.

After the terrorist attacks of September 11, 2001, America responded by destroying the government haven that terrorists had found in the Taliban regime in Afghanistan. Toward this action, there was almost a national consensus, with only a minority of disagreement. Sharper, however, was the debate that met the decision to wage war in Iraq to depose Saddam Hussein and establish democracy in that nation. Whether one agrees or disagrees with the decisions to conduct war in both these theaters, there is no doubt that America is now engaged in prolonged combat, perhaps for many years. We are learning again that this reality carries a heavy price, a cost to our national character beyond the projections of budgets or expenditures. We are learning again that our decisions exact a toll, not just on those enemies who would destroy us, but on our own values, resolve, and will.

Why is this important as we approach Advent this year? In the time of the prophet Isaiah, Israel was learning about itself as it struggled through the crucible of war. Inured for years to the consequences of its actions by the promise of Davidic kingship, Israel dared to think itself immune from attack by outside neighbors. As many biblical scholars agree, a stream of thought runs through Isaiah that posits, "Surely God is with us because of his promise to David to maintain his throne forever; we have nothing about which to worry."

Israel was trading on God's blessing, believing that God's grace was due more to their righteousness than to God's boundless love. In this, they made a crucial error; God would not have the divine character misconstrued. In an ironic connection to our own situation, God allowed Assyria, the greatest superpower of the day (located in modern northern Iraq) to conquer, though not completely destroy, Israel. In the wake of this disaster, Israel engaged in a wrenching theological debate, asking itself: what hope is there for us now? Israel realized that the war it had brought upon itself had a greater cost than could be calculated by money alone; it cut to the very core of their national being, and required a reassessment of their relationship to God.

As a result, Israel realized something critical: it desperately needed to rediscover its hope in God. This is no mean feat for a people. To collectively awaken to a lack of hope consigns a culture to certain destruction, yet how many have succumbed to such national suicide? Israel, however, moved beyond hopelessness and renewed its sustaining trust in God. For other peoples this may have seemed a naively desperate ploy to stave off collapse, but for Israel, who knew—really knew—God's sustaining power, this was the prescription for recovery. They returned to an eschatological hope in the certain triumph of God over the kingdoms of that day or any day. Essentially, Israel awakened its liturgical consciousness and remembered that beyond its current circumstances, God offered an alternative vision of time that no other nation could see. Israel remembered that beyond the earthly power of Assyria, God controls destiny through the in-breaking of God's kingdom. Indeed, in liturgy, God's people engage not simply in passive memory, but in the active expression of hope.

As a result, Israel sang anew of "the day of the Lord," a great day, an almost cosmic day, when God will turn the existing order of peoples on its head and when tiny Israel will be the conduit for God's grace in the world. Rather than great nations being defined by military, economic, or political influence, Israel will be the path through which people ascend the mountain of the Lord to seek God's face. Moreover, old things will pass away as God metes out justice based on faithfulness and obedience to God; where nations respond by abandoning their previous ways, to the point of using instruments once destined for war to till the land in harvest. Indeed, this was, and is, an alternative view of time worthy of song and praise, one that inspires hope when hope fades in the light of unimagined circumstances.

So this Advent, as our nation lives with its decisions to stand and fight a war with which our children shall live, where do we as a church find hope? This Advent, what do we as the people of God say to the nation and world around us? With ancient Israel, as the people of God, we offer an alternative vision of time. We see that beyond mere circumstance, a day is coming when God will reorder time to consummate his kingdom through the second coming of God's Messiah, our Lord, Jesus Christ. We too look to that day when we ascend the mountain of the Lord and creation is reordered to reflect God's desire to give life to those whom God loves. Truly, then, we hope in that promise and watch for its occurring. In the words of the ancient church's breath prayer, "Even so, Lord, come." Amen. (Timothy S. Mallard)

Seeing That Everyone Is Fed

First in a Series of Four: Watching for the Light

Matthew 24:32-44

The Christian world has always been fascinated with the subject of the end times. When I was a young teen, my Sunday school teacher was absolutely taken with Hal Lindsey's *The Late Great Planet Earth*, and even sent a copy home with each of us for further study. Infected by our teacher's enthusiasm, my brothers and I pored over the little book's pages as if it were the latest comic book sensation. Within those pages, we were taught to believe the meaning of the end times could be discerned.

The Hal Lindsey generation wasn't the first to find the subject of Jesus' return alluring. During the great plague of Europe in the middle of the fourteenth century, prophets predicted Christ's appearance within ten years. Two centuries later, Luther predicted the final conflict would align the reigning pope with the Turks against the Reformation Church. John Knox predicted 1547 was the year for Christ's return; for others, the year was 1830 and then 1847. A New England farmer's eschatological prediction (either 1843 or 1844) went askew but gave birth, in the meantime, to an entire religious movement: the Adventist Church. The Watchtower movement held out for 1874, then 1914. Even John Wesley weighed in—his choice was 1836.

Speculation as to Jesus' return has been an occupation—sometimes a preoccupation—of the church from its infancy. Matthew presents Jesus as both a cultivator of such expectation and a naysayer against it. On the one hand, "From the fig tree learn its lesson" (24:32). On the other, "About that day and hour no one knows" (v. 36). Jesus clearly encourages a certain forward-leaning disposition toward God's coming reign; the future is to be seen as trustworthy, hopeful, and true to God's promise of redemption. Even so, there is an equally clear admonition not to go off the deep end with speculations and predictions. It's as if Jesus is saying, "Look toward the future, but stay in the present."

How are we to balance the "then" and the "now," the sense of leaning forward with the sense of being grounded in the present? Walden Pond gave Henry David Thoreau much to ponder, explore, and write about. In one journal entry he made this observation of that beautifully numinous body of water: "Walden is blue at one time and green at another, even from the same point of view. Lying between the earth and the heavens, it partakes of the color of both" (Henry David Thoreau, *Walden* [New York: Houghton Mifflin, 1995], 172). Blue and green, partaking of the heavens and of the earth—all in the same place; Thoreau has gifted us with a metaphor for a Christian community that lives both expectant and grounded, hopeful and helpful. We are blue and we are green, we partake of heaven and earth, Christ's promise from the future and Christ's mandate for the present.

It is perhaps clear enough what it means to "partake" of the future hope offered by the gospel. Gospel hymns, end-times literature, and apocalyptic texts all do their part to take us there. Our own souls' longing for redemption, echoing creation's own "groaning in travail" (Romans 8:22 RSV), resonates with these other sources of future-leaning blue.

What about the green dimension of life—the groundedness, the helpfulness, the here-and-now dimension? What about the sensible dismissal of predictions and prognostications, which Jesus prescribes; the turning of our energies to the work of our hands over and above the wishes of our hearts?

With characteristic lyricism, at once as obscure as night and as plain as day, Jesus presents us with a parable (vv. 45-51). In it, a slave is put in charge of the master's household while the master is away. We feel a sense of expectancy, an assumption of eventual, if not immediate, return. The "blue" aspect of faithful living has found its way into the tale. But what of the time in between? As the slave waits for the master's return, what is expected, we might say, of the expectant? The answer is, curiously, both strikingly obvious and remarkably hidden from view; the slave is responsible for the nourishment of the others in the household. It seems that partaking of the green of earth—the present, here-and-now reality—becomes a matter of seeing that *all* have "partaken," that is, been fed. As has been the case from time immemorial, it turns out that the true moral measure in the economy of life is the kitchen!

As we know, kitchens come in all shapes and sizes. There are kitchens in cozy, safe, loving homes, filled with laughter and simmering dishes and aromas by day, as quiet as a cat by night. But there are also kitchens where soup is served up to the homeless, and all hope is held in a cup.

Jesus has a most rudimentary and unglamorous prescription for keeping ourselves prepared for the coming of Christ in glory and judgment: be certain everybody is fed.

It's worth remembering at this point that "the other great commission" of Matthew's Gospel is found just a chapter beyond these apocalyptic pages, in Matthew 25: "Lord, when did we see you hungry, and feed you?" (see v. 44). Seeing that the hungry are fed seems to be very much on Jesus' mind, and he wishes it to be very much on ours as well, particularly when we think about the end times. Instead of partaking of the scintillating religious science of dates and predictions, Jesus would have us ask the homelier, but far more morally relevant question, "Is everyone being fed?" And Jesus would mean by that everyone—from the least to the greatest. Warmed with a blanket? Cheered with a visit? Remembered with a card? Clothed? Hugged? Delivered from danger? Loved?

For Matthew, the operative question is not "When is Jesus coming?" but "What shall we do in the meantime?" The answer? Not fascination with the future, but attention to the now. And we begin here, at the Lord's Table, where all are welcome, and everyone is fed. (Paul L. Escamilla)

Worship Aids

Advent Wreath Explanation

The Advent wreath is a simple circle of evergreen, a sign of everlasting life, and a symbol of God's never-ending love. Its four candles, one lit each Sunday prior to Christmas, encircle a central white Christ candle—a sign of God's light birthed into the world, which is lit on Christmas Eve and Christmas Sunday.

Congregational Response to the Lighting of the Advent Wreath

We light this candle as a symbol of Christ, the Prince of Peace. May we make room for the peace of Christ in our hearts, our homes, and our relationships. O come, O come, Emmanuel.

Words of Assurance

People of God, claim your inheritance and celebrate God's gift. In the name of the Christ, you are granted grace, peace, and forgiveness. Amen.

Benediction

Leader: Peace is a conscious choice.

People: Peace is a deliberate action, an act of self-control, a perspective maintained.

Leader: Go forth to live as a people of peace, in the name of the Prince of Peace, Jesus the Redeemer.

All: Amen.
(Gary G. Kindley)

DECEMBER 9, 2007

❧❧❧

Second Sunday of Advent

Readings: Isaiah 11:1-10; Psalm 72:1-7, 18-19; Romans 15:4-13; Matthew 3:1-12

Witness the Coming of Our King
Isaiah 11:1-10

Advent helps the church remember its theological heritage in the promises of God. The church stakes its message on the certainty that God will do what God has said God will do: return and bring the kingdom to fruition. Of Jesus, we claim this promise in the Apostles' Creed:

> he ascended into heaven,
> is seated at the right hand of the Father,
> and will come again to judge the living and the dead.
> (*The United Methodist Hymnal* [Nashville: The United Methodist Publishing House, 1989], 882)

In Advent, the church lives by what it professes, and the world measures our witness against our beliefs.

Where do we hear this promise of God again, with fresh understanding? God's character is in full view in the text from Isaiah for this Sunday. This passage, a messianic hymn extolling the reign of God's chosen servant, is broken into three very clear sections of poetry bracketed by declarations of fact.

First, the announcement: a new person, a hopeful king, will arise from the line of David. Using the analogy of a shoot coming forth from a stump (cf. Isaiah 6:13), the image is clear: Israel, like a previously living tree, has been felled by the ax of faithlessness. Yet God, Isaiah declares, will bring new life from and into David's kingly line through his chosen servant. Because God has acted, this king shall embody the ideal characteristics of Israel's great rulers, even qualities of wisdom, understanding, counsel,

315

might, and knowledge and fear of the Lord. Because God's Spirit is the means for bringing God's kingdom about, this king will be close to the heart of God.

The effect of this king's holiness will be to decisively alter how he reigns. Isaiah uses the device of contrasting human physical qualities to illustrate how this king will rule in a countercultural way. He shall see and hear, but he shall not decide by his senses; rather, the king will decide based on the qualities of holy character with which God has imbued him. Thus righteousness, equity, and faithfulness will be new standards. Because he so rules, the poor and dispossessed will now be at the center of communal life. These same qualities will ensure the destruction of the wicked, presumably those who once segregated the poor and landless. God's divine king will invert the social order to reflect the human care and compassion God has always desired but previous kings could not or would not impart.

Beyond how this king will rule, however, is the effect he will have on creation, for he will invert not only human culture but also the temporal order. The king's reign will restore God's design for all the earth, such that predator and prey shall coexist peacefully, and children will play without harm amid life-threatening danger. The pain and misery of sin will be no more, as the qualities of knowing God will suffuse all earthly life. In essence, this king will help redeem both people and creatures to the state God always intended. Isaiah ends this poem with a final declaration: this king will act as a standard for the in-breaking and triumph of the reign of God.

Yet in the words of one my preaching professors, "So what?" As we proclaim again the claims of our sacred text, Christians must always ask the question that nonbelievers ask, one born of a skeptical estimation of the wider spiritual truth of the Bible. If Isaiah's prophecy is true, then what of it? Without trying to succumb to reductionism, we should wrestle with explaining our belief in practical terms. I see the following threads of meaning from this text.

First, we are not in control of time. While former seminary students might recall the difference between chronological and eschatological time (e.g., Greek *chronos* versus *kairos*), it always bears repeating: God's time is not our time, and God is not done reorienting the world toward God's vision for creation. Isaiah reminds us that in God's sight, the Day of the Lord is not an ordinary day but an event of cosmic proportions.

Such a claim is always fresh, always dangerous, and always necessary to hear.

Second, what we see in the world now is not all that there will be; God has a different vision for us beyond sin and death. In the comfort of developed nations, this message plays poorly, but in the plight of developing nations, this is a radical cause for hope. We must affirm again, however, that each person, no matter the temporal circumstances, desperately needs this message. As people steeped in sin and death, we need—desperately need—God to redeem us from the reality of our finite existence, to provide a way of salvation for body and soul that we cannot provide for ourselves. Isaiah reminds us again that indeed the day of the Lord offers such hope.

Third, as we admittedly read this text with postressurection eyes, the church historically has witnessed that Jesus Christ is the manifestation of Isaiah's prophecy. While it remains a mystery that the Day of the Lord has not yet occurred, Christians understand that in light of Christ's promised second coming, the conditions are set for the Day of the Lord to occur. In the proclamation that Christ will come again to claim Christ's people (Acts 1:11) and to judge the nations (Revelation 19:11-16), the church affirms that it is Jesus Christ whom Isaiah foretold, and God has begun to do that which God once promised.

This Advent, then, we as the people of God renew the claim of this text to a world that may have closed its ears to its power. God is in control of time, God has a different vision for the world than what we see, and God has begun to redeem creation in Jesus Christ our Lord. Indeed, may God give us "eyes to see" and "ears to hear" the word that God offers the world this Advent. Amen. (Timothy S. Mallard)

Turning Around

Second in a Series of Four: Watching for the Light

Matthew 3:1-11

Harold Beck used to tell the story of the truck driver, tired from a long day's driving, who pulled into a lonely truck stop and sidled up to the counter. In a minute or two a waitress came out from the kitchen and said, "What'll it be?" The truck driver said, "All I want is a kind word and a piece of apple pie." The waitress disappeared into the kitchen and returned with a slice of pie. She set the dish on the counter and started back into the kitchen. The truck driver said, "And the kind word?" The waitress turned around, leaned over the counter, and said, "If I were you, I wouldn't eat the pie."

This waitress might have been related to John the Baptist, who could have been the inspiration for that line in *The Black Crows'* song: "Got a head full of sermons and a mouth full of spiders." When John opens his mouth, you can almost see the spiders crawling out: "You brood of vipers! Who warned you to flee from God's wrath? Bear fruit that befits repentance. Even now the axe is lying at the root of a tree that bears your name. Repent!" (see Matthew 3:7-10).

Wait a minute—this is supposed to be Christmas! In the middle of a season where we're supposed to be celebrating life and love and peace on earth, how did we get John the Baptist? If you've been around the Bible very long, then you know how we got him, because you know that when it comes to matters of the Spirit, before good news is ever good news, it always feels like bad news first. John has a word to give us that looks like spiders crawling out of his mouth, but by the end of the day, we may find that what he's really offering when he warns us against eating the pie is a sustenance far more nourishing than we ever could have imagined.

That word *Repent!* is a strong one, isn't it? It's a good, solid New Testament word, but it's also a word that, if we have some bad history with it, may leave some of us edging toward the door.

Repent means, literally, "to turn around," and John is calling for the people who have followed him out into the wilderness to do just that—to turn their lives around. But what does that mean?

The first thing I'd suggest it means is that we take a close look at where we are in life, deciding then if change is called for. After all, if we are watching for the light of Christmas, the first thing that light will likely reveal to us is the shadows it casts around and even within us.

Calling, by definition, always requires another's voice, and the call to change is no different. It is not, therefore, our own self-examination that is likely to be the most successful inventory of our lives. The people who love us most have the power to confront us the most honestly. Husbands, wives, siblings, parents, children, close friends—these are the only ones who care more about our deep well-being than about pleasing us, and so they hold the unique capacity to present us with "turnaround" messages that may be off-putting, but also happen to be true.

Who loves you fiercely enough to be that honest with you? And what are you giving them in thanks? A stiff neck, or a listening ear? E. Stanley Jones saw the value of those who gave him "turnaround" messages of whatever sort. He used to speak of his critics as "the unpaid guardians of my soul." Are there any unpaid soul guardians in your life right now? Do you value them as E. Stanley Jones did his?

Perhaps there is someone telling you, "I know you love shopping and giving, and Christmas is a wonderful time for that, but would you please remember that what those you love want most from you is not your stuff but yourself?"

Maybe you are the scrooge in the bunch, spending the whole month of December in a folded-arms posture uttering your favorite saying, "Humbug!" Maybe somebody's "turnaround" word to you is to loosen up, lighten up, open up to the possibilities of the Spirit of God working in and through the season in a way that transcends or even transforms what you may consider merely a tawdry commercial spectacle.

Maybe our way of repenting is by "turning around" some of our purchasing power, and instead of buying gifts for the gifted, purchasing blankets for a homeless shelter or books for the women's shelter. Maybe it's making a special gift to a special nonprofit ministry or to the church, or to a family in need. Maybe it's giving your afternoon to the nursing home instead of the mall, volunteering on an affordable housing committee or with a tutoring team.

What is the Spirit nudging you to do and be? And who is the Spirit's spokesperson, that unpaid guardian of your soul, whose kind word may just begin in an altogether unendearing but lifesaving way, "If I were you ..."

John the Baptist gets up in our faces year after year, and his message is always the same: those who would know Jesus Christ in a powerful, life-transforming way must turn away from the stale pie the world offers, seductive as it is, and choose in its place the surpassing feast that's really worth stopping the truck for and promises to nourish us to eternal life.

Christmas is for celebrating, not scowling. If there is joy around us, it bears repeating. Maybe you need eyes for seeing and a heart for understanding that behind our materialism is a yearning to find ways to express how much we love the people who are close to us and even, perhaps, the whole world of God's domain.

No one is better able to hold that lantern up to our lives than somebody who loves us fiercely enough to get in our faces and say what John said to the people that day: "Look at your life! Wake up and turn around!"

He gets free guardianship of his soul from those people who stare him in the face and tell him what's wrong with him, or what he's not getting done, or where he's missing the mark in his work. Anyone do that to you on a regular basis?

I don't mean the call of discipleship is to buy ourselves into a frenzy, waste our time and energy hurrying and scurrying here and there just for the sake of "getting into the spirit" of Christmas.

Your words, your presence, your embrace, maybe a handwritten letter, a phone call—is someone giving you that message right now? (Paul L. Escamilla)

Worship Aids

Congregational Response to the Lighting of the Advent Wreath

We light this candle as a sign of hope. As a people of hope, let us bear witness to the hope that is eternal through Christ our Lord.

Call to Worship

> Leader: Christ came to bring us salvation and joy and has promised to come again.
>
> **People: Whether we discover Christ in a stranger among us,**
>
> Leader: Or the face of one in desperate need,
>
> **People: Let us pray that we may always be ready to welcome him. Amen.**

Benediction

Advent is about anticipation. Live this week with anticipation. Expect great things from God. You will not be disappointed! (Gary G. Kindley)

DECEMBER 16, 2007

✵✵✵

Third Sunday of Advent

Readings: Isaiah 35:1-10; Psalm 146:5-10; James 5:7-10; Matthew 11:2-11

Volcanoes and Paradise Islands
Isaiah 35:1-10

I've always had a fascination with volcanoes. As a small child my picture of a volcano was of a tall mountain off in the distance on a tropical island that was fun to look at and amazing to see as it erupted. But I remember watching the Discovery Channel one day and seeing the pictures of live volcanoes in action. Yes, it was just like I had thought in many ways, and I marveled at the pictures of the lava as it erupted. But what I didn't bargain for were the pictures after the eruption was over. It wasn't the picture of the paradise island I had in mind; all you could see was total and pure devastation of anything and everything that stood in the way of the lava.

I began to wonder how my picture of a paradise island with a volcano on it got so skewed, because all I saw after the eruption was black soot that had destroyed everything, not some sandy beach and tropical backdrop.

I imagine the Israelites might have had some questions about the promised land, their paradise island, and the volcanoes that had seemed to erupt all around them as their world came crashing down in the midst of captivity. As Israel looked around, the picture they had to view was no longer a land flowing with milk and honey, but a land now covered in the black soot of war and the destruction of captivity. The promise of Scripture, though, is that God doesn't leave us in the blackness of soot, death, and destruction.

Learning more about volcanoes helped me to understand this quality about God. As I learned more about volcanoes, I found out that the black

321

soot does eventually change into the paradise island I imagined. Somehow, in God's creativity, God provides a way for that which is unproductive to become productive again. Somehow, after the lava from a volcano has hardened to where it seems as if nothing will ever grow there again, God provides a way for the nitrogen in the air to be absorbed and, over a long period of time, the molten lava becomes fertile soil in which vegetation can grow and thrive. The volcano that had been the picture of destruction will eventually help to produce the paradise island where everything is productive once more.

We serve a God who continues to create and find newness of life amid that which has been destroyed. In our passage, God wasn't finished with the work God began in the Israelites, and Isaiah begins to outline the reversal of the sad state of Israel. Isaiah does so by suggesting that the approaching glory of the Lord is literally bursting into life. Isaiah says, "The wilderness and the dry land shall be glad, the desert shall rejoice and blossom" (Isaiah 35:1). The prophet continues by suggesting that all of those who are considered lowly in this life will be restored to wholeness. From that which has been dry, bubbling springs will break forth, and there will be more vegetation than anyone can imagine. Isaiah envisions that day when there will be no more sorrow and sighing, for joy and gladness will break forth and the redeemed will walk on a highway called the "Holy Way" (v. 8).

Such it is for the people of faith as we await the coming of the Christ Child this Christmas. When the volcanoes that we used to think were fun to look at explode all around us and all that is left is darkness and infertility, may the words of Isaiah lift our eyes to the God who brings light into darkness and the birth of God's Messiah into that which was thought to be infertile. And maybe somehow, in God's hands, the volcanoes of life can become paradise islands for those who will wait on the Lord. (Ryan Wilson)

Hope Is Wearing a Rugby Shirt

Third in a Series of Four: Watching for the Light

Matthew 11:2-11

About twenty years ago there was a popular bumper sticker that read *I FOUND IT*. Remember that? I don't know where it originated, or where it has gone, but *I FOUND IT* was on a lot of bumpers. It was a faith statement, a declaration of identity, a witness for the gospel offered to the unchurched tailgater.

I remember driving behind someone one day whose bumper displayed the *I FOUND IT* sticker on one side, and on the other side a different message: *DON'T FOLLOW ME—I'M LOST, TOO.*

Now I know who was driving that car—it was John the Baptist. Just a week ago, in our hearing, John was declaiming large truths with utter clarity and conviction: "The Messiah is coming. . . . The mountains will be leveled, . . . the valleys raised up, . . . the crooked places made straight, . . . the rough places plain. . . . Repent and believe." But since that time John has landed in prison, and it's a question mark rather than an exclamation point that ends his sentences these days: "Is this Messiah the same One that I heralded before in the wilderness? The One who will lower mountains and raise up valleys? Is this Messiah the One who is to come, or shall we wait for another?"

Suddenly the knight of faith is shown to have a crack in his armor. The driver who boldly sported the *I FOUND IT* sticker has added another to the opposite side: DON'T FOLLOW ME—I'M LOST, TOO. Are you the One?

Maybe John became jaded by the endless procession of so-called messiahs that had been paraded through Palestine over the years, over the centuries—people claiming this, promising that. Here was one more, and so far, things hadn't changed much.

Perhaps John was discouraged in his faith. After all, remember where he is—in prison—and why he's there—because he did the right thing: stood up to royalty, confronted Herod about marrying his brother's wife.

Maybe John simply had different expectations for the Messiah, expectations Jesus didn't meet in a specific way. John was hoping for real fireworks and folderol when the Messiah came—military might, apocalyptic signs, earthmoving changes.

From his prison cell, John sent his disciples to inquire of Jesus, "Are you the one who is to come, or are we to wait for another?" (Matthew 11:3). Jesus responded to John's friends by saying, "Go and tell John what you've heard and seen: the blind see, the lame walk, the lepers are cleansed, and the poor have good news brought to them" (see vv. 4-5).

Did you notice that there's nothing in that litany of which John is not aware? Everything Jesus tells him is already common knowledge, the sort of thing John would already know. It's as if Jesus is saying, "What you see going on around you—simple things, familiar things, loving-God-and-neighbor things—these are the signs that the Messiah has come." No razzmatazz, no rending of the veil, no prophet ecstasies, no beatific vision—just the ordinary, ongoing work of participating in the kingdom through words and deeds.

In 1995 Jean-Dominique Bauby was at the center of the fashion world. He was the editor and chief of *Elle* magazine in Paris, a bright star in the constellation of glitterati in Europe and across the world. In October of that year, he suffered a massive stroke that left him paralyzed, restricting his movement to the use of his left eye. He was admitted to a rehabilitation hospital along France's northern coast, near Calais. Bauby was fed with a spoon like a baby, shaved and bathed, wheeled around in a wheelchair, lifted into bed each night and out of bed each morning.

After months of therapy, Bauby was still able to bat only one eye; that was all. Even so, with that one eye Bauby eventually relayed his experience, "dictating" an entire book by blinking one letter at a time to an assistant. In that book, *The Diving Bell and the Butterfly*, he recounts a day when his therapist was wheeling him to therapy and accidentally stepped off the elevator on the wrong floor. For no reason in particular, the therapist wheeled him over to an outdoor terrace to have a look around, Bauby's first time out of doors since his injury. From that terrace, through his one good eye, he could vaguely make out something in the distance, far beyond the hospital grounds. It was a lighthouse, situated on the banks of the Calais coast, painted in the customary wide red and white horizontal stripes. He recounts that at first glance, the thought that entered his mind was "rugby shirt," because of the striped pattern. Only after that initial mental impression did another follow—here is a lighthouse, a beacon, a symbol of hope (Jean-Dominique Bauby, *The Diving Bell and the Butterfly* [New York: Alfred A. Knopf, 1997]).

Rugby shirt. Lighthouse. Hope. In that order. That may well be the gospel order too. That's certainly the way Jesus presented things to John, "Go and tell John that the routine work of obedience and compassion is going forward." As plain as they are, mundane even, these are the sort of signs, it seems, that truly usher in the kingdom; these are the signs that the Messiah has come: love is being shared, the poor are being cared for, those who mourn are being comforted, the sick are healed. A note to a friend, a phone call to a neighbor, a visit to someone we suspect may be particularly lonely right about now; an extra financial gift at the end of the year for the work of the gospel in the church and in the world. Go and tell John that at the moment hope is not wearing royal vestments, or military brass, or Superman's cape, or angel's wings. At the moment, hope is wearing a rugby shirt. (Paul L. Escamilla)

Worship Aids

Congregational Response to the Lighting of the Advent Wreath

We light this candle as a reminder of Christ's great love. May we be living reminders of God's love to the world by our words and our actions.

Call to Worship

Advent is for expectation. Come now with expectancy and open eyes. Let us look for God and realize the surprises of the Spirit.

Pastoral Prayer

Holy God of birth and life, this season is alive with joy and blessing. The sounds and sights of Advent remind us of hope that is born into the world by your love. May that truth be more than merely a season but a daily reality. May Christmas be more than a time of commerce but a period for renewed commitment. In living our lives, may we live large enough that grace is made real, that our service is sanctified, and that we realize we can never out-give you. In the name of the Christ Child and Savior. Amen. (Gary G. Kindley)

Benediction

"The grace of the Lord Jesus Christ, the love of God, and the communion of the Holy Spirit be with all of you" (2 Corinthians 13:13). (David N. Mosser)

DECEMBER 23, 2007

✖✖✖

Fourth Sunday of Advent

Readings: Isaiah 7:10-16; Psalm 80:1-7, 17-19; Romans 1:1-7; Matthew 1:18-25

Set Apart Instead of Set Aside
Romans 1:1-7

With two little girls running around our house, it has been fascinating to watch as they play with different toys and dolls. Christmastime is interesting, because whenever there are new toys around, they gravitate toward the new toys and "set aside" toys they have had for a while. After the newness wears off though, they play with all of the toys as equals again.

I have also noticed that the girls "set apart" certain toys or dolls for various occasions. If they are playing with their kitchen set, there are certain dishes and baking utensils that receive special placement and attention. If they are playing with their baby dolls, there are specific dolls, bottles, and blankets that have specific roles as they play.

As Paul is writing to the Romans, he wants to emphasize that the Gentiles have not been "set aside," but rather, he himself has been "set apart" (Romans 1:1) to deliver the good news to the Gentiles. First, Paul wants to establish that he has been "set apart" by God for a specific ministry. This would include him in the line of the prophets and others in the Hebrew Scriptures whom God "set apart" for God's work. To his credit, Paul begins by claiming the status of a servant of Jesus Christ, indicating that he is writing to serve the community in Rome. Then, I think, Paul wants to give them his credentials by calling himself an apostle, a title that indicated some authoritative commission. With this title of apostle, Paul suggests that he has been "set apart" for the gospel of God.

Second, in verses 3 and 4, Paul borrows a confession that was probably found in the early church, which describes Jesus as the Son of God. From the viewpoint of the flesh, the confession makes it clear that Jesus was from the line of David, a key point for anyone who was knowledgeable in the Hebrew tradition. From the viewpoint of the Spirit, the confession makes it clear that through the Resurrection, Jesus was declared to be the Son of God. Paul uses this confession to be clear about Jesus' identity.

Paul then tells the church at Rome that he is proclaiming the gospel of God's own Son, and that through his proclamation, Paul is hoping to "bring about the obedience of faith among all the Gentiles for the sake of his name" (v. 5). Jesus Christ, who was "set apart" by God, is calling for the Gentiles to accept an invitation to become part of the gospel story. God has not "set aside" the Gentiles, but rather God has "set apart" Paul to be God's messenger to the Gentiles. It is through God's Son, Jesus Christ, that the Gentiles can see clearly where they are included in the story.

While God "set apart" the Jewish people as God's chosen people, God never intended their chosenness to be exclusive. This fact was demonstrated through the power of the Resurrection and now through God's servant Paul, who is specifically called to proclaim the gospel to the Gentile world.

Just as my girls "set apart" certain toys for specific occasions, God sets us apart for certain areas of service. As we reach the fourth Sunday of Advent, we are reminded that God's love is much broader than we have ever imagined. The Jews thought God's love was inclusive only of them, but through Jesus Christ, Paul suggests that God has clearly spoken that all who obey through faith have been included. God doesn't "set aside" certain groups over others, but rather, God will "set apart" certain groups and certain people to accomplish God's mission of love and redemption in God's world. And that's good news to anyone who might have thought Christmas wasn't for him or her. (Ryan Wilson)

The Manger of the Heart

Fourth in a Series of Four: Watching for the Light

Matthew 1:18-25

Open your Bibles to Matthew chapter 1 in the King James Version, and behold the most organized presentation of "begats" you've ever laid eyes on. Abraham begat Isaac, Isaac begat Jacob, Jacob begat Judah. . . . Anyone who commits the very opening pages of their story to that kind of a list appreciates order. David begat Solomon, Solomon begat

Rehoboam—direction. Jechoniah begat Salatheil, Salatheil begat Zerubbabel—symmetry.

One name after another—nearly fifty in all—strung like pearls on a necklace. At the very end of the necklace are the showcase pearls, to whom all this order and symmetry leads—Joseph and Mary betrothed. These two could have made the cover of *Bride* magazine. They have all the right pedigrees, all the right family backgrounds. With their addition to the strand, the pearl necklace is complete.

But then something happens that is not only unforeseen but unimaginably wild. A bird flies in through an open window, and looking for some filler for its nest, spots the necklace. The little wren nips a few times at the string holding that perfected pearl necklace together, and on the last nip breaks it apart, sending the pearls bouncing and rolling in every direction, all over the floor, beneath the furniture, through the floor grate, under the door.

In Matthew, that bird has a name: the Holy Spirit. In our prayers over the baptismal font, we say, "When nothing existed but chaos, you swept across the waters and brought forth order, brought forth life." Over the opening pages of Matthew we could say the very opposite prayer, "When nothing existed but order, you flew in and scattered things from here to kingdom come."

Mary has turned up pregnant, and for all Joseph knows, he's been betrayed by his betrothed. If Mary and Joseph were cover material for *Bride* magazine before, now they're more likely to appear in the *Enquirer*. Can't you see it? Star couple in trouble—she turns up pregnant; he attempts damage control—wedding canceled.

We can only imagine what Joseph must be thinking: *a few days ago we had our whole community behind us and our whole lives ahead of us. Now it's all over. Our engagement is broken; our covenant is broken; our hearts are broken.* It is only when Joseph follows the wisdom of the ages and sleeps on it that we arrive at the real story: it is the Holy Spirit who has nibbled away at that neat, orderly necklace of past and posterity until it broke, scattering all that hope and hard work across the floor. Mary's womb holds a life that will be Jesus, Savior. When Joseph awakens from his dream, he has a new understanding that in the chaos stirred up by the Holy Spirit, all shall be well.

Doesn't that make a great story? If only it could be confined to the pages of a book, to a moment in time two thousand years ago. If only that wren of holy mischief had died out with Joseph and Mary, but we have it on good authority that the bird responsible for all that hullabaloo back in Joseph's day is alive and well, and is in fact looking for material for her nest. In fact, it seems that, particularly at Christmas, the bird is still surprising people by what she yanks on and tugs at.

Did you know that wrens commonly return to the same nest they built the previous year? Yet rather than settling down and nesting in a perfectly good nest, they take it apart, piece by piece, and then build another nest in the very same location—often using the very same materials they've just discarded. What kind of efficiency is that?

It's God's kind. For as good as tradition is, tradition isn't good enough in and of itself to accomplish God's purposes. A long, beautifully arranged litany of "begat's" is not what God is looking for. What God is looking for is life!

You may have had a special moment of spiritual awakening last year at Christmas, or in 1987 when you were just a bright-eyed child, or way back during the depression. You may have your spiritual milestones set one beside the other like pearls, carefully arranged, and put up for safekeeping.

Just as the wren salvages material from the old nest for putting into the new one, there are elements of that earlier faith experience that find their way into the new nest. Yet, as far as God is concerned, when it comes to holy encounter, yesterday is not recent enough. God calls us every morning, every Sunday, every Christmas to open our hearts again, turn our minds again, yield up our lives again to that life-giving relationship.

Christmas becomes a natural moment for the un-nesting/re-nesting work of God, perhaps because the image of a life being miraculously planted and nurtured in Mary's womb allows us to imagine new life being planted and nurtured within us. The wren that was at work that first Christmas is still at work this Christmas, seeking to rebuild a nest right where the old one was, right there in your very heart, and in mine. A scrap of this, a scrap of that; a twig from the family tree; a flower petal from the garden of memory; some grass from the ragged meadow of a grief still tender. A time of closeness to God we can faintly remember, and wish to know again; the goodness and blessedness and beauty of our lives.

That wren is busy in your heart and mine, dismantling and reassembling, plucking up and planting, scattering shreds of the old nest and gathering those shreds together for the new one—right in the middle of our hearts. As it begins to take shape, we may begin to notice it looks less and less like a nest, and more and more like a manger. (Paul L. Escamilla)

Worship Aids

Congregational Response to the Lighting of the Advent Wreath

We light this candle as a symbol of Christ, our joy. As people of faith, may we celebrate with joy God's gift of love and all of the blessings God brings to life.

Call to Worship

The time is near. The Advent approaches. The Redeemer arrives. Prepare. Listen. Look. Expect. Worship.

Litany for Advent

Leader: Take off your shoes.

People: Tiptoe in silence.

Leader: A miracle awaits.

People: Get ready.

Leader: Watch closely.

People: Hold your breath.

Leader: Wonder arrives.
(Gary G. Kindley)

Pastoral Prayer

When the church prays, O God, we pray to you who created the earth and the heavens. Indeed, you created all that is, and was, and will come to be. Give us the forgiveness to again face the world and the grace to be forgiving people. We encounter many troubling circumstances in life, yet your promise is to always be with us in each and every situation in which we may find ourselves. Help us be a thankful people, for you have given us much over which to give thanks. Grant us a peace to face life and be

sisters and bothers to those in need. Send your Holy Spirit as we anticipate the birth of the One who shows us the path that leads to you. May
we remember that Christ is the greatest, most surpassing gift ever given.
May we celebrate your gift of the incarnate Christ with glad and generous hearts. Amen. (David N. Mosser)

DECEMBER 24, 2007

✺✺✺

Christmas Eve

Readings: Isaiah 9:2-7; Psalm 96; Titus 2:11-14; Luke 2:1-20

When God Shows Up
Luke 2:1-20

A Sunday school teacher asked her class why Joseph and Mary took Jesus with them to Jerusalem. A small child replied, "They couldn't get a babysitter." There is a young person who looks at life with a practical bent. Thank goodness, so does God. God knew we needed the Incarnation, so God showed up.

It seems to me that Christmas is about showing up. The Magi showed up. They could have stayed in their own country. They could have published a paper (or scroll) about their astronomical and astrological findings. They could have sent someone else to check things out, but no, the Magi showed up. It was not an easy trek. There were no Holiday Inns or exit signs marking restaurants along the way. There was no highway patrol to protect from robbers and muggers. Still, the Magi went anyway, because they decided to show up.

In contrast, Herod ran away. Herod sent someone else. Herod stayed at the palace and relied on others to do his dirty work. He sent soldiers to eliminate any possible threat, and left Rachel weeping for her children. The cries of anguish of mothers throughout Judea condemned Herod's cowardly absence.

Joseph and Mary showed up. It was not an easy journey for them. No physician of the first century would advise traveling while pregnant, but they showed up. Caesar's census compelled them. Faithfulness propelled them. The call of God upheld them, and they showed up.

The shepherds showed up. Frightened but faithful to heed the news of the angelic choir, they showed up. Accustomed to tending sheep rather than attending a baby's birth, they still showed up. They did what they had to do, what they were asked to do, what they could do. The shepherds tended their flocks, and attended the birth of One to whom countless throngs would flock, and they showed up.

Simeon showed up. He waited to see the salvation of God's people. He knew that he would not die until he did. He waited with patience, fidelity, and wisdom. When his eyes beheld the Christ Child, he knew what God had already promised. He realized that God always shows up as promised. Simeon had waited to see the promise show up.

Most of our journey is about showing up. God showed up, and our lives are changed forever. Faithful living, sacrificial service, committed discipleship are all about arriving at the foot of the cross and standing before the empty tomb. Once we have encountered those truths, we know that God has shown up and so must we.

We are a people on a journey, and like children in the backseat of the family van, we are constantly wondering, "Are we there yet?" Life is not solely about our destination. Life is, most of all, about our journey.

The leading factor in at-risk kids' becoming incarcerated or addicted, or dying prematurely, is lack of education—dropping out of school. They don't start school as children who plan to drop out. They quit due to frustration, inability to read, lack of a mentor, or lack of parental support. The best way to help these kids is to show up. Think of what might happen if you bother to show up.

Consider the difference in someone's journey when you simply show up. Change the life of a child forever by showing up. Volunteer. Tutor. Serve. Give. Pray. Witness. Lobby. Lead. The Sunday school is the largest volunteer organization in the world, yet there can be no Sunday school if teachers don't show up. The American Red Cross is usually the first on the scene of disasters, yet they would be almost totally ineffective if their volunteers failed to show up. The church is the body of Christ, yet there would be no church if you failed to show up to worship, witness, and serve.

Live out the faith you proclaim. Announce to the world the arrival of God. God showed up for us; it is our time to return the favor. (Gary G. Kindley)

Poor Mary
Luke 1:39-45

Luke's gospel goes to great lengths to compare and contrast two women central to the birth of Jesus: his mother, Mary, and her cousin Elizabeth. The fact that these two women are cousins is just about all they have in common, until an angel visits them both. Elizabeth is well to do; Mary is not. Elizabeth lives in the city; Mary lives in the country. Elizabeth belongs to a priestly family that can trace its lineage all the way back to Aaron; Mary's family tree is not so grand. Elizabeth's husband is high priest; Mary's husband is a carpenter. Elizabeth lives in the City of David; Mary lives in Nazareth. Remember the phrase, "Can anything good come from Nazareth?" Nazareth was clearly the wrong side of the tracks.

Zechariah had been chosen to be high priest that year. While he was in the "holy of holies" an angel appeared to him and announced that he and Elizabeth were going to have a baby. When he finally emerged from the Temple, everyone knew something unusual had happened because Zechariah was speechless. Six months later, the same angel appeared to Mary and announced, "You're going to have a baby too, just like your cousin Elizabeth." Mary had heard of her cousin's miraculous pregnancy and now without warning, the same miracle had been given to her. They had much to talk about, so off Mary goes to Jerusalem.

Mary is the kind of woman who would not attract much attention: shy, unassuming, and poor. If we think about the poor at all, we hardly ever imagine good fortune or blessings. In fact, we seldom think of them at all. Many believe the poor get what they deserve. But Mary's story challenges all our well-worn assumptions. The Bible says Jesus identified with the poor. He even went so far as to say that when the kingdom comes, it would be the poor who would be given places of honor at the banquet table. We look at the poor and make all kinds of judgments. God looks on the poor and sees beloved children.

Early Protestants believed that, if you were poor, you deserved to be. The poor were prime examples of human depravity in the eyes of some. In those days it was believed that the material life was a reflection of the spiritual life. If you had nothing, it was because you were lazy or immoral. However if you were prosperous, you were blessed by God. The poor were not even worth noticing. So what does it mean that Mary—poor Mary—is chosen above all women to be the mother of Jesus? What does it mean for the rest of us if God sent God's son into the world to live among the poor?

What images come to mind when you think of the poor? Is it someone you would invite home for dinner? Have you ever visited in the home of someone who is genuinely poor? Not many of us could say yes. When Mary sings, "My soul doth magnify the Lord, . . . for he hath regarded the low estate of his handmaiden" (Luke 1:46-48 KJV), it means that God looks upon everyone, and in God's eyes we are all equal.

Remember the stable where Jesus was born? A congregation I once served was surprised to be reminded that in the stable would be animals and animal smells, not just sweet-smelling hay and the soft glow of candles that we see on Christmas cards. Can't you just hear the innkeeper saying, "Those people would be better off in the stable anyway"?

But who was it that came to the stable first? In Luke it was not the rich and powerful, but simple shepherds. Matthew tells us about the wise men and their costly gifts, but Luke says the shepherds were the first visitors, not the rich and powerful. There is a reason Luke tells us the story of Jesus' birth this way. It is to remind us that God knows each of us personally, and declares each one precious, from the greatest to the least. (Robert D. Penton)

Worship Aids

Call to Worship

Leader: Joseph took Mary to Bethlehem,

Children: And God showed up!

Adults: A star shone in the heavens,

Children: And God showed up!

Adults: Shepherds were tending their flocks,

Children: And God showed up!

Adults: Angels announced Christ's arrival,

Children: And God showed up!

Leader: We gather this night to worship,

All: And God showed up!

Invocation

Holy Christ, in the wonder of this hour, we celebrate your birth. In the mystery of the Incarnation, we celebrate your grace. In the holiness of this holiday, we proclaim your hope. We gather to worship, to remember, and to praise! Amen.

Benediction

Go into the night as a people who are changed! Proclaim the Incarnation! Receive the grace of God! Live as Christ's disciples! Go! (Gary G. Kindley)

DECEMBER 30, 2007

❦❦❦

First Sunday after Christmas

Readings: Isaiah 63:7-9; Psalm 148; Hebrews 2:10-18; Matthew 2:13-23

Do You Trust Your Dreams?
Matthew 2:13-23

Matthew is the opening Gospel in the current ordering of the New Testament, but many scholars speculate that it may have been the second or third Synoptic Gospel written (Mark being the first). Most biblical researchers recognize that Matthew contains textual material both from Mark and from a sayings source comprising Jesus' words, known as Q (for the German word for "source," *Quelle*). Matthew displays a scrupulous understanding of Jewish religious culture that we do not find in the other Gospels, at least to this extent. The Gospel of Matthew was likely written in the 70s C.E., and it is quite appropriate for Jewish readers who have come to Christianity.

According to Matthew, the Magi from the East, perhaps Persia, visit Jesus and Mary. They offer Jesus gifts, and Herod asks them to return to him so that he may learn where the child is. Ignoring Herod's request, they instead return to their own country by another route.

In today's lesson from Matthew, an angel appears to Joseph three times in a dream. The dream guides Joseph and directs his steps. Initially, the nocturnal visitor suggests to Joseph that he should take Mary and Jesus to Egypt. Next, in another of Joseph's dreams, an angel of the Lord instructs him to take the holy family back to Israel. Finally, the nighttime messenger advises Joseph to go to Nazareth and bypass Judea. So, Joseph takes his family to the district of Galilee, and the family settles down in a town called Nazareth.

Three times Joseph follows a dream's directives. Joseph's trustful following must have taken a lot of courage. It is funny how a dream can shape a person's destiny. Or how even a metaphoric use of a dream, such as the August 28, 1963, "I Have a Dream" speech given by Martin Luther King, Jr. can help fashion the destiny of an entire nation. To those steeped in the Christian tradition, King's speech sounded suspiciously like a sermon. Some social historians of American history believe that King's speech was one of several decisive factors that turned the tide against segregation in the United States. These historians believe that King's speech made possible the social emancipation of African Americans that Abraham Lincoln's Emancipation Proclamation legally authorized one hundred years before. Dreams, even today, continue to impact a people's destiny.

How do we, people of modernity, appropriate this narrative and its implications from Matthew's Gospel? What are dreams for people of this century?

Psychologists and psychiatrists in recent years give dream interpretation a "born-again" prominence. For example, scholars take C. G. Jung's work in dream interpretation with a new seriousness. Scientific research into nature's dreaming function provides further evidence. Scientists believe that only phenomena having practical functions in nature exist; therefore, dreaming must serve a function in nature because dreaming is scientifically verifiable.

But let's put aside the scientific community for a minute. They are, after all, plowing the earlier, fertile fields of biblical writers. The Bible reminds us that dreams play a major role in the stories about Abraham, Jacob, Daniel, and Joseph, among others. Early Christian literature is also full of references to dreams. In one of many examples, Tertullian wrote, "Almost the greater part of mankind get their knowledge of God from dreams" (Tertullian, "A Treatise on the Soul," in *Latin Christianity: Its Founder, Tertullian* [vol. 3 of *The Ante-Nicene Fathers*; New York: Charles Scribner's Sons, 1905], 226). Expanding the operational definition of dreams to include terms like "vision," "trance," and "being in the spirit," there are more than seventy references to this phenomenon—experiences that include children, women, and men.

Indifferent to what modern psychology or the ancient Scriptures suggest about dreams, however, many modern folk put no stock in dreams. How do we deal with this attitude and at the same time hear this passage from Matthew speaking the word to us—today?

First, we need to admit that "the unconscious" is a very powerful force in our lives. Most of us are motivated by drives and perceived needs difficult to name. Paul puts this concept best, although in negative terms: "I do not understand my own actions. For I do not do what I want, but I do the very thing I hate" (Romans 7:15). As sophisticated, logical, and modern people, this part of our personalities profoundly disturbs us. If we even recognize the existence of the unconscious, we think we are contaminating our more pure, more reasonable selves.

Second, and dovetailing with the issue of reason's contamination, are our fears raised by the whole issue of the unconscious. We are afraid of what our unconscious will reveal about us to ourselves. Many people do not want to know too much, choosing to discount anything that probes too deeply into our lives as a form of parapsychology or a pursuit reserved for "weirdos." In our most honest moments, nevertheless, we sense that our dreams are speaking to us, regardless of our attempts to suppress them.

The Bible in general—and this passage from Matthew in particular— reminds us that God speaks in a variety of ways and in a multitude of experiences. This truth follows clearly what the writer to the Hebrews relates to readers: "Long ago God spoke to our ancestors in many and various ways by the prophets, but in these last days he has spoken to us by a Son" (Hebrews 1:1-2). That Joseph paid heed to his dreams is a tribute to his faith. With twenty-first-century hindsight, we see that Joseph's discernment had practical implications for the holy family's survival. Those who move families may be "mindless dreamers," but, after all, in following his dream, Joseph saved the Savior.

Christmas reminds us that God's good grace comes to us as a gift. The promptings of God's Spirit come to us as gracious parts of God's holiness and wholeness. Often we require the gift of discernment in order to receive this word and world of goodness. We must run the risk of overcoming our own unconscious fears to hear this word. Perhaps better said, we can permit God to speak to us.

In the end, Joseph prevailed on behalf of his family at the most practical level because he was willing to trust and heed the voice and direction of God. We will never be too modern for a gift such as this one. It is the gift that keeps on giving. Amen. (David N. Mosser)

Decisions and Directions
Romans 12:2

If the phone rings and the voice on the other end asks, "How do you get to Albuquerque?" one of the first responses is "Where are you starting from?" On any journey one needs to know the destination, where you are going; and the point of origin, where you are starting from. Only when those two facts are established can the middle be planned. Even for those who claim to wander with no definite plans, a decision is made as the vehicle leaves the driveway: "East, south, west, or north."

Tomorrow is the last day of the year, with Tuesday a new beginning. At midnight we are each presented with a brand-new year. Much like the first day of school with new pencils and notebooks, we have a new calendar—some entries already made, but for the most part, blank. How will you fill them?

Perhaps a brief look over our shoulders to the past 365 days is in order—where are we coming from? This question may be difficult to answer. It means being honest with yourself about yourself.

The Diné (Navajo) language has more than three hundred thousand words meaning "to go," while the English language has only one verb. For the English speaker, modifiers describe how one goes—fast, slowly, now, and so on. A description of a person in Diné always includes motion; she may be going along, starting out, on her way to a specific point, or moving away from. Many times the motion is relative to another object; she is moving over there, closer to the rock than to me. In a sense, a description of a person describes a journey.

For the Diné, like many Native American nations, directions are very important and meaningful. I was taught that one says the directions in only one sequence, always starting with the east, then following the movement of the sun. Each direction represents a time of the day, a time in one's life journey, and seasons.

East is the direction where the sun begins its journey. My mother would arise before dawn, go straight outside, and await the rising sun. The traditional eight-sided hogan has only one door facing east and no corners. The sun's rays enter the hogan to chase any spirits out of the house. With eight sides, there are no corners for them to hide in. As soon as the sun's rays broke the horizon, my mother would greet them with a prayer on her lips while releasing pollen to bless the new day she had been given. East also represents the new life, infancy. East, at the end of the cycle, also represents old age and transition to the "Other Side."

South is the summertime, noontime, and the end of childhood. In the traditional Diné, teenagers did not exist. One puts away childish things at about age ten to eleven. Puberty means a change of mind-set, and adulthood is welcomed through ceremonies and ageless rituals. Again, prayers and pollen are offered at this time of day.

West is the season of fall and, in the life cycle, the time of young adulthood. It is a time of added responsibility. The color red, representing the sky at sunset, is associated with the west. Another prayer and more pollen are offered at dusk. Time is spent in reflection upon whom we have met, what we have done, and preparing for what needs to be done.

North is the wintertime, middle age, and nighttime. It is a time to get ready for the next stage of the journey, old age, and death. It is a time when one must be very aware of who is coming behind you; have they been taught all they need to know?

The cardinal directions also include up and down. Most Native people see themselves as part of the entire universe, a universe that moves and in which nothing stands still. A full cycle, coming back to where we started, to begin anew.

The new year is a new beginning. The Preacher in Ecclesiastes tells us that there is nothing new under the sun (Ecclesiastes 1:9). I would argue that we, as God's creations, are new, and given something new every twenty-four hours and every 365 days. Every time we learn something new about ourselves or about God's creation, we have the potential, perhaps even the responsibility, to grow and change.

The idea of determining one's direction at this time of year is not new. That's what resolutions are: setting goals for a new direction for ourselves. Whether it is to get in better shape, to spend more time in the Word, to pay off a credit card, or just to get those photographs in some kind of order, the desired end result defines the plan of action.

Any new path requires strength, self-discipline, sacrifice, and faith. Perhaps that is why the elders greeted each day with prayers and pollen; they knew they could not do it alone. In some Native communities, they call the Christian walk the "good Red road." My prayer for you is that you take some time to greet the day with prayer and pollen to bless it. Determine your "good Red road" and while walking on it, if you find it is too hard, ask for help. Throughout the Scriptures, the fellowship refers to its members as brothers and sisters. Asking for help is not a sign of weakness, but rather a symptom of wisdom. Knowing yourself, your strengths and weaknesses, is the point of origin. As the ball drops in Times Square tomorrow night, may you find the time, the courage, and the desire to be honest with yourself as you realize your own personal starting point and look to your Creator to know in which direction to take your next step. (Raquel Mull)

Worship Aids

Call to Worship

The New Year dawns with potential and possibility. We come together today to say farewell to all that this year has held, and to embrace the future that still lies ahead. We come together as a people of faith who are here to worship God. (Gary G. Kindley)

Prayer of Confession

On this last day of our calendar year, O God of goodness and light, illumine a path for us by which we may walk in faithfulness. Too often we have lost our way. Too often we have lived out of our pride and stubbornness and failed to turn to you in our times of need. You have given us all that we need to live sober lives in a right mind. Impel us to sin no more and give us a more perfect knowledge of your divine ways in the world. Help us accept the forgiveness you offer if we but only ask for it. Grant us the opportunity to celebrate this coming year with a faithfulness that we scarcely knew we had in us. Power this celebration through your Holy Spirit—the greatest gift you can offer us today. In Jesus' name we pray. Amen. (David N. Mosser)

Words of Assurance

Release the burdens of the past. Relinquish control from that which is only in God's hands. Allow the peace of God to dwell in you. You are forgiven. Accept the gift. Relax in the warmth of God's embrace.

Benediction

Let go of yesterday. Embrace tomorrow. Live in the moment. Fear not. Amen. (Gary G. Kindley)

III. APPENDIX

SPECIAL SERVICES

Commissioning a Mission Trip

Prayer

To the Holy Spirit, who sent the apostles into the world to spread the gospel, we pray for the new adventure of these men and women who choose to serve as the apostles before them. We offer thanks to God for the courage and determination of each person. Protect them. Help each person find the words and the actions that will change the lives of people they meet. Amen.

Sermon

Hebrews 12:1-4

We are gathered to provide a spiritual and emotional send-off to our mission team. Their journey will lead them to the place God is asking them to go, and the passage will not be a simple one. Just as Jesus prepared his disciples to go to all parts of the world to share the message they spent three years learning from their Teacher, so have these people been prepared to share their message and to give time and energy to the poor and needy.

Early cartographers that traveled to new frontiers were uncertain of what lay ahead of them. Maps from the fifteenth century often end at the last point of exploration. Then you see drawings of dragons. In some cases, you might even see the words "Beyond here, there be dragons." The unknown has long been a frightening thing to human beings. For years, mapmakers masked their own fears of venturing farther by simply explaining away the unexplored territory with the unexplainable.

Missionaries today have the courage to go forward. They do not let adversity get in the way of meeting the needs of other people. Missionaries who face up to the hills and valleys caused by the unknown have earned our respect and our prayerful support. Today we begin a special prayer process, remembering these people every hour and day until they return safely to us again. Perhaps they will not meet every objective, but we know they will give it their all, and as the author of Hebrews wrote, they will "run with perseverance the race that is set before [them]" (Hebrews 12:1).

Each Olympics has its own set of stories, and perhaps each one of you has your favorite. Mine has long been the example of Dan Jansen. Three times, he qualified for the Olympics. Three times, he was favored to win the 500-meter speed-skating event. Each time, he lost his footing and slipped during the race. Each time, the Olympic championship was lost. Dan Jansen returned in 1994 for the last time, knowing clearly that it was now or never for him. He prepared to skate the 500-meter race. He slipped. He fell. He did not win.

He had entered the 1,000-meter speed-skating event, a longer, more difficult event, and not the one he had trained so hard to win. Well, you know the story. He won. In winning, he won much more than the gold medal. He found something inside that demonstrated his own endurance.

Dan Jansen had an ability to withstand profuse internal and external pressure. All who watched the race that day could sense the incredible relief as he gathered up his daughter in one arm, carried the American flag in his other hand, and took his victory lap after winning the gold in the 1,000 meters.

I wonder how often Dan Jansen said, "I can't continue to do this." I see a parable of our Christian life in his story and a parallel to our members who embark on this mission trip. There are times in our lives when we grow weary and fainthearted. The author of Hebrews is concerned about those who lose their heart, those who do not or cannot continue.

But the author suggests that we look "to Jesus the pioneer and perfecter of our faith, who for the sake of the joy that was set before him endured the cross, disregarding its shame, and has taken his seat at the right hand of the throne of God" (Hebrews 12:2). As these courageous and spirited people depart from this place, we pray that they remain on solid footing, continue to be upright, and win for the sake of those they serve. God's blessings on each of you. Amen.

Closing Prayer

God of the mission fields, hear our prayer as we seek your intervention in the lives of these people who leave here today to serve you. Grant them courage and strength to remain sturdy messengers and caregivers to the needy they go to help. Protect them, O God, and return them safely home and to us. We pray this in the name of the great protector of all missionaries throughout the ages, Jesus the Christ. Amen. (Ted McIlvain)

Funeral

Greeting

Dear friends, we have gathered in this time and place to worship God and to celebrate the life of *(Name)*. As we gather, we trust in the peaceful presence of the Holy Spirit that walks with us in our grief and helps us in our time of need. Although we come here in sorrow, we also come giving God thanks for the life and memories of *(Name)*.

We believe that God, through Jesus Christ, conquered death, not only for the person of Christ, but for all of us who believe in God's name. So we come witnessing to our faith, even in the midst of death, because there is life eternal in Jesus Christ our Lord and Savior.

Opening Prayer

Gracious and eternal God, you have created and sustained all things in life, in death, and in life beyond death. Come and be present with us this day as we celebrate the life of *(Name)*. We especially ask your blessing upon this family and these close friends as they experience the pain of loss at this time.

Guide them to an assurance of your love and allow them to remember the blessings that *(Name)* brought into their lives. Help each of us this day to turn our eyes to you, for comfort, for peace, and for a new joy that is promised through the resurrection of your Son, Jesus the Christ. Amen.

Sermon

Romans 8:14-18

These words from the book of Romans offer us a new perspective on the life we live and on the death that *(Name)* has now experienced. This scripture helps us understand that God's adopting love is not bound by the realities of our human world. God's love is beyond our earthly experience. It transcends the human realm and connects us with the divine. We are called the children of God, and if children, then we are open to the blessings and promises created through the resurrection of Jesus Christ.

When we find ourselves grieving the loss of a loved one, it is easy to think of death as the first disciples did the day after Jesus was crucified. We can see death as the end, the final word in a great story of someone's life. We might even act as the disciples did and go into hiding and mourn without hope.

But death is not an end. Death is a part of the divine relationship between God and humans. The scripture tells us that we share in the experience with Christ. We share in the suffering realities of this world, but we also share in the glory of heaven to come. As Paul writes, the glory to come does not begin to compare to the minor suffering of this world.

So instead of focusing on the worldly sorrow we feel at the loss of a loved one, we as Christians are called to celebrate the adoption we have through Christ, which leads to a glory that far surpasses any human experience. As people of faith, we still grieve our losses, but we do not grieve as though this event is an ending.

We grieve for ourselves and for lost time, but at the same moment we celebrate for *(Name)* and for ourselves, who have the ability to be heirs to God's glory. We do not hide and mourn without hope, but we express our loss with the knowledge that God's eternal love, and divine gift of Christ, makes all things new, even death. Amen.

Closing Prayer

Loving God, you have accepted us into your family and have provided a way for us to know you. Help us this day to claim, not only the suffering and death of Jesus Christ but also Christ's glorious resurrection. Help us to understand that we are connected to that event by your loving grace.

Receive *(Name)* into your loving arms, and give us the assurance that someday we will all feast at the glorious banquet you have prepared for us. In doing so, may that part of our Apostles' Creed be made a reality as we celebrate the "communion of the saints." In this, as in everything, we lift our prayers in the holy and sanctified name of Jesus Christ. Amen. (Chris J. Hayes)

Funeral for a Teen Suicide

Call to Worship

Where the Spirit of the Lord is, there is comfort in the face of sorrow and hope in the shadow of despair. Let us gather to claim God's promises and to offer comfort and hope to those who grieve.

Invocation

Merciful God, we claim the resurrection promise of Christ, our Lord, at this hour of loss. We are adrift in the tides of life's turmoil apart from your saving grace. Claim us, comfort us, redeem us, and carry us as we journey through the valley of the shadow of death to the place of resurrection. Amen.

A Homily for a Teen Suicide

John 11; Revelation 21:1-6

(The opening of this homily assumes the setting is a funeral chapel rather than a sanctuary or a church auditorium.)

We are gathered today in a place we would rather not be, for a reason we wish were not true, to do that which we dread to have happen. We are here to face the reality of death that has come too soon for someone whom we love—a friend, child, student, teammate, grandchild, and child of God.

Death is something before which we shrink, and we try to mask our fear of its truth with floral tributes and ribbon. Whenever we face death, when we stand before the reality of our mortality, it is a compelling opportunity to consider the very nature of life and death. As Christians, we see death very differently than do other mortals.

Christians are called to remember to whom they belong and to always consider death in the light of resurrection. Indeed, this is considered more than a funeral service today; it is a service of death and resurrection. Therefore let us consider both whenever we stare death in the face.

Whether it is a body that we bury, or ashes that we inter or scatter, we must remember what it is that we need to bury in death. We need to bury what is a leftover of every human relationship: things we did that we wish we could undo, things we said that we wish we could take back, and things we failed to do or say before the time ran out. These are the things that we need to bury—"ashes to ashes and dust to dust."

We take with us those things that even death cannot rob from us: precious memories, sacred moments, joyous laughter, and tender times. These we hold close for eternity and we remember.

Death, even death that comes too soon or with such waste, need not be an enemy or an end. The Revelation of John tells us that death is a door to another part of our journey where suffering, crying, and pain are no more (see Revelation 21:4). Today, we release one we love, who stands today, and for all eternity, in the loving embrace of the everlasting arms of the Lord.

In the eleventh chapter of the Gospel of John, the often-read story of the raising of Lazarus captures both the grief of death and the amazing hope of Christ. In John 11:21, Martha, with a tone of accusation, says to Jesus, "Lord, if you had been here, my brother would not have died." Jesus turns her allegation into an opportunity for proclamation when he says to her, "I am the resurrection and the life. Those who believe in me, even though they die, will live, and everyone who lives and believes in me will never die" (John 11:25-26).

It would be easy for us, like Martha, to finger-point at this tragic time. "If only …" "If someone …" "If I had …" "If God had …" Instead, we must follow Christ's example of pointing to the greater reality of the resurrection faith. Indictments, blaming, and guilt are not needed here, but rather compassion, comfort, and grace.

Whenever death comes in this way, we worry and wonder. Life is sacred; God cherishes life so much that we are created to share in its wonder. When someone's soul becomes so troubled, their thoughts so dark, they can see no light at the tunnel's end, suicide seems, to them, the only answer. We worry about condemnation from God for such an act and we fear for the very soul of the one who chooses that answer.

Fear not; God's grace is sufficient for times such as these. Fear not; God is our judge and the judge of all. Fear not; put aside our narrow judgment that we might focus on the wide embrace of God's immeasurable grace. God does not condemn those whose bodies—or whose minds—have robbed them of health and wholeness. Let us never confuse illness for lack of faith or lack of courage. God is the Great Physician who understands our needs. God makes our spirits whole again when illness drags our minds over the cliff of despair.

Struggles, such as physical health or mental illness, are not the exclamation points of a life. Struggles are instead the parentheses of life, a part of the story but not its conclusion. Let us not focus on how our loved one has died but rather celebrate how our loved one has lived.

Let us offer hope and comfort to this family. Let us speak of the truth of God and the hope of Christ's redeeming love. Let us live as witnesses to faith, proclaimers of life, bearers of hope, and believers in grace.

Near the entrance of the tower of the University of Texas is an inscription from the Gospel of John, chapter 8. It reads, "You will know the truth and the truth will set you free." The inscription is only a partial quotation and is taken out of context. The quotation, from verses 31 and 32 of John chapter 8 reads: "[Jesus said,] 'If you continue in my word, you are truly my disciples; and you will know the truth, and the truth will make you free.'"

The truth for us to know transcends this world. It is a truth that not even death can take away. It is not merely about a law or a rule; it is about a relationship. It is a relationship of grace offered for each one of us, if only we will open our hand and claim the gift.

This is the truth that we claim today. This is the truth that sets us free. This is the truth that nothing can stop and that death cannot kill.

The truth is that in life, and in death, and in life beyond death, God is with us. We are not alone. Thanks be to God! Amen.

Benediction

Peace and comfort be unto you. Claim the power that God's Spirit offers. Live in hope and peace, and in the Truth that is Christ, our Lord. Amen. (Gary G. Kindley)

Funeral for the Death of a Child

Prayer

God of the children, we praise you and ask you to comfort the friends and family of (*Child's Name*) as they gather in this place to grieve and to worship. God, help the memories to be strength to all of us in this room, and comfort us through your words of assurance.

Look upon this gathering, God, and see the suffering that is here. Let these worshipers feel your spirit as it descends to give consolation. Hear the prayers of their hearts reaching out to you to calm the spirit of parents and family members, and to reassure others who feel the pain from the loss of (*Child's Name*).

God, we offer thanksgiving for the promise of life eternal. We seek your presence as we begin the process of letting the joys of knowing (*Child's Name*) bring delightful visions of play and laughter. We thank you for the courage you will bring to each of us as we release this child to your presence this day. Amen.

Sermon

Mark 10:13-16

I believe that all children are born with the natural desire and instinct to discover truths that adults may no longer seek. I believe that every little boy or girl is going to see the world—"just as soon as I can cross the street." I believe that every child can creatively rearrange spinach ten different ways on a dinner plate before announcing that he/she is full. I believe that every child has a God-given inquisitiveness that mystifies those who receive the multitude of questions. I believe that God shows himself to all of us each time a child laughs, feels better when Daddy kisses a boo-boo, or reaches out for another hug just before drifting off to sleep.

From the scripture, Mark relates Jesus' feelings toward children as they come into his presence. He expressed his displeasure to those who attempt to keep the little ones away. He wanted children to come to him because he loved each one. Their attitude of wanting to learn and grow must have been most appealing to him because it is a manner pleasing to his God and our God. Jesus acts out of his compassion. He embraces and blesses the children. He feels their uncompromising faith and reassures his genuine concern for them. I believe (*Child's Name*) is experiencing his love now.

This scripture does not deal with the desperation of parents, family members, and friends as they let go of this child. I get a sense that Jesus is aware that emotional healing is more than physical; it is a life-changing event. Christians know that prayer and surrounding ourselves with God's people on earth will help us through the loss of loved ones.

Grief may well be the price we all pay for love. There are few answers as to why the pain exists and fewer ways to make them go away. Christians, however, are comforted by God's promise of a heavenly home for all of God's children. Life stopped short of its potential is perhaps the greatest loss in human existence. Yet life does go on for those who loved and cared for (*Child's Name*). The continuation of our lives and the evidence of genuine care for others around us are the greatest ways to allow (*Child's Name*)'s time on earth to be meaningful. We will experience moments when the presence of this child would make the experience so much more momentous; we may even say that the sunset we want to share or the family gathering is hollow without (*Child's Name*).

When someone we love dies, our world is changed in an instant. When a child dies, we also feel powerless. Parents and friends, this may be the first time in your lives that you believe you have no control or cannot make it feel better inside. As God's people, we depend on relationships in our lives just as God expects a relationship with each of us. Through a loss of my own, I have found that it is most important to find someone who will listen to your story of grief. This is a highly effective road to healing for most people.

I believe that (*Child's Name*) is celebrating a new union with God even as we gather here to bid him/her farewell. We can find comfort in the fact that (*Child's Name*) is welcomed into the presence of God and his/her spirit will unite with the spirits of loved ones who went before and will rejoice over loved ones who will follow.

God makes a promise to us all. John writes about that promise in the book of Revelation, saying, "The Lamb at the center of the throne will be their shepherd, and he will guide them to springs of the water of life, and God will wipe away every tear from their eyes" (7:17). I believe it should be so for all of us who celebrate the life of (*Child's Name*).

Prayer

Loving God, we have celebrated the life of (*Child's Name*). We have united to worship you and ask your blessings on this family. Now we ask for you to accept the spirit of this young life into the heavenly family. We pray for family and friends here and away. Give them strength and courage as they begin to live lives with an empty space that (*Child's Name*) once filled. These things we pray in the name of your Son, Jesus Christ. Amen. (Ted McIlvain)

Homecoming

Call to Worship

Leader: Welcome home!

People: God calls to us, whoever we are.

Leader: God calls, "Welcome home!"

People: God calls us to a purpose that propels us forward.

Leader: Where God calls us, it is home!

People: God calls. Listen! Search for the home where our purpose and our peace can be found.

All: God is calling, O sinner, come home!

Invocation

Wherever the Spirit of the Lord is, we are home! Thank you, God, for calling us, claiming us, naming us, and housing us. You have created a place for us on this planet and in the paradise yet-to-come. Call to us, Lord God, that we might listen. Lead us, Lord God, that we might follow. Open the door, Lord God, as we knock to enter your kingdom. We say with the psalmist, "I would rather be a doorkeeper in the house of my God than live in the tents of wickedness" (Psalm 84:10). Amen.

Where God Has a Purpose for You

John 21; 1 Kings 17:1-24

Some time ago, I had the opportunity to return to the church of my childhood. It was there where I was baptized, where I learned to sing in the children's choir, and where I was a part of the youth group until I graduated high school. When I went back for the reunion service, everything seemed smaller.

As a child, I was impressed by the pulpit, which seemed to tower above the front pew. What an awesome thing it was to sit even higher than the pulpit in the choir loft behind it, whenever the children's choir sang in the service. As an adult, the pulpit was much less impressive than I had remembered it to be. Still, there was something comforting about going back to my "home church."

After the crucifixion and resurrection of Christ, Peter and six of the disciples returned home (see John 21). It was not the home where they stayed in Jerusalem, but the place where Jesus first found most of them—in Galilee. What do you do when your world is turned upside down and you are uncertain what tomorrow will bring? For Peter, the answer was obvious. Peter went fishing.

It was not an easy, let's-coast-out-in-the-boat-and-toss-a-hook-in sort of fishing. It was a haul-out-the-large-nets-and-haul-in-as-big-a-catch-as-you-can, hard-work sort of fishing. Peter and the others needed to let off some steam, and focus. So they returned to their roots and got back into their comfort zone—they went home.

Home is a safe place, a place of miracles, and a place of growth. Home is a place to hunker down and remember who you are. The prophet Elijah discovered that. He learned that home is not necessarily from where you have come, as much as it is where you find you belong. Home can be wherever God has a purpose for you.

There was famine in the land (see 1 Kings 17). These were difficult times. It was especially difficult for people who were "the least of these," such as a widow and her young son. They did not have much to start with, and having a guest ask for hospitality seemed an imposition. Still, the widow knew the importance of hospitality. In welcoming a stranger, you sometimes discover God's messengers. Sarah and Abraham had learned that lesson. The widow of Zarephath was about to realize it for herself.

Elijah asked the young widow for a place to stay, and promised that there would always be enough food if only she was willing to share. She was faithful and generous. Elijah and God kept their promise. She gave herself and her jar of flour away, and it never ran out; in return, she got her son back from the grip of death. Illness and death came to their home, but so did Elijah, a prophet of God. Her son's body died, but Elijah prayed and healed him.

Because this single mother was faithful and kind, she received into her home a man who needed a home for a time. Because she opened a door, God opened a window of salvation that saved her son, her soul, and Elijah.

Home is not necessarily from where you have come as much as it is where you find you belong. Some believe that they have no home because the home of their childhood was one of abuse or abandonment. Some believe that they have no home because their memories of home are thoughts they would rather not remember. Home is more than where we once were. Home can be wherever God has a purpose for you.

Consider your present and your future. Consider the now and the not-yet. Consider what God may have in store for you and consider where God might be calling you as your new home. Home can be wherever God has a purpose for you.

Welcome home! God is waiting! Amen.

Benediction

We go forth to our homes to come again to God's house. We go forth as builders of God's kingdom. Go and invite so that others might enter. Go forth and build the kingdom of God. Amen. (Gary G. Kindley)

Stewardship (Mark 12:38-44)

Invocation

Lord God, may something shake us up today, so that we might worship beyond our complacency and believe beyond our doubt. Stir us up, Holy Spirit. Open our eyes to see differently. May we have a fresh faith, renewed vigor, open hearts, and open minds. Give us ears to listen for Christ's message to us today, and the courage to obey and follow. Amen.

When We Are Poorer Than We Realize

Mark 12:38-44

It is a paradox that love can yield hatred, but it is true. The love of money may have birthed greater enmity and strife than any other love we can imagine. Perhaps *love* is not the proper word to use, for *lust* and *avarice* seem more appropriate here.

Jesus begins this passage by speaking out against arrogance. "Beware!" he cautions in the first word from his mouth. It is a dire warning against a common sin that has led to great destruction. The self-centered nature of the human condition is so prevalent that we attempt to make God fit our image. Anthropomorphism, it is called. It is what we do when we want to lower the bar of Christian discipleship. Instead of living up to God's standards, we attempt to make God fit our own.

Jesus takes a seat across from the place where the litmus test of true faith occurs: the treasury. A pastor once told me about a private investigator he had in his congregation. The investigator said that he could tell almost anything about someone by simply looking at checking account and credit card statements. Where our treasure is, that is where our heart follows. Jesus also said that (Matthew 6:21).

As Christ sits opposite the place where people make their offering to God, he observes the many kinds of people who come by. The rich people put in large sums. It is not that what they give is not important; it is more the motive of their gift about which Jesus expresses concern. When one of the least of these—a poor widow—comes to make an offering, Jesus takes action. He calls a meeting of all the disciples who are around and makes a proclamation. Those who have much have given out of their abundance. She, who has little, gave out of sacrifice.

Who are the rich? We would like to think they are people who have more than we do. In truth, most all of us are rich. Middle-class, everyday Americans are wealthier than most people on the planet. Most of us own more than one coat or sweater, and have a few extra pounds that bear witness to our not having missed many meals. As long as we believe that we are not the wealthy of whom Jesus speaks, we can ignore the admonition—or can we?

Jesus taught a great deal and often about possessions, money, and wealth. He knew that things often stand in our way of being God's people. Money has been a blessing and a curse for the church.

More good has been done as a result of financial support of missions and ministries than many would ever have dreamed. Still, untold numbers of people have been "turned off" by financial appeals from Christian ministries. And there are unscrupulous "evangelists" whose insipid and conniving sermons are designed to line their pockets rather than the streets of heaven. Salvation is far from those whose motives have little to do with God's kingdom. Martin Luther, fed up with the manipulative theology of the church that sold "indulgences" to pay for papal construction, gave birth to the Protestant Reformation. Money and religious manipulation is neither a recent phenomenon nor exclusive to television preachers.

So what is our excuse for poor stewardship? Do we give as an act of worship or to meet IRS guidelines? Are we trying to impress someone or are we seeking to bless God? Do we give begrudgingly or with a grateful and joyous heart? What excuse will we make this year for failing to support Christ's church and charitable causes with as much of our resources as we spend on entertainment and dining out? Millions of children could be fed with only 1 percent of what Americans spend on movies, videos, and DVDs.

The widow gave out of sacrifice, not abundance, yet she experienced abundance in her sacrifice. Such is the nature of the kingdom of God. Let those who will listen, hear.

Offertory Prayer

Holy God, you are always about the task of blessing us, so we need not ask. This day we ask that we may be a blessing to you. Open our hearts, stir our souls, and excite our spirits. May we be prodded just enough to do something about that which we claim to believe. Teach us to serve. Compel us to give. Commend us to share. Forgive us when we fail you. These things we pray in the name of the One who gave everything for love's sake. Amen.

Benediction

Give as if you have everything. Serve as if you owe everyone. Love as one of God's holy ones. Be a disciple of Jesus Christ. Amen. (Gary G. Kindley)

Stewardship (1 Corinthians 12:12-26)

Opening Prayer

Gracious and loving God, you give all good things for our use and into our care. Open our hearts that we may receive these blessings with humility and gratitude. Open our minds that we may understand how deeply blessed we are. Open our hands to give back to you from our abundance. Amen.

Sermon

1 Corinthians 12:12-26

Stewardship is more than giving and pledging budgets. Stewardship is more than a season of the year. Stewardship should be an everyday focus of our lives as Christian disciples. Stewardship is simply using God's gifts to the best of our abilities. With God's help, we can use and offer the gifts God has given us to show others the love and grace of God that we have experienced.

Too often, stewardship is associated with only money or church budgets. If we were all good stewards, there would be no need to worry about church budgets or funding ministries. However, there would be many more important things we would not have to worry about as well.

We would not need to worry about people feeling lost or lonely. We would not worry about poverty and the feelings of helplessness. We would not need to worry about many things that cause our world so many aches. If we all recognized and used the gifts and talents that God has given us, then the world would be full of caregivers, volunteers, hospitality, and generosity.

Stewardship is about understanding that everyone has been gifted by God and that the gift can be used to be the hands and feet of Christ in the world. For some people, this may be the gift of personality and friendliness; while for others, this may be the gift of financial know-how and prosperity. However, for all of us, there is a gift or two that we can give back to God and God's people. What gift have you been given from God?

Too often, we minimize the gifts that do not look exciting or meaningful to us. God's message to us through Paul's pen in 1 Corinthians is that all gifts, no matter what our perception may be, are important to the body of Christ. To be the true body of Christ, as God intends for us to be, we must understand and appreciate the variety of gifts God bestows upon all of us.

We must also realize that we are all called to use these gifts to the glory of God, and we are called to be good stewards of these gifts. I cannot tell you what your gifts are, but I know that we all have important gifts, and when we do not use them to the best of our abilities, we hurt the whole body. As people of God, we are called to give back of our gifts and ourselves.

During this focus on stewardship, remember that you have a part. It may seem small to you or others, or you may believe that your part is more important than anyone else's component, but in the model God sets forth for us, all parts are of equal value, and all must work together to do the work of Christ in the world.

We give to God and to others, because God has given us so much. Let us never forget that what we have is exceedingly important to God and can be important to others, if we are good stewards as God intends us to be. Thanks be to God for the gifts we have been given. Amen.

Prayer

Giving God, for all the good gifts you give, we thank you. For the wisdom to recognize and celebrate the value of all gifts, we beseech you. For the responsibility of caring for and using those gifts in meaningful and loving ways, we ask your guidance and strength. In the name of Jesus the Christ we pray. Amen. (Chris J. Hayes)

Hanging of the Greens—for Advent

Greeting

Sisters and brothers in Christ, as we prepare for the coming of the Light of the World, we prepare our church and our homes with symbolic light. Tonight as we light the Chrismon trees and the Advent wreath, we remember the love of God sent to us in the light of Christ Jesus. Let us prepare our hearts for the coming of the Lord! Glory to God in the highest!

Prayer

God of creation and God of redemption, send your blessing upon your people everywhere. Allow us to experience the mystery of this season, and the hope that the Christ Child brings. Be present in all our celebrations, and never let us forget that we celebrate because of your gift to us. Bless this worship space. We pray that it might lead this congregation and other people to see your light more clearly this Christmas season. In the name and Spirit of Jesus the Christ we pray. Amen.

Sermon

Use the Advent lections, or any of the following: Jeremiah 23:5-6; Isaiah 9:2, 6-7; Isaiah 53:1-6; John 1:1-5, 9-14

From the very beginning of creation, God desired a relationship. God created the earth and all that is in it, but something was missing. So God created humans, woman and man, in God's own image, so that they could have a relationship with each other and so God could have a relationship with humanity.

The story of creation is a story full of relationships—a relationship between God and the creation, and the many relationships among the creatures. Through sin, God's relationship with the humans was blocked. Obviously, this hurt the Creator, who had made these persons for relationship with God.

Out of love, God began trying to reconnect with God's creation. The Lord sent varied and numerous judges, kings, and prophets to call the people of promise back into a relationship with their God. All of these efforts reveal, for the created people, a way back to God. However, these efforts at revelation of the divine fell short of a permanent answer.

God then sent God's only Son into the world, so that the people of the world might know God once again. God wants a relationship with people so passionately that God was willing to sacrifice Jesus Christ.

It was more than mere sacrifice. It was the Word of God coming to the people so they could hear and see again the goodness and the love that God has for them. This Advent season, we celebrate the birth and the life of Jesus Christ. In the life of Christ, we see ways to reconnect with God, through prayer and service, and ways to reconnect with one another as God's holy and good creation.

Tonight as we light the trees and celebrate the coming of the Christ Child, let us never forget God's purpose in giving us this gift. Jesus Christ was given to bring us back home into a relationship with God. This was not only the desire of God some two thousand years ago; it is God's ultimate desire today!

God wants us to see these lights and sing the songs of the season for a purpose, to reconnect our lives with the divine. This is the goal of Advent and Christmas. To find the relationship with God that was always intended. Amen.

Prayer

God of Christmas, help us to remember just how much you love us and long to be in a relationship with us. Help us to focus on you during this busy time of year. As we light up our homes and our church, allow our thoughts to turn to the true Light of life, Jesus the Christ. Make us one with you and with one another. May we see this Advent and Christmas season the power of love and light in Jesus Christ. Amen. (Chris J. Hayes)

CLASSIC SERMONS

What Does God Look Like?
by Robert E. Goodrich, Jr.

At the time he delivered The Protestant Hour sermons, Robert E. Goodrich, Jr. was pastor of First Methodist Church in Dallas, Texas.

The year was 1963 ... Pope John XXIII died and Paul VI was elected. The Soviet Union sent a woman into space. The Vietnam conflict became more intense.

Moviegoers raved over *The Birds, Tom Jones,* and *Dr. Strangelove.* Peter, Paul, and Mary sang "Puff, the Magic Dragon" and "Blowin' in the Wind" as American youth tuned them in on the radio.

The biggest story of 1963 was the assassination of President John F. Kennedy. The president was shot on the streets of Dallas in his open limousine. Lee Harvey Oswald was arrested hours later.

Dr. Martin Luther King addressed 200,000 persons in Washington with his famous "I Have a Dream" speech. Civil rights leader Medgar Evers was assassinated. A bomb exploded in a Birmingham, Alabama, church, killing four girls. Civil rights struggles dominated the headlines of our nation's news.

In 1963 black people were being mentally and physically abused. They raised their hands high and cried for civil rights.

And where were the churches? Dr. Eugene Carson Blake of the United Presbyterian Church, along with fellow clergy, addressed a crowd in a Baltimore amusement park that forbade black attendance. Dr. Blake and his fellow church leaders gathered together with a simple biblical idea, that all people, regardless of race, are created in the image of God. That leaves us with one big question: what does God look like?

❧❧❧

On a visit to Russia, a friend of mine was talking with a young woman bus driver. "I understand that in America nearly everybody believes in God," she said. He answered that about 90 percent of the people claim to believe in him. The young woman thought for a moment and then asked, "Tell me, what does your God look like?"

She was asking a crucial question for all of us. What does he look like ... in character? What is the shape of his love, his goodness, his judgment?

Many persons hold a picture of God in their hearts, which makes me wonder how on earth they could ever love him, or even respect him. When tragedy comes, for example, they immediately begin to ask, Why did God do this to me? Why did he take my husband? We had so many plans and dreams! Why did he send this lingering illness upon my child?

I was on the Texas coast about twelve months after hurricane Carla had wrought her terrible destruction. There were rows of homes still so water-damaged that their owners had not been able to return to them. And though a year had passed, more than once I heard the question "Why do you think God sent this upon us? We must have been doing something terribly wrong." What does God look like for them?

A young man in a hospital wrote to his pastor a letter, which included these sentences: "For months I have been on this bed with time to think. Tell me, sir, in view of the facts of life, have I any reason to love God? I believe some God exists but be good enough to tell me why I should love him."

So everywhere there are persons who don't bother with the church because frankly they do not like the kind of God whom they imagine is worshiped in the church. They carry a picture of him fashioned from hearsay, or from fragmentary experiences remembered from Sunday school days, or from the words of some traveling revivalist in other years. They would say to us, "We don't want to believe in your God! We have outgrown your childish ideas of a sort of super-man sitting out on the rim of the universe somewhere, running things like a king, pulling the strings on life so that everybody's real name would be Punch and Judy! Nor do we like the idea that from up there somewhere he sends sorrow and suffering and pain upon persons in order to get even with them or to punish them or to test their faith. And furthermore, we don't like your ridiculous idea of a glorified private-eye always watching us so that he can put down a checkmark or a gold star by our name in his big black book!"

To be sure, this composite picture sounds overdrawn, and yet the various ideas out of which it is made are present all around us. But what does God really look like?

Perhaps it is foolish to try to deal with such a subject within the space of these few minutes, but we can at least make a beginning. Granted that it is impossible for the finite mind to encompass the infinite: we cannot completely picture him or express him in human language or thought. But we can have the spirit of the man who said to Jesus, "Lord, I believe; help thou mine unbelief." There is much beyond our power of understanding or comprehension, but on the other hand, there are surely some things we can grasp. And we can make an effort to bring into sharper focus a picture of the God of the Christian faith as seen in the revelation of Jesus Christ. Lord, I believe; help thou mine unbelief!

Let's begin with that idea that God is a super-king, a manlike dictator, sitting off somewhere on the rim of the universe pulling the strings of life.

In a paper on religion, a college student described her struggle with such a picture. She said that as a child in church, she used to be fascinated with the angels in the stained-glass windows. She would imagine that she could see a great throne-room with the soft, billowy clouds for the floor and the bright blue sky for the ceiling. Seated down at one end of the room in a huge chair was a bewhiskered old gentleman, in the fashion of a patriarch of Israel, who she was sure was God. In and out of the room floated pink and blue and lavender angels. "But one day," she concluded, "I grew out of my visions in pastels and found myself left with nothing at all . . . nothing."

This is the final and inevitable result of trying to believe in a manlike God. And yet most of us began as children with a picture of him that was a strange blend of Father Time and Santa Claus and Daddy! As we grew in wisdom and understanding, however, we put away childish things and have come to believe with Jesus Christ that "God is a Spirit, and they that worship him must worship him in spirit and in truth." He is not a God who is just up there, he is down here; he is not just out there, he is in here. We believe he is everywhere present, always.

When a friend of mine asked his little son to say grace at the table, he came forth with these words: "God is good, God is great, clear across the Lone Star state." But you and I know that he must be a God who is not limited to these fifty states, or to this continent, or even to this earth. We believe that he is a Spirit, always near, everywhere present, no matter where we go.

But if this is what he looks like, why do we go on referring to him as having manlike qualities? Why do we talk of "the everlasting arms," or of "walking with him, talking with him"? Why do we speak of "the eyes of God" or the "hand of God"?

We do this because, for one thing, we are hopelessly limited to the language of our experience. In a sense, we are earthbound in our efforts to express that which reaches far beyond the earth.

But a more important reason is that human personality is the highest that we know. Within the range of our knowledge, it alone can plan and create and love and sacrifice. And I think we reason correctly when we conclude that surely God is more like a man than like a jellyfish, or a chair, or a tree. To picture God in the terms of our experience is not to limit him to human nature. It is rather to say, "I believe; help thou mine unbelief."

Furthermore, we are persuaded that we can often see him reflected in human personality. After all, the word became flesh and dwelt among us! Surely the Incarnation was a part of the eternal revelation.

A college sophomore—which, as you know, is the wisest of all men—came home for the Christmas holidays loaded with arguments with which to puncture the religious faith of his parents. These arguments had been gleaned from his first acquaintance with biology and geology on the college level. Now he could hardly wait to launch his attack. Sitting in front of the fire after dinner, waiting for an opening, he looked at his mother, noting the deep lines in her face and hands, which somehow recalled for him the personal battles she had fought and won through her faith. Then he turned toward his father, and something brought to his mind the memory of that habit which had nearly ruined their home; it had been conquered through faith. Suddenly, all of his arguments began to vanish in the presence of this witness to the power of faith expressed in human personalities. One could not argue with a living fact!

We will go on describing God in terms of human personality, even though we know that he is Christ-like, not manlike; even though we know that he is not up there but is down here, not out there but in here. God is a Spirit everywhere present, always.

Another element of that composite picture was the idea that God orders suffering and pain, paralysis, and even death upon persons just to get even with them or test their faith. Is this what he looks like?

In James Agee's novel *A Death in the Family*, the young husband is killed in a senseless one-car accident; a little bolt came loose and the car swerved off the highway. Later in the evening the brother of the new young widow came to be with her. As he entered the room his first comment was: "Now ... what about that idiot God of yours!"

If God decrees and directs such tragedies, then the phrase would seem to fit. When a man does such a thing he is removed from society, put behind bars, or judged sick in mind and spirit. If on the one hand God loves us, and with the other hand afflicts us with such monstrous suffering, then he would be schizophrenic! It is not a criminal God but a Christ-like God in whom we believe!

This leaves questions, however, which someone might put like this: "If he is a God of love who cares about us, then why does he allow such natural catastrophes as hurricanes, tornadoes, earthquakes, and the like, these things which are sometimes legally defined as 'acts of God'? They take a tragic toll; why does he allow them?"

Let's imagine that we possess the power to banish these things. But before we do it, perhaps we should remember that there is a relation between the tornado tearing the sky and the wheat which grows in the field, between a hurricane and a rose. They are all part of one great body of natural law. To make it impossible for an earthquake to happen might also make it impossible for grain to grow. Perhaps this is not only the best possible world; it may be the *only* possible world.

Conceivably our questioner might say, "All right, then, we'll keep natural law with its consequences: but if he loves us, why doesn't God banish sin? It would be such a wonderful world if there were no such thing as sin!"

Let's imagine that it is also within our power to banish the possibility of sin. But before we do it, perhaps we should consider that if we do away with the possibility of evil, we do away with the possibility of good. *Virtue* and *honor* and *nobility* would become words with no meaning. No wonder a young man in the midst of a discussion on this subject finally said, "I demand the right to be damned!" You see, the right to be saved and the right to be damned go together.

So now our questioner might agree that we do better to keep the possibility of sin. "But if God loves us," he would say, "couldn't he at least do away with pain? This is what spoils so much of life—headaches and backaches and toothaches and heartaches with their own special kind of suffering! Why doesn't God banish pain?"

Once again, let's imagine that we have such power. We would banish pain from the world! But before we do away with its possibility, I have a newspaper clipping that puzzles me. It describes a little girl in a northern city who has already received this great blessing; she can feel no pain. Cut her, burn her, stick a pin in her, it would not matter; she has no capacity to feel pain. So is she called "blessed"? Well, strangely, the article describes her as a tragic case and tells how medical scientists are doing everything in their power to restore to this girl the capacity to feel pain! Strange? Not when we remember that the capacity to feel pain is the sign of sensitivity; no pain, no joy; no tears, no laughter; no sorrow, no rejoicing.

Then perhaps we do better to keep even this capacity to feel pain. This may be the only possible world in which men can become great in character, deep in sympathy and understanding, all so that they may become sons of God.

What does God look like? Please do not misunderstand. The point is that he does not arbitrarily send these tragedies upon us; they are within his will in the sense that, so far as we can see, without their possibility, our life in this world would not be possible. He does not send them; but if we do not shut him out, God will come with the tragedy or pain to help us to use them and not waste them. This is the pattern in which he used even the Cross.

A father whose daughter was stricken with polio told me that he thought it was one of the great things that had happened to their family. I asked him what on earth he meant by such a statement. He explained that there were several reasons. "For one thing, we are so proud of our daughter—the way she has handled this illness in her own spirit. And then," he continued, "we're grateful for the way in which our family has been drawn together in this experience; we have never been so close as a family. It is as if we have discovered each other. And third, we never guessed that we had so many friends here in the city; people who cared enough about us to send flowers and food and messages. And then, for the first time we really know what the Church and our faith really mean. I don't know what we would have done without them. And so . . . for these reasons we think polio is one of the great things that has happened in our family."

I could never believe God sent polio upon a child in order to teach a family these lessons, or to test their faith, or reveal it to them. But when that tragedy entered, they did not shut him out; and he helped them to use it and not waste it.

One other part of the composite picture is the concept of God as "heavenly private-eye," or as divine bookkeeper, always watching so that he may put down some mark by our name in his big black book!

In my grandparents' home, there was a picture I despised as a child growing up. In the center of the large frame there was one great big eye. Arranged around this eye were the symbols of civilization: trucks and plows and tractors and engines and factories—all sorts of things. Even as a child I reasoned that this was some sort of a representation of God; that great big all-seeing eye. But, frankly, I simply didn't like the thought of a one-eyed God! But what I disliked most of all was the way in which ... well, if I were to take a supply of dried leaves or coffee grounds or grapevine out behind the barn, and roll it up carefully in some tissue paper and put it in my mouth, then just as I would get the match up to light it ... around the corner of the barn would come that terrible, terrible eye!

Some people imagine that this is the way God sees us; as an eye always out to catch us and condemn us. I do believe he sees us ... however, not with an eye to condemn, but with an eye of love that never lets go of us. But never think that it is not a terrible thing to be loved like this! When we are loved, then everything we do is judged in the light of that love. Whenever I have an unworthy thought, or contemplate an ugly or evil deed, I do not suddenly think of a judgment day out in the future. I think of those who love me and believe in me. And I stand judged in the light of their love!

What does God look like? One who sees us, not with an eye to catch us and condemn us, but with an eye of love which never gives up, never lets go. Like a shepherd who watches over his sheep, like a father whose eyes keep searching the road for some sign of the prodigal coming home, a love like a mother's love.

A young man once came to me with the request that I write a letter to a little town up in New England to learn if his mother was still alive and living there. "I used to send her a card or a message on Mother's Day, but I haven't done it in a long time," he explained. "I don't even know if my mother is still living. Would you find out for me? If she is still there, I'm going to send her a card this year."

Of course I would write the letter for him. I sent it by airmail the same afternoon. Within four days, I think, I had an answer. She was still at the same address. In her letter to me, this mother said, "So that is where that no-good son of ours is living. He violated every principle we had in our home. He's turned his back upon everything we have tried to do for him. He has disgraced our name. You tell that boy I never want to see him again . . ."

Do you think this is what that mother wrote? Then you don't know mothers. Instead, she said, "So that's where our boy is. How long would it take me to get to Texas from here? Tell him that we love him." A mother's love, you see, never gives up.

Like a shepherd; like a father; like a mother's love. So the love of God never gives us up, never lets go. And in the light of such a love are we judged.

What does God look like? This is the crucial question. Any picture we hold will be partial, incomplete; we cannot encompass the eternal. But we can measure our every thought of him by what we see in Jesus Christ. He is not up there but is down here; he is a Spirit everywhere present, always. Measuring by Christ, we know that God does not order suffering and send tragedy upon us; rather, when it enters our life, if we do not shut him out, he will come with it to help us use it and not waste it. Measuring by Christ, we know that he sees us not with an eye of condemnation, but with an eye of love that never lets go and waits the day when we may say at last:

> Just as I am, thy love unknown,
> Hath broken every barrier down;
> now, to be thine, yea, thine alone,
> O Lamb of God, I come, I come.

(*Protestant Hour Classics 1953–1988* [Nashville: Abingdon Press, 1992], 25-35).

The Folly and Danger of Being Not Righteous Enough
by George Whitefield

Ecclesiastes 7:16—"Be not righteous overmuch, neither make thyself over-wise: why shouldst thou destroy thyself?"

Nothing is more frequent, than while people are living in a course of sin, and after the fashion and manner of the world, there is not notice taken of them; neither are their ways displeasing to their companions and carnal relations: but if they set their faces Zion-ward, and begin to feel the power of God on their hearts; they then are surrounded with temptations from their friends, who thus act the devil's part. The enemies, the greatest enemies a young convert meets with, my dear brethren, are those of his own house. They that will be godly, must suffer persecution; so it was in Christ" time, and so it was in the Apostles time too; for our Lord came not to send peace, but a sword. Our relations would not have us sit in the scorner's chair; they would not have us be prodigals, consuming our substance upon harlots; neither would they have us rakes (a dissolute [loose in morals or conduct] person) or libertines, but they would have us be contented with an almost Christianity. To keep up our reputation by going to church, and adhering to the outward forms of religion, saying our prayers, reading the word of God, and taking the sacraments; this, they imagine, is all that is necessary for to be Christians indeed; and when we go one step farther than this, their mouths are open against us, as Peter's was to Christ: "Spare thyself, do thyself no harm."

And of this nature are the words of the text. They are not the words of Solomon himself, but the words of an infidel speaking to him, whom he introduces in several parts of this book; for Solomon had been showing the misfortunes which attended the truly good, as in the verse before our text.

Upon this the infidel says, "Be not righteous over-much, neither be thou over-wise; why shouldst thou destroy thyself?" i.e. Why shouldst thou bring these misfortunes upon thyself, by being over strict? Be not righteous over-much; eat, drink, and be merry, live as the world lives, and then you will avoid those misfortunes which may attend you, by being righteous over-much.

This text has another meaning; but take it which way you will, by brethren, it was spoken by an unbeliever; therefore it was no credit for the person who lately preached upon this text, to take it for granted, that these were the words of Solomon: the words of an infidel was not a proper text to a Christian congregation. But as David came out against Goliath, not armed as the champion was, with sword and spear, but with a sling and stone, and then cut off his head with his own sword; so I come out against these letter-learned men, in the strength of the Lord Jesus Christ; and, my dear brethren, I trust he will direct me to use my sling, so that our enemies may not gainsay us; and by the sword of God's word, cut off the heads of our Redeemer's enemies.

But though they are not the words of Solomon, yet we will take them in the same manner the late writer did; and, from the words, shall,

FIRST, Show you what it is, not to be righteous over-much, that we may not destroy ourselves.

SECONDLY, I shall let you see what it is to be righteous over-much. And then,

THIRDLY, Conclude with an exhortation to all of you, high and low, rich and poor, one with another, to come to the Lord Jesus Christ.

FIRST, The first thing proposed, is to show you what it is not to be righteous over-much. And here,

It is by no means to be righteous over-much, to affirm we must have the same Spirit of God as the first Apostles had, and must feel that Spirit upon our hearts.

By receiving the Spirit of God, is not to be understood, that we are to be inspired to show outward signs and wonders, to raise dead bodies, to cure leprous persons, or to give sight to the blind: these miracles were only of use in the first ages of the church; and therefore Christians (nominal Christians, for we have little else but the name) may have all the gifts of the Spirit, and yet none of the graces of it. Thou, O man, mayest be enabled by faith to remove mountains; thou, by the power of God, mayest cast out devils; thou, by that power, mayest speak with the tongues of men and angels; yes, thou mayest, by that power, hold up thy finger and stop the sun in the firmament; and if all these are unsanctified by the Spirit of God, they would be of no service to thee, but would hurry thee to hell with the greater solemnity. Saul received the spirit of prophesying, and had another heart, yet Saul was probably a cast-away. We must receive the Spirit of God in its sanctifying graces upon our souls; for Christ says, "Unless a man be born again, he cannot see the kingdom of God." We are all by nature born in sin, and at as great a distance from God, as the devils themselves. I have told you often, and now tell you again, that you are by nature a motley mixture of the beast and devil, and we cannot recover ourselves from the state wherein we have fallen, therefore must be renewed by the Holy Ghost. By the Holy Ghost, I mean, the third Person of the ever blessed Trinity, co-equal, co-essential, co-eternal, and consubstantial with the Father and the Son; and therefore, when we are baptized, it is into the nature of the Father, into the nature of the Son, and into the nature of the Holy Ghost: and we are not true Christians, till we are sanctified by the Spirit of God.

Though our modern preachers do not actually deny the Spirit of God, yet they say, "Christians must not feel him"; which is in effect to deny him. When Nicodemus came to Christ, and the Lord Jesus was instructing him, concerning the new birth, says he to our Lord, "How can these things be?" Nicodemus, though a master of Israel, acts just as our learned Rabbis do now. The answer that Christ gave him should stop the mouths of our letter- learned Pharisees: "The wind bloweth where it listeth, and we hear the sound thereof, but cannot tell whence it cometh, nor whither it goeth." Now till the Spirit of God is felt on our souls as the wind on our bodies, indeed, my dear brethren, you have no interest in him: religion consists not in external performance, it must be in the heart, or else it is only a name, which cannot profit us, a name to live whilst we are dead.

A late preacher upon this text, seems to laugh at us, for talking of the Spirit in a sensible manner, and talks to us as the Jews did to Christ: they said, "How can this man give us his flesh to eat?" So he asks, "What sign or proof do we give of it?" We do not imagine, that God must appear to us, and give it us: no; but there may be, and is, a frequent receiving, when no seeing of it; and it is as plainly felt in the soul, as any impression is, or can be, upon the body. To what a damnable condition should we bring poor sinners, if they could not be sensible of the Spirit of God; namely, a reprobate mind and past feeling?

"What proof do they give?" says the writer. What sign would they have? Do they expect us to raise the dead, to give sight to the blind, to cure lepers, to make the lame to walk, and the deaf to hear? If these are what they expect, I speak with humility, God, by us, hath done greater things than these: many, who were dead in sin, are raised to scripture-life: those, who were leprous by nature, are cleansed by the Spirit of God; those, who were lame in duty, not run in God's commands; those, who were deaf, their ears are unstopped to hear his discipline, and hearken to his advice; and the poor have the gospel preached to them. No wonder people talk at this rate, when they can tell us, "That the Spirit of God, is a good conscience, consequent thereupon." My dear brethren, Seneca,

Cicera, Plato, or any of the heathen philosophers, would have given as good a definition as this. It means no more, than reflecting that we have done well. This, this is only Deism refined: Deists laugh at us, when we pretend to be against notions, and yet these men use no other reason for our differing from them, than what is agreeable to Deists' principles.

This writer tell us, "It is against common-sense to talk of the feeling of the Spirit of God." Common-sense, my brethren, was never allowed to be a judge; yea, it is above its comprehension, neither are, nor can the ways of God be known by common-sense. We should never have known the things of God at all by our common sense: no; it is the revelation of God which is to be our judge; it is that we appeal to, and not to our weak and shallow conceptions of things. Thus we may see, it is by no means to be righteous over-much, to affirm we must have the Spirit of God as the Apostles had. Nor,

SECONDLY, Is it to be righteous over-much to frequent religious assemblies.

The preacher, upon this text, aims at putting aside all the religious societies that are in the kingdom: indeed, he says, "You may go to church as often as opportunity serves, and on Sundays; say your prayers, read the word of God; and, in his opinion, every thing else had better be let alone: and as for the Spirit of God upon your souls, you are to look upon it as useless and unnecessary." If this, my brethren, is the doctrine we have now preached, Christianity is at a low ebb indeed; but God forbid you should thus learn Jesus Christ. Do you not forbear the frequenting of religious assemblies; for as nothing helps to build up the devil's kingdom more than the societies of wicked men, nothing would be more for pulling of it down, than the people of God meeting to strengthen each other's hands; and as the devil has so many friends, will none of you be friends to the blessed Jesus? Yes, I hope many of you will be of the Lord's side, and build each other up in Christian love and fellowship. This is what the primitive Christians delighted in; and shall not we follow so excellent an example? My brethren, till Christian conversation is more agreeable to us, we cannot expect to see the gospel of Christ run and be glorified. Thus it is by no means to be righteous over-much, to frequent religious assemblies. Nor,

THIRDLY, Is it to be righteous over-much, to abstain from the diversions and entertainments of the age.

We are commanded to "abstain from the appearance of evil," and that "whatsoever we do, whether we eat or drink, we shall do all to the glory of God." The writer upon this text tells us, "That it will be accounted unlawful to smell to a rose": no, my dear brethren, you man smell to a pink and rose too if you please, but take care to avoid the appearance of sin. They talk of innocent diversions and recreations; for my part, I know of no diversion, but that of doing good: if you can find any diversion which is not contrary to your baptismal vow, of renouncing the pomps and vanities of this wicked world; if you can find any diversion which tends to the glory of God; if you can find any diversion, which you would be willing to be found at by the Lord Jesus Christ, I give you free license to go to them and welcome; but if, on the contrary, they are found to keep sinners from coming to the Lord Jesus Christ; if they are a means to harden the heart, and such as you would not willingly be found in when you come to die, then, my dear brethren, keep from them: for, indeed, the diversions of this age are contrary to Christianity. Many of you may think I have gone too far, but I shall go a great deal farther yet: I will attack the devil in his strongest holds, and bear my testimony against our fashionable and polite entertainments. What satisfaction can it be, what pleasure is there in spending several hours at cards? Strange! That even people who are grown old, can spend whole nights in this diversion: perhaps many of you will cry out, "What harm is there in it?" My dear brethren, whatsoever is not of faith, or for the glory of God, is a sin. Now does cards tend to promote this? Is it not mispending your precious time, which should be employed in working out your salvation with fear and trembling? Do play-houses, horse- racing, balls and assemblies, tend to promote the glory of God? Would you be willing to have your soul demanded of you, while you are at one of those places? Many of these are, (I must speak, I cannot forbear to speak against these entertainments; come what will, I will declare against them) many, I say, of these are kept up by public authority; the play-houses are supported by a public fund, and our newspapers are full of horse-races all through the kingdom: these things are sinful; indeed they are exceeding sinful. What good can come from a horse-race; from abusing God Almighty's creatures, and putting them to that use he never designed for them: the play-houses, are they not nurseries of debauchery in the age? And the supporters and patrons of them, are encouragers and promoters of all the evil that is done by them; they are the bane of the age, and will be the destruction of those who frequent them. Is it not high time for the true ministers of Jesus Christ, who have been partakers of the heavenly gift, to lift up their voices as a trumpet, and cry aloud against these diversions of the age? Are they not earthly, sensual, devilish? If you have tasted of the love of God, and have felt his power upon your souls, you would no more go to a play, than you would run your head into a furnace.

And what occasions these place to be so much frequented, is the clergy's making no scruple to be at these polite places: they frequent play-houses, they go to horse-races, they go to balls and assemblies, they frequent taverns, and follow all the entertainments that the age affords; and yet these are the persons who should advise their hearers to refrain from them; but instead thereof, they encourage them by their example. Persons are too apt to rely upon, and believe their pastors, rather than the scriptures; they think that there is no crime in going to plays or horse-races, to balls and assemblies; for if there were, they think those persons, who are their ministers, would not frequent them: but, my dear brethren, observe they always go disguised, the ministers are afraid of being seen in their gowns and cassocks; the reason thereof is plain, their consciences inform them, that it is not an example fit for the ministers of the gospel to set; thus, they are the means of giving that offense to the people of God, which I would not for ten thousand worlds: they lay a stumbling-block in the way of their weak brethren, which they will not remove, though it is a stumbling-block of offense. "Woe unto the world because of offenses, but woe unto that man by whom the offense cometh." The polite gentlemen of the age, spend their time in following those diversions, because the love of God is not in their hearts; they are void of Christ, and destitute of the Spirit of God; and not being acquainted with the delight there is in God and his ways, being strangers to these things, they run to the devil for diversions, and are pleased and delighted with the silly ones he shows them.

My dear brethren, I speak of these things, these innocent diversions, as the polite part of the world calls them, by experience; perhaps none, for my age, hath read or seen more plays than I have: I took delight in, and was pleased with them. It is true, I went to church frequently, received the sacrament, and was diligent in the use of the forms of religion, but I was all this while ignorant of the power of God on my heart, and unacquainted with the work of grace; but when God was pleased to shine with power upon my soul, I could no longer be contented to feed on husks, or what the swine die eat; the Bible then was my food; there, and there only I took delight: and till you feel this same power, you will not abstain from the earthly delights of this age, you will take no comfort in God's ways, nor receive any comfort from him; for you are void of the love of God, having only the form of godliness, while you are denying the power of it; you are nominal Christians, when you have not the power of Christianity.

The polite gentlemen say, "Are we to be always upon our knees? Would you have us be always at prayer, and reading or hearing the word of God?"

My dear brethren, the fashionable ones, who take delight in hunting, are not tired of being continually on horseback after their hounds; and when once you are renewed by the Spirit of God, it will be a continua pleasure to be walking with, and talking of God, and telling what great things Jesus Christ hath done for your souls; and till you can find as much pleasure in conversing with God, as these men do of their hounds, you have no share in him; but when you have tasted how good the Lord is, you will show forth his praise; out of the abundance of your heart your mouth will speak.

This brings me to the second thing proposed, which is an extreme that very seldom happens:

SECONDLY, To show what it is to be righteous over-much, And here,

FIRST, When we confine the Spirit of God to this or that particular church; and are not willing to converse with any but those of the same communion; this is to be righteous over-much with a witness: and so it is, to confine our communion within church-walls, and to think that Jesus could not preach in a field as well as on consecrated ground; this is judaism, this is bigotry: this is like Peter, who would not go to preach the gospel to the Gentiles, till he had a vision from God: and when his conduct was blamed by the disciples, he could not satisfy them till he had acquainted them with the vision he had seen. And, therefore, we may justly infer, the Spirit of God is the center of unity; and wherever I see the image of my Master, I never inquire of them their opinions; I ask them not what they are, so they love Jesus Christ in sincerity and truth, but embrace them as my brother, my sister, and my spouse: and this is the spirit of Christianity. Many persons, who are bigots to this or that opinion, when one of a different way of thinking hath come where they were, have left the room or place on the account: this is the spirit of the devil; and if it was possible that these persons could be admitted into heaven with such tempers, that very place would be hell to them. Christianity will never flourish, till we are all of one heart and of one mind; and this would be the only means of seeing the gospel of Jesus to flourish, more than ever it will by persecuting those who differ from us.

This may be esteemed as enthusiasm and madness, and as a design to undermine the established church: no; God is my judge, I should rejoice to see all the world adhere to her articles; I should rejoice to see the ministers of the Church of England, preach up those very articles they have subscribed to; but those ministers who do preach up the articles, are esteemed as madmen, enthusiasts, schismatics, and underminers of the established church: and though they say these things of me, blessed be God, they are without foundation. My dear brethren, I am a friend to her articles, I am a friend to her homilies, I am a friend to her liturgy; and, if they did not thrust me out of their churches, I would read them every day; but I do not confine the Spirit of God there; for I say it again, I love all that love the Lord Jesus Christ, and esteem him my brother, my friend, my spouse; aye, my very soul is knit to that person. The spirit of persecution will never, indeed it will never make any to love Jesus Christ. The Pharisees make this to be madness, so much as to mention persecution in a Christian country; but there is as much of the spirit of persecution now in the world, as ever there was; their will is as great, but blessed be God, they want the power; otherwise, how soon would the send me to prison, make my feet fast in the stocks, yea, would think they did God service in killing me, and would rejoice to take away my life.

This is not the Spirit of Christ, my dear brethren; I had not come to have thus preached; I had not come into the highways and hedges; I had not exposed myself to the ill treatment of these letter-learned men, but for the sake of your souls: indeed, I had no other reason, but your salvation; and for that (I speak the truth in Christ, I lie not) I would be content to go to prison; yea, I would rejoice to die for you, so I could but be a means to bring some of you to Jesus: I could not bear to see so many in the highway to destruction, and not show them their danger: I could not bear, my brethren, to see you more willing to learn, than the teachers are to instruct you: and if any of them were to come and preach to you, I should not envy them, I should not call them enthusiasts or madmen; I should rejoice to hear they had ten thousand times more success than I have met with; I would give them the right hand of fellowship; I would advise them to go on; I would wish them good luck in the name of the Lord, and say as Christ did, when the disciples informed him of some casting out devils in his name, and were for rebuking of them, "Forbid them not, for they that are not against us are for us"; or as St. Paul says, "Some preach Christ of envy, and some of good-will; notwithstanding, so Christ is but preached, I rejoice; yea, and will rejoice." The gospel of Jesus, is the gospel of peace. Thus you may see, that to be righteous over-much, is to be uncharitable, censorious, and to persecute persons for differing from us in religion.

SECONDLY, Persons are righteous over-much, when they spend so much time in religious assemblies, as to neglect their families. There is no license given by the blessed Jesus, for idleness; for in the very infancy of the world, idleness was not allowed of. In paradise, Adam and Eve dressed the garden, Cain was a tiller of the ground, and Abel was a keeper of sheep; and there is a proverb amongst the Jews, "That he who brings his son up without a business, brings him up to be a thief:" and therefore our Savior was a carpenter; "Is not this the carpenter's son," said the Jews: and St. Paul, though brought up at the feet of Gamaliel, was a tent-maker. Labor, my brethren, is imposed on all mankind as part of the divine curse; and you are called to be useful in the society to which you belong: take care first for the kingdom of God, and all things necessary shall be added. To labor for the meat that perisheth, is your duty; only take care, that you do not neglect getting the meat for the soul: that is the greatest consequence, for this plain reason, the things of this life are temporal, but those of the next are eternal. I would have rich men to work as well as poor; it is owing to their idleness, that the devil hurries them to his diversions; they can be in their beds all the morning, and spend the afternoon and evening in dressing, visiting, and at balls, plays, or assemblies, when they should be working out their salvation with fear and trembling. Such a life as this, occasions a spiritual numbness in the soul; and if Jesus Christ was not to stop those who thus spend their time, they would be hurried into eternity, without once thinking of their immortal souls. But Jesus Christ has compassion upon many of them, and while they are in their blood, he bids them "live." And though I preach this doctrine to you, yet I do not bid you be idle; no, they that do not work should not eat. You have two callings, a general one, and a special one: as we are to regard the one in respect of our bodies, so we are to regard the other on account of our souls. Take heed, my brethren, I beseech you, take heed, lest you labor so for the meat that perisheth, as to forget that meat which endureth for ever. Seek the things of God first; look well to obtain oil in your lamps, grace in your hearts. I am not persuading you to take no care about the things of the world, but only not to be encumbered with them, so as to neglect your duty towards God, and a proper concern for your souls. It is meet, it is right, it is your bounden duty, to mind the calling wherein God hath placed you; and you may be said to be righteous over-much not to regard them. This brings me,

THIRDLY, To give you another sign of being righteous over-much; and that is, when we fast and use corporal authorities, so as to unfit us for the service of God.

This, my brethren, you may think there is no occasion at all to caution you against, and indeed there is not a great necessity for it; however, many persons, upon their first being awakened to a sense of their sin, are tempted to use authorities to that excess which is sinful. It is our duty to fast, it is our duty to fast often, and it is what we are directed to by Jesus Christ himself; but then we are to take care to do it in a proper manner: to bring our bodies under for the service of God, is that which we are commanded by our Lord Jesus Christ.

The late preacher upon this text, runs into great extremes, and charges us with saying and acting things of which we never thought; but I do not regard what he said of me: I do not mind his bitter invectives against my ministry; I do not mind his despising my youth, and calling me novice and enthusiast; I forgive him from my very heart: but when he reflects on my Master; when he speaks against my Redeemer; when Jesus Christ is spoken against, I must speak, (I must speak indeed, or I should burst:) when he gives liberty to persons to take a cheerful glass, and alledges Christ for an example, as in the marriage-feast, saying, "Christ turned water into wine, when it is plain there had been more drank than was necessary before"; what is this, but to charge Christ with encouraging drunkenness? It is true, the Governor says, "Every man in the beginning sets forth good wine, and when men have well drank, that which is worse; but thou hast kept the good wine until now": but it does not at all follow, that it was not necessary, or that there had been a sufficient quantity before: I would not speak thus slightingly of one of my Master's miracles, for the whole world. And we may observe, that as Christ chiefly visited poor people, they might not have wherewithal to buy a sufficient quantity of wine; for having more guests than were expected, the wine was expended sooner than they thought; then the Mother of Jesus tells him, "They have no wine"; he answers, "Woman, what have I to do with thee? My hour is not yet come." After this he commanded them to fill the water-pots with water, and they filled them to the brim, and this water he turned into wine: now it does not follow, that there was more drank than was necessary; neither would the Lord Jesus Christ have continued in the house if there had. But we have an excellent lesson to learn from this miracle: by the water-pots being empty, we may understand, the heart of man being by nature destitute of his grace, his speaking and commanding to fill them, shows, that when Christ speaks, the heart that was empty of grace before, shall be filled; and the water pots being filled to the brim, shows, that Christ will fill believers hearts brim full of the Holy Ghost: and from the Governor's observing, that the last wine was the best, learn, that a believer's best comforts, shall be the last and greatest, for they shall come with the greatest power upon the soul, and continue longest there: this, this my dear brethren, is the lesson we may learn from this miracle.

But one great inconsistency I cannot avoid taking notice of in this late learned preacher. In the beginning of his sermon, he charges us with "laying heavy burdens upon people, which they are not able to bear"; in the latter part he charges us with being Antinomians, whose tenets are, "So you say you believe in the Lord Jesus Christ, you may live the life of devils." Now, he charges us with being too strict, and by and by with being too loose. Which side, my brethren, will you take? Thus you see, when persons forsake Christ, they make strange mistakes; for here can be no greater opposition of sentiments than this letter-learned writer has made: as opposite as light and darkness, good and evil, sweet and bitter. And, on this account, to find out these lettered-learned gentlemen's notions of the new-birth, I put a paragraph in my Journal; and, blessed be God, I have obtained my desires, and have plainly perceived, that the persons who have lately written concerning the new-birth, know no more of it than a blind man does of colors, nor can they have any more notion of it, (by all their learning, falsely so called) than the blind man, who was to give an account what the sun was, and, after a considerable time allowed for study, he said, "It was like the sound of a trumpet." And till they are taught of God, they will be unacquainted with the new-birth; therefore, if you have a mind to know what the devil has to say against us, read Dr. Trapp's sermons.

It is with grief I speak these things, and were not the welfare of your souls, and my Redeemer's honor at stake, I would not now open my mouth, yes I would willingly die (God is my judge) for the person who wrote such bitter things against me, so it would be a means of saving his soul. If he had only spoken against me, I would not have answered him; but, on his making my Redeemer a pattern of vice, if I was not to speak, the very stones would cry out; therefore, the honor of my Redeemer, and love to you, constrains me to speak. It is of necessity that I speak, when the divinity of Jesus Christ is spoken against, it is the duty of ministers to cry aloud, and spare not. I cannot forbear, come what will; for I know not what kind of divinity we have not among us: we must have a righteousness of our own, and do our best endeavors, and then Christ will make up the deficiency; that is, you must be your own Savior, in part. This is not the doctrine of the gospel; this not the doctrine of Jesus: no; Christ is all in all; Jesus Christ must be your whole wisdom; Jesus Christ must be your whole righteousness. Jesus Christ must be your whole sanctification; or Jesus Christ will never be your eternal redemption and sanctification. Inward holiness is looked on, by some, as the effect of enthusiasm and madness; and preachers of the necessity of the new-birth, are esteemed as persons fit for Bedlam. Our polite and fashionable doctrine, is, "That there is a fitness in man, and that God, seeing you a good creature, bestows upon you his grace." God forbid, my dear brethren, you should thus learn Jesus Christ!

This is not the doctrine I preach to you: I say, salvation is the free gift of God. It is God' free grace, I preach unto you, not of works, lest any one should boast. Jesus Christ justifies the ungodly; Jesus Christ passed by, and saw you polluted with your blood, and bid you live. It is not of works, it is of faith: we are not justified for our faith, for faith is the instrument, but by your faith, the active as well as the passive obedience of Christ, must be applied to you. Jesus Christ hath fulfilled the law, he hath made it honorable; Jesus Christ hath made satisfaction to his Father's justice, full satisfaction; and it is as complete as it is full, and God will not demand it again. Jesus Christ is the way; Jesus Christ is the truth; and Jesus Christ is the life. The righteousness of Jesus Christ, my brethren, must be imputed to you, or you can never have any interest in the blood of Jesus; your own works are but as filthy rags, for you are justified before God, without any respect to your works past, present, or to come. This doctrine is denied by the learned rabbis; but if they deny these truths of the gospel, they must not offended, though a child dare speak to a doctor; and, in vindication of the cause of Jesus Christ, a child, a boy, by the Spirit of God, can speak to the learned clergy of this age.

If I had a voice so great, and could speak so loud, as that the whole world could hear me, I would cry, "Be not righteous over-much," by bringing your righteousness to Christ, and by being righteous in your own eyes. Man must be abased, that God may be exalted.

The imputed righteousness of Jesus Christ is a comfortable doctrine to all real Christians; and you sinners, who ask what you must do to be saved? How uncomfortable would it be, to tell you by good works, when, perhaps, you have never done one good work in all your life: this would be driving you to despair, indeed: no; "Believe in the Lord Jesus Christ, and you shall be saved": therefore none of you need go away despairing. Come to the Lord Jesus by faith, and he shall receive you. You have no righteousness of your own to depend on. If you are saved, it is by the righteousness of Christ, through his atonement, his making a sacrifice for sin: his righteousness must be imputed to you, otherwise you cannot be saved. There is no difference between you, by nature, and the greatest malefactor that ever was executed at Tyburn: the difference made, is all owing to the free, the rich, the undeserved grace of God; this has made the difference. It is true, talking at this rate, will offend the Pharisees, who do not like this leveling doctrine, (as they call it); but if ever you are brought to Jesus Christ by faith, you will experience the truth of it. Come by faith to Jesus Christ; do not come, Pharisee-like, telling God what you have done, how often you have gone to church, how often you have received the sacrament, fasted, prayed, or the like: no; come to Christ as poor, lost, undone, damned sinners; come to him in this manner, and he will accept of you: do not be rich in spirit, proud and exalted, for there is no blessing attends such; but be ye poor in spirit, for theirs is the kingdom of God; they shall be made members of his mystical body here, and shall be so of the church triumphant hereafter. Acknowledge yourselves as nothing at all, and when you have done all, say, "You are unprofitable servants." There is no salvation but by Jesus Christ; there is no other name given under heaven amongst men, whereby we may be saved, but that of the Lord Jesus. God, out of Christ, is a consuming fire; therefore strive for an interest in his Son the Lord Jesus Christ; take him on the terms offered to you in the gospel; accept of him in God's own way, lay hold on him by faith.

Do not think you are Christians; do not flatter yourselves with being righteous enough, and good enough, because you lead moral decent lives, do no one any harm, go to church, and attend upon the outward means of grace; no, my brethren, you may do this, and a great deal more, and yet be very far from having a saving, experimental knowledge of Jesus Christ.

Beg of Christ to strike home upon your hearts, that you may feel the power of religion. Indeed, you must feel the power of God here, or the wrath of God hereafter. These are truths of the utmost consequence; therefore, do not go contradicting, do not go blaspheming away. Blessed be God, you are not such cowards to run away for a little rain. I hope good things of you; I hope you have felt the power of God; and if God should bring any of you to himself through this foolishness of preaching, you will have no reason to complain it was done by a youth, by a child; no; if I could be made an instrument to bring you to God, they may call me novice, enthusiast, or what they please, I should rejoice; yea, and I would rejoice.

O that some sinner might be brought to Jesus Christ! Do not say I preach despair; I despair of no one, when I consider God had mercy on such a wretch as I, who was running in a full career to hell: I was hastening thither, but Jesus Christ passed by and stopped me; Jesus Christ passed by me while I was in my blood, when I was polluted with filth; he passed by me, and bid me live. Thus I am a monument of God's free grace; and therefore, my brethren, I despair of none of you, when I consider, I say, what a wretch I was. I am not speaking now out of a false humility, a pretended sanctity, as the Pharisees call it: no, the truth in Christ I speak, and therefore, men and devils do your worst; I have a gracious Master will protect me; it is his work I am engaged in, and Jesus Christ will carry me above their rage.

Those who are come here this night out of curiosity to hear what the babbler says; those who come to spend an idle hour to find something for an evening-conversation at a coffee-house; or you who have stopped in your coaches as you passed by, remember that you have had Jesus Christ offered to you; I offer Jesus Christ to every one of you: perhaps you may not regard it because it is in a field. But Jesus Christ is wherever his people meet in sincerity and truth to worship him: he is not confined to church walls: he has met us here; many, very many of you know he has; and therefore you may believe on him with greater confidence.

Can you bear to think of a bleeding, panting, dying Jesus, offering himself up for sinners, and you will not accept of him? Do not say, you are poor, and therefore are ashamed to go to church, for God has sent the gospel out unto you. Do not harden your hearts: oppose not the will of Jesus.

O that I could speak to your hearts, that my words would center there. My heart is full of love to you. I would speak, till I could speak no more, so I could but bring you to Christ. I may never meet you all, perhaps, any more. The cloud of God's providence seems to be moving. God calls me by his providence away from you, for a while. God knows whether we shall ever see each other in the flesh. At the day of judgment we shall all meet again. I earnestly desire your prayers. Pray that I may not only begin, John-like, I the spirit, but that I may continue in it. Pray that I may not fall away, that I may not decline suffering for you, if I should be called to it. Be earnest, O be earnest with God in my behalf, that while I am preaching to others, I may not be a cast-away. Put up your prayers for me, I beseech you. Go not to the throne of grace, without carrying me upon your heart; for you know not what influence your prayers may have. As for you, my dear brethren, God knows my heart. I continually bear you on my mind, when I go in and out before the Lord; and it is my earnest desire, you may not perish for lack of knowledge, but that he would send out more ministers to water what his own right-hand hath planted. May the Ancient of Days come forth upon his white horse, and may all opposition fall to the ground. As we have begun to bruise the serpent's head, we must expect he will bruise our heel. The devil will not let his kingdom fall without raging horribly. He will not suffer the ministers of Christ to go on, without bringing his power to stop them. But fear not, my dear brethren, David, though a stripling, encountered the great Goliath; and if we pray, God will give us strength against all our spiritual enemies. Show your faith by your works. Give the world the lye. Press forward. Do not stop, do not linger in your journey, but strive for the mark set before you. Fight the good fight of faith, and God will give you spiritual mercies. I hope we shall all meet at the right- hand of God. Strive, strive to enter in at the strait gate, that we may be born to Abraham's bosom, where sin and sorrow shall cease. No scoffer will be there, but we shall see Jesus, who died for us; and not only see him, but live with him forever.

Which God, of his infinite mercy, &c.

The Works of the Reverend George Whitefield [London, 1771–1772].

CONTRIBUTORS

Tracey Allred
2729 Mountain Woods Drive
Birmingham, AL 35216

Guy Ames
Chapel Hill United Methodist
    Church
2717 West Hefner Road
Oklahoma City, OK 73120

Stephen Bauman
Christ Church United Methodist
520 Park Avenue
New York, NY 10021

Meredith Remington Bell
313 North Center Street
Arlington, Texas 76011

B. J. Beu
3810 67th Avenue Ct. Northwest
Gig Harbor, WA 98335

Scott Bullard
1207 Melrose
Waco, TX 76710

Thomas Lane Butts
First United Methodist Church
324 Pineville Road
Monroeville, AL 36460

Kenneth H. Carter Jr.
Providence United Methodist
    Church
2810 Providence Road
Charlotte, NC 28211

Paul L. Escamilla
Spring Valley United Methodist
    Church
7700 Spring Valley Road
Dallas, TX 75254

Dan L. Flanagan
Saint Paul's United Methodist
    Church
324 South Jackson Street
Papillion, NE 68046

Travis Franklin
1111 Herring Avenue
Waco, TX 76708

Roberto L. Gómez
El Mesias United Methodist
    Church
P.O. Box 4787
Mission, TX 78573-4787

Robert Gorrell
First United Methodist Church
P.O. Box 1632
Ardmore, OK 73402

Drew J. Gunnells Jr.
1205 Dominion Drive East
Mobile, AL 36695

Tracy Hartman
3400 Brook Road
Richmond, VA 23227

Chris J. Hayes
First United Methodist Church
313 North Center Street
Arlington, TX 76011

Don Holladay
P.O. Box 2054
Portales, NM 88130

Bob Holloway
First United Methodist Church
P.O. Box 88
Graham, TX 76450

Karen Hudson
5709 Drayton Drive
Glen Allen, VA 23060-6381

Laura Hollandsworth Jernigan
1776 Stonecliff Court
Decatur, GA 30033

Randy Jessen
First United Methodist Church
420 North Nevada Avenue
Colorado Springs, CO 80903

Wendy Joyner
Fellowship Baptist Church
P.O. Box 1122
Americus, GA 31709

Gary G. Kindley
First United Methodist Church
5601 Pleasant Run Road
Colleyville, TX 76034

Mike Lowry
University United Methodist
  Church
5084 DeZavala Road
San Antonio, TX 78249

Timothy S. Mallard
Combat Maneuver Training
  Center
CMR 414, Box 2018
APO AE 09173

John Mathis
High Hills Baptist Church
211 South Halifax Road
Jarratt, VA 23867

Ted McIlvain
Texas Christian University
Adjunct Faculty, Communication
  Studies
P.O. Box 298045
Fort Worth, TX 76129

Lance Moore
First United Methodist Church
915 Pine Street
Foley, AL 36535-2150

David N. Mosser
First United Methodist Church
313 North Center Street
Arlington, TX 76011

Raquel Mull
2210 Silver Southeast
Albuquerque, NM 87106

Douglas Mullins
1545 Cohasset Drive
Cincinnati, OH 45255

Timothy Owings
402 Congressional Court
Augusta, GA 30907

Robert D. Penton
First United Methodist Church
324 Pineville Road
Monroeville, AL 36460

William A. Ritter
First United Methodist Church
1589 West Maple Road
Birmingham, MI 48008

Henry Roberts
First United Methodist Church
6 East Wright Street
Pensacola, FL 32501

Cindy Guthrie Ryan
2134 Wedgewood Drive
Grapevine, Texas 76051

Carl L. Schenck
Manchester United Methodist
Church
129 Woods Mill Road
Manchester, MO 63011-4339

Mary J. Scifres
3810 67th Avenue Ct. Northwest
Gig Harbor, WA 98335

Jeffrey Smith
Woodway First United Methodist
Church
9191 Woodway Drive
Waco, TX 76712

Thomas R. Steagald
Marshville United Methodist
Church
P.O. Box 427
Marshville, NC 28103

Eradio Valverde Jr.
First United Methodist Church
129 West Hutchison
San Marcos, TX 78666

Ronda Wellman
P.O. Box 773
Graham, TX 76450

Mark White
5576 Scott's Pond Drive
Williamsburg, VA 23188

Victoria Atkinson White
5576 Scott's Pond Drive
Williamsburg, VA 23188

Jennifer H. Williams
Christ United Methodist Church
6570 Mifflin Avenue
Harrisburg, PA 17111

Ryan Wilson
Trinity Baptist Church
210 West South Sixth Street
Seneca, SC 29678

Philip D. Wise
Second Baptist Church
6109 Chicago Avenue
Lubbock, TX 79424

Sandy Wylie
P.O. Box 986
McAlester, OK 74502

SCRIPTURE INDEX

❧❧❧

OLD TESTAMENT

NEW TESTAMENT

CONTEMPORARY AND TRADITIONAL RESOURCES FOR WORSHIP LEADERS

The ABINGDON WORSHIP Annual 2007

EDITED BY MARY J. SCIFRES & B. J. BEU

A must for traditional and contemporary worship!" As pastors, we recognize that few worship planners have as much time and creative energy to spend planning services of worship as they would like. . . . *The Abingdon Worship Annual 2007* provides pastors and worship planners the liturgical elements to put a complete service of worship together," say Mary J. Scifres and B. J. Beu in the 2007 volume of *The Abingdon Worship Annual.* The *Annual* provides lectionary-based resources for creating moving and coordinated worship experiences for both traditional and contemporary worship styles. Each dated entry includes: lectionary readings, calls to worship, praise sentences and contemporary gathering words, opening and confessional prayers, benedictions, and blessings. *The Abingdon Worship Annual 2007* is a must-have sourcebook offering countless opportunities for meaningful and insightful worship.

"Commendations to Abingdon Press for offering two fresh ecumenical resources for pastors."
For *The Abingdon Preaching Annual*—"Anyone who dares proclaim a holy word week in and week out soon realizes that creative inspiration for toe-shaking sermons quickly wanes. Multitasking pastors who are wise seek out resources that multiply their own inductive initiatives."
For *The Abingdon Worship Annual*—"Not only the sermon but also the whole service dares to be toe-shaking . . . and the *Worship Annual* is a reservoir of resources in that direction."
—The Rev. Willard E. Roth, Academy of Parish Clergy President, *Sharing the Practice: The Journal of the Academy of Parish Clergy*

 Abingdon Press